Y0-CDA-334

COLS
WRIGHT STATE UNIVERSITY
UNIVERSITY LIBRARY
0 0013 0154655 0

Assessment of Special Children

Joseph C. Witt
Louisiana State University

Stephen N. Elliott
University of Wisconsin, Madison

Frank M. Gresham
Louisiana State University

Jack J. Kramer
University of Nebraska, Lincoln

Assessment of Special Children

Tests and the Problem-Solving Process

Scott, Foresman/Little, Brown College Division
SCOTT, FORESMAN AND COMPANY
Glenview, Illinois Boston London

Library of Congress Cataloging-in-Publication Data

Assessment of special children: tests and the problem-solving process
/ Joseph C. Witt . . . [et al.].
p. cm.
Bibliography: p.
Includes index.
ISBN 0-673-39755-6
1. Handicapped children — Education. 2. Handicapped children —
Psychological testing. 3. Problem solving. 4. Special education.
I. Witt, Joseph C.
LC4015.A73 1988
371.9 — dc19 87-35446
CIP

1 2 3 4 5 6 7 8 9 10 – RRC – 93 92 91 90 89 88 87

Printed in the United States of America

Credit

To my parents, Wilma and Garlen Witt

J.C.W.

To the memory of Ed Argulewicz, who always reminded me of the importance of individual differences; to my loving wife, Anita; and to my two "special" children, Dustin Rhodes and Andrew Taylor.

S.N.E.

To my parents, Metz and Julia Gresham

F.M.G.

To Jeannie, Jamie, and Jessica—my best friend and our special contributions

J.J.K.

Preface

Purpose of the Text

How is it possible to convey fully the degree to which the assessment of special children is a rich, rewarding process? As authors we wanted to write an interesting and readable text. We were concerned that an encyclopedic listing of tests and an overemphasis on the technology (e.g., statistics) of assessment might overshadow the more important and interesting features of the field. We wanted to present stories of children like Rhonda K., who, because of cerebral palsy, had very poor control of her arms and legs and was thought to be mentally retarded. However, skillful testing with nontraditional methods indicated she was in fact a very bright young girl who could benefit from a much higher level of instruction than traditional tests had suggested. This practical focus, based on our experience, is interwoven with a clear, accurate, and readable description of all the essential information one would expect to find in an introductory text on assessment in special education.

We have stressed the application of assessment in two ways. First, there is a strong emphasis on the linking of assessment with intervention and instruction through a *problem-solving process*. In fact, this book evolved out of a perception that specialists wanted a source of information that would link assessment to intervention and the solution of important educational problems. The goals are therefore to describe how assessment data can be obtained and used by individuals engaged in the problem-solving process within educational settings and to integrate the assessment process typically used in schools with test instruments. Application has also been stressed through the frequent discussion of actual case studies, examples, and special sections entitled "Focus on Practice" that show real people dealing with real problems.

To describe a field as broad and diverse as assessment and still convey that it is an organized and coherent body of knowledge, it was necessary to maintain a unity from chapter to chapter by emphasizing the following common themes:

Linking Assessment and Intervention

The book is based on the assumption that when a child is referred for assessment, the goal is to solve the child's problem by developing appropriate academic or social interventions. Thus, the focus is on using tests within a problem-solving process. For too long, giving tests has been equated with problem solving, but the link between assessment and intervention must be explicitly planned and practiced. The text first details the assessment process and then examines ten common areas of concern, such as reading, math, language, and preschool readiness, to illustrate how to understand a child experiencing problems in each of these domains.

Using and Interpreting Tests

A second purpose of the text is to help test users master assessment fundamentals so that instruments can be administered and interpreted correctly. Because assessment data play a major role in determining how children will be educated, they can be harmful as well as helpful, depending on their use. Irrevocable damage can be done by individuals misinformed about the limitations of tests, and thus every test user is responsible for knowing what tests can and cannot do.

Audience for This Book

Special education professionals taking their first course in assessment are the audience for this book. We have assumed no previous knowledge of or work in educational measurement or statistics. The book is designed for individuals who will be working with special needs children and who must be able to use and interpret both standardized and informal tests. This text will also benefit counselors, school psychologists, educational administrators, speech and language pathologists, social workers, and others directly or indirectly involved in the education of preschool children, children with behavior problems, and those with mild or severe handicaps.

The Student Workbook

The workbook that accompanies this text can be used by the instructor for in-class exercises, homework assignments, or self-instruction modules for students to supplement their understanding of the material covered in class. It includes objective and subjective exercises designed to help students transfer their knowledge to actual situations. Because learning assessment theory and techniques can sometimes be dry and uninteresting, in both the workbook and the text attempts have been made to communicate the relevance of the material to give students a reason to develop more than rote mastery of basic skills and principles. The workbook exercises were accordingly written to be entertaining as well as instructive. They include applied exercises, vocabulary drills, and sample questions from both multiple-choice and essay tests. The exercises can serve as a springboard for class discussion. In short, instructors can use the workbook either directly or indirectly.

The Instructor's Manual

The instructor's manual has two basic features. First, it offers suggestions for enhancing lectures for each chapter as well as supplemental readings and other materials to help make the course relevant and interesting to students. Second, the manual contains multiple-choice, true-false, and short-item essay questions to assist instructors in the preparation of examinations.

Acknowledgments

A number of people have been extraordinarily generous with their time, energy, and wisdom during the writing of this book. We are hopelessly in debt to these individuals and gratefully acknowledge their efforts here.

A book cannot be influenced more fundamentally than in the conception of the idea. The idea for this book came from Mylan Jaixen, then Senior Editor with Little, Brown and Company. Mylan embodies all the qualities one would hope for in an editor and continuously provided advice and support until he left Little, Brown late in the writing of the text. After Mylan's departure and the merger of Little, Brown with Scott, Foresman, we were very fortunate to fall into the capable and experienced hands of Chris Jennison at Scott, Foresman, who helped us refine the manuscript. Cynthia Chapin of Little, Brown skillfully guided the text through the production process.

Several professionals provided thoughtful and helpful reviews of one or more of the three drafts of this book. We gratefully acknowledge Bob Algozzine, University of Florida; Miriam Cherkes-Julkowski, The University of Connecticut; Kathryn Gerken, The University of Texas; Mary Frances Landers, Wright State University; Bruce Ostertag, California State University, Sacramento; Robert Rueda, University of Southern California; Robert J. Sheehan, Cleveland State University; Corinne Smith, Syracuse University; Sue Warren, Boston University; and Richard Weisenfeld, Boston College.

Our students have been a constant source of inspiration, and we would like to note especially Brian K. Martens, William T. McKee, Mary Boone Von Brock, Colleen Fitzmaurice, and Melissa Pardue, who contributed intellectual stimulation if not actual research and production efforts.

We must also gratefully acknowledge James Geer, Chairman of the Department of Psychology, and David Harned, Dean of the College of Arts and Sciences at Louisiana State University, for providing a supportive and comfortable environment that offered freedom and resources needed to accomplish our work.

Finally, but most especially, we want to thank our families for their patience, understanding, and encouragement during the completion of this book.

J.C.W.
S.N.E.
F.M.G.
J.J.K.

Brief Contents

Contents

Assessment of Special Children

Part One

Foundations of Assessment

Whether one is building a house or teaching fifth-grade math, it is both necessary and important to set a proper foundation. A good foundation is also important to school-based assessment of children for special education, and this first part of the book introduces basic assumptions and terminology upon which the remainder of the book will be based. This part also provides a context within which assessment can be placed.

This book is mostly about children—children who are experiencing problems of one type or another. Individuals working directly with these children both want and demand solutions to the problems. In Chapter 1 assessment is presented as a vital source of the information needed to address these problems. More specifically, assessment should yield information that helps identify the nature of the problems, the factors that may be contributing to them, and, most importantly, possible remedies.

In Chapter 2, problem solving is placed within the context of the laws and regulations that govern the education of handicapped children. These laws govern not only the day-to-day functioning of the special education assessment process but also its very existence. The application of the various laws and regulations is described to explain how the assessment process works.

Chapter 3 introduces additional terminology used throughout the book. By the time you complete this chapter, you should have a richer understanding of why we assess, the legal foundation of the assessment process, and the context within which that process exists.

Chapter 1

Assessment and the Solving of Problems

Learning Objectives

1. Distinguish between the content and process of assessment.
2. Describe and be able to apply a problem-solving model.
3. Explain the use of the Centra and Potter model in the identification of factors related to student learning.
4. Explain the application of a funnel analogy to the assessment process.
5. List and describe the five major decisions for which assessment data are used.

The ability to solve complex problems is critical to the successful functioning of teachers, psychologists, and others involved in the schooling of children. Central to the process of problem solving is *assessment*, the collecting and synthesizing of information about a problem.

Assessment means different things to different people. Many laypersons as well as professional educators believe standardized testing and assessment are synonymous terms. Assessment, however, involves much more than testing. Most teachers will tell you they assess students by observing classwork and performance on classroom tests. Speech clinicians may argue that the best way to assess children is to listen to them talk. Psychologists tend to emphasize testing, yet they also use direct observation and clinical interviews as common means of assessment. All these perceptions of what assessment involves are accurate yet incomplete.

Assessment should be viewed as an ongoing process that involves the use of an array of materials, techniques, and tests across a variety of time periods and situations. Teachers, parents, counselors, psychologists, speech clinicians, and even children can be involved actively in *the process of* assessing the strengths and weaknesses of a child experiencing a problem at school. Thus assessment, particularly for purposes of special or remedial education, is multifaceted and should be a team process whereby professionals and laypersons work cooperatively toward the solution of a problem.

Any study of assessment theory and practice must take into account inherent unknowns, inconsistencies, and ambiguities. One must be prepared to take a cautious approach to the use and interpretation of assessment instruments since some very practical consequences can result from the problems intrinsic to our measuring systems, as these examples will illustrate:

1. A speech clinician and a special education teacher have each evaluated a five-year-old boy but disagree on the source of his difficulty. The speech clinician feels that the child has a language delay, while the special education teacher insists that he is retarded. The speech clinician suggests the child only appeared retarded on the tests because of his language problems. The special education teacher insists that the language delay is indicative of retardation. How can two individuals evaluate the same child, review essentially identical assessment information, and reach such different conclusions?
2. Following a recent district desegregation, fifteen third-grade students newly transferred to Bailey School are referred for reading evaluations because they are struggling in the basal reading series. According to their records, they all had been functioning at grade level in reading at their old schools. What could account for this discrepancy in the students' ability between schools? Is something wrong with all fifteen students, the teacher, or the curriculum?
3. A group of specialists in a suburban school district have been asked to assess the effectiveness of special education classes. Part of the group believes that the goal of the classes is the academic progress of the students, which therefore is the only factor that should be assessed. The remainder of the group argues that any assessment of effectiveness should consider an array of factors including teacher experience, type of student handicap, and length of special program. What should be done to resolve these differing viewpoints and to assess the programs?
4. The parents of a young girl are becoming increasingly confused. They suspect their child is having difficulties in math but when the child was given a math test at school, her scores indicated she was progressing normally. The parents then had their child tested by a private consultant who reported that her math ability was at least one grade level behind that of her peers. The parents wonder how two tests claiming to measure "math ability" could yield such discrepant results.

A major goal of this chapter is to suggest that assessment practices can and should vary according to the type of problem that precipitated assessment.

Assessment is a tool that is useful if, and only if, it contributes to the solution of problems.

The Processes of Assessment and Decision Making

Assessment requires the collection and interpretation of many pieces of information. A primary goal of any assessment is to determine what a student can and cannot do and how that student learns best in order that successful interventions can be designed. To accomplish this goal efficiently and effectively, a systematic plan is needed for the collection and interpretation of data. Such a plan functions like a road map, since it can provide direction and landmarks for moving from the problem state to the intervention state in the delivery of psychoeducational services.

The activities and decisions that occur during assessment can be thought of as *process* components, while the information collected represents *content* components. For example, the decision to use interview and direct observation techniques instead of a test to assess a disruptive student represents a process component, whereas the information derived from the interview and observation would represent a content component. The focus of this chapter is on the process components of assessment. We will explore the steps involved in an individual assessment and how to use the assessment information to make decisions about students. Later chapters will focus on the content components of assessment relating to intelligence, reading, math, and adaptive behavior. Knowledge of the process of assessment may be generalized across all types of assessment situations. Thus, it is a prerequisite to knowledge of the various content domains.

Problem Solving and the Role of Assessment

Assessment is never an end in itself. Rather, as part of the problem-solving process, assessment is used in screening, classifying and placing, progress monitoring, programming, and determining program effectiveness. Numerous psychologists and educators have written about problem-solving strategies; however, less has been written about how such strategies or schemes apply to assessment.

Before examining a general model of problem solving, we must define the term "problem." Most people think of a problem as something negative, subaverage, or at least bothersome. Although this is often true, there are numerous situations in which individuals are functioning well above average but still have problems or concerns. For example, a student may be functioning several grades above average in math yet experience significant difficulties when

FOCUS ON PRACTICE
The Problem Identification Interview

The identification and definition of a problem is the first and probably the most important step in problem solving. Therefore, Witt and Elliott (1983) outlined a series of objectives that can be used to guide a consultant's interview with a parent or teacher that is intended to define a problem. These objectives are described briefly below:

1. *Explanation of problem definition purposes.* The parent or teacher should be told what is to be accomplished during the interview and why problem identification is important. (Example statement: "I would like to talk with you a few minutes about John and his behaviors that bother you most. In order to help you, we will need to assess his behaviors, when and how often they occur, and what factors in your classroom (or home) influence them.")
2. *Identification and selection of target behaviors.* The parent or teacher should be asked to focus his attention on the problematic aspects of a student's difficulties. (Example statement: "Please describe exactly what John is doing that has caused you concern.") When individuals identify multiple problems, it is necessary to determine which to address. (Example statement: "Which of these concerns is most pressing to you now?")
3. *Identification of problem frequency, duration, and intensity.* After a target behavior has been defined, it is helpful to assess its basic characteristics: How often does it occur (frequency), how long does it last (duration), and how strong is it (intensity)? (Example statements: "How many times did John cry last week?" "How long does each crying session last?" "Does he cry loud enough for everyone in the room to hear him?") To interpret descriptions of frequency, duration, and intensity, we usually ask the parent or teacher to compare the target child's behavior with that of other children. In addition, a consultant should have knowledge of normative expectations to which the child's behavior can be compared.
4. *Identification of the conditions under which the target behavior occurs.* The assessment of environmental factors that occur in conjunction with a target behavior is often helpful in understanding the problem. (Example statement: "How do

continued

placed in an accelerated math program. In addition, the student's self-concept may be influenced negatively as a result of the failures in the accelerated program. "Problem" is thus a relative concept and can be said to exist when an individual (child, teacher, or parent) reports a significant discrepancy between a target person's current level of performance and a desired level of performance.

A number of aspects of this definition require elaboration. First, the person reporting the problem may or may not be the target person; regardless, the reporter in most cases would be considered a component of the problem.

FOCUS ON PRACTICE *continued*

you and the class react to John's crying?") Use of a simple model of behavior, such as the ABC model, can help unravel many problems. This model construes behavior (B) to be a function of antecedent (A) and/or consequent (C) events. Thus, once a behavior has been identified, a consultant looks at events that chronologically precede and follow it.

5. *Identification of the required level of performance.* Obtaining a description of the behavior required of a student is as important as obtaining a description of the student's problem behavior. (Example statement: "What would you consider to be an acceptable frequency for this out-of-seat behavior?") Once a desired or expected level of performance is identified, it serves as a goal to work toward.
6. *Identification of the student's strengths.* Learning what a child does well is often more useful than learning what a child does not do or does poorly. (Example statement: "What does John do best when interacting with his classmates?") Developing interventions that use a student's strengths helps to increase the probability of a successful treatment.
7. *Identification of behavioral assessment procedures.* All interventions require some assessment or recording of behavior. Thus, a consultant should help a teacher or parent decide what, how, when, and where behavior will be recorded and who will do the recording.
8. *Summary of the interview.* The final step should include a summary of the important points discussed and a review of individuals' responsibilities. This can be accomplished by reviewing or restating the definition of the target behavior, the method of recording behavior, and the person responsible for data collection.

The eight objectives outlined should not be viewed as steps through which the consultant should rigidly or mechanically progress. To do so could be detrimental to the interpersonal processes between a consultant and the parent or teacher with whom the consultant is working.

Adapted from "Assessment in Behavioral Consultation: The Initial Interview" by J. C. Witt and S. N. Elliott, 1983, *School Psychology Review, 12*, pp. 42–49.

Second, the determination of whether a problem involves a "significant discrepancy" is initially not questioned; however, once the current and desired levels of performance are defined operationally, this significant discrepancy becomes the focal point of assessment. This approach to problem definition is based on the belief that such problems grow out of the unsuccessful or discrepant interactions between persons (for example, child and peers, child and teacher, child and parent, and parent and teacher). Thus, the person targeted as having a problem and his or her interactions with the environment must be examined first to understand and then to change the problem behavior. Several models have been developed for problem solving by professionals in educational settings.

A General Model of Problem Solving

Many special educators and psychologists have used a general problem-solving model that has been conceptualized as a seven-step process by Gutkin and Curtis (1982):

1. Define and clarify the problem.
2. Analyze factors that may be causing the problem.
3. Brainstorm alternative strategies for solving the problem.
4. Evaluate and choose among the alternatives.
5. Specify responsibilities of those involved in solving the problem.
6. Implement the chosen remedial strategy.
7. Evaluate the effectiveness of the solution and repeat the process if necessary.

Within this process the first step is to achieve a clear, objective definition of the problem. Once a problem has been identified and defined, the helper or consultant and the referral agent are ready to analyze factors that may be influencing the targeted problem. After a comprehensive assessment of the problem and the factors influencing it, some intervention designed to treat the problem must be developed and implemented. Finally, after a suitable time period, the intervention plan is evaluated to determine its effectiveness.

Assessment plays a central role in this model in that assessment data are used in several steps to assist in decision making. This model also illustrates that a comprehensive assessment should result in an intervention designed to resolve the problem. Adherence to this process does not ensure a successful problem solution, but it does increase the chances that one will be reached.

Problem Solving Within the Assessment Phase

In the problem analysis stage, one must examine the nature of the problem and the environmental factors that may influence it. Then one must decide what specific questions one needs to ask to help solve the problem. For example, if a student is having difficulty in reading, one question could be, "Is the student's visual acuity adequate?" This is then stated as an hypothesis: "The student has poor visual acuity that interferes with reading." This hypothesis is tested and action taken. If it is incorrect (that is, if testing reveals the student has good vision), another hypothesis is generated. Hypotheses can be tested by observational techniques, standardized norm-referenced and criterion-referenced tests, behavioral checklists, and informal tests using curriculum material. This process can be thought of as a funnel. Such an analogy is instructive because the assessment process progresses from a wide perspective on a problem to a narrower, more well-defined perspective. The various hypothesis testing techniques flow through the funnel differently and aid in making screening, diagnostic, and programming decisions at three critical or structural points.

Elliott and Piersel's (1982) depiction of the assessment process as a funnel is illustrated in Figure 1.1. Assessment techniques are arranged in order of specificity of instructional information provided and types of decisions for which the techniques contribute information. As the assessor continues to refine hypotheses, data collection techniques become more specific to a focal child and his or her particular learning environment. Therefore, assessment becomes more direct and serves as a link to intervention.

Operationalizing the assessment funnel. The assessment of students often ends prematurely at the diagnostic or classification phase. Consequently, service providers, whether teachers, psychologists, or counselors, are left with little more than a label (such as "learning disabled") and general information about a student's strengths and weaknesses. The formulation of an intervention or Individualized Educational Plan (IEP) remains to be done, and may become a very subjective task when it should not be. Too often it seems that testers test and teachers teach but they do not share meaningful information. The basic point is that service providers want to know specifically what to do for and with children!

An example of a reading problem may help to illustrate the assessment process. Experienced educators and psychologists may hypothesize accurately about a given reading problem on the basis of data collected from interviews, classroom observations, or referral forms. However, since reading is a complex process, most professionals will probably need to initiate some systematic observation and testing before really knowing the sources of a student's reading difficulties. A good place to start any assessment is with an investigation of a student's sensory capabilities, particularly vision and hearing, and prerequisite learning skills and behaviors. Important prerequisite behaviors include attending to task, following directions, and correcting oneself. Such characteristics are fundamental to educational progress and are often the source of faulty learning or inappropriate behavior. Such behaviors can be assessed with classroom observations and individualized testing.

Following the assessment of sensory capabilities and prerequisite learning behaviors, the assessor is ready to examine a student's basic reading skills. This can be accomplished by a combination of standardized tests and classwork samples. The assessor's task is facilitated by looking for an error pattern (that is, frequent mistakes resulting from a knowledge or skill deficit) on tests of reading and classwork samples. Once an error pattern is detected, the assessor needs to determine the *reliability* and *generalizability* of the errors. Reliability refers to the consistency with which an error occurs, while generalizability

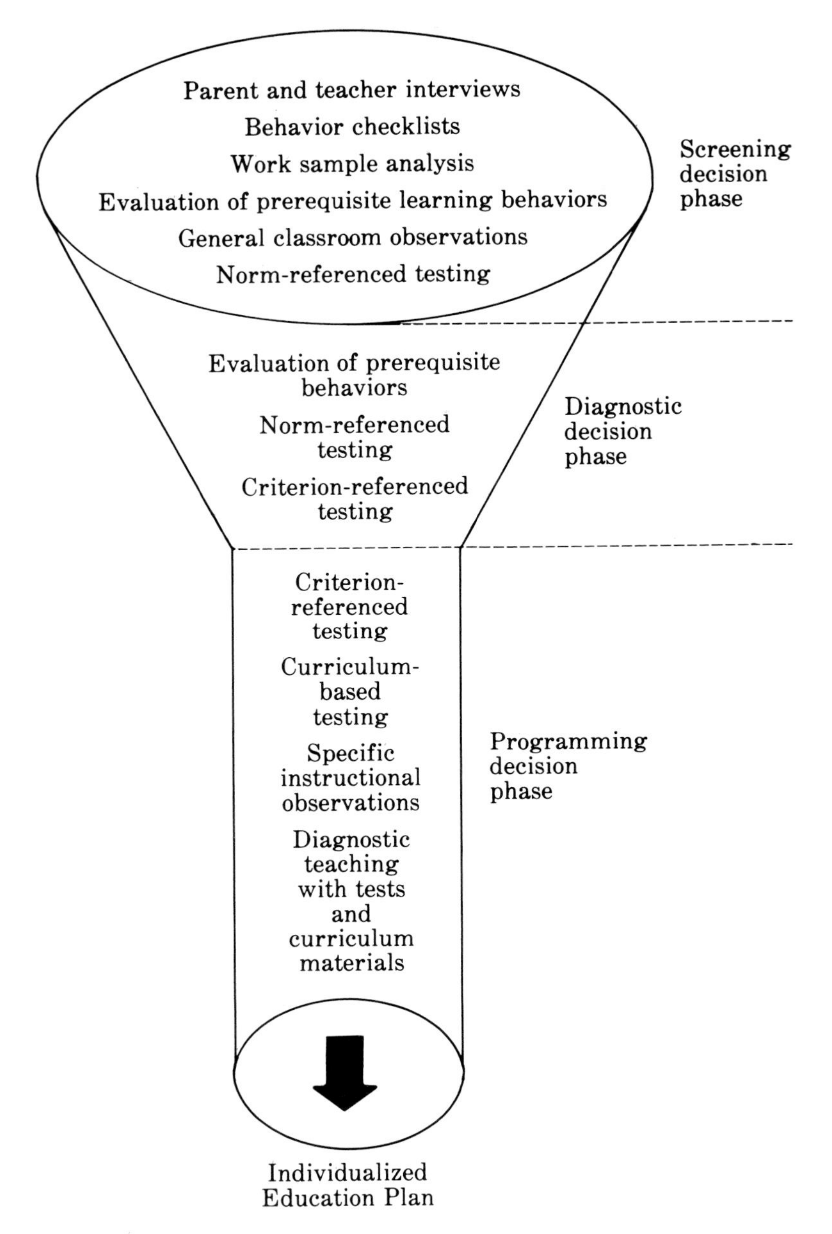

Figure 1.1 The assessment funnel. (From "Direct Assessment of Reading Skills: An Approach Which Links Assessment to Intervention" by S. N. Elliott and W. C. Piersel, 1982, *School Psychology Review, 11*, pp. 267–280. Copyright 1982 by National Association of School Psychologists. Reprinted by permission.)

involves the presence of an error in various forms and across types of tasks and materials. In the process of determining the reliability (test-retest) and generalizability of any given error pattern, an assessor answers important questions such as: Are errors due to a lack of knowledge (for example, that the vowel *a* says its name when it is long as in the word *make*)? Are errors specific to unfamiliar words or do they also occur with familiar words of similar structure or meaning? Do the same errors occur when words are isolated, as when presented in the context of a sentence?

Techniques that are used to determine the reliability and generalizability of an error are referred to as *testing the limits* and *diagnostic*, or *trial, teaching*. In our model of assessment, these techniques are used sequentially. That is, once testing is completed, high-frequency errors such as vowel confusion, inappropriate syllabification, incorrect sound-symbol relations, and failure to apply the rule of the final *e* are identified, and items similar to missed representative test items are administered in at least two fashions: according to the way the test item was administered initially and with some additional coaching. This combination of procedures aids in determining whether the error is reliable (consistent) and whether it can be removed with minimal additional structure from an instructor. When a student is unable to solve a reading task correctly after several attempts and with minimal instruction, trial teaching should be initiated.

In trial teaching, an assessor's goal is to teach the student skills to solve new problems from curriculum materials similar to those missed on the initial tests. Trial teaching usually is brief (ten to fifteen minutes), intensive, individualized instruction on the correct application of a skill. It is characterized by task analysis techniques, instructor modeling, instructor guidance in problem-solving strategies, and reinforcement of success. As a result of trial teaching, the assessor should be able to comment on the generalizability of a skill or knowledge deficit (that is, which words or conditions are affected) and instructional factors and materials that can or cannot be used with the student in future remedial activities.

Based on the funnel model of assessment and the brief example concerning reading, it should be clear that meaningful assessment is time-consuming and requires an assessor or team of assessors to possess collective knowledge of learning and behavior beyond that necessary to score and interpret standardized tests. Knowledge of factors that may influence learning and behavior is critical to a comprehensive and flexible approach to assessment. In the next section, we will examine two general models for understanding students' behavior that are useful during the problem analysis phase of assessment. Other models specific to various content areas of assessment such as reading or math will be explored in later chapters.

Conceptual aids for analyzing a problem. A comprehensive analysis of a student's problem requires the use of several methods to collect data about the relationship between student and environment (including school, teacher, class materials, and types of tasks). Centra and Potter (1980) developed a model for investigating school and teacher variables that influence students' achievement (see Figure 1.2). This model includes examples of variables and their expected relationships to each other and to student learning outcomes. Such a model provides a valuable framework for hypothesizing about students' school performances.

In the Centra and Potter model, school factors include differences between schools and school districts and conditions within an individual school. Teacher factors include characteristics such as experience, verbal aptitude, and classroom behavior. Although this model highlights school and teacher factors, it does not disregard peer group and parental influences. Three student-oriented factors complete the model: student behavior, student characteristics, and student learning outcomes.

The model contains two types of relationships: causal and correlational. A causal relationship exists if one variable or factor is thought to cause another. A correlational relationship is present when two variables occur together but one does not cause the other. For example, a child's height and reading ability are usually correlated because as children get taller, they also tend to become better readers. However, this is only a correlational relationship since neither variable causes the other. Instead both variables are probably related to some third variable, such as aging. (This will be discussed in depth in Chapter 4.) In Figure 1.2, expected causal relationships are indicated by the straight arrows. The curved arrow between teacher characteristics and within-school conditions represents a correlational rather than a causal relation. The double arrows going in opposite directions signify a causal relationship in either direction. For example, not only does teaching performance affect student behavior but also the reverse is true: Student behavior in response to teacher behavior probably causes many teachers to adjust their own behavior.

According to Centra and Potter (1980), their model indicates that "student behavior and student learning outcomes are most directly affected by student characteristics, teaching performance, and within-school conditions" (p. 275). Thus, when trying to solve a student's learning or behavior problem, an assessor would be wise to investigate the relationship among student characteristics, performance of the student's teachers, and within-school conditions such as class size and rules.

Goslin (1963) developed a useful model for understanding factors that may influence a person's test performance (see Figure 1.3). In this model, a test score is viewed as the end product of constitutional and environmental factors as well as of intervening variables such as personality, situation, test demands, and random variation factors.

The Goslin model provides an assessor with a framework for hypothesizing about a person's test performance. When used with other models, such as that of Centra and Potter, an assessor can maximize the probability that the assessment is sensitive to the many factors that can affect human behavior. In the following section, we discuss another major influence on the decision-making process: the type of decision that must be made.

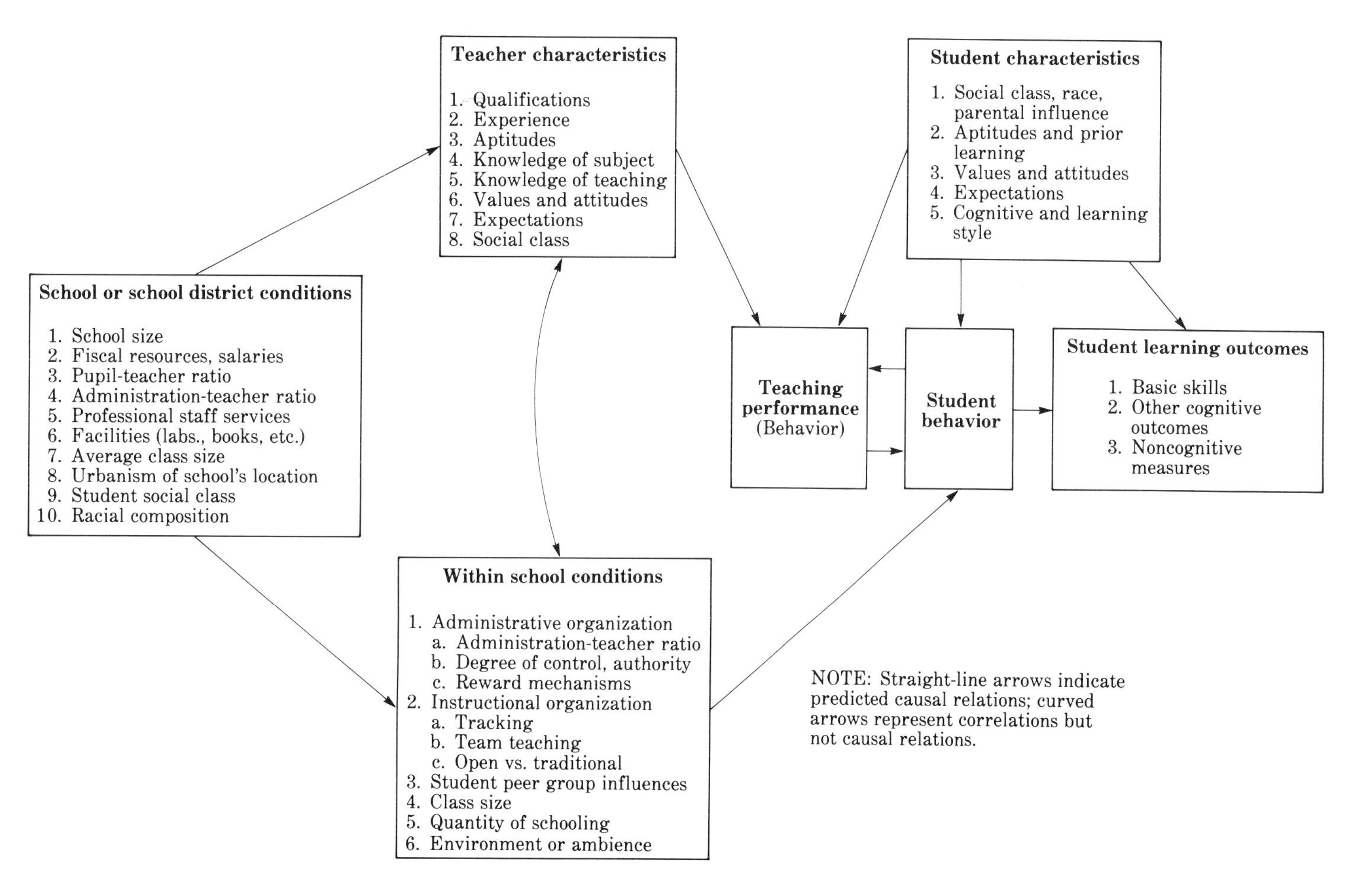

Figure 1.2 Structural model of school and teacher variables influencing student learning outcomes. (From "School and Teacher Effects: An Interrelational Model" by J. A. Centra and D. A. Potter, 1980, *Review of Educational Research*, *50*, p. 277. Copyright 1980 by the American Educational Research Association. Reprinted by permission.)

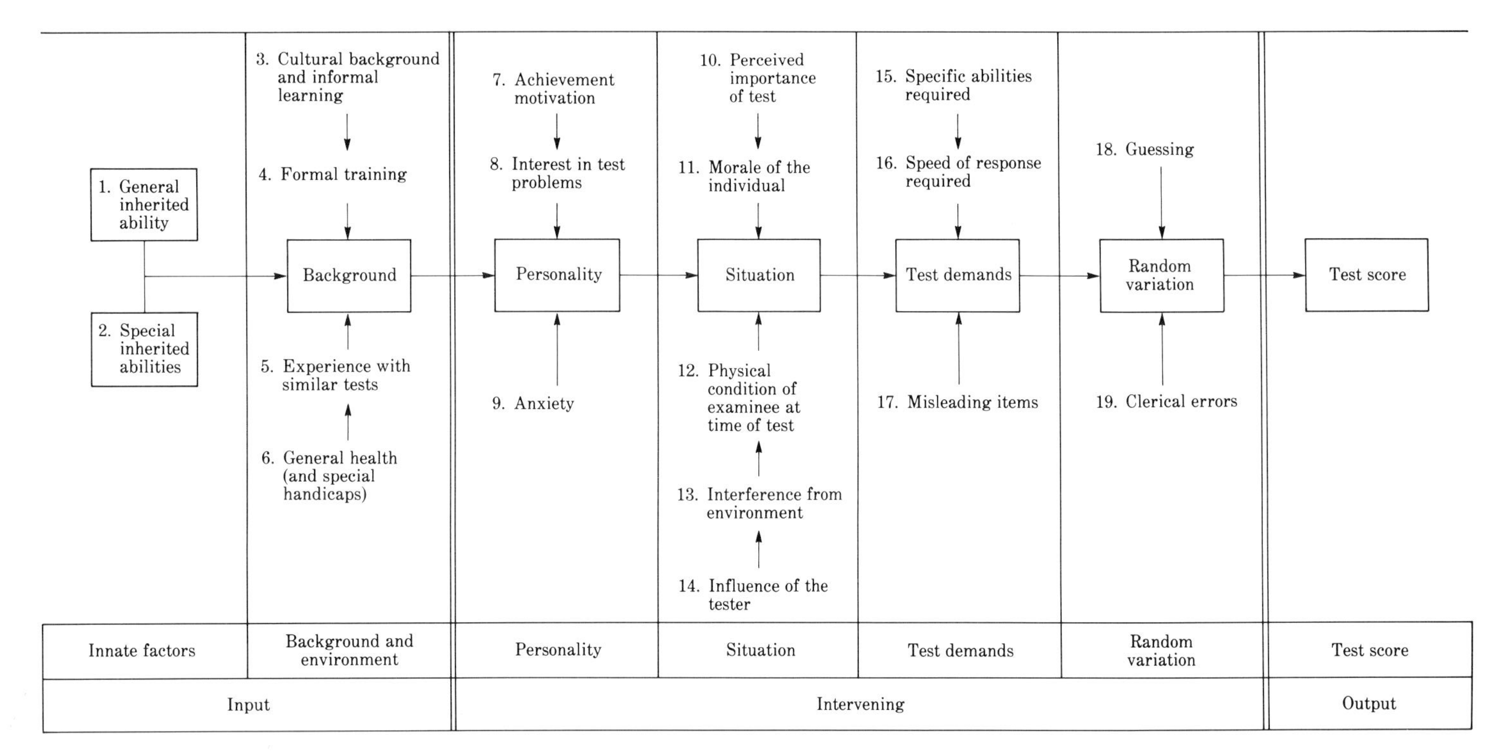

Figure 1.3 Paradigm for the analysis of variables that may influence learning and behavior. (From *The Search for Ability: Standardized Testing in Social Perspective* (p. 130) by D. A. Goslin, 1963, Russell Sage Foundation. Copyright © 1963 by the Russell Sage Foundation. Reprinted by permission of Basic Books, Inc., Publishers.)

Purposes of Assessment

The overriding purpose of all assessments is to gather information to facilitate effective decision making. Within education, assessment is used to help make at least five kinds of decisions: screening, classification and placement, student progress, programming or instruction, and program effectiveness decisions (Hawkins, 1979; Ysseldyke, 1979). Each requires the collection of a variety of data on students' backgrounds, interests, and abilities as well as on the environmental conditions and expectations of their families and school. The type of data collected to make any of these decisions can be very similar. In other words, academic achievement data (such as scores on standardized achievement tests, grades, or classwork samples) or behavior rating data can be used to help make any of the five kinds of decisions. It is the criteria or standards used to interpret the data that vary across the five kinds of decisions.

Screening Decisions

Screening is a procedure in which an entire population of students, such as those entering kindergarten, are evaluated to determine whether they may need additional assessment from educational, psychological, or medical specialists. Abilities and skills assessed during a screening process are generally considered to be basic or prerequisite to success in regular education settings. Therefore, individuals who cannot or do not perform at least at a specified level of competency on screening tasks are labeled "at risk" and are usually targeted for a more detailed, individualized examination of their abilities.

Assessment for educational screening purposes is generally carried out by teachers and involves brief tests, skill inventories, and behavioral checklists. These instruments are characterized by ease of administration, brevity, and only moderate levels of reliability. In addition to teachers, speech, vision and hearing specialists are routinely involved in screening. Many school systems also require regular health screenings of students.

Classification and Placement Decisions

Students whose abilities or behaviors seem to differ significantly from those of "normal" peers are often targeted by teachers or parents for consideration for placement in special instructional programs. Some of these students have persistent learning difficulties, others have behavioral or emotional disorders, and still others are intellectually gifted or talented. Of course, assessment will indicate that some of the students referred have no serious difficulties and do not require special services. Regardless of the reason for the referral, if an appropriate referral is made it becomes the collective responsibility of educators, parents, and specialists to gather data on which to base informed decisions.

A classification decision technically is separate from a placement decision and in fact must precede it with regard to special education actions. Historically, psychologists have been responsible for the classification or, more specifically, the diagnosis of individuals' learning and behavior problems, while educators have decided where to teach such individuals. However, with the passage of the Education for All Handicapped Children Act of 1975, Public Law No. 94-142, eligibility, classification, and placement decisions must now be made by teams of knowledgeable professionals and parents. Such a legal requirement provides a strong rationale for the development of assessment knowledge and skills in all teachers.

Although a classification decision is a very serious action intended to help students obtain needed services, it can have adverse effects if improperly used (Hobbs, 1975). Therefore, for intelligent classification and placement decisions to be made, specific and accurate data must be gathered concerning a student's ability and present educational setting (for example, materials, seating arrangement, and teacher's methods). Assessment information typically used to make such decisions includes direct behavior observations, scores from individually administered intelligence and achievement tests, behavior rating scales, and class performance indicators such as work samples.

Student Progress Decisions

The educational development of a student or a group of students is generally of much interest to parents, teachers, and students themselves. In fact, a good teacher continuously monitors and evaluates student progress in numerous areas. On a daily basis, students' work samples and classroom performance provide information for progress decisions. However, since the learning of many concepts and skills requires considerable time, most progress decisions can be made only after significant time has elapsed. Data concerning student progress are likely to consist of standardized group achievement tests, curriculum-based checklists of objectives accomplished, and teachers' subjective reports of growth. Students receiving special or remedial services are often given the same test at the beginning and end of each school year to enable educators to document their progress more accurately.

Programming or Instructional Decisions

Teachers need information about a student's abilities, curriculum content, and teaching methods to make intelligent programming or instructional decisions, for such decisions are complex and cannot be made automatically since students with similar abilities do not always learn in the same way (Cronbach & Snow, 1977; Ysseldyke, 1977). Therefore, a student's progress within a particular curriculum and under given instructional methods must be assessed regularly if effective programming decisions are to be reached.

Standardized intelligence and achievement tests have often been used to develop instructional programs for exceptional students, but unless these tests correspond well with the content of a given curriculum, such use must be questioned. Instead, direct assessment of a student's performance on classroom materials and teacher-prepared tests can provide detailed, reliable information for specific programming decisions.

Program Effectiveness Decisions

Assessing the effectiveness of an educational program is difficult because generally more than one student or educator is involved and the criteria for determining effectiveness are often undefined. Nevertheless, educators must be accountable for their programs. Hence, program evaluation has become a major activity of educational administrators and psychologists. Assessment data such as those used to make decisions about students' progress are particularly helpful in making decisions about a given program's effectiveness. Of course, data from individual students must be integrated to obtain an overall picture of the educational impact of a program. Published investigations of the effectiveness of various special education programs have appeared recently in several major educational and psychological journals and provide interesting reading (see, e.g., Carlberg & Kavale, 1980; Sindelar & Deno, 1978). Since assessment for classification and placement is likely to be the goal of most readers of this text, we will examine a typical school-based referral process in some detail in the next chapter.

Summary

This chapter, like this entire text, is based on a relatively simple premise: The purpose of assessment is to facilitate problem solving. In schools this problem-solving process is usually applied to children who are not progressing at an expected level or rate. Special education services have been developed as a primary method by which problems are solved. It is important to keep in mind, however, that the original purpose of special education is to solve problems. In too many cases, determining whether a child qualifies for special education is the beginning and end of this problem solving. The teacher who refers a child for assessment but is told the child does not qualify for special education services may be left with no alternative solutions. The problem is not solved. It still exists. The method of solving the problem (the special education refer-test-place sequence) has become an end in itself. But the goal is always to solve the problem. Assessment can provide information to accomplish this goal, but assessment is *not* an end in itself.

Chapter 2

Assessment and the Law

Learning Objectives

1. Identify major legal decisions that form the basis for the Education for All Handicapped Children Act of 1975, Public Law 94-142.
2. Describe major provisions of P.L. 94-142 that prescribe activities prior to and during the assessment phase of the special education process.
3. Describe major provisions of P.L. 94-142 that control the process of making classification and placement decisions.
4. Describe the major components to be included in an Individualized Education Plan.
5. List the major steps that a school district would take when applying P.L. 94-142 on a day-to-day basis.

Most school districts currently provide a relatively wide array of special education services for children with mild to severe handicaps. We do not have to go back much more than ten years, however, to discover this level of service to handicapped children did not always exist. In fact, at one time most handicapped children were denied *any* type of education. Parents were encouraged to find an institutional setting for the child or do what they could at home. Now, schools have elaborate procedures not only to admit and educate all handicapped children but also to search for such children whose parents may not be aware that services are available.

What has brought about this marked change in school attitudes in such a short period? Could it be that benevolent school districts have suddenly become aware of the learning potential of children with even the most severe handicaps? Have school districts proactively taken steps to ensure that all children receive the education to which they are entitled? Unfortunately most school systems have been neither benevolent nor proactive in responding to the needs of handicapped children. Instead, parents of handicapped children have argued successfully in one lawsuit after another that it is illegal to deny handicapped children their basic right to an education. Thus, school systems have been required to provide an education to all children. In this chapter we describe how the law has influenced how we conduct assessment, classification, and intervention activities with potentially handicapped children.

Legal Influences on Assessment and Special Education

Court Decisions Establishing a Free and Appropriate Public Education

The issue at the heart of all the litigation between parents of handicapped children and school systems has been that *all* children have a basic right to an education. The legal basis used by parents to establish this right is the Fourteenth Amendment to the United States Constitution, which forbids any state from denying "to any person within its jurisdiction the equal protection of the laws." This is frequently referred to as the equal protection clause and has been interpreted by the courts as directing schools to provide equal educational opportunities to all students.

The first and most significant court decision invoking the equal protection clause was *Brown* v. *Board of Education* (1954). Although *Brown* was filed in behalf of nonhandicapped black students, the logic behind the case has been subsequently used in defending the rights of handicapped children. *Brown* was filed because it was believed that black children were not receiving an education equivalent to that given to white children. In its ruling, the United States Supreme Court agreed with this argument and stipulated that black students must receive an equivalent education using equivalent resources and the like. This decision is relevant to handicapped children because in this case the court considered students to be a class of persons in society. According to the Constitution, all members of a class must be treated equally. In cases involving handicapped children, *Brown* has been used as a precedent to argue that handicapped and nonhandicapped students should be defined as a class and must therefore be treated equally. Just as the Court indicated in *Brown* that black children had been denied equal protection because of an unalterable and unchosen trait, their race, in subsequent cases involving handicapped children the Court has stipulated that such children have been denied an equal education because of an unalterable and uncontrollable trait, their handicap.

Among the major post-*Brown* cases that helped gain equal education for handicapped children, the most important were *Pennsylvania Association for Retarded Children (PARC)* v. *Commonwealth of Pennsylvania* (1972) and *Mills* v. *Board of Education of the District of Columbia* (1972). In *PARC* the suit was filed because Pennsylvania state law relieved a board of education "from any obligation to educate a child whom a public school psychologist certified as uneducable or untrainable" and permitted "an indefinite postponement of admission to public school of any child who has not obtained a mental age of 5 years" (*PARC*, 1972, p. 282). The United States Supreme Court struck down this state law, stipulating that all mentally retarded children are capable of benefitting from an education and the state has the responsibility to provide all such children between the ages of six and twenty-one years access to a free education.

After the *PARC* decision, the Court heard the *Mills* case, in which the school system did not deny that all children had the right to a free education but rather that the system lacked the financial resources to fulfill its obligation to handicapped children. While acknowledging that the education of severely handicapped children can be very expensive, the Court did not accept this as an excuse for failing to provide an education to handicapped children, ruling that

> if sufficient funds are not available to finance all of the services and programs needed and desirable in the system then the available funds must be expended equitably in such manner that no child is entirely excluded from a publicly supported education consistent with his needs and ability to benefit therefrom. The inadequacies of the District of Columbia public school system, whether occasioned by insufficient funding or administrative inefficiency, certainly cannot be permitted to bear more heavily on the "exceptional" or handicapped child than on the normal child. (*Mills*, 1972, p. 348F)

In both the *PARC* and *Mills* cases, the Court went beyond establishing that handicapped children had a right to a free and appropriate public education, for it imposed many procedural and due process requirements on school systems. Due process is a means of assuring that schools perform as the law mandates. For example, in the *PARC* decision, the court declared that the state must locate all retarded children in the state, that those children should be placed in as normal an environment as possible, and that their progress should be reviewed yearly or at the parents' request. In both *PARC* and *Mills*, the Court recognized that the advances granted to parents by the law would be a hollow victory if due process procedures were not also specified. These procedures make it clear to school systems that parents are to be involved and may challenge decisions made by the system.

The Education of All Handicapped Children Act of 1975

The *PARC* and *Mills* cases as well as many subsequent decisions have had a profound effect on who is educated, how they are educated, and which due process procedures are available to safeguard the children and their parents. The most obvious result was the recognition by Congress that federal legislation and funding would be necessary to guarantee a free and appropriate public education for all children. Congress accordingly enacted the Education of All Handicapped Children Act of 1975, Public Law 94-142 which goes far beyond simply establishing each child's right to an education by specifying the process through which education must occur (for example, describing the steps in the assessment process and declaring that children must be educated in the least restrictive environment). The seven major provisions of this law are summarized in Table 2.1. Its importance for individuals concerned with the assessment and placement of handicapped children cannot be overstated, because it literally directs their daily activities.

The law has been a two-edged sword in the field of special education. On one hand, it has created a vast network of services for handicapped children who were often denied any publicly supported education prior to the 1970s. On the other hand, it has made the assessment of children more complex. Generally, this increased complexity is not unnecessarily constricting. In fact, in most cases what was once simply good educational practice is now the law!

From time to time concern is focused on the expense of educating handicapped children, and there are calls within United States Congress to repeal P.L. 94-142. This often causes fear among those whose employment in special education is dependent upon the existence of the law. However, such fear is probably unfounded for three reasons. First, P.L. 94-142 is based directly on case law, which in turn is influenced by the United States Constitution. Thus, as long as a free education is offered to nonhandicapped children, a free and appropriate public education must also be granted to handicapped children. Congress cannot alter this right unless it amends the Constitution. Second, many states have adopted laws that are highly similar to P.L. 94-142. Many are even more procedurally specific than the federal law and would remain in effect even if the latter were changed. Finally, there is still considerable support in Congress for P.L. 94-142. Originally, the bill passed by a margin of 87 to 7 in the Senate and 404 to 7 in the House. Evidence of the continued support for the law in Congress is provided by the passage in October 1986 of the Education of the Handicapped Amendments, Public Law 99-457, which serves to amend P.L. 94-142 by requiring states to provide special education services to not only school-aged children but also preschoolers as young as three years. In sum, the fundamental philosophy of P.L. 94-142 will influence the profession of special education and the delivery of psychoeducational services for years to come.

Table 2.1 Major Provisions of P.L. 94-142

Free and appropriate public education

All children are entitled to a free and appropriate public education, regardless of the nature or severity of their handicap.

Nondiscriminatory assessment

Requires the establishment of procedures to assure that testing and evaluation materials and procedures utilized for the purposes of evaluation and placement of handicapped children will be selected and administered so as not to be culturally or racially discriminatory.

Development of an Individual Education Plan (IEP)

Requires the development of a written IEP for each handicapped child that will include a statement of current levels of educational achievement, annual and short-term goals, specific educational services to be provided, dates of initiation and duration of services, and criteria for evaluating the degree to which the objectives are achieved.

Due process

Requires an opportunity to present complaints with respect to any matter relating to the identification, evaluation, or educational placement of a child. Specific due process procedures include: (a) written notification to parents before evaluation, (b) written notification when initiating or refusing to initiate a change in educational placement, (c) opportunity to obtain an independent evaluation of the child, and (d) an opportunity for an impartial due process hearing.

Privacy and records

Requires that educational and psychological records pertaining to a child remain confidential except to those individuals who are directly involved in a child's education and who have a specific reason for reviewing the records. Further the law provides an opportunity for the parents or guardian of a handicapped child to examine all relevant records with respect to the identification, evaluation, and educational placement of the child.

Least restrictive environment

Requires to the maximum extent appropriate that handicapped children be educated with children who are not handicapped in as normal an environment as possible.

Related services

Required support services (e.g., psychological, audiology, occupational therapy, music therapy) are required to assist the handicapped child to benefit from special education.

Adapted from Education of all Handicapped Children Act of 1975, P.L. 94-142, *Federal Register*, pp. 42474–42518.

Legal Influences in the Assessment Phase

Parental Consent

Legal regulation of the education of handicapped children starts even before assessment begins. The law requires that parental approval is necessary before the evaluation of any child for potential placement in special education. Under ordinary circumstances, a regular classroom teacher who is administering tests to the entire class for the purpose of improving educational programming within the classroom does not need to obtain parental permission to give the tests. Likewise, permission is not usually required for a school district to administer routine educational tests to all children. In general parental permission is usually not required if a test is administered to all children, if it does not reveal information that is educationally irrelevant (for example, questions about drug use), and if the test is not used to change a child's educational placement.

According to P.L. 94-142, parental permission is required when an educational agency proposes to initiate (or refuses to initiate) or change the classification, evaluation, or educational placement of a child or the provisions of a free and appropriate public education for the child. Thus, parental permission is a legal necessity when a child is singled out and removed from the classroom to be tested by a psychologist, speech clinician, or special education teacher, regardless of whether the child eventually is placed in special education. Parents have a right to know when a potential change is being considered.

It is not enough simply to tell parents that an evaluation of their child is planned. The notice must also meet the legal requirements of informed consent, which means that parents must be informed in writing, in their primary language, of the purpose of the evaluation, the specific tests that will be administered, what they measure, how the information will be used, and the likely outcomes of such an assessment.

Nondiscriminatory Assessment

By far the most intense involvement in assessment by courts and legislatures has been to establish procedures to assure that assessment materials and procedures utilized for the evaluation and placement of handicapped children will be selected and administered so as not to be culturally or racially discriminatory. The impetus for the development of law in this area has its roots in the civil rights struggles of the 1950s, when minorities fought for and won the right for their children to have the same education as white children, as in *Brown*. Many schools, however, sought to circumvent the rights of minority children by placing them in "special" classrooms on the basis of their performance on standardized tests. The courts (see, for example, *Larry* v. *Riles*, 1979) have often concluded that the intelligence and achievement tests used to place these children are biased or discriminatory and result in a disproportionate number of minority children in special education classrooms. Many tests have been considered discriminatory because of the lack of minority group children in the sample on which they were standardized and because children from minority cultures tend to achieve lower scores than middle-class white children (cf. Reynolds, 1982).

The isssue of discriminatory assessment has not received a fair appraisal in the courts because many of the individuals responsible for making decisions have appeared to ignore the scientific evidence concerning assessment instruments and have instead relied upon intuition and inference. *Larry P.* concerned the overrepresentation of minority students in special education classrooms. The plaintiffs portrayed the "culturally biased" intelligence test as the primary reason that black children were placed in "isolating," "inferior," "dead-end," and "stigmatizing" classes for the educably mentally retarded. The logic of this statement has been questioned, and the court has been faulted for not inquiring as to why so many black children are even brought into the referral process (MacMillan & Meyers, 1980). Perhaps this occurs because these children often are not able to learn from standard curricula and teaching practices and because schools may lack sufficient educational options for remedying children's deficits.

The problem of deciding intuitively whether a test is biased has been examined by Reschly and Sabers (1979), who argued that evaluating a test without reference to research can lead to inaccurate conclusions. They pointed out, for example, that the widely criticized item from the Wechsler Intelligence Scale for Children–Revised, "What is the thing to do if a boy (girl) much smaller than yourself starts to fight with you?" may actually be easier for black children to answer than for white children. Without consulting the research on this particular question, it would be easy to conclude that it was biased against poor children because turning your back on anyone who hits you in the ghetto would not be an intelligent thing to do. Determining whether a test is biased is a complex social and psychometric issue that has challenged researchers from many scientific disciplines.

Public Law 94-142 contains a good summary of the legalities influencing assessment. This law emphasizes the use of a wide range of assessment information that is collected by a variety of professionals so as to be as culturally fair as possible. Table 2.2 provides an overview of portions of the law relevant to testing and assessment.

Access to Records

Public Law 94-142 as well as another federal law, the Family Educational Rights and Privacy Act (FERPA) of 1977 (often referred to as the Buckley Amendment), govern the handling of records in educational settings. These laws require that all public educational institutions

1. allow parents access to all official educational records related to their child and provide an interpretation of the records if necessary;

Table 2.2 Major Requirements Concerning Testing and Assessment in P.L. 94-142

1. Each State educational agency shall insure that each public agency establishes and implements procedures which meet the requirements of this law.
2. Testing and evaluation materials and procedures used for the purposes of evaluation and placement of handicapped children must be selected and administered so as not to be racially or culturally discriminatory.
3. Before any action is taken with respect to the initial placement of a handicapped child in a special education program, a full and individual evaluation of the child's educational needs must be conducted in accordance with the requirements of this law.
4. State and local educational agencies shall insure, at a minimum, that tests and other evaluation materials:
   a. Are provided and administered in the child's native language or other mode of communication, unless it is clearly not feasible to do so;
   b. Have been validated for the specific purpose for which they are used; and
   c. Are administered by trained personnel in conformance with the instructions provided by their producer.
5. Tests and other evaluation materials include those tailored to assess specific areas of educational need and not merely those which are designed to provide a single general intelligence quotient.
6. Tests are selected and administered so as best to ensure that when a test is administered to a child with impaired sensory, manual, or speaking skills, the test results accurately reflect the child's aptitude or achievement level or whatever other factors the test purports to measure, rather than reflecting the child's impaired sensory, manual, or speaking skills (except when those skills are the factors which the test purports to measure).
7. No single procedure is used as the sole criterion for determining an appropriate educational program for a child.
8. The evaluation is made by a multidisciplinary team or group of persons, including at least one teacher or other specialist with knowledge in the area of suspected disability.
9. The child is assessed in all areas related to the suspected disability, including, where appropriate, health, vision, hearing, social and emotional status, general intelligence, academic performance, communicative status, and motor abilities.
10. In interpreting evaluation data and in making placement decisions, each public agency shall:
    a. Draw upon information from a variety of sources, including aptitude and achievement tests, teacher recommendations, physical condition, social or cultural background, and adaptive behavior.
    b. Insure that information obtained from all of these sources is documented and carefully considered.
    c. Insure that the placement decision is made by a group of persons, including persons knowledgeable about the child, the meaning of the evaluation data, and the placement options.
    d. Insure that the placement decision is made in conformity with the least restrictive environment rules.
11. If a determination is made that a child is handicapped and needs special education and related services, an individualized education program must be developed for the child.

Adapted from Education of All Handicapped Children Act of 1975, P.L. 94-142, *Federal Register*, pp. 42474–42518.

2. allow parents to challenge records that may be inaccurate or misleading; and
3. obtain the written consent of parents before releasing a child's records to a third party.

Basic to understanding the regulations contained within these laws is the legal definition of "educational records." Simply stated, educational records are any records directly related to a student that are maintained by an educational institution. Stated even more simply by Trachtman (1972), a record is "anything put in writing for others to see" (p. 45). Obviously all reports and other official documentation of evaluation, classification, and placement should be open for parental inspection. Frequently school districts appoint an individual to review the records with parents so that explanations and interpretations can be offered if needed.

To follow the law is not always a straightforward matter, and the issue of access to records provides an excellent example of the problems that may be encountered. The fact that FERPA allows parents to see the educational records of their child runs counter to the rights of some test publishers, who argue that test forms and test protocol must not be shown to anyone except qualified professionals because to do so would jeopardize test security. Since many of these test protocols contain actual test items, publishers are concerned that parents might tell others about test content, thus jeopardizing the validity of the test. Individuals who provide interpretations of test results to parents can usually avoid problems by telling parents the general type of items on the test and giving examples that are similar but not identical to the ones actually on the test.

Although FERPA allows parents wide latitude in having access to records, it is quite specific in denying access to all other persons except those who have a "legitimate educational interest" in the child. For example, if a child moves from one school system to another, the new system may want to know the results of special education evaluations conducted by the former district. However, no records can be released unless the parents give written permission. Parents have the right to know what records are being disclosed and to whom and the purposes of the disclosure. In addition, parents have the right to a copy of all records being disclosed. An issue that arises with some frequency involves telephone requests for information about a child with whom an educational specialist has had some contact. The caller may or may not have permission to see the records and could be an individual from another school district or the private sector (such as a speech pathologist or psychologist) or even a relative of the child. According to FERPA, it is clearly not prudent to provide information over the telephone. First, it is difficult to be completely certain to whom you are talking. Second, although the caller may have the child's best interests in mind, the law requires parental permission be obtained before information is released. Third, the specialist must exercise reasonable care in assuring that information is disclosed to parties who have obtained such permission.

Legal Influences in the Classification and Placement Phase

Multidisciplinary Decision Making

After the assessment phase has been completed, the classification phase typically begins with a group of professionals coming together to make decisions about classification and placement. P.L. 94-142 is very specific about how this process should occur. Specifically, P.L. 94-142 states that "the evaluation is made by a multidisciplinary team or group of persons, including at least one teacher, or other specialist with knowledge in the area of suspected disability." The law further requires each school to "insure that the placement decision is made by a group of persons, including persons knowledgeable about the child, the meaning of the evaluation data, and the placement options" [P.L. 94-142, Section 121a.523(c)]. Thus, educational decision-making teams comprised of teachers, parents, and support personnel (e.g., psychologists, counselors, nurses, physical and occupational therapists, speech pathologists, and social workers) have been required to ensure such a mandate is carried out. Children can also be a part of this team, although based upon our experience they are rarely present during formal team meetings.

According to Fenton, Yoshida, Maxwell, and Kaufman (1979), teams should try to accomplish eleven goals for every student with special needs:

1. Determine the student's eligibility for special education.
2. Determine whether sufficient information about the student exists before the placement team makes decisions affecting the student's instructional program.
3. Evaluate the educational significance of such data.
4. Determine the student's placement.
5. Formulate appropriate year-long educational goals and objectives for the student.
6. Develop specific short-term instructional objectives for the student.
7. Communicate with the parents about changes in the student's educational program.
8. Decide which information is needed for the future review of the student's program and progress.
9. Establish the date for the placement team's review.
10. Review the continued appropriateness of the student's educational program.
11. Review the student's educational progress.

The implicit rationale for a team approach to special education decision making is the belief that a group decision provides safeguards against individual errors in judgment while enhancing adherence to due process requirements (Pfeiffer, 1980). According to Pfeiffer (1981), "the key elements of a multidisciplinary team are a common purpose, cooperative problem-solving by different professionals who possess unique skills and orientation, and a coordination of activities" (p. 330). Thus, multidisciplinary teams provide a number of benefits beyond those provided by a single individual, including:

1. greater accuracy in assessment, classification, and placement decisions;
2. a forum for sharing differing views;
3. provisions for specialized consultative services to school personnel, parents, and community groups; and
4. the resources for developing and evaluating individualized educational programs for exceptional students.

Classification and Diagnosis

A major goal of the multidisciplinary decision-making process is to determine if a child is handicapped and whether he qualifies for placement in special education. Although they are often used interchangeably, the terms "classification" and "diagnosis" refer to different processes. Within an educational setting, classification involves the ordering or grouping of the attributes, characteristics, or behaviors of children into distinct categories. Effective classification systems use objective criteria or rules to decide whether a particular child belongs in a specific category. For example, to be classified as mentally retarded a child must have a score that is less than 70 (or 2 standard deviations below the mean) on a comprehensive intelligence test and significantly subaverage adaptive behavior. In this case, test scores provide relatively objective criteria upon which to base a decision to classify a child as mentally retarded. Classification is thus the system used to categorize the characteristics and behaviors of children.

Diagnosis follows from classification and is the process of assigning a child to a particular category within the classification system. In education, the development of the classification system has involved the establishment of a series of categories such as mentally retarded, learning disabled, and behavior disordered. The diagnostic process that evolves from this classification scheme requires that the attributes of a particular child be compared with the criteria that define each category. Diagnosis is thus simply the process of assigning a child to one of the classification categories (such as mentally retarded).

Classification in educational settings. Although a number of educational classification systems are available, one derived from the federal guidelines (that is, P.L. 94-142) is used almost without exception throughout the United States. This system, which is typically interpreted in a slightly different manner by each state's department of education, is widely used because funding from the federal government to state governments and from state governments to local school districts is based upon the system. Thus, local school districts are reimbursed by state governments for each child classified as handicapped. Typically, children with the more severe handicaps entitle their school district to more funding than do children with mild handicaps. A listing of the various categories recognized by the federal government is presented in Table 2.3. The descriptions of the various handicapping conditions were taken verbatim from P.L. 94-142.

Evaluation of the educational classification system. Ysseldyke and Thurlow (1984) have collected considerable data on how well the educational classification system works. They found that approximately 5 percent of the elementary school population is referred for evaluation during any given year. Once a student is referred, 92 percent are evaluated, and 73 percent of the students who are evaluated are actually placed in special education. Thus teachers who refer a student for evaluation appear to have an astoundingly high prediction rate, that is, most students who are referred for testing are diagnosed as handicapped and placed in special education. Ysseldyke and Thurlow attribute this phenomenon not to the keen eye of teachers but instead to negative features of the diagnostic process itself. They characterize the multidisciplinary decision-making process as a "search for pathology" during which it is "assumed that *if* a teacher refers a student, then the student must have a problem; it is assumed that the task of the decision making team is to find the problem" (Ysseldyke & Thurlow, 1984, p. 125). This perspective, although probably true in many cases, is quite pessimistic and fails to acknowledge the ability that teachers develop for identifying children experiencing problems (Hoge, 1983).

Children diagnosed as handicapped are most frequently placed in situations involving part-day services in a resource room with the remainder of their time in school being spent in the regular classroom. According to Ysseldyke and Algozzine (1982), the overall outcome of the educational classification process, which often involves the use of psychometrically inadequate tests, is the overinclusion of children on a one-way street into special education programs.

Needless to say, the educational classification system has been a matter of intense debate. Critics have strongly suggested that it has a number of serious shortcomings and that classification of children in this way should be abandoned. Although proponents of the system recognize that it could be improved, they also argue that it offers a number of advantages, including several administrative necessities, not the least of which are record keeping and a means for funding. Readers interested in an extensive discussion of issues surrounding the classification of children should consult other sources, including the Project on the Classification of Exceptional Children, a comprehensive and systematic analysis of the educational classification system. This project, coordinated by Nicholas Hobbs and funded by the federal government, was eventually published as *Issues in the Classification of Children* (Hobbs, 1975) and, although somewhat dated, should be required reading for anyone involved with handicapped children.

Table 2.3 Handicapping Conditions as Defined by P.L. 94-142

(1) "Deaf" means a hearing impairment which is so severe that the child is impaired in processing linguistic information through hearing, with or without amplification, which adversely affects educational performance.

(2) "Deaf-blind" means concomitant hearing and visual impairments, the combination of which causes such severe communication and other developmental and educational problems that they cannot be accommodated in special education programs solely for deaf or blind children.

(3) "Hard of hearing" means a hearing impairment, whether permanent or fluctuating, which adversely affects a child's educational performance but which is not included under the definition of "deaf" in this section.

(4) "Mentally retarded" means significantly subaverage general intellectual functioning existing concurrently with deficits in adaptive behavior and manifested during the developmental period, which adversely affects a child's educational performance.

(5) "Multihandicapped" means concomitant impairments (such as mentally retarded-blind, mentally retarded-orthopedically impaired, etc.), the combination of which causes such severe educational problems that they cannot be accommodated in special education programs solely for one of the impairments. The term does not include deaf-blind children.

(6) "Orthopedically impaired" means a severe orthopedic impairment which adversely affects a child's educational performance. The term includes impairments caused by congenital anomaly (e.g., clubfoot, absence of some member, etc.), impairments caused by disease (e.g., poliomyelitis, bone tuberculosis, etc.), and impairments from other causes (e.g., cerebral palsy, amputations, and fractures or burns which cause contractures).

(7) "Other health impaired" means limited strength, vitality or alertness, due to chronic or acute health problems such as a heart condition, tuberculosis, rheumatic fever, nephritis, asthma, sickle cell anemia, hemophilia, epilepsy, lead poisoning, leukemia, or diabetes, which adversely affects a child's educational performance.

(8) "Seriously emotionally disturbed" is defined as follows:

- (i) The term means a condition exhibiting one or more of the following characteristics over a long period of time and to a marked degree, which adversely affects educational performance:
  - (A) An inability to learn which cannot be explained by intellectual, sensory, or health factors;
  - (B) An inability to build or maintain satisfactory interpersonal relationships with peers and teachers;
  - (C) Inappropriate types of behavior or feelings under normal circumstances;
  - (D) A general pervasive mood of unhappiness or depression; or
  - (E) A tendency to develop physical symptoms or fears associated with personal or school problems.
- (ii) The term includes children who are schizophrenic or autistic. The term does not include children who are socially maladjusted, unless it is determined that they are seriously emotionally disturbed.

(9) "Specific learning disability" means a disorder in one or more of the basic psychological processes involved in understanding or in using language, spoken or written, which may manifest itself in an imperfect ability to listen, think, speak, read, write, spell, or to do mathematical calculations. The term includes such conditions as perceptual handicaps, brain injury, minimal brain disfunction, dyslexia, and developmental aphasia. The term does not include children who have learning

Table 2.3, *continued*

problems which are primarily the result of visual, hearing, or motor handicaps, of mental retardation, or of environmental, cultural, or economic disadvantage.

(10) "Speech impaired" means a communication disorder, such as stuttering, impaired articulation, a language impairment, or a voice impairment, which adversely affects a child's educational performance.

(11) "Visually handicapped" means a visual impairment which, even with correction, adversely affects a child's educational performance. The term includes both partially seeing and blind children.

Adapted from Education of All Handicapped Children Act of 1975, P.L. 94-142, *Federal Register*, p. 42476.

Legal Influences in the Intervention Phase

Individualized Education Plan

After a child has been assessed and classified, P.L. 94-142 requires that a team of individuals, including the child's parents, develop an Individualized Education Plan, or IEP, which is a written document describing the goals, objectives, and procedures that will be used to provide an appropriate education for the handicapped child. The plan must contain at least the following types of information (see Table 2.4 for a sample IEP):

1. a statement of the child's present levels of educational performance;
2. a statement of annual goals, including short-term instructional objectives;
3. a statement of the specific special education and related services to be provided and the extent to which the child will be able to participate in regular education programs;
4. the projected dates of the initiation of their services and their anticipated duration; and
5. objective criteria and evaluation procedures for determining, at least annually, whether the short-term instructional objectives are being achieved.

After the IEP is developed, the special education and related service personnel who will implement the objectives are given copies of the final document to guide their interventions. There are at least two major problems with a follow-up evaluation of an IEP. First, the review of an IEP is required only annually. Although it is possible to review goals more frequently, the process of meeting with a number of different professionals can be time-consuming and expensive. The problem, however, with only a yearly review is that the needs of and goals for a child can change several times during that period. Although P.L. 94-142 calls for the specification of short-term objectives, it provides no formal mechanism for monitoring the realization of these objectives or changing them as they are determined to be ineffective or inappropriate. Therefore, there is a high probability that problems with an IEP will not be discovered

Table 2.4 A Sample Individual Education Program

Date January 5

(1) Student	(2) Committee		
Name: Joe S. School: Tall Trees Elementary Grade: 5–7 Current Placement: Regular class Date of Birth: 11/4/77 Age: 10	*Name* Mr. Havlichek Mr. White Dr. Gory Mrs. Green Mrs. S. IEP From 1/20/88	*Position* Principal Regular Teacher School Psychologist Resource Teacher Parent To 6/1/88	*Initial*

(3) Present Level of Educational Functioning	(4) Annual Goal Statements	(5) Instructional Objectives	(6) Objective Criteria and Evaluation
MATH *Strengths* Can successfully compute 3-digit addition and subtraction facts without regrouping. Can complete an oral or written sequence of 4-digit numbers. *Weaknesses* Frequently makes computational errors on problems with which he has had a great deal of experience. Cannot successfully compute division problems.	*MATH* 1. To complete an oral or written sequence of 5-digit numbers with 0 in 10's, 100's or 1000's place. 2. To correctly add a 3-digit plus a 3-digit number with carrying in the 10's and 100's place.	*MATH* 1. Will complete oral and written sequence with 4, 5-digit number with no zeroes, with 90% accuracy. 2. Will complete oral and written sequence with 4-digit numbers with 0 in the 10's place and 0 in the 100's place, with 90% accuracy. 3. Will complete an oral and written sequence of 5-digit numbers with 0 in 10's place, 0 in 100's place and 0 in 1000's place. These tasks must be completed, with 90% accuracy. 4. Solves addition problems of 1-digit plus 2-digit numbers with carrying, with 90% accuracy. 5. Solves addition problems of 2-digit plus 2-digit numbers with carrying, with 90% accuracy.	*MATH* 1. Keymath at beginning and end of this 2-month period 2. Teacher-made CRT 3. Teacher observation

SOCIAL COMPETENCE *Strengths* Joins in team games with enthusiasm. Is able to cooperate with team members appropriately during team games. *Weaknesses* Demonstrates poor self-concept by making derogatory statements about himself. Lacks respect for other classmates during quiet work periods by talking out loud. Demonstrates lack of self-discipline with out-of-seat behaviors during work periods.	*SOCIAL COMPETENCE* 1. Joe will develop desirable behaviors (good manners, responsibility & self-discipline) such that he is able to interact appropriately with teachers & peers. 2. Joe will increase positive interpersonal behavior such that he is able to make friends in his class. 3. Joe will develop a more positive self-concept by increasing his success experiences.	*SOCIAL COMPETENCE* 1. Joe will give examples of and use socially acceptable language 90% of the time. 2. Joe will give rules of and practice etiquette in these situations: in the classroom, in cafeteria, on playground, as a guest, in a store, 90% of the time. 3. Joe will display self-discipline when placed in a tempting situation (e.g., finishing work before play, returning or reporting found articles) 90% of the time. 4. Joe will demonstrate that he can be trusted by successfully completing a task without delay or persuasion 90% of the time. 5. Joe will give 6 examples of good friendship while practicing new and positive behaviors toward peers during 80% of the school day. 6. Joe will discuss and give 5 examples of good and bad family relations between parents & children with 80% accuracy.	*SOCIAL COMPETENCE* Observation Teacher-made written tests Discussion with teacher Role play Observation Teacher-made tests Role play and discussion.

(continued)

Table 2.4, *continued*

(3) Present Level of Educational Functioning	(4) Annual Goal Statements	(5) Instructional Objectives	(6) Objective Criteria and Evaluation
READING *Strengths* Can identify the main idea of a paragraph from a 2nd grade reader. Comprehends written reading material at 2nd grade level. Reads 90% of words from Durrell Reading List at 2nd grade level. *Weaknesses* Cannot identify the meaning of certain words after having read them in a sentence. Unable to sound out an unknown word successfully when seeing it for the first time. Has difficulty with the comprehension skills of sequencing and inferring details when reading 2nd grade material.	*READING* 1. Joe will read paragraphs correctly and demonstrate comprehension skills. 2. Joe will demonstrate understanding of the visual clues to long & short vowel sounds by identifying correctly letters that are clues to vowel sounds.	*READING* 1. Given paragraphs and matching sets of multiple choice questions, he will complete the questions with 90% accuracy. 2. Given a 3-paragraph story, he will number the sentences in the order in which they sequentially occurred. 3. Given a paragraph containing clues to character's emotions, he will identify the emotions of the character correctly. 4. Will complete study sheets on *O*, *E*, and *Y* in final syllable or end of word, with 90% accuracy. 5. Will complete study sheets on *ai*, *ay*, *ea*, *ei*, *ie*, *oa*, and *oe* in the accented syllable, with 90% accuracy. 6. Will complete study sheets on identifying one consonant preceding a final *ie*, with 90% accuracy.	*READING* Teacher-made questions Teacher-made material Teacher-made material Teacher-made CRT Teacher-made CRT Teacher-made CRT

(7) Educational Services to Be Provided

Services Required	Date Initiated	Duration of Service	Individual Responsible for the Service
Regular Reading — Adapt	4/10/88	6/1/88	Mrs. Jones
Resource Room	4/10/88	6/1/88	Mrs. Green
Counselor Consultant	To be arranged		Not available at present

Extent of time in the regular education program: 60% increasing to 80%
Justification of the educational placement:

It is felt that the structure of the resource room can best meet the goals stated for Joe; especially coordinated with the regular classroom.

It is also felt that Joe could profit enormously from talking with a counselor. He needs someone with whom to talk and with whom he can share his feelings.

(8) I have had the opportunity to participate in the development of the Individual Education Program.
I agree with the Individual Education Program (   )
I disagree with the Individual Education Program (   )

____
Parent's Signature

until an entire year has passed and it is time for the annual review of the IEP. Of course, active parental involvement in their child's education enhances the accountability of educators and increases the probability the objectives are accomplished or adjusted when needed.

A second major problem with the review of an IEP is that school personnel are often concerned that their professional credibility will be damaged if a child's educational objectives are not achieved. They have this concern despite explicit statements in the regulations governing special education that educational personnel will *not* be held accountable if educational objectives are not met. This fear among school personnel can lead to the establishment of only minimal annual goals that can be easily attained.

Least Restrictive Environment

In making placement and intervention decisions, multidisciplinary teams must take care to insure that education occurs in the least restrictive environment, which is best defined within the context of a continuum of educational services for handicapped children. One such continuum is illustrated in Figure 2.1. The figure is organized from top to bottom, with services at the top (that is, those provided in the regular classroom) being less restrictive than those at the bottom (that is, those provided in a residential school). The idea behind the principle of least restrictive environment is that children must be educated in as normal an environment as their handicap allows. Thus, children with minor handicaps such as a minor reading problem can be educated in their home school where they socialize with their neighborhood friends. Children with very severe handicaps such as autism may require placement in a school that specializes in that handicap.

Education in the least restrictive environment is sometimes referred to as mainstreaming because many mildly handicapped children are pulled out of their regular education classes for part of the day and placed in a resource room where they receive specialized services for handicaps such as learning disabilities or mild mental retardation. The remainder of the day they are "mainstreamed," or placed with other, normal children for socialization and instruction in subjects in which their deficits do not interfere with their ability to benefit from the teaching.

Appropriate Education

The major purpose of the entire special education referral, assessment, and placement process is to insure that handicapped children receive an appropriate education. Typically, this is a straightforward process, and the multidisciplinary team designs a program individualized for a child's unique strengths and weaknesses. Occasionally, however, as in all decision-making processes, there is disagreement as to what represents the most appropriate educational services. The definition of the term "appropriate" has thus become a major issue.

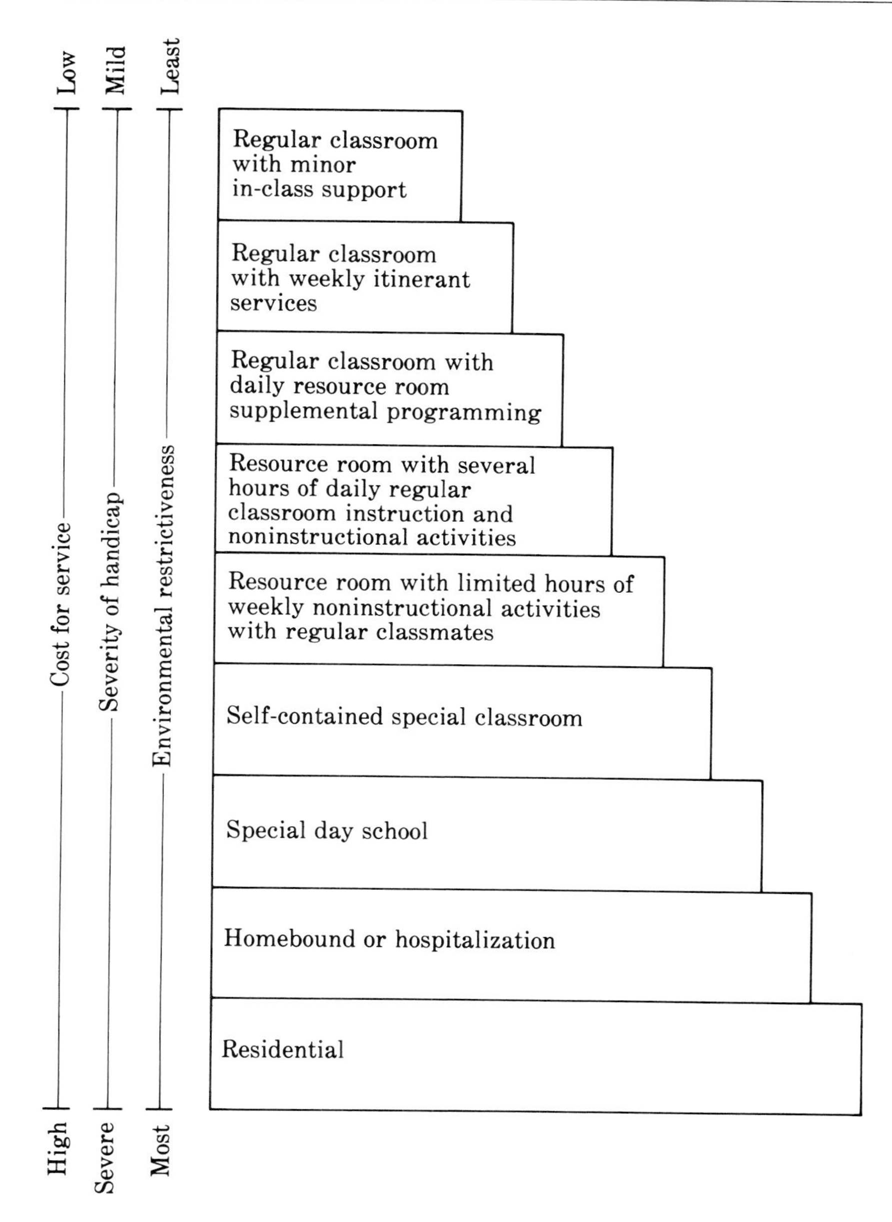

Figure 2.1 Continuum of special education services along three dimensions. (From *Encyclopedia of Special Education* by C. R. Reynolds and L. Mann, 1987, New York: John Wiley and Sons. Copyright 1987 by John Wiley and Sons. Reprinted by permission of John Wiley and Sons, Inc., Publisher.)

Such disagreements have usually been between parents and the school system. Parents, for example, may want their child to be placed in a special school in another state that has an excellent reputation for handling problems similar to the ones their child is experiencing. The local school system may refuse to pay for placement in such a setting, saying they can provide an appropriate education within the district. Does a school system have an obligation to provide the best possible education for a child or only an appropriate education?

In response to this question, the United State Supreme Court has come down on the side of the school system in the case of *Hendrick Hudson District Board of Education* v. *Rowley* (1982). The Court ruled that a school system must provide an appropriate but not necessarily an ideal educational program for a child and that "the requirement that a state provide specialized services to handicapped children generated no additional requirement that the services so provided be sufficient to maximize each child's potential 'commensurate with the opportunity provided to other children'" (p. 198).

Psychoeducational Assessment Procedures in Schools

From the above discussion it should be obvious that the special education referral, classification, and placement process has become a highly regulated process due to federal legislation such as P.L. 94-142. The question remains, however, as to how the various aspects of the law can be translated into step-by-step procedures whereby the needs of children and teachers are provided for within an orderly process that takes into account the legal issues bearing upon special education. In the remainder of this chapter we describe a generic process, typical of those used in many school districts throughout the United States, for the accomplishment of these goals. Figure 2.2 depicts a flow chart that describes the procedural steps typically taken by psychologists and special educators in the evaluation and treatment of students. A brief discussion of each step should provide an overview of a complete psychoeducational service model, thus highlighting the interrelationships among consultation, assessment, and intervention services.

Step 1: Determine appropriateness of referral. A referral, whether formal or informal, is a signal to an assessor that a student is perceived to be experiencing a problem. The assessor's task is to determine whether the referral is "appropriate." The definition of an "inappropriate" referral will vary. However, some documentation of the perceived problem or concern as well as an enumeration of previous teacher- or parent-directed interventions is usually necessary before an assessor should get involved. If the referral is deemed inappropriate and does not warrant direct or indirect involvement by school district personnel, it should be either referred back to the person making the request

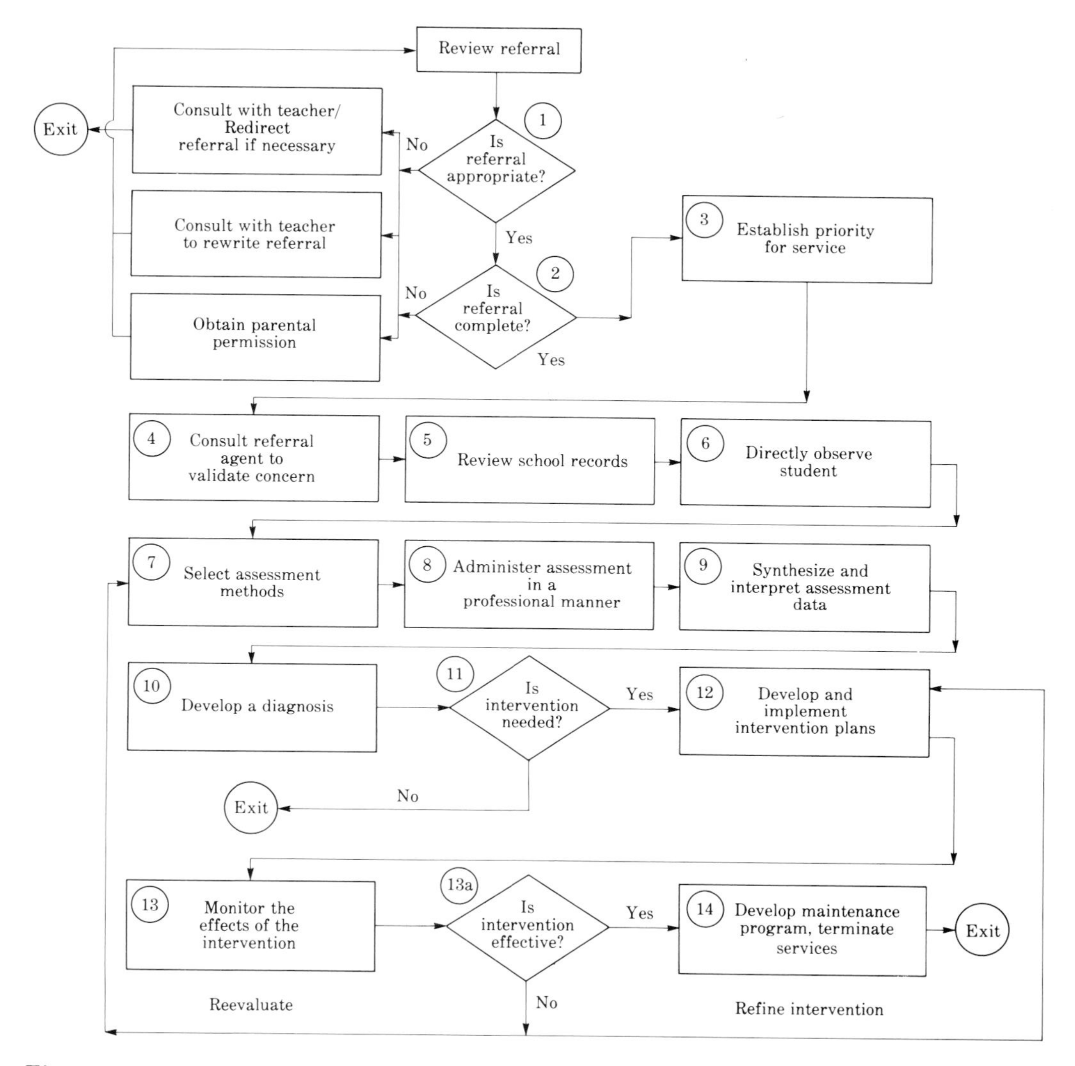

Figure 2.2 Flow chart of consultation-assessment-intervention service system. (From *School Psychology: Essentials of Theory and Practice* by C. R. Reynolds, T. B. Gutkin, S. N. Elliott, and J. C. Witt, 1984, New York: John Wiley and Sons. Copyright 1984 by John Wiley and Sons. Reprinted by permission of John Wiley and Sons, Inc., Publisher.)

or directed to another service system or agency. If no service is needed, an explanation should be made to the person who made the referral.

Step 2: Review referral for essential components. If the referral is judged to be appropriate, the assessor must determine whether it has all the essential components applicable to psychoeducational services, including a clear, behavioral statement of the problem and the written permission of the student's parents or legal guardians if a psychologist or educational diagnostician will be working directly with the student.

If the referral is incomplete, the assessor should initiate the steps needed to secure the necessary information. This will most likely involve returning the referral to the referring agent for revision. In the interim, consultation with teachers or parents, record reviews, and classroom observations could be initiated.

Step 3: Establish service priority. The demands for psychoeducational services are usually such that some individual or group of individuals must make decisions about who receives priority in acquiring services. Some systems utilize a severity-of-problem scale, while others use the date of referral to prioritize potential recipients. Typically, the assessor reviews referrals and other time investments with a principal or special education coordinator before prioritizing cases. When an appreciable delay between initial referral and expected date of service is anticipated, it is advisable to notify parents and teachers involved in the case.

Step 4: Consult with referral agents. The assessor should meet at least once with the individual who referred a student to clarify and validate the child's problem before further interactions take place. This step is particularly necessary when there has been a significant delay between the referral date and the assessor's initial involvement. When the referral agent is not a parent, the assessor might also contact the parents or legal guardians to ensure cooperation and to gather information. If nothing more, this step provides for enhanced communication among assessors, parents, and teachers, all of whom are critical in the assessment and intervention phases.

Step 5: Review school records. Prior to an evaluation or intervention, the assessor should review and analyze a student's cumulative records. Information gleaned from such records can be classified as relating to the student's (a) sensory system (such as vision and hearing) integrity, (b) academic progress, (c) history of physical health, (d) history of emotional health, and (e) family or social history. A review of school records should be supplemented by interviews with parents, school personnel, or other significant individuals.

Step 6: Direct student observations. Observations of a student in different settings and by different observers provides valuable information for decision making, whether one actually records specific behaviors or simply attempts to better understand a student interacting within a particular setting. When testing is likely to occur, unobtrusive observation may be impossible unless it takes place prior to working with the student directly. Thus, conducting observations prior to meeting a student reduces the probability of the student behaving differently because of your presence and thereby enhances the meaningfulness of the observation.

Step 7: Select assessment methods. Selection of assessment instruments and strategies should be based on the student's stated problem and the assessor's competencies. If a student requires an assessment beyond the competencies of a given assessor, that professional is ethically obligated to refuse to use procedures beyond her level of competence and to refer the case to someone skilled in using the methods or tests.

Step 8: Administer assessment professionally. The assessor should administer all tests and collect observations or ratings according to recommended procedures. In other words, when administering and scoring standardized instruments or using nonstandardized assessment methods, assessors should adhere to the procedures outlined in test manuals or documented in the professional literature.

Step 9: Synthesize and interpret assessment data. Once all the assessment data have been collected and quantified, the assessor is responsible for analyzing and interpreting the results with respect to the stated problems. The results are usually communicated in a written report and a verbal summary at a multidisciplinary staff meeting. Assessors should be aware of their colleagues' knowledge so as to write reports in an understandable and meaningful manner. Oral or written reports laden with technical terms and jargon may confuse or even antagonize others. Communication to all parties is facilitated by providing objective and concrete evidence to support interpretations. Information and interpretations should also account for measurement error and recognize the limitations of particular instruments. Finally, assessors should not rely solely on their written reports or verbal summaries if behavior change in a student is a desired outcome of the evaluation; follow-up discussions or notes to those who will provide direct services are often necessary to ensure understanding and correct implementation of such recommendations.

Step 10: Develop a diagnosis. At the conclusion of the interpretation of assessment data, the assessors are responsible for formulating a psychological-educational diagnosis whenever classification or eligibility for services is a consideration. In most states, guidelines for determining handicapping conditions (such as learning disabled, behaviorally impaired, and educably mentally handicapped) have been developed by state departments of education or mental health agencies that assist psychologists and educators in determining classification criteria.

Step 11: Decide if intervention is needed. Decisions about interventions usually follow a comprehensive consultation or assessment of a student. An assessor formulates an opinion regarding the need for intervention, whether functioning as an assessment team member or individual consultant. When a team is involved, other members of the team should have input about intervention plans. When the assessor is the primary or only person consulting with a teacher, parent, or other individual on a case, responsibility for determining the need for intervention effectively rests with the assessor and referring adult. In every case, *not* to implement an intervention must be considered a viable option since some problems will solve themselves if left alone. Determining which problems demand attention and which do not is one of the most difficult of lessons for professionals eager to help.

Step 12: Develop and implement intervention plans. The assessor, along with others (assessment team members or consultees), develops potential intervention plans for implementation in the least restrictive environment. These intervention plans should (a) correspond to the student's problem statement and diagnosis, (b) be practical, (c) contain behavioral objectives, and (d) be communicated in sufficient detail for implementation. If a student is to be enrolled in special education, the intervention plan would be included in an IEP.

Step 13: Monitor effects of intervention. Assessors should try to measure the results of interventions that they have helped to develop. Periodic monitoring allows for corrections or adjustments in services and provides valuable feedback about diagnosis and intervention plans. According to P.L. 94-142 and most state special education regulations, follow-up in the form of a psychological reevaluation must occur at least every three years. Reviews of students' IEPs are to occur annually, and thus provide another opportunity for assessors to receive feedback and have input into the refinement of services. However, three-year reevaluations and annual IEP reviews are insufficient for maximal use of follow-up information, so we suggest weekly monitoring of interventions initially after implementation and monthly contacts thereafter to monitor a client's progress.

Step 14: Determine if psychoeducational services should be terminated. After an intervention has been in place for a reasonable period and improvement has been documented, the assessor should formulate an opinion concerning the necessity of continuing the intervention. Although a decision may be made to develop a generalization and maintenance plan, if generalization has occurred already, termination of services may be in order.

This fourteen-step procedural model of psychoeducational services for referred students should be viewed as a flexible process. It is an attempt to organize typical services in a logical sequence. In addition, feedback or refinement loops are available at each major decision point allowing for redefinition of a problem, further assessment of a student, or redesigning of an intervention.

Summary

The law has been a double-edged sword for individuals providing services to handicapped children. For the most part, the laws have been very helpful in securing services for these children. However, they sometimes cause the system to become rigid and inflexible and provide services in ways that may not be optimal. In the present system, children must be evaluated in specific ways and labeled as handicapped before they can receive services. Some who need services still do not qualify under the existing guidelines. There are many critics of the present system who insist that all children who need help should receive it. Opponents of that proposal say a system is necessary to keep account of the money spent on special education. The prudent psychoeducational specialist will remember that the laws governing special education are useful tools for problem solving and advocating an appropriate education. It is important to understand the laws so they may be used and applied to one's advantage.

Chapter 3

Assessment Models, Approaches, and Assumptions

Learning Objectives

1. Compare and contrast the medical and behavioral-ecological models of child behavior.
2. List the strengths and weaknesses of each major approach to educational assessment.
3. Discuss the meaning and importance of each of the major assumptions of assessment.
4. Describe the importance of the linkage between assessment and intervention.
5. Describe how working on an assessment team can be made more difficult by different theoretical orientations.

Professionals in various fields develop frameworks or theories for understanding their highly specialized world. Different frameworks or theories lead to different decisions about assessment methods and different interpretations of data. One's theoretical orientation may dictate whether to test, which tests to give, what to test, and how to interpret the tests. Consider, for example, a situation in which a child is referred by his teacher for evaluation because of hyperactivity. The child is evaluated by a team of specialists with different types of training and frameworks for viewing behavior. The basic questions are "What is causing the hyperactivity?" and "What can be done to reduce the problem?" A social worker may see the problem as a result of difficulties in the home. A behavioral consultant may review her observations and suggest the child is overly active because of insufficient teacher control in the classroom. The school nurse may recall that the child eats chocolate "all day long" and attributes the problem to poor nutrition. The psychologist may consider the problem a result of minimal brain dysfunction.

One solution to the lack of consensus among the specialists about the cause of the child's hyperactivity would be for the specialists to acknowledge their own respective frameworks and try to understand the child's functioning from a variety of perspectives. Such an approach is necessary because the same professional frameworks that give order to our decision making can cause a failure to consider all variables for a given case objectively. If you have only one way of viewing the world, you will attempt to mold the world to be consistent with your view.

The purpose of this chapter is to introduce several theoretical perspectives on human behavior and subsequent approaches to assessment. In addition, we will consider the different types of assessment information that can be collected, the various purposes for which they can be used, and the major methods of assessment.

Perspectives on Human Behavior

Human behavior is quite predictable. Determining, for example, why Sarah behaves "appropriately" one day but not the next can be accomplished through a systematic assessment process if you understand the factors that influence human learning and behavior. Psychologists and educators have contributed significantly to the understanding of human behavior by developing theories or models that help to explain an individual's behavior in a given situation. In this section, we use two general models of human behavior to illustrate the importance of theory for assessment: the medical model and the behavioral-ecological model.

A useful model of human behavior should provide a theoretical framework for increasing our understanding of individuals' past actions and predicting their future behaviors. A study of models of human behavior is important because they can influence one's beliefs about why people behave as they do. Consider, for example, the phrenologist who believes that behavior is determined by the size and location of bumps on the head. This view of behavior dictates the subject matter for assessment (bumps on the head); the phrenologist would thus see no benefit in administering a personality test.

It is useful for assessment to categorize human behavior into three broad categories: motoric, cognitive, or physiological. Clearly, these categories are not entirely separate and distinct, nor should it be inferred that one category of behavior can occur without a corresponding action in the other two categories. These three categories, however, do provide a framework for focusing on different types of behavior. The two models of human behavior we have chosen to discuss focus on these categories differentially, with motor and cognitive behavior receiving the most attention.

The Medical Model

The medical model of behavior is illustrated by the psychoanalytic theory of Sigmund Freud and other later analysts. A central postulate of this model is that actions or behaviors are best understood through the intensive study of intrapsychic states. According to the theory, one's intrapsychic state is significantly influenced by early life events, particularly those in the first five years of life. The medical model focuses on an individual's thoughts or cognitions as they influence deviant behavior. It assumes (a) that behavior that deviates negatively from normative standards is a reflection of a personal disease, or disturbance, disorder, or dysfunction; and (b) that treatment must bring about changes within the individual (Reger, 1972). The first assumption implies that children who cannot be maintained or accommodated in a regular education program are suffering from an internal psychoeducational disorder. The second assumption implies that such children are deviant and that educational treatments should be designed to modify them. Educational "cures" seem most frequently to take the form of special classes that tend to isolate the "diseased" child from normal or healthy children. The utility of the medical model for education has been seriously challenged (Szasz, 1960; Zubin, 1967). Reger (1972) has very succinctly summarized some of the problems with the model:

> When a child is seen as a "patient" in school, when he is looked at as a carrier of a medical-model illness (or deviation, etc.), then the teacher and the school are relieved of much of the responsibility for the child. If he makes little or no progress, it is because of him and his condition rather than the school teacher. (pp. 11–12)

The Behavioral-Ecological Model

The behavioral-ecological model of human behavior acknowledges the impact of other people and environmental factors in shaping a child's behavior. The major assumption of this model is that human behavior is primarily a function of the interaction between environmental events and individual characteristics of people (Lewin, 1951; Skinner, 1953). With this model, deviant behavior is viewed as inappropriate rather than as an illness or intrapsychic disturbance. Assessors subscribing to this model would probably assess all three categories of behavior but focus primarily on observable motoric behavior.

Obviously, a behavioral-ecological model would cause one to examine different variables than a medical model. Assessment procedures selected within this framework would focus on environmental variables rather than on internal child variables. Given the complexity of the learning and adjustment problems of school children, behavior is clearly a function of many factors, and a comprehensive assessment thus requires that one have substantial knowledge and skills as well as the ingenuity of a good detective. In the next section, several approaches to this assessment "mystery" are described.

Approaches to Assessment

A theory determines the types of variables that will be measured during the assessment process. The assessment of different types of variables in turn leads to the use of different approaches to assessment. Major approaches to assessment include norm-referenced assessment, criterion-referenced assessment, informal assessment, and ecological assessment. They differ not only with respect to what is measured but also with respect to how it is measured. This section provides a critical analysis of the various approaches to assessment, including a discussion of the strengths and weaknesses of each.

Norm-Referenced Assessment

Perhaps the most common approach to testing is norm-referenced assessment. It derives its name from the method in which test scores get their meaning by comparison to a representative group of scores. For example, a test score of 86 is considered good if it is higher than 95 percent of the scores with which it is compared, but it is not so good if it is lower than 70 percent of the other scores.

In the development of norm-referenced tests, a large, collectively representative sample of the general population is tested. These people are referred to as the norm group. On the most common children's intelligence tests, such as the Wechsler Intelligence Scale for Children-Revised (WISC-R), the norm group has an average score of 100 (this is the result of a rather complex transformation process whereby raw scores are transferred to a scale with a mean of 100). The properties of this test have been extensively studied, and the test manual suggests, for example, that less than 5 percent of the population score above 130. Because it is norm-referenced, any WISC-R score can be meaningfully interpreted by comparing it to the norm group. Norm-referenced assessment can be used to answer the following types of questions: How does Sarah compare in reading comprehension to the rest of the class? Does Dustin have the math aptitude needed for a college engineering program? Are Julie's SAT scores high enough to qualify her for admission to the university of her choice?

Advantages of norm-referenced assessment. Norm-referenced tests are widely used in special and remedial education for several reasons. First, many decisions involve categorizing children as "exceptional" or "special." These are essentially norm-referenced decisions because information is needed (and sometimes is required by law) on who is legally eligible for special services and who will probably be in greatest need of such services. Second, norm-referenced assessment provides information that is easily communicated to parents and others unfamiliar with tests. Telling parents that their child is in the lower 5 percent of the population with respect to hearing ability is usually more meaningful than providing data about their child's deciBel (loudness) levels. Third, norm-referenced tests have received the most attention in terms of technical data and research. They have a long and proud history, and their usefulness for a wide range of purposes (such as problem identification and screening) is well documented.

Disadvantages of norm-referenced assessment. A major difficulty with norm-referenced assessment is that it typically provides information that may be too general to be useful in everyday classroom teaching activities. Many educators disregard the prognostic and interpretative types of data provided by standardized tests because the information is often not directly applicable to developing daily instructional activities or interventions. What does knowing a child's WISC-R score or grade equivalent in reading specifically tell a teacher about what and how to teach? Does the child need to learn initial consonants or is he having difficulty with comprehension?

Another problem is that because most norm-referenced tests are designed for a broad national use, there is often a discrepancy between what is taught in an individual classroom and what is tested. For example, the spelling subtest of the Peabody Individual Achievement Test (PIAT) requires the respondent to choose the one word, out of a list of four, that is spelled incorrectly. The problem with this test is that most classroom spelling tests require the respondent to *write* words from memory as they are dictated by a teacher. Thus, the PIAT would provide information that not only lacks the specificity to guide remediation but also would probably be inaccurate unless a child's ability to recognize a correctly spelled word corresponded perfectly to her ability to recall and write spelling words from memory.

A third problem with norm-referenced tests is that they tend to promote and reinforce the belief that the locus of the problem is within the child because their primary purpose is to compare one student with another. However, although a child may differ from the norm, the real problem may not be within the child but in the teaching, placement, or curriculum. Educational specialists must begin to assess teacher behaviors, curriculum content and sequencing, and other variables not measured by norm-referenced tests.

Criterion-Referenced Assessment

Whether a child can perform a particular skill is the question criterion-referenced assessment seeks to answer. In contrast to norm-referenced assessment, which compares, or references, one person's performance with others', criterion-referenced assessment seeks to determine which individuals have reached some preestablished level. Typically, skills within a subject are hierarchically arranged so that those that must be learned first are tested first. In math, for example, addition skills would be evaluated (and taught) before multiplication skills. These tests are usually criterion referenced because a student must achieve competence at one level before being taught at a higher level; criterion-referenced tests help to determine if a person is ready to move on to the next level. No effort is made to determine how much better or worse than the criterion a student performs but merely to assess, in a pass-fail manner, if a student possesses a certain skill.

Criterion-referenced assessment can be further illustrated by referring to differences in the methods used by some graduate and professional schools to evaluate students. A medical school, for example, may be concerned that everyone achieve surgery skills at some established criterion level (for example, the patient must recover in a minimal amount of time with no complications). However, some professional schools may use a norm-referenced approach in which they admit more students than they expect to graduate and then "weed out" the weaker ones by administering difficult tests and passing only those with the highest scores.

Advantages of criterion-referenced assessment. The primary usefulness of criterion-referenced assessment is in identifying a child's specific skills. Since most skills have been extensively studied and broken down into a series of steps or hierarchies, the test results could be used to determine the next most logical skill to teach. Thus, the implications for teaching are more direct with criterion-referenced tests than with norm-referenced tests.

A related advantage is the ability to use criterion-referenced tests in formative evaluation, which means assessing a child regularly, usually daily, when skills are being learned. This makes it possible to note student progress, determine if instruction is effective, and help plan the next skill to be taught. Since the focus is on skills instead of comparison with others, knowing what to teach and how to measure it becomes simplified.

Disadvantages of criterion-referenced assessment. The primary problem with this form of assessment is establishing a suitable criterion. If a test were needed to determine whether students had mastered high school mathematics, for example, there is the problem of determining exactly which skills should be included in the test. Some may feel that geometry must be included, while others may disagree. After it is decided to measure a particular skill, the level at which the skill must be performed for the student to pass must be determined. Should a student pass the test if 90 percent of the questions are answered correctly or only if 100 percent are correct? These decisions must be carefully considered, because setting inappropriate criteria may cause a student to struggle unnecessarily with a concept.

Advocates of criterion-referenced testing assume that a child who fails to master a concept does so because of lack of exposure to the material. It is further assumed that additional instruction related to the concept will enable a child to pass the test. However, these assumptions may be inaccurate for some youngsters in special education, because additional instruction of the wrong type may not benefit some children and may result in repeated failures.

A potentially troublesome aspect of this form of test is that the skills assessed may become the goals of instruction rather than selected samples exemplifying what the child should know. Teachers may then narrow the focus of their instruction and simply teach in accordance with what is measured on the test, which can result in a loss of the richness and variety that characterize good instruction.

Ebel (1975) summarized well some additional problems with criterion-referenced tests:

> Criterion-referenced testing has the appeal of novelty and innovation. It may seem to offer more meaningful measures of achievement, as well as escape from some of the problems inherent in norm-referenced measurements. But it creates special problems. . . . There is the problem of repeated testing of those who do not reach criterion at first, plus the problem of creating multiple parallel test forms for use in the repeated testing. There is the problem of reporting only two levels of an achievement that exists at many different levels, and of treating an achievement ever so slightly above the criterion as completely satisfactory, while achievement ever so slightly below is treated as completely unsatisfactory. There is the problem of producing, distributing, and using detailed, bulky, and quite ephemeral reports on which objectives a student achieved success and on which he did not. (p. 85)

Informal Assessment

Watching grandparents interact with their grandchildren is a good opportunity to see a wide range of assessment activities. For example, a three-year-old might be asked to count to ten, to follow simple directions, to color with crayons, or to name the animals in a book. Such tasks may or may not be present at that age, but grandparents derive a great deal of satisfaction whatever the outcome. This type of assessment is ongoing and occurs in a very flexible and open social atmosphere. The tasks are obviously not standardized.

Similarly, teachers who analyze a child's writing for error patterns, special education teachers who observe a child in the regular classroom, speech therapists who just listen to a child talk, and psychologists who look at a child's mannerisms during oral reading may all be using informal assessment. Informal in this instance refers to the fact that this form of assessment is not a standardized and prespecified process but rather adapted to the individual child and situation. Such techniques tell how a child learns and what a child knows. The selection of the word "informal" to describe a model of assessment may be problematic, however, for it may lead to some unfortunate misunderstandings. The term is intended to refer to the content of assessment (that is, the type of measures used and the way in which they are used) and the use of such content rather than the process. The process is really behavioral assessment and represents a very structured and systematized problem-solving approach (see, for example, the systems suggested by Eaves & McLaughlin, 1977, and Elliott & Piersel, 1982). Specifically, the intent is to emphasize the use of curriculum-based tests, behavioral observations, and trial teaching in the assessment of children.

Individuals who utilize informal assessment seem to view themselves as detectives. If a child is experiencing failure, assessment consists of collecting clues and facts about what contributes to the problem. Is it a problem with the child such as a lack of ability or low motivation or with the task being too difficult, insufficiently explained, or not worth learning? Or is it a problem with the setting such as poor teaching or the lack of a quiet place to study? A good detective attempts to evaluate every area that might possibly contribute to the problem. A major assumption of this approach is that the closer the evaluation is to the actual situation in which the child is experiencing difficulty, the more accurate the identification processes and remedial interventions.

Advantages of informal assessment. The primary benefit of informal assessment over either norm-referenced or criterion-referenced assessment is its relevance to developing instructional or intervention activities. In general, norm-referenced tests can be used to select those who who need instruction, and criterion-referenced tests help to determine what needs to be taught. Informal assessment practices also provide information about what a child needs to learn, but they do so using the actual materials and stimuli that the child encounters daily. Additionally, informal assessment is unique in providing information about how instruction should be given. By experimenting and playing detective, one can determine whether a child should be seated at the front or back of the room, what reinforces her, and when performance is best and worst.

Another reason that informal assessment is so applicable to instruction is that only very small inferences are needed to use the test data for instruction. Compare, for example, the degree of inference required to apply data from a nationally standardized norm-referenced test of reading ability versus information from a test derived from the reading book the child uses in class. Naturally the use of classroom materials increases the applicability of assessment results to instructional activities. Since informal assessment typically occurs in the child's natural environment, assessors do not have the problem of generalizing the results from one situation to another. For example, consider a child who is being evaluated for a behavior problem. One evaluator may take the child into a quiet office for interviewing and formal testing. Another person may choose to observe the child in the classroom and on the playground under a variety of conditions. It is easy to question the degree to which the formal testing generalizes since it was conducted in a small, quiet room on a one-to-one basis. Even the informal aspects of this situation are suspect because whether the child behaves normally during the individual session may have little relevance to how he may behave in a classroom with twenty-five other children who may encourage and reinforce his behavior. The observations, on the other hand, may easily be generalized since they took place in the child's actual environment.

Another major advantage of informal assessment is its flexibility. It can be utilized nearly any time, any place, and with any problem. Virtually the only limits are the users' knowledge of specific subjects or behaviors and the means of gathering reliable data. *Little* problems occur very frequently when working with children. It is usually best to check out such difficulties before they become *big* problems. The flexibility of informal assessment enhances its use over other types of assessment because users can take whatever materials are available and obtain a quick and simple check in a problem area. In general, fast and economical assessment procedures are preferred to those that are equally effective but require more personnel and material resources.

Disadvantages of informal assessment. One drawback to informal assessment is that it places a great deal of burden on the examiner to select appropriate tasks, be a good detective, and to correctly interpret the results in the absence of a test manual or formal guidelines. Informal assessment also requires good training in the content area in which assessment occurs and good problem-solving skills. For example, if a teacher notices that a kindergarten child is consistently reversing the letters *b* and *d*, does this mean that the child might have a learning disability? In this case, a *little* knowledge (that *b* and *d* reversals are bad) might cause problems because *b* and *d* reversals are relatively common among kindergarten and first-grade children and reflect developmental immaturity rather than a learning disability. Users of norm-referenced tests do not have this problem of interpretation because standards are provided.

A related problem with informal assessment is that the values and biases of the assessor can influence testing. For example, most people believe that boys are more aggressive and create more problems in school than girls. The difficulty with this and other biases is that judgment does not always correspond with reality. Observations of primary-grade children, for example, indicate that girls display as many deviant behaviors as boys but that teachers are more likely to respond to boys' misbehavior in a negative way (Patterson, 1982). Similar biases affect how informal assessment methods are chosen, implemented, and interpreted. Systematically approaching informal assessment and being aware of personal biases may help reduce bias as much as possible.

Finally, informal assessment does not have the long history of supportive research and theory enjoyed by criterion-referenced and norm-referenced assessment. Consequently, informal assessment has not often been included in training programs. Although many practitioners use it on an ongoing basis, few have received any formal training in informal assessment. Its outward simplicity compared with the grand statistical underpinnings of formal testing cause some individuals to question its adequacy. Although research suggests that educational programming can be accomplished just as effectively with informal assessment as with standardized testing (Lovitt & Fantasia, 1980), some are still reluctant to adopt informal assessment procedures.

Ecological Assessment

Anyone who has ever worked with children is aware of some of the complex interrelationships that exist between student and teacher, student and student, student and environment, teacher and community, and the like. Children are affected by other children, approaching holidays, the subject matter they are learning, the social mores of their community, their family situation, and even world economic conditions, especially if their parents are unemployed. It may be impossible to assess every factor that can influence student learning and behavior, but it is possible to move beyond an almost exclusive focus on the child. Ecological assessment must include an analysis of the child as well as the teacher (for example, does the teacher use appropriate feedback and instructional techniques), the teacher's expectations (for example, does the teacher expect the child to be perfectly still and docile), the environment (for example, is the temperature at the proper level and are the desks arranged in a manner consistent with what the teacher wants to accomplish), and the task (for example, was the material worth learning and related to the content).

Consider a teacher who is concerned about the number of students who have begun to turn in incomplete assignments during the last month. Previously, the rate of assignment completion had been excellent for the entire class. An analysis of the situation suggests the problem really began when construction was initiated on a new wing of the school. The building activities were clearly visible to the students through an open window, and many enjoyed watching the progress. An easy solution would be to close the curtains or turn the students' desks away from the window. However, a less complete, child-centered analysis may have resulted in the time-consuming and possibly less successful remedy of modifying student behavior in spite of an environment that encouraged off-task behavior.

Ecological assessment is not a category of tests nor even a theory of assessment. Instead, it is more of a viewpoint of assessment. Virtually any type of criterion-referenced, norm-referenced, or informal test could be used in an ecological approach, for it offers the freedom to utilize assessment devices in unique and creative ways. The Centra and Potter model (see Figure 1.2) illustrates the wide range of variables that can influence student learning and behavior, many of which can be measured using a variety of assessment approaches.

Advantages of ecological assessment. The ecological model has four major advantages over other forms of assessment. First, because it is a process of assessment, it is more than a collection of tests: It is a way of viewing all forms of assessment. Second, it has helped to expand the focus of assessment. Rather than simply focusing on the child, an intensive study of the student is made in relationship to the environment. Third, ecological assessment increases our awareness of the complexity of human behavior. Finally, this model causes us to question the validity of simplistic and mechanical assessment practices that diagnose a child's problem on the basis of only one or two standardized tests.

Disadvantages of ecological assessment. The most obvious problem in using ecological assessment is its complexity. Instead of administering a test or observing one or two behaviors, an evaluator is faced with the additional possibilities of interviewing other adults, observing the child in multiple situations, and collecting and synthesizing a large amount of information. This process may be too time-consuming or impractical for many situations. Professionals using the ecological approach must be careful to collect enough information so that the problem can be understood yet not so much that it cannot be used or comprehended.

A second problem with this form of assessment is the lack of adequate instruments. To a large extent, assessors are left on their own to determine what and how to assess. A related problem is the lack of research into factors such as the seating arrangement or the type of instruction that significantly affect learning.

General Assumptions in the Assessment of Children

Some of the ambiguity surrounding assessment practices can be directly attributed to the fact that various individuals approach assessment with differing assumptions concerning how and when tests can be utilized. This problem is further complicated by the lack of any one universally accepted theory guiding the development, use, and interpretation of tests. However, despite the many different perceptions of assessment, a core of widespread assumptions still exists. A review of these assumptions provides a basis for the examination of assessment in content areas that follows in later chapters.

Assumption 1: Individual Differences Among Children Derive Their Meaning from the Situation in Which They Occur

In assessing the many attributes and behaviors of a particular child, it is very likely that the child will differ, perhaps markedly from his peers on at least one dimension. It must be determined if we should be concerned about such differences. The answer is that it depends upon the child's situation and the expectations placed upon the child in that situation. Behaviors considered normal in one setting may be considered abnormal in another, and skills considered adequate in one school may cause problems in another school. The point is that tests can determine if a child is different from the norm but not if this difference is a problem!

Children differ on innumerable attributes, some of which are important while others are not. For example, a child's hearing is measured frequently during the school years, and those with a hearing loss are identified because this is a problem that may interfere with learning. However, some children have a quite different hearing abnormality: They are able to perceive extremely high-pitched sounds (i.e., those in excess of 20,000 cycles per second). At present, this capability has no practical importance in our society (except perhaps to people who test dog whistles). Children who cannot hear sounds in this range are not considered hearing impaired because there is no expectation that they should be able to hear sounds at such high frequencies. Suppose, however, that it suddenly became important for children to be able to hear sounds of 20,000 cycles per second. Children who could hear at such frequencies would be valued highly by our culture, whereas those who could not would probably be viewed as less capable and possibly marked for placement in classrooms for the hearing impaired.

Consider the more realistic example of a child who moves from the Watts neighborhood of Los Angeles, (an inner-city ghetto) to Scarsdale, a suburb of New York City (an upper-class, professional community). According to a nationally standardized reading test, the child's reading ability would be approximately a half-year below grade level, yet when he was in Watts his reading ability was not considered a problem. In fact, there he was a good student. However, in Scarsdale he is immediately referred for specialized programming because perhaps the average child in that community scores over one year *above* grade level on the national test. The obvious conclusion is that a test score becomes most meaningful when the conditions and expectations under which the child must operate are known.

Assessment data must also be interpreted in terms of developmental norms, which evaluate a child's performance relative to what other children that age are doing. For example, an interview with a mother indicates that she is concerned about her five-year-old son who is frequently disobedient at home. Reference to developmental norms suggests that such behavior is relatively normal for children that age. In fact, 56 percent of normal boys are considered disobedient at one time or another. Similarly, kindergarten and first-grade children are referred frequently to speech clinicians because of problems articulating the letters *s* and *r*. Generally, however, speech therapy is not initiated with such young children because the problems often disappear with another year or two of experience in the natural environment.

It is important to assume that test data derive their meaning from the social context because viewing test scores as meaningful by themselves can lead to their misuse. It is important to state this explicitly because all too often tests that are interpreted naively and mechanically do more harm than good. Simply because a child may score in the impaired range on a particular test should not be sufficient evidence to label the child as handicapped. Most importantly, a test score in the impaired range does not always correspond to impaired performance in other situations.

Assumption 2: Tests Are Only Aids to Decision Making

The assumption that test data will be only a portion of the information used to make a decision about a child is related to the first assumption and pertains to how test data are used. Unfortunately, in practice, test data are frequently the *only* information considered. Children are placed in programs based upon very specific criteria based on exact scores. For example, a score of 130 or above on an intelligence test may be needed for placement in a program for gifted youngsters, and a score of 129 simply will not suffice. Perhaps if other criteria were examined, a child with a 129 IQ may be more suited to the program than a child with an IQ in the 140 range. Tests are simply not accurate enough, nor do they measure a wide enough range of variables, to be used as the sole criterion for most decisions. They are only samples of behavior, and common sense must be used in judging their contribution to decisions.

A simple decision, such as placement in the proper reading group, may be fraught with difficulty if a test score is the major determiner. Two children with scores indicating they read at the third-grade level may have quite different reading abilities, especially if they were given different tests or were tested in different aspects of reading. One child may have approached the task with a cavalier attitude and, because of carelessness, responded incorrectly in some relatively minor areas. Another child may have approached the test very anxiously and struggled all the way through, as evidenced by grimacing, stammering, and statements suggesting self-doubt. A test score may suggest that the two children should be in the same reading group, yet it may be very difficult to teach them in the same manner and at the same rate. In addition to knowing a test score and the manner in which it was achieved, it may be helpful to have information that is not in any test (for example, whether the child learns best in a group or one-to-one situation, whether the child responds best in written form or orally, and whether the child could be taught more effectively by a teacher or a peer). Good educational programming is seldom based on test scores alone but instead considers the complex array of variables that influence student learning.

This problem can be partially overcome by making sure an adequate sample of behavior is included in assessment. For example, the assessment of intelligence should measure a wide range of behaviors that have been associated with the construct of intelligence. In addition, it is important that the child is properly motivated and puts forth an optimal or nearly optimal effort. By doing this, it is possible to predict more accurately what the child can do given proper motivation in the classroom.

Assumption 3: A Primary Reason to Conduct an Assessment Is to Improve Instructional or Intervention Activities

What are the goals of assessment? To find out how to eliminate a problem? To find out why a child performs as she does? To determine the appropriate placement for a child? Some may argue that determining etiology and finding the cause of a problem are primary reasons for conducting an assessment. In ordinary educational practice, this is true, however, only to the extent that assessment also points to an effective treatment for the child's problem. Knowing a child's educational classification may help decide how to teach or work with the child, but such classifications do not provide information for planning daily lessons. For example, knowing a child has a learning disability does not lead to the same level of treatment specificity as does knowing the child has a medical problem, such as phenylketonuria (PKU). On this topic, Howell, Kaplan, and O'Connell (1979) have noted:

> When the problem is academic deficiency, the variables for classification are less specific. . . . Yet educators have tended to treat students who fail academically as if they have enzyme deficiencies. That is, they have sought to label students and then make treatment statements from the label. . . . Of course, our educational labels are far from precise. (p. 16)

Consider a teacher or a psychologist who knows only that a child has one of the labels listed in Table 3.1, which were drawn from Smith and Neisworth (1975), who recorded the labels used in several special education journals to classify children in need of special education. How should a child who is "primitive" be taught? How does it help to know that a child completes his assign-

Table 3.1 Labels Applied to Children with Special Educational Needs

1. Academically handicapped
2. Acting out
3. Adjunctive
4. Aggressive
5. Antisocial
6. Aphasia
7. Autistic
8. Behavior-disordered
9. Below-average learner
10. Brain-damaged
11. Cerebral dysfunction
12. Child with educational problems
13. Child with failure sets
14. Culturally deprived
15. Delinquent
16. Educable mentally retarded
17. Educationally disabled
18. Ego-development deficiency
19. Emotionally disturbed
20. Emotionally handicapped
21. Emotionally maladjusted
22. Exceptional
23. Genotypically retarded
24. Hyperactive
25. Hyperkinetic
26. Impulse-ridden
27. Latent development
28. Learning-disabled
29. Low cognitive capacity
30. Low IQ
31. Mentally defective
32. Mentally handicapped
33. Minimal brain dysfunction
34. Neglected
35. Neurotic
36. Overgratified
37. Overstimulated
38. Perceptually handicapped
39. Physically handicapped
40. Primitive
41. Psycholinguistically disabled
42. Psychopathic
43. Psychotic
44. Retarded development
45. Schizophrenic
46. Slow learner
47. Socially defective
48. Socially deprived
49. Socially disruptive
50. Socially handicapped
51. Socially impaired
52. Socially maladjusted
53. Socially rejected
54. Speech and language latency
55. Symbiotic disorder
56. Trainable
57. Withdrawn

From *The Exceptional Child: A Functional Approach* (p. 147) by R. M. Smith and J. T. Neisworth, 1975, New York: McGraw-Hill. Copyright © 1975 by McGraw-Hill Book Company. Reprinted by permission.

ments in a sloppy fashion because he is "impulse-ridden." Labels are useful only to the extent that they lead to a successful treatment. If there is a prescribed treatment for the "primitive" child, then using that label is advantageous; however, if no such prescription is available, such labels may actually interfere with treatment by clouding the variables that influence the problem.

All too often educational specialists have considered their job to be completed when they have labeled the child to determine the classification and made some general recommendations. This attitude may be partially attributable to the categorical system of special education established in most states and the heavy demands on specialists to conduct large numbers of assessments. By law a child must be classified as eligible to receive special education services. Thus, some specialists may communicate *only* the appropriate categorical label and leave teachers and therapists, who do most of the direct, daily work with the child, to develop the individualized educational programming.

Assumption 4: The Assessor Is Properly Trained

Since many potential sources of error exist in administering and interpreting tests and other assessment devices, it is extremely important that they be administered by individuals who are knowledgeable about both assessment and human behavior. For example, an acquaintance of the authors told of a college student who was gaining experience administering tests to children in a small rural school. In discussing the results of the testing with the college student, our friend learned that two Native American students would not respond to any test questions. Our friend then readministered the test but allowed more time than usual for answering each question. Although perhaps thirty seconds were required for the students to respond to each question, they did eventually respond, and very accurately. They simply needed more time to respond than white middle-class children. A person less familiar with the response times of individuals from some Native American tribes may have assumed a lack of knowledge on their part. Thus, skill in administering an assessment device encompasses more than the simple mechanics of test giving and requires knowledge and training in many aspects of human behavior.

The lack of highly skilled assessors has been a major problem in special education because of the sudden and dramatic demand for individuals in this field after the passing of P.L. 94-142. As a result, states allowed people to become "provisionally" or temporarily certified. Master's degree programs in speech pathology, school psychology, and special education sprang up to meet the demand for practitioners. Some of these programs have provided adequate training, but others have not.

Ample evidence exists that many in the field of special education are inadequately trained in assessment practices. Bennett and Shepard (1982), for example, reported that, on the average, a sample of learning disability specialists missed 50 percent of the items on a test reflecting their knowledge of basic measurement (such as reliability, validity, and use of norms). This lack of skill often translates into the misuse of tests and misinterpretation of assessment information.

The assumption that a person doing an assessment is properly trained implies that people can be trained at different levels. At one level, regular classroom teachers are well trained to administer a number of assessment instruments. In fact, in many cases they are the persons of choice to conduct an assessment, for they are familiar with the classroom materials and the demands that will be placed on the child, have access to almost unlimited samples of the child's behavior, and have more contacts with the child than almost any other individual (Moran, 1978). At a more complex level, more specialized tests, such as individually administered intelligence tests, require supervised training to learn to administer. Most professional codes of ethics admonish individuals to administer only those tests for which they have the training and skills.

Assumption 5: All Forms of Assessment Contain Error

Information provided by lie detectors is inadmissible as evidence in court because of an error rate of between 10 percent and 25 percent (Bersoff, 1983). Unfortunately, many of the tests administered to school children contain even greater error. It is simply not possible to measure such variables as anxiety, motivation, intelligence, and self-concept without some degree of error.

Error is introduced into the assessment of children by several factors. First, tests themselves often have low reliability and validity. A common and frustrating example is that different reading and math achievement tests provide different grade equivalent scores. Second, the *same* test may indicate different results when administered to the same child on different occasions. Test scores should be expected to fluctuate slightly because the child will remember some of the items and may feel more at ease when the test is repeated. Marked variations in scores can result because of other factors as well. For example, a child may feel more motivated on one occasion than another or the conditions under which the test is given may change from one testing to another.

The assumption that error is present in all forms of evaluation influence practice in two primary ways. First, it mandates that we be aware of and try to minimize factors that might contribute to inaccurate test scores. Every effort should be made to see that an assessment reflects the attribute being measured to the fullest possible extent. Second, the presence of errors makes it all the more necessary to use and interpret test data in a cautious and professional manner. Fortunately, with standardized tests we can statistically estimate error. This point provides a convenient springboard to the next two chapters in which technical procedures used in determining the worth of a test will be introduced.

Summary

The goal of this chapter was to introduce some terms that are used throughout the text and to show how one's theoretical orientation and assumptions influence the testing process. It would be worthwhile to take a few minutes and characterize your own thinking about human behavior in general. It is important to recognize that one's own view of the world may differ markedly from those of others with whom you must work. A person who believes that children's behavior is caused by intrapsychic forces is likely to develop different assessment plans and interventions than someone who believes behavior is a function of environmental influence.

How do we go about settling differences between people with contrasting points of view about human behavior? An obvious choice would be to examine research relevant to each position. If the effectiveness of various interventions has been evaluated, one then has a basis for recommending an assessment or intervention procedure. In many cases, however, a person's belief system will not be altered by data or any other form of persuasion. In working with others this is a problem not easily resolved.

Part Two

Technical Issues in Assessment

After reading material that was similar to what follows in this part, a student remarked, or more accurately complained, that her goal—her *only* goal—was to help people and that the technical issues surrounding assessment seemed to offer little that was relevant to that goal. This student, along with many others, equates helping with working directly with special needs children. To some the specialized technology that often accompanies these efforts seems antithetical to such a goal. However, given the structure of the system through which children are helped, providing quality assistance without a strong grounding in the technical issues is an impossibility. Measurement and statistics can be used either for or against children. Those who want to help children must understand such concepts in order to argue their side in the inevitable battles over the needs of children versus the needs of the system.

Part Two extends the discussion of foundational concepts begun in Part One. This material is presented separately because of its specialized and technical nature. Chapter 4 discusses the basic statistical concepts needed to understand, utilize, and interpret tests and test results. Chapter 5 can be viewed as a consumer's guide to the selection of tests because it discusses the three key ingredients to any test: reliability, validity, and norms. Finally, Chapter 6 introduces the topic of computerized assessment, which, although new to special education and psychological assessment, has already had a marked impact on the field. Since the use of computers in assessment is expected to increase, it is important to understand the issues that underlie the use of the technology.

Chapter 4

Basic Statistical Concepts

Learning Objectives

1. Describe the four types of measurement scales.
2. Describe and interpret the following measures of central tendency: mean, median, mode.
3. Define variability and interpret both the range and standard deviation.
4. Interpret the meaning of standard scores and percentiles.
5. Interpret the type and degree of association between two variables.

During the early 1980s millions of people throughout the world spent countless hours almost oblivious to events occurring around them. The focus of their rapt attention was the Rubik's Cube, which outsold virtually every other puzzle or game in existence. The Rubik's Cube heightened interest in puzzles of all types, and prompted *Psychology Today* magazine to commission Dr. Robert Sternberg and Janet Davidson (1982) of Yale University to study the types of people who spend their time solving these puzzles. They tested the hypothesis that people who are good at puzzles and brain teasers are more intelligent than those who are not good at solving puzzles.

Sternberg and Davidson discovered that puzzle solving and intelligence (as defined by IQ) were highly correlated, thus indicating that people who solve certain types of puzzles are more intelligent than people who cannot solve the puzzles. Even more unusual was the fact that the time it took to solve the puzzles had a higher correlation (that is, a stronger relationship) with IQ than did the number of puzzles solved correctly. The unusual aspect of this finding was that more intelligent people took *longer* to solve the puzzles than less intelligent people. Thus, the higher their IQ, the longer the individual took to solve a puzzle. This certainly seems to go against common sense, because one would expect that bright people solve problems more quickly than individuals with lower intelligence.

What do these results mean? Can we say that practice in solving puzzles causes you to be more intelligent? If someone is a poor problem solver, can we predict that the person is less intelligent? Should we recommend that a course in puzzle solving be introduced in every high school in the country? Why does it take smart people longer to solve puzzles? These and many more important questions can be asked about the findings. This chapter is intended as an introduction to the methods and techniques test developers and statisticians use to answer questions of this kind.

The Methods of Data Analysis

One of Mr. Barton's high school students brought Sternberg and Davidson's *Psychology Today* article to class. Students questioned whether a test of puzzle solving could really be indicative of intelligence and whether more intelligent people really took longer to solve problems, so Mr. Barton decided to launch an investigation. As a first step, he constructed a twenty-five-item test composed of brain twisters taken from Sternberg and Davidson's article. (Sample items are displayed in Table 4.1.) He then administered the test to twenty

Table 4.1 Sample Items from Mr. Barton's Test

Questions

1. Water lilies double in area every twenty-four hours. At the beginning of the summer there is one water lily on a lake. It takes sixty days for the lake to become covered with water lilies. On what day is the lake half-covered?
2. If you have black socks and brown socks in your drawer, mixed in the ratio of 4 to 5, how many socks will you have to take out to make sure of having a pair of the same color?
3. How could two men play five games of checkers and each win the same number of games without any ties?
4. A bottle of wine costs $10. The wine was worth $9 more than the bottle. How much was the bottle worth? (Hint: The answer is *not* $1.)

Answers

1. Fifty-ninth day
2. Three socks
3. They were not playing with each other.
4. The bottle was worth $0.50 and the wine was worth $9.50.

Adapted from "The Mind of the Puzzler" by R. J. Sternberg and J. E. Davidson, 1982, *Psychology Today, 16*, pp. 37–44.

students and noted the number of puzzles they were able to solve correctly. In addition, he recorded the time required by each student to solve the puzzles. Finally, he obtained the students' IQ scores. All of this information is displayed in Table 4.2.

At first glance Table 4.2 is a confusing array of numbers. What do all these scores mean? Is IQ related to puzzle-solving ability? Are Mr. Barton's results similar to Sternberg and Davidson's original findings? How do you tell? Some way of summarizing these scores must be found so that we can get an overall picture. In the sections below we will introduce some terminology and a process for summarizing and understanding these data. The information will be useful in learning to apply statistical concepts to your own data and for reading research reports, but it is even more important in interpreting the statistical terminology found in tests and test manuals. The discussion begins with an overview of scales of measurement.

Measurement Scales

As a first step in clarifying the data it is important to determine what kinds of measurement scales were used. Measurement can be defined as assigning numbers to objects or events according to a set of rules. Clearly not all types of measurement are the same. Measuring the size of an atom, for example, re-

Table 4.2 Data from Mr. Barton's Test

Student	Number of puzzles solved correctly	Average amount of time spent on each puzzle (in seconds)	IQ score
Tommy	6	101	111
Jane	4	69	90
Linda	5	65	92
Larie	8	114	115
Anita	8	100	108
Sarah	7	64	99
Dustin	8	107	102
Bob	7	90	100
Mary	7	87	107
Katie	6	62	94
Ron	8	105	103
Deb	10	161	121
Mitzi	10	141	141
Wade	7	88	106
Wes	8	106	107
Brendon	8	89	99
Megan	9	121	110
Edna	9	110	118
Bunny	11	161	136
Flo	12	170	182

quires a vastly different type of measurement than measuring a student's knowledge about spelling rules. The types of measurement can be classified within a hierarchy according to the precision of the measurement and the types of arithmetical operations that can be performed. The four types of measurement scales are nominal scales, ordinal scales, interval scales, and ratio scales.

Nominal scales. Sometimes the scores assigned to people have a qualitative rather than a quantitative meaning. Qualitative measurement is referred to as nominal scale measurement and represents the least sophisticated level of measurement because the scores are simply used for grouping people, objects, or events into categories. Examples of nominal scales are Democrat–Republican, Chevy–Ford–Chrysler, and girl–boy. Some statisticians claim that nominal measurement is not measurement at all because the only measurement operation is the judgment of whether something is equal to (=) or not equal to (≠) other members of the category.

Many times nominal data will be in the form of numbers, but the numbers still do not imply that something has been measured. For example, a researcher may say Female = 1 and Male = 2. In this case the numbers are much like the numbers on football players' jerseys, and they possess no numerical qualities. It would be inaccurate to say that it takes two females to equal one male. It would be equally inaccurate to average the numbers on football players' to determine the winning team. With nominal level measurement, numbers simply refer to the names of objects or people.

Ordinal scales. The term "ordinal" implies a rank ordering of the characteristic being measured. In a horse race, for example, we indicate which horses came in first, second, and third; the higher the ranking, the faster the horse. Here the relative magnitude is meaningful in that numbers are assigned according to the amount of the characteristic being measured (for example, speed in a horse race). If Bjorn Borg, Jimmy Connors, Arthur Ashe, and Ann Landers would play in an imaginary tennis tournament, their rank order of finish should reflect their tennis skill. If Borg finished first, he would do so because he performed better than Connors, who came in second. If Connors finished second it is likely that he did so because he played better than Ashe, who finished third. Because Ann Landers is not known for her tennis ability, she would likely finish fourth. Thus, when these individuals are assessed according to their tennis skills, the fact that one received a higher ranking is based upon their ability. Contrast this with nominal scales, in which the numbers on the football jerseys did not have any meaning in terms of magnitude.

It should be noted that equal intervals do not usually exist between rankings. In the tennis tournament described above, there is a much greater difference in tennis ability between Landers and Ashe (ranked fourth and third, respectively) than between Connors and Ashe (ranked second and third, respectively). Similarly, the interval between kindergarten and second grade is greater in terms of the number of basic academic skills learned in that time period than between tenth and twelfth grades.

Measurements on an ordinal scale, however, tell us nothing about how much better Borg was than Connors, only their relative ranking. Ordinal measurements may thus yield deceptive results when manipulated arithmetically. For example, if the director of a tennis tournament decided to make pairings for doubles based upon the average ranking of the partners, he might pair ranks 2 and 3 against ranks 1 and 4, giving both teams an average ranking of 2.5. Unfortunately, the magnitude of the difference between Ann Landers (fourth place) and Arthur Ashe (third place) is so great that the pairings would not be equal. The team of Connors and Ashe would probably be far superior to the Borg and Landers team.

Interval scales. Unlike the ordinal scale, equal differences between scores can be treated as equal units when using an interval scale. Interval scale measurement is rare in educational assessment and most common in the physical sciences, when measuring temperature with an ordinary thermometer. The 10 degree difference between the temperatures of 30°F and 40°F is assumed to be the same as the difference between 80°F and 90°F. The zero point in interval measurement, which indicates that zero amount of the attribute exists, is arbitrary. With temperature, for example, the zero point is not the beginning of the scale. Further, when the thermometer reads zero, it is incorrect to say that there is a total absence of temperature.

Ratio scales. Like the interval scale, in the ratio scale there is equal distance between the variables being measured. The major difference is that with a ratio scale a true or real zero point exists. Measurements of height, weight, and length exemplify ratio scales that have a zero point and equal units.

A second difference between ratio and interval scales is the computation of arithmetical operations. Addition and subtraction produce meaningful results with both types of scales. However, multiplication and division yield understandable results only when a true zero point exists, and these operations are appropriate only for ratio level measurement. Thus, it would not be accurate to say that 10°C (Centigrade) is twice as hot as 5°C because temperature is an interval scale. However, it would be correct to say that 10 feet is twice as long as 5 feet, because length is a ratio scale. Table 4.3 summarizes the major characteristics of each of the four kinds of scales. The scores on Mr. Barton's test would most likely be ordinal data. It would be wrong to say that a child who scored 120 on an IQ test is twice as smart as a child who scored 60. Also, there is no evidence for equal intervals between ranks.

Frequency Distributions — Organizing the Data

Now that we have some understanding of the type of data with which Mr. Barton was dealing, we are ready to discuss some statistical procedures that will help us interpret the data. The next step in trying to summarize the puz-

Table 4.3 Characteristics of Measurement Scales

Scale	Characteristics
Nominal scale	Mutually exclusive categories
Ordinal scale	Mutually exclusive categories Magnitude
Interval scale	Mutually exclusive categories Magnitude Equal intervals
Ratio scale	Mutually exclusive categories Magnitude Equal intervals Absolute zero point

Table 4.4 Frequency Distribution of Puzzles Solved Correctly in Mr. Barton's Test

Score	Number of students
4	|
5	|
6	||
7	||||
8	|||||
9	|||
10	||
11	|
12	|

zle-solving data might be for Mr. Barton to construct frequency distributions and graphs. The frequency distribution for the number of puzzles solved correctly is presented in Table 4.4. First, the scores were ranked from highest to lowest, and then the number of students who achieved each score was tallied. Already the scores are becoming easier to understand. For example, it is apparent that most students tend to score around the middle of the distribution, with a score of 8 being about average.

For an even clearer picture of the score distribution, we can draw graphs to represent the data visually. Figure 4.1 displays the number of puzzles solved correctly in the form of a bar graph, or histogram, and Figure 4.2 presents the same data using a frequency curve polygon. By looking at the graphs it is easy to compare scores.

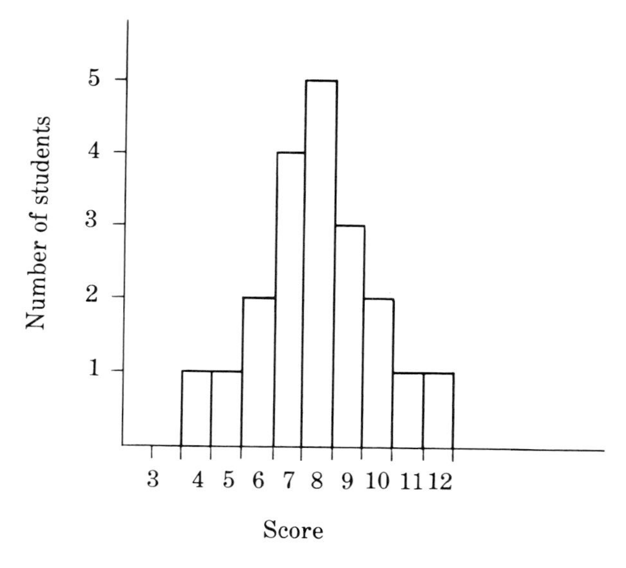

Figure 4.1 Bar graph of the frequency distribution of puzzles solved correctly in Mr. Barton's test.

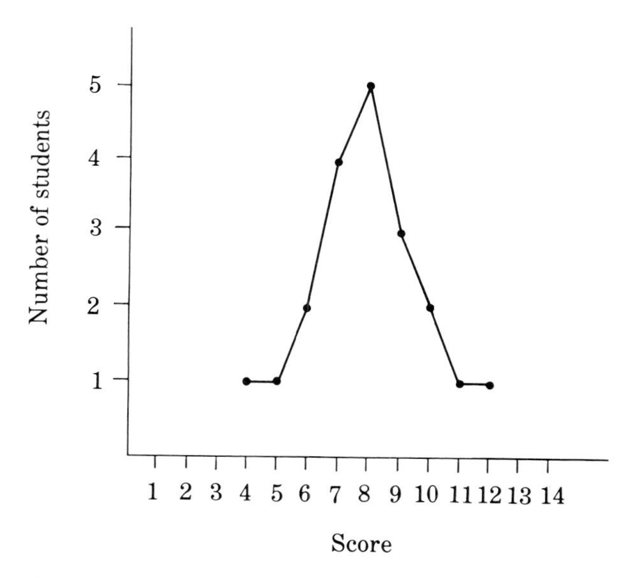

Figure 4.2 Frequency curve polygon of puzzles solved correctly in Mr. Barton's test.

Central Tendency — The Mean, Median, and Mode

Three different statistics are used to describe the central tendency, or average, of the frequency distribution: the mean, median, and mode. A measure of central tendency is needed because it is useful to have one point that is representative of the distribution. Perhaps the best-known measure of central tendency is the mean. To calculate the mean you add all the scores and divide by the total number of scores. The procedure used to calculate the mean number of puzzles solved correctly and mean IQ in Mr. Barton's class is presented in Table 4.5, which also introduces some basic statistical symbols.

Each puzzle-solving score is represented by the letter X. When the twenty X's are added, this summing process is shown as ΣX; the Greek capital letter sigma, Σ, is a symbol for "sum the scores that follow." In Table 4.5, IQ is rep-

Table 4.5 Computation of the Mean Number of Puzzles Solved Correctly and Mean IQ in Mr. Barton's Test

Student	Number of puzzles solved correctly (X)	IQ (Y)
Tommy	6	111
Jane	4	90
Linda	5	92
Larie	8	115
Anita	8	108
Sarah	7	99
Dustin	8	102
Bob	7	100
Mary	7	107
Katie	6	94
Ron	8	103
Deb	10	121
Mitzi	10	141
Wade	7	106
Wes	8	107
Brendon	8	99
Megan	9	110
Edna	9	118
Bunny	11	136
Flo	12	182
	$\Sigma X = 158$	$\Sigma Y = 2241$
	$N = 20$	$N = 20$
	$M = 7.9$[a]	$M = 112.05$[b]

[a] $M = \frac{\Sigma X}{N} = \frac{158}{20} = 7.9$

[b] $M = \frac{\Sigma Y}{N} = \frac{2241}{20} = 112.05$

resented by the letter Y, and thus ΣY means to add the Y scores. N simply refers to the number of people in each group, and when divided into ΣX yields the mean (M). Now if the students were to ask Mr. Barton how the class performed on the test, he could simply report the mean, which was 7.9 puzzles solved.

Although the mean is by far the most frequently used measure of central tendency, the median and mode are also reported, especially when data are ordinal or nominal. The mode is the score that occurs most frequently in the distribution. In Table 4.2, for example, the score of 8 is the mode, for it occurs most often. The median is the middle score — the one that divides the distribution in half: 50 percent of the scores fall above it and 50 percent fall below it. For example, suppose a test was administered to seven students who obtained the following scores: 12, 5, 10, 4, 9, 2, 6. If we reorder the scores from low to high (2, 4, 5, 6, 9, 10, 12), it is clear that the median is 6 because there are as many scores below it (2, 4, 5) as above it (9, 10, 12). It is the middle score and represents the fiftieth percentile.

Variability — The Range and Standard Deviation

To know only a person's raw score is of little value. Knowing where that score falls in relation to the mean is a little more helpful but can still be misleading. Scores are much easier to interpret if both the central tendency and the variability of the distribution are determined.

Variability refers to the extent to which scores differ from one another. If a test were given and the resulting scores were all the same, as would occur if everybody scored a perfect score, the distribution would have no variability. Suppose that you have two sets of data: $A = 3, 5, 7$ and $B = 1, 5, 9$. Notice that distributions A and B each have the same mean (5) but that they differ in the amount of variability. Distribution A is less variable around the mean than distribution B. Figure 4.3 displays ways in which the relationship between variability and central tendency can vary. Descriptions of two common measures of variability follow.

Range. The easiest way to calculate the variability of a distribution, or the range, is to subtract the lowest score from the highest score. To calculate the range of IQ scores in Mr. Barton's class (see Table 4.5), you would subtract the lowest IQ, 90, from the highest IQ, 182. This yields a range of 92. The range is limited in its ability to reflect the variability of a distribution.

Standard deviation. An index of the degree of variability in a distribution without the limitations of the range is the standard deviation. Understanding standard deviation is prerequisite to understanding and interpreting virtually all standardized tests. Conceptually, the standard deviation is a logical way to measure the variability of a distribution. If we want to assess the degree to which scores in a distribution differ from one another, it seems logical to base

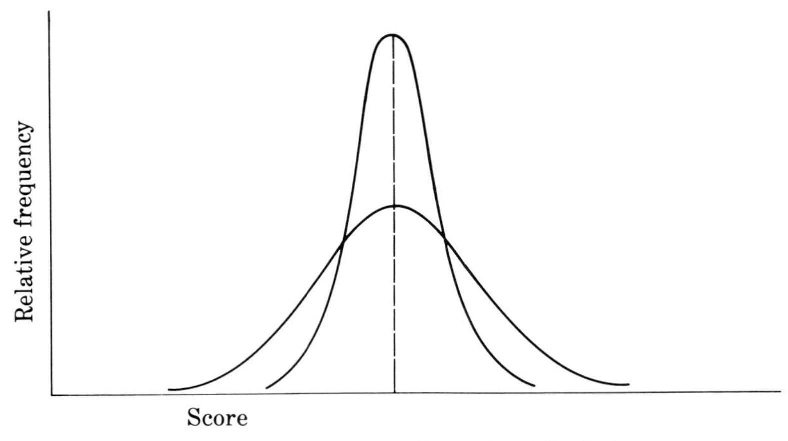

(a) Equal means, unequal standard deviations

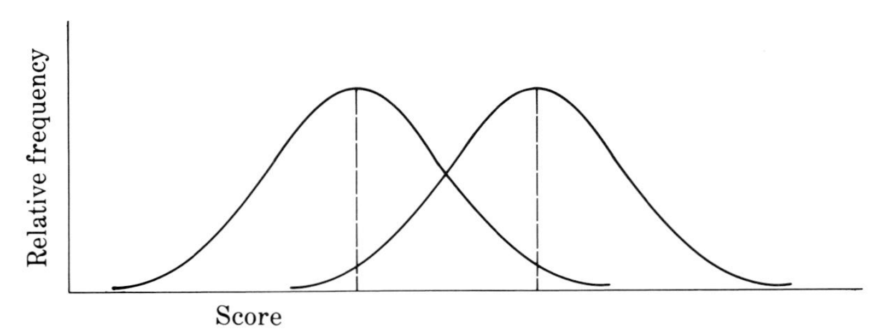

(b) Unequal means, equal standard deviations

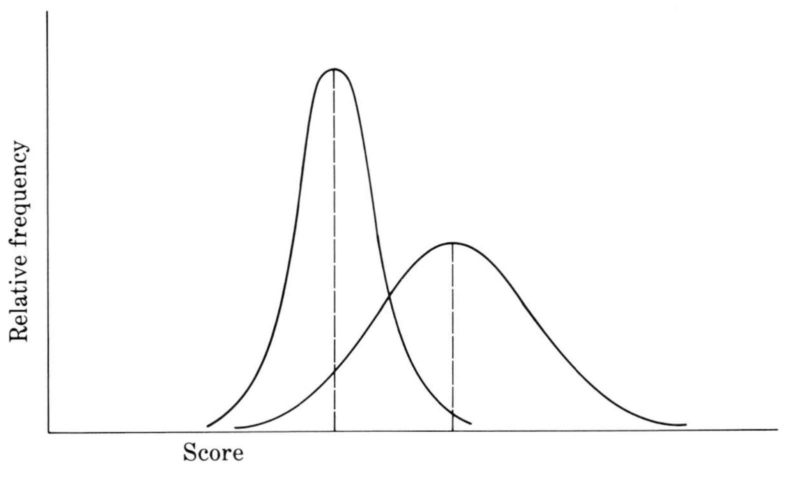

(c) Unequal means, unequal standard deviations

Figure 4.3 Variations in normal distributions.

our assessment upon the extent to which scores deviate from the central value of the distribution. That is, one subtracts each score from the mean of the distribution. Table 4.6 shows how this is accomplished for the puzzle scores of the children in Mr. Barton's class.

The first step is to calculate the mean (M). Next, each student's score (X) is subtracted from the mean. These new scores, symbolized by the lowercase letter x, measure the distance of each score from the mean. At this point it may seem plausible simply to find the average variability by adding all of the x scores and dividing by the total number of scores. Unfortunately, when you add the distance scores for an average distance score, you will always get a sum of zero, because the mean is the algebraic middle of the distribution. Instead, the distance scores must first be squared and then summed, thus eliminating the negative values. The average deviation of the squared distance scores (x^2) is then calculated as

$$\frac{\Sigma x^2}{N}$$

Since the distance scores were originally squared, this result is in the form of squared units. To return to regular units you take the square root. Thus, the standard deviation (SD) is determined as

$$\sqrt{\frac{\Sigma x^2}{N}}$$

The standard deviation for the number of puzzles solved correctly is 1.89. The meaning of this number will become more apparent as you read the next section on the normal curve.

The Normal Curve

The standard deviation is a particularly useful tool when used in conjunction with the normal distribution, or normal curve. For example, IQ test scores in the general population tend to conform to a normal distribution (see Figure 4.4) with a mean of 100 and a standard deviation of 15. Since IQ scores form a normal distribution, we know that approximately 34 percent of the scores fall between the mean and one standard above the mean. Thus, approximately 68 percent of the population scores between 85 and 115 on IQ tests and approximately 96 percent scores between 70 and 130.

The normal or bell-shaped curve seen in Figure 4.4 represents the distribution of such a large number of human attributes that it is used frequently in psychoeducational work, especially in educational measurement. If we were to examine the distribution of people on many physical or psychological attributes

Table 4.6 Computation of the Standard Deviation of the Puzzle Scores in Mr. Barton's Class

Student	Number of puzzles solved correctly (X)	Mean number of puzzles solved correctly (M)	$X - M = x$	x^2
Tommy	6	7.9	−1.9	3.61
Jane	4	7.9	−3.9	15.21
Linda	5	7.9	−2.9	8.41
Larie	8	7.9	.1	.01
Anita	8	7.9	.1	.01
Sarah	7	7.9	−.9	.81
Dustin	8	7.9	.1	.01
Bob	7	7.9	−.9	.81
Mary	7	7.9	−.9	.81
Katie	6	7.9	−1.9	3.61
Ron	8	7.9	.1	.01
Deb	10	7.9	2.1	4.41
Mitzi	10	7.9	2.1	4.41
Wade	7	7.9	−.9	.81
Wes	8	7.9	.1	.01
Brendon	8	7.9	.1	.01
Megan	9	7.9	1.1	1.21
Edna	9	7.9	1.1	1.21
Bunny	11	7.9	3.1	9.61
Flo	12	7.9	4.1	16.81

$$\text{SD} = \sqrt{\frac{\Sigma x^2}{N}} = \sqrt{\frac{71.8}{20}} = 1.89$$

(for example, height, weight, intelligence, and graduate school aptitude), a natural pattern would appear. This pattern is such that most people are about average, a few are moderately above or below average, and even fewer have extremely high or extremely low scores. If we plotted such a distribution it would resemble the familiar normal curve (see Figure 4.5). Every normal curve has a single peak near the middle of the distribution, indicating frequently occurring scores, and then trails off in each direction, indicating that as we move away from the mean, we encounter fewer scores. We can take this a step further and say that the likelihood of obtaining a score near the middle of the distribution is very good but that it is much less likely that people will score at the extreme ends of the distribution. Hence, IQ scores of 100 are fairly common but not many people have scores above 140. Flo, in Mr. Barton's class, whose IQ is 182, is an extremely rare individual.

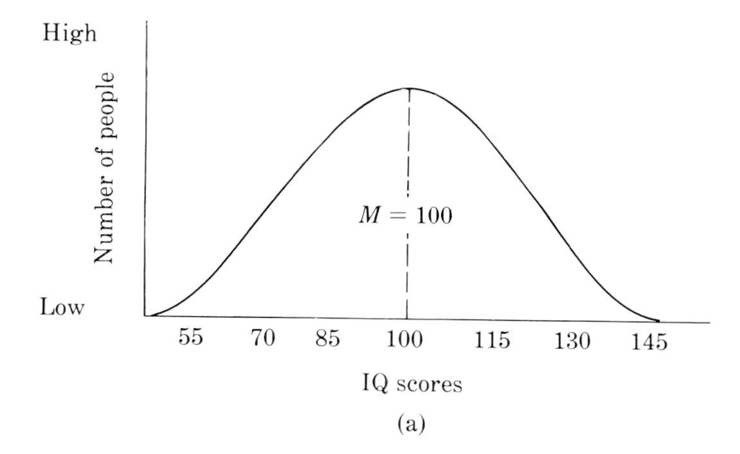

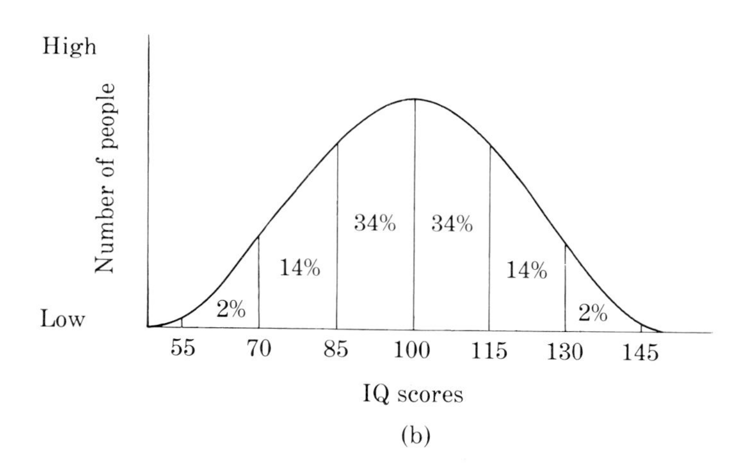

Figure 4.4 The normal distribution of IQ scores.

Standard Scores

One of the most frequent uses of the normal curve is to determine the degree to which an individual's score is unusual by comparing it to those of others. For example, many parents of preschoolers believe firmly that their child is "gifted." One such child, Megan, was recently tested with a popular preschool "intelligence" test. She earned a score of 600. Her parents were sure that any child who could score 600 must surely be gifted, and they eagerly awaited an interpretation of the test.

Since intelligence is normally distributed in the population, we can use the theoretical properties of the normal curve to determine whether Megan is in

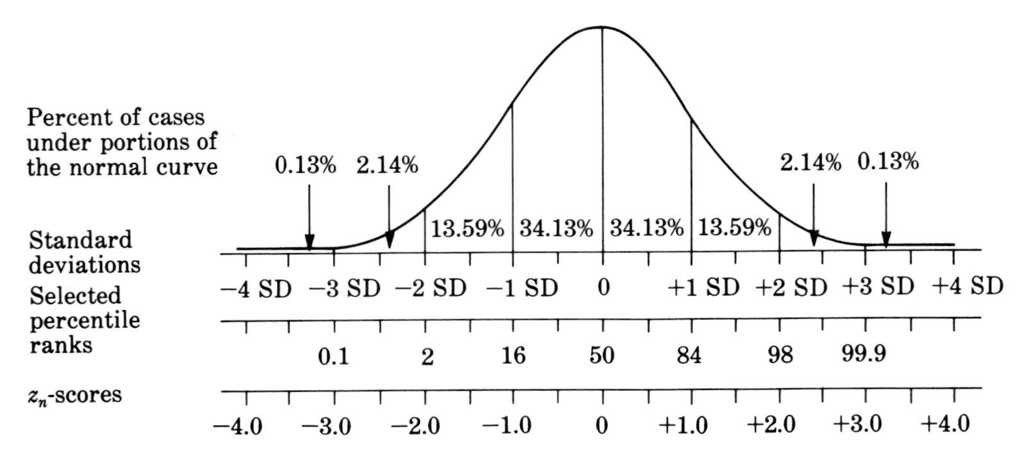

Figure 4.5 The normal curve.

fact gifted. This is most easily accomplished through the use of a standard score, or *z*-score, which indicates the number of standard deviation units a particular raw score is either above or below the mean. Recall that approximately 16 percent of people score one or more standard deviations above the mean. We can convert a raw score to a *z*-score by the following formula:

$$\frac{X - M}{\text{SD}}$$

where X = child's score, M = mean of distribution, and SD = standard deviation of distribution. On the test given to Megan, the mean is 500 and the standard deviation is 100. Thus, Megan's *z*-score is determined as follows:

$$z = \frac{600 - 500}{100} = 1.00$$

From her *z*-score it would appear that Megan is above average but not gifted. Since the *z*-score is in standard deviation units, a score of 1.00 indicates that Megan is one standard deviation above the mean. The normal curve (Figure 4.5) shows that one standard deviation above the mean is better than the scores of about 84 percent of the population and thus not really rare. If only those in the top 2 percent of the population are defined as gifted (as is fairly common in education), a *z*-score of 2.00 would be needed for a child to be labeled "gifted." To have a *z*-score of 2.00, Megan would need a raw score of 700:

$$z = \frac{700 - 500}{100} = 2.00$$

By using a similar procedure with other scores, even though they may have different means and standard deviations, it is possible to determine exactly how extreme a particular score is. If we return to Mr. Barton's data, we can see that Mitzi's z-score for number of puzzles solved correctly ($z = 1.06$) is an above-average score. This score is calculated as follows:

$$z = \frac{10 - 8}{1.89} = 1.058 = 1.06$$

Standard scores are also useful if we have a person's scores on two tests and want to know on which test the individual performed better. The use of standard scores allows us to convert the two tests to a common scale. For example, if Mary scored 32 on Test A, with a mean of 28 and a standard deviation of 4, and she scored 88 on Test B, with a mean of 85 and a standard deviation of 6, which was the relatively better score? Figure 4.6 displays her scores graphically. We can see that her score on Test A is relatively farther from the mean than her score on Test B. That is, a greater percentage of persons scored lower than Mary on Test A than on Test B. Thus, Mary did relatively better on Test A. It would of course be inefficient to plot distributions of scores on both tests to answer questions of this type. Standard scores can be used to answer such questions more effectively:

$$z\text{-score on Test A} = \frac{32 - 28}{4} = \frac{4}{4} = 1$$

$$z\text{-score on Test B} = \frac{88 - 85}{6} = \frac{3}{6} = .5$$

Since her z-score is higher for Test A, it is apparent that she did relatively better on that test.

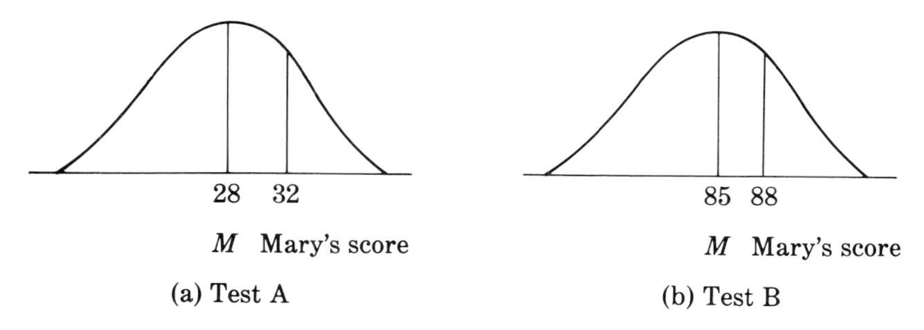

Figure 4.6 Mary's scores on two tests.

Percentiles

Percentiles are a more common and understandable way of expressing a person's relative position in a distribution than are standard scores. A percentile is the point on a distribution below which a given percentage of the scores are found. For example, the forty-fourth percentile is the point on the distribution below which 44 percent of the cases fall. By definition, the percentile rank for the median is fifty because 50 percent of the cases fall at or below the median. As another example, a score of 36 on a given test is at the sixtieth percentile if 60 percent of the scores are below it. On a different test, a score of 36 might be at the twentieth-percentile because only 20 percent of the cases fall at or below it (see Figure 4.7).

Percentiles are popular because they appear easy to understand and interpret and are relatively easy to calculate. However, one problem in understanding and interpreting percentiles is that they are frequently confused with percentages, especially by parents and students. In testing, percentages usually refer only to the percentage of correct or incorrect answers.

Correlation — A Measure of the Relationship Between Two Variables

Let's return to Sternberg and Davidson's (1982) findings that puzzle-solving ability is related to intelligence and that the higher the IQ, the more time taken for puzzle solving. Sternberg and Davidson used correlation to assess the relationship between puzzle solving and intelligence. Correlation is simply a mea-

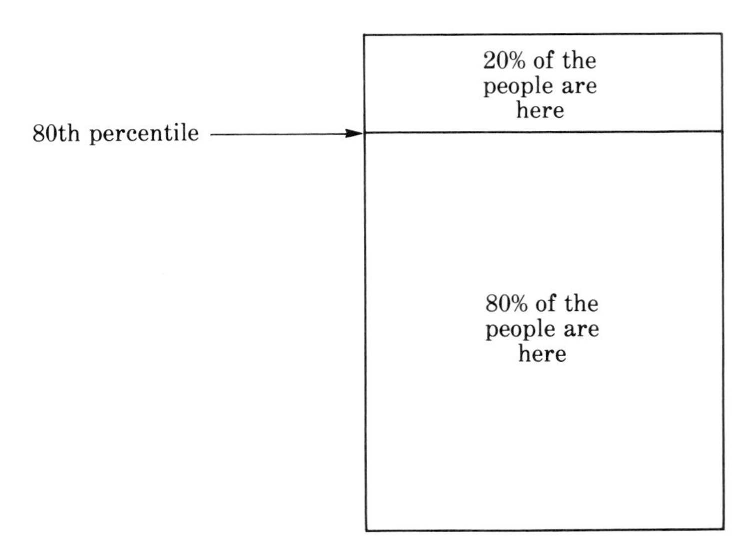

Figure 4.7 Illustration of a percentile.

sure of how things are related to one another. In this context, "related" means that people who score one way on the puzzle-solving test tend to score in a predictable way on the IQ test. If high scores on one test tend to correspond with high scores on the other test, the two tests are said to have a *positive correlation*. If high scores on one test tend to correspond with low scores on the other test, the tests are said to have a *negative correlation*. If scores on one test have no relationship to scores on the other test, we say there is *no correlation* between the tests. The Pearson product moment correlation, symbolized by r, is the most common method of assessing the correlation between variables. The correlation coefficient can range from -1.00 to $+1.00$. The smaller the correlation coefficient, whether positive or negative, the weaker the relationship between variables. Correlations close to zero would mean there is little or no relationship between variables. Positive numbers, such as $+.87$, denote positive relationships while negative numbers, such as $-.87$, indicate a negative correlation. The positive or negative *sign* of the correlation does not indicate the strength of the relationship, only the direction. Two variables that had a negative correlation coefficient of $-.92$ would thus be more strongly related than two variables that had a $+.36$ correlation.

The correlation data for Mr. Barton's experiment are presented in Table 4.7. Examine the table closely and try to determine the type of relationship, if any, between puzzle solving and IQ. Those with a sharp eye may have been able to detect that a positive relationship exists. However, when analyzing a large number of scores, it is usually difficult to tell by visual inspection the type of relationship between two variables. *Scatterplots* are often used for this purpose. To construct a scatterplot of the data of Table 4.7, we plot each pair of X and Y scores as a geometric point (see Figure 4.8). This scatterplot represents the puzzle-solving and IQ scores for the twenty students in Mr. Barton's class. It is apparent from the scatterplot that a positive relationship does exist. If the relationship were negative, it would resemble the scatterplot in Figure 4.9. Notice that as scores on one test increased, those on the other decreased. However, in Figure 4.8, as scores on the IQ test increased, so did puzzle-solving scores.

Sternberg and Davidson reported the relatively high positive correlation of .66 between number of puzzles solved correctly and IQ. How would we compute a similar correlation for Mr. Barton's data? Table 4.7 shows the steps for calculating the Pearson product moment correlation, which describes the relationship between the two sets of scores. Note that there $r = .84$, which is higher than the correlation of .66 obtained by Sternberg and Davidson. Mr. Barton was also interested in knowing if those students with higher IQ scores took longer to solve puzzles. Try figuring this out on your own from the data in Table 4.2. You should discover that the correlation is .85.

Correlation takes some time and work to understand, but it will aid you in grasping other concepts in this book. Although it is not essential to know how to calculate a correlation coefficient, it is important to understand what a correlation means.

Table 4.7 Computation of Pearson Product Moment Correlation (r) for Mr. Barton's test

Number of puzzles solved correctly (X)	X^2	IQ (Y)	Y^2	XY
6	36	111	12,321	666
4	16	90	8,100	360
5	25	92	8,464	460
8	64	115	13,225	920
8	64	108	11,664	864
7	49	99	9,801	693
8	64	102	10,404	816
7	49	100	10,000	700
7	49	107	11,449	749
6	36	94	8,836	564
8	64	103	10,609	824
10	100	121	14,641	1,210
10	100	141	19,881	1,410
7	49	106	11,236	742
8	64	107	11,449	856
8	64	99	9,801	792
9	81	110	12,100	990
9	81	118	13,924	1,062
11	121	136	18,496	1,496
12	144	182	33,124	2,184
$\Sigma X = 158$	$\Sigma X^2 = 1{,}320$	$\Sigma Y = 2{,}241$	$\Sigma Y^2 = 259{,}525$	$\Sigma XY = 18{,}358$

$$r = \frac{N\,\Sigma XY - \Sigma X\,\Sigma Y}{\sqrt{[N\,\Sigma X^2 - (\Sigma X)^2]\,[N\,\Sigma Y^2 - (\Sigma Y)^2]}}$$

$$r = \frac{20 \times 18{,}358 - 158 \times 2{,}241}{\sqrt{[[20 \times 1{,}320 - (158)^2]\,[20 \times 259{,}545 - (2{,}241)^2]]}}$$

$$r = \frac{13{,}082}{15{,}551.52} = .84$$

Summary

In this chapter we have described a variety of techniques for organizing test scores and other data. Data management techniques are dictated to some extent by the level of measurement used: nominal, ordinal, interval, or ratio. The first step in organizing data is to develop a frequency distribution that specifies how many people received a particular score. Techniques for describing the frequency distribution include those that describe its central tendency (mean, median, and mode) and those that reflect the variability in the distribution (range and standard deviation). Standard scores and percentiles tell about how a particular person did relative to others. The chapter concluded with a discussion of correlation, which assesses the relationship between two variables.

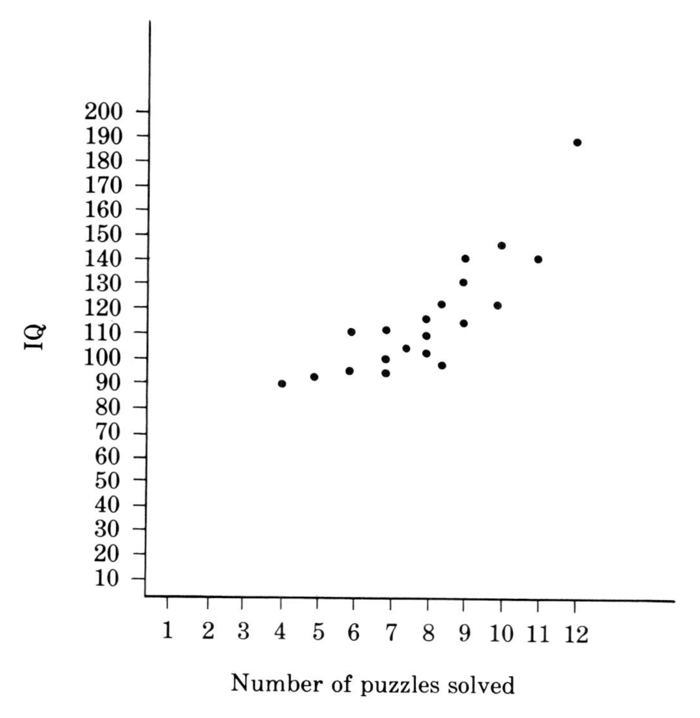

Figure 4.8 Scatterplot of the IQ and puzzle-solving scores of Mr. Barton's students.

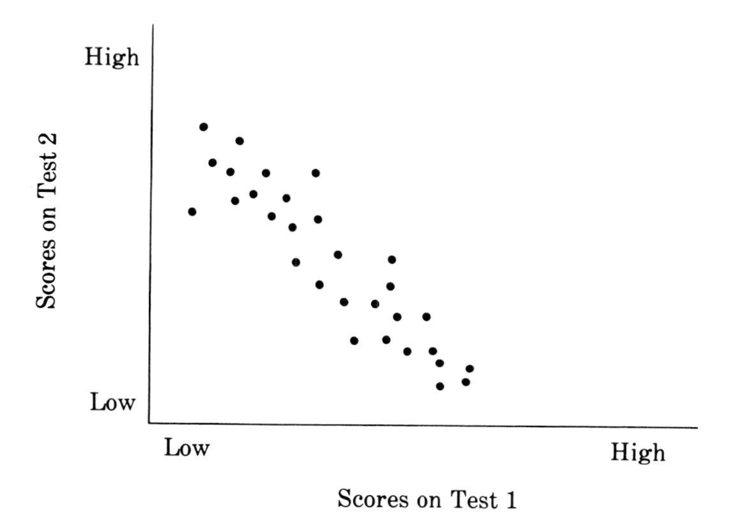

Figure 4.9 Scatterplot of a fictitious negative relationship.

Some people feel that statistics makes everyone the same, that is, it reduces people to numbers and these numbers do not convey the uniqueness of any one person. Although it is true that statistics can be misused, it is important to keep in mind that statistical analyses would not be needed if everyone were the same. It is because of the rich variety among individuals that statistics, when properly understood and used, can be helpful.

Chapter 5

Essential Characteristics of Tests: Reliability, Validity, and Norms

Learning Objectives

1. List sources of error in test scores.
2. Define each major type of reliability.
3. Define each major type of validity.
4. List the major criteria by which a normative sample can be evaluated.
5. List and describe sources of information for use in the evaluation of tests.

The Department of Mathematics at Johns Hopkins University in Baltimore conducted a talent search in the spring of 1975 to locate eleventh-grade students who showed exceptional promise in math. Teachers in the area were contacted and invited to send their brightest math students. Julian C. Stanley, director of the Study of Mathematically Precocious Youths at Johns Hopkins University heard about the contest and asked to nominate some children. His was a special case, because the students he had in mind were not in any of his classes and he was obviously not an eleventh-grade teacher. His only prior dealings with students had been three years earlier, when he had administered the mathematical part of the College Entrance Examination Board's Scholastic Aptitude Test (SAT-M). Stanley received permission to submit nominees, and eventually ten of his suggestions took the math department's test. The results of the contest were astonishing:

> Among the 51 people who entered the contest, the 10 chosen by [Stanley based on their scores on] SAT-M ranked 1, 2, 3, 5.5, 7, 8, 12, 16.5, 19, 23.5. Points earned by the top three were 140, 112, and 91. The highest scoring

> person nominated only by a teacher scored 83. Just 3 of 10 ranks, 2, 5.5, and 19, had also been nominated by their teachers. The No. 1 contestant was not nominated by his teacher. He is quite able mathematically but had been far from the top of the 396 entrants in my March 1972 SAT-M contest. Most of the higher scorers from that testing had already skipped beyond the 11th grade and therefore were not eligible to enter the math department's contest. (The ablest of them, a 16-year-old Hopkins student, had already completed a junior-year course in mathematical analysis with a final grade of A.) (Stanley, 1976, p. 313)

The results were so astounding because teachers who had known their students for almost an entire year could not compete with three-year-old SAT-M scores in selecting the best math talent. In fact, one of the teacher nominees received only two points, whereas the lowest rank of the SAT-M nominees was 23.5 out of 51.

This represents a striking example of the value of tests. However, before we conclude that the test was far superior to the teacher in determining talent, let's keep in mind that the contest was really just another test. A cynic would say that the only math talent identified by the test was the ability to take another test.

Not all tests are as good as the SAT-M; some have inadequate norms and poor standardization, and many do not have any demonstrated validity. How can you distinguish between good tests and poor tests? How can you select a test that is suitable for your purposes? What are some of the characteristics of good tests? This chapter discusses three technical components that contribute to the quality of a test: reliability, validity, and norms.

Reliability

At the Olympics in Mexico City during the summer of 1968, Bob Beamon won a gold medal by broad jumping over twenty-eight feet. This was about three feet further than any human being had ever jumped. Some sports authorities now recognize that jump as the single greatest athletic accomplishment ever. Until much later, no one, including Beamon himself, even came close to equaling that record. If the event is examined objectively, the question must be asked, "Did the jump represent Beamon's true jumping ability or was it a rare fluke?" Since Beamon's jumps before and after the record setter were nowhere close to twenty-eight feet, we may assume the jump was a fluke. That is, a rare combination of factors may have combined and resulted in the record-setting performance. We might conclude that the jump was not an accurate representation of Beamon's jumping ability because it could not be repeated.

An only slightly less rare event occurred in the 1976 Olympics, when Nadia Comenich of Romania scored a perfect ten points in gymnastics competition. However, her score did appear to be a much more reliable indicator of her true athletic ability, because the fourteen-year-old performer repeatedly received ratings of ten in various other competitions.

Whether we are measuring athletic ability or spelling skill, there is concern about the degree to which the result is a true measure of a person's ability. In the terminology of educational and psychological measurement, this is a concern about *reliability*. Reliability involves the degree to which we get the same result when repeatedly measuring the same thing. Since Nadia Comenich's achievements were repeated and Bob Beamon's were not, we would say that her score was a reliable measure of her gymnastics skill but that his broad jump was not a reliable measure of his jumping ability.

The same kind of logic can be applied to educational and psychological tests. For example, Jill and Toni studied together for a midterm physics exam, and both seemed to know the material equally well. However, when the test was given, Toni scored much higher than Jill. In talking they discovered some reasons for the difference in scores. Jill had had a cold and did not sleep well the night before. Further, she had had a bad case of test anxiety and said she had not been able to think clearly. Toni, on the other hand, was feeling great the day of the test. In addition, some of the examples on the test involved the application of physics problems to automobiles. Since Toni is in an automotive repair class this term and Jill is not, her score, relative to Jill's, could have been enhanced. They both said that they had had to guess at some of the answers, but Toni had evidently guessed correctly more often. This illustrates a case in which both students had about the same true ability in physics but extraneous factors caused them to receive different scores.

Learning some basic terminology will allow us to explain what happened to Jill and Toni more precisely. We can divide each of their scores into two parts. The first, and preferably the major, part of their score reflects their knowledge about physics. This score is referred to as a *hypothetical true score*. It is called hypothetical because there is really no way we can determine their actual knowledge of physics. The other part of their scores, or the error score, consists of all factors that caused their scores to fluctuate, including guesses, fatigue, and anxiety. Theoretically, it is impossible ever to know a person's true score because some error factor is always present.

Symbolically, we represent a person's score, X, as follows:

$$X = T + E$$

where

X = test score
T = true score
E = error score

This equation, while quite theoretical, represents a most essential concept for the practitioner: *Every score obtained in assessing a child contains some de-*

gree of error. Even the best test may over- or underestimate a child's true ability. This is a critical piece of information if important educational decisions are made on the basis of the obtained score. In many states, one criterion for classifying a student as mentally retarded is an IQ score of 69 or below. What if the child scored exactly 69? Given that there is some error in the test score, caution must be exercised in deciding to label the child as retarded. Certainly the error could have worked in the child's favor, and the true IQ may be only 63. However, if the error worked against the child, the true IQ may be closer to 75. In a problem-solving process involving a child's placement, factors such as illness or motivation, which could have affected the test performance and thus inflated or deflated the error component, should be considered. Test scores are not unalterable facts but instead are subject to error, just as a teacher's judgments are liable to fluctuate.

Tests are not the only form of assessment for which reliability must be a concern. Simply observing a child in class is also subject to such problems. If two people were to observe the same child, would they see the same things? Would they agree that a certain behavior occurred or failed to occur? Unless observations are highly structured, two people are likely to disagree about what they saw. Although this chapter will primarily focus on reliability as it applies to standardized tests, the reader should bear in mind that reliability is *always* a concern, whether the assessment takes the form of standardized tests, informal tests, interviews, or observations.

Types of Reliability

You are likely to encounter many of the numerous methods for computing test reliability as you read test manuals. The more common methods include test-retest, equivalent form, split-half, and internal consistency.

Test-retest reliability. Recall that reliability refers to the extent to which we get the same result when repeatedly measuring the same thing. A logical way to establish the reliability of a test would then be to measure the same person twice and compare the results. This is precisely what is done in the test-retest procedure. Table 5.1 illustrates this process using a kindergarten screening test that was administered to the same twenty children on a Monday and again on the following Friday. (Note: Reliabilities are rarely if ever computed on only five scores, but only five are utilized here.) Correlations are computed for both sets of scores, yielding the reliability coefficient r_{xx}. This symbol is used to designate reliability because the Pearson product moment correlation r is often used for assessing reliability. The subscript $_{xx}$ refers to the correlation of a test x with itself.

Although the test-retest method is useful, it is very seldom used in the actual computation of reliability because it can over- or underestimate the reliability coefficient. A spuriously high reliability coefficient may be obtained when the second test is given too soon following the initial testing, because

Table 5.1 Test-Retest Reliability of a Kindergarten Screening Test

Student	Number of answers correct	
	Test	Retest
1	9	10
2	7	6
3	5	1
4	3	5
5	1	3

$$r_{xy} = \frac{N\,\Sigma XY - (\Sigma X)(\Sigma Y)}{\sqrt{[N\,\Sigma X^2 - (\Sigma X)^2][N\,\Sigma Y^2 - (\Sigma Y)^2]}}$$

$$r = \frac{150}{\sqrt{(200)(230)}}$$

$$r = .70$$

students may recall their first responses and tend to respond in the same way (Blood & Budd, 1972). If the test-retest interval is too long, however, the reliability coefficient may be artificially low, because a person's true score may change during that time as, for example, additional skills may be learned. Another problem with the test-retest method is that having students take the same test twice is an inefficient use of time.

If a test-retest reliability coefficient is reported in a test manual, the interval between testings must also be reported. The evaluation of the length of the interval is a subjective process. If a relatively stable trait, such as intelligence, is being measured, a longer interval may be used. However, when assessing a skill such as arithmetic ability, which can change relatively quickly when learning new material, the value of r_{xx} is likely to be reduced with long intervals.

Equivalent-form reliability. If a test of math aptitude is being constructed, one way to assess a person's true ability would be to construct a test using all possible math questions. Of course this is impractical because such a test would contain millions of questions beginning with simple number recognition and continuing through advanced mathematical theory. Most math tests thus sample only a few of all possible items. If the sample is representative of the larger domain of items, we can generalize from the sample to the domain. Given the extremely large number of potential tests measuring math aptitude, it should be possible to construct several equivalent tests. Each would be a measure of math aptitude, and although they would have different items, each should provide equally good estimates of a person's true score.

Using this example, it seems logical to determine correlations betwee

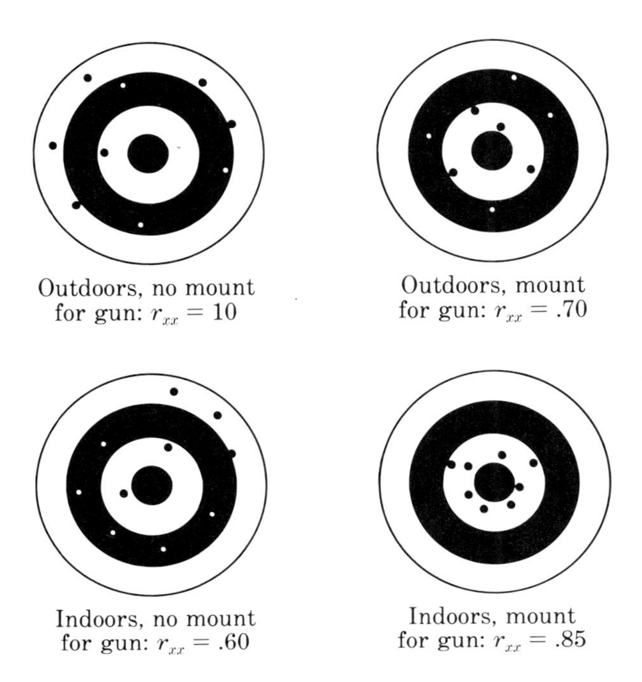

Figure 5.1 Analogy of equivalent-form reliability using shots at a bull's-eye. (Adapted from *Psychology* by H. Gleitman. By permission of W. W. Norton and Company, Inc. Copyright © 1981 by W. W. Norton and Company, Inc.)

the two alternative forms of the same test as a measure of reliability. This method of reliability computation is referred to as equivalent- or parallel-form reliability. If the test is reliable, the scores on separate tests should be relatively consistent. Figure 5.1 illustrates this process using an analogy suggested by Gleitman (1981). The bull's-eye represents a person's true score. Each shot aimed at the bull's-eye symbolizes an attempt at measuring a person's true score. When the instrument firing the shots is reliable, each measure will be close to the bull's-eye. However, much more scatter is present when the measurements come from an unreliable source.

Although the use of equivalent forms as a measure of reliability can be more easily justified from a theoretical perspective, this method shares some of the shortcomings of the test-retest method, including requiring students to sit through two test sessions, and determining the appropriate length of the interval between testings. In addition, it is difficult to construct a second form that is truly equivalent, because both tests should have identical means and standard deviations.

Split-half reliability. In one sense, the split-half method is identical to the equivalent-forms method. Split-half reliability is determined by dividing one test into two parts of equal lengths. One common method of dividing the test is in terms of odd and even numbered questions. Each person then receives a score for both sets of questions. The "equivalent forms" in this case are the halves of the same test. The reliability coefficient is derived by determining the correlation between the halves.

A primary difference between this method and equivalent-form reliability is that with this method the length of the test is halved. This can be a problem because longer tests are generally more reliable than shorter ones because they are less affected by factors that can increase measurement error, such as guessing. The Spearman-Brown formula has been developed to correct for the shorter test length and is reported frequently in test manuals.

Compared to the test-retest and equivalent-form methods of calculating reliability, the split-half approach has the advantage of requiring only one test administration. Because the data are thus available even if the test-retest procedure is used, most test manuals that report reliability will give a split-half reliability coefficient, regardless of other methods used. However, split-half reliabilities may be somewhat inflated because these estimates do not reflect errors of measurement due to changes in the student over time. For example, error related to a student's particularly bad mood on test day would not be reflected with the split-half procedure, because the entire test would probably be affected by the mood.

Internal consistency. Although split-half reliability measures the internal consistency of a test, it is used less often today than the Kuder-Richardson Formula 20 (KR-20) and coefficient alpha, which are also derived from a single test. These procedures reflect the degree to which an individual's test performance is consistent from item to item. Under most conditions both procedures yield roughly consistent results (Lindeman & Merenda, 1979).

The Standard Error of Measurement

The methods of calculating the reliability coefficient reported above help to answer the questions, "How consistently do we get the same result when repeatedly measuring the same thing?" Another reliability question deals with the amount of variation expected in a score, or "How much confidence can we place in this score?" This is an important issue in interpreting the meaning of a score. If a person's score is 69, are we reasonably sure that it represents a true score?

The standard error of measurement can answer these questions, as the example of Bob Beamon's Olympic broad jump can illustrate. Recall that Beamon made one jump of over twenty-eight feet, a distance much further than he jumped before or since. If we examine his feat more closely, we can see that it was not a reliable measure of how well he could routinely jump. Table 5.2 presents data on ten hypothetical jumps Beamon could have made prior to his record jump and ten jumps he might have made following the Olympics. Figure 5.2 displays a graph of these data. Note that there is some variability in the jumps perhaps related to factors such as motivation, anxiety, illness, and

Table 5.2 Bob Beamon's Broad Jumps Before and After His Olympic Jump

Hypothetical jumps before Olympics (feet)	Hypothetical jumps after Olympics (feet)
24	26
23	23
24	24
25	25
25	24
25	24
23	25
26	25
24	26
24	25

weather. Notice also that the higher scores in the distribution are statistically rarer. It is thus clear that the 28-foot jump is not representative of his jumping ability. Which distance is representative? Measurement theory dictates that the mean of this distribution is the most logical reflection of Beamon's true jumping ability. Excluding the 28-foot jump, Beamon's mean from Table 5.2 is 24.5 feet. Any of the jumps that deviate from this measure of his true jumping ability would be attributable to error. In other words, if Beamon were in perfect condition each time he jumped and if all other factors remained constant, he would always jump the same distance.

If we wanted to measure the variability of Beamon's jumps, the standard deviation would be the appropriate means. In this case the standard deviation would be a measure of the degree to which Beamon's jumps deviated from his true jumping ability. In measurement terminology, the extent to which a particular jump deviates from his true jumping ablity is considered error, because Beamon would jump the same distance each time if sources of error did not cause variations. In a sense, the standard deviation would characterize the amount of error in the distribution. This special type of standard deviation is called the standard error of measurement, although it is really a standard deviation of measurement error. The standard error of measurement, or SEM, is directly related to the reliability of a test and is calculated as follows:

$$\text{SEM} = \text{SD}_x \sqrt{1 - r_{xx}}$$

where

SD_x = standard deviation of obtained scores
r_{xx} = test reliability

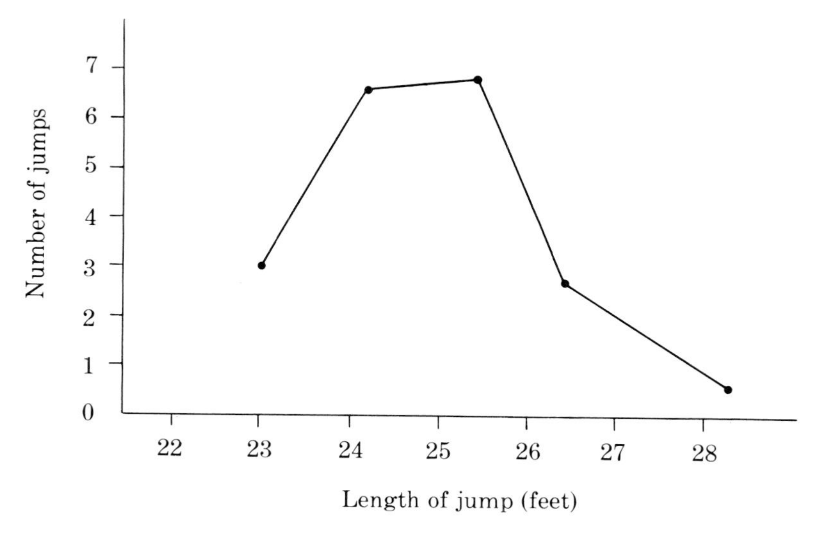

Figure 5.2 Graph of Bob Beamon's Olympic broad jump and jumps before and after.

Tests that have higher reliability coefficients have a lower SEM. This means that more confidence can be placed upon scores from reliable tests because they have less error. In other words, there is less variability of obtained scores around the true score. However, a relatively larger standard deviation tends to increase the standard error of measurement.

A practical use of the standard error of measurement. All test scores contain some degree of error. It is difficult to communicate the concept of test error to laypeople who try to interpret educational and psychological tests. Many tend to believe that a person's obtained score is the true score. In actuality, the person is likely to obtain a *different* score if given the test again. To the extent that a test is reliable, the magnitude of the difference between the two test scores will be small. The SEM can be used to communicate this rather complex array of information to others in a relatively straightforward manner using *confidence intervals.*

A confidence interval provides a range of scores rather than an exact score. Instead of indicating that John has an IQ of 110, we would say that John's IQ is between 105 and 115. In this way, we indicate that his score is probably within 5 points of 110 but not exactly 110.

We can increase the precision of our communication by indicating our degree of confidence that the true score will be within the interval. For example, we might say that we are 68 percent confident that John's score is between 105 and 115. We are able to make this type of statement by applying our knowledge of the normal curve. Recall that 68 percent of the cases in a distribution fall within one standard deviation of the mean. When using the SEM, we can say that 68 percent of the time the true score will fall within one SEM of the obtained score (and about 16 percent of the scores would be above and another 16 percent below the confidence interval).

To establish a confidence interval, the first step is to select the degree of confidence desired. The most commonly used intervals are the 68 percent and the 95 percent confidence levels because they correspond with one and two standard deviations, respectively. Next, the z-score associated with the particular level of confidence is selected. For example, the z-score corresponding to the 95 percent confidence level is 1.96. This z-score is then multiplied by the SEM to yield one-half of the confidence interval. This one-half interval is then added to and subtracted from the obtained score. An example from the Wechsler Intelligence Scale for Children (WISC-R) (Wechsler, 1974) will illustrate. On the WISC-R the SEM for children eleven and a half years old is 2.96. If a child of that age obtains an IQ score of 100 on the test, the 95 percent confidence level is derived by multiplying the z-score corresponding to the 95 percent level (1.96) by the SEM (2.96) to obtain a value of 5.8. Typically, this value is rounded off and then both added to and subtracted from the obtained score. In this example, we would say that we are 95 percent confident the student's score is 100, plus or minus 6. Alternatively, we could say that we are 95 percent certain that the *range* of scores from 94 to 106 contains the child's true IQ.

It should be noted that as the confidence interval increases, the band of scores must become wider. However, it is not possible to establish 100 percent confidence boundaries.

Some test users may resist the use of confidence intervals because they make for unduly tenuous statements. However, people do change, and our assessment procedures have not reached a level of precision that enables us to communicate more precisely. To do otherwise misinforms the recipient of test information. The use of confidence intervals may prevent such nonsense as rigidly adhering to a single criterion of 130 IQ for placement in a program for the "gifted" that puts one child who has an IQ of 131 in such a program and denies admission to another child with an IQ of 129. In actuality, the range of true scores for both children overlaps markedly.

Factors Affecting Reliability

The reliability of a test can be affected by a variety of factors. Table 5.3 lists the more common factors that can influence test scores and thus the reliability of a test. Some factors, such as whether a child guesses on questions, are not under the control of the person giving the test. Others, such as ambiguous instructions, can be eliminated by careful test design and administration. In reporting test results to others it is important to note factors that may have influenced the reliability of the test scores. Motivational lapses in those being tested, for example, are some of the more common reasons given for poor test performances.

Table 5.3 Factors Affecting Test Reliability

I. Lasting and general characteristics of the individual
   1. General skills (e.g., reading)
   2. General ability to comprehend instructions, testwiseness, techniques of taking tests
   3. Ability to solve problems of the general type presented in this test
   4. Attitudes, emotional reactions, or habits generally operating in situations like the test situations (e.g., self-confidence)

II. Lasting and specific characteristics of the individual
   1. Knowledge and skills required by particular problems in the test
   2. Attitudes, emotional reactions, or habits related to particular test stimuli (e.g., fear of high places brought to mind by an inquiry about such fears on a personality test)

III. Temporary and general characteristics of the individual (systematically affecting performance on various tests at a particular time)
   1. Health, fatigue, and emotional strain
   2. Motivation, rapport with examiner
   3. Effects of heat, light, ventilation, etc.
   4. Level of practice on skills required by tests of this type
   5. Present attitudes, emotional reactions, or strength of habits (insofar as these are departures from the person's average or lasting characteristics—e.g., political attitudes during an election campaign)

IV. Temporary and specific characteristics of the individual
   1. Changes in fatigue or motivation developed by this particular test (e.g., discouragement resulting from failure on a particular item)
   2. Fluctuations in attention, coordination, or standards of judgment
   3. Fluctuations in memory for particular facts
   4. Level of practice on skills or knowledge required by this particular test (e.g., effects of special coaching)
   5. Temporary emotional states, strength of habits, etc., related to particular test stimuli (e.g., a question calls to mind a recent bad dream)
   6. Luck in the selection of answers by "guessing"

Validity

Validity, or the extent to which a test fulfills its function, is the *sine qua non* of educational and psychological tests. Put another way, a test is valid if it measures what it is supposed to measure. Reliability, you will recall, refers to how consistently and accurately a test measures *something*. What the "something" is really does not matter in determining reliability. Thus, a test can have high reliability and yet not be valid for your particular purpose. Reaction time, for example, can be very reliably measured, but it is not a valid measure of intelligence. Reliability is a necessary, but not a sufficient, condition for validity. This means that a test *must* be measuring a trait or skill consistently *before* it can be considered to measure what it is supposed to measure.

When we measure height, there is little question about the validity of a tape measure for this purpose. However, other concepts are not so easily defined. For example, suppose we want to measure a child's motivation. Most people would agree that motivation is an important determinant of how a child functions in school. If you think of various children with whom you are acquainted, you can probably categorize some as "motivated" and others as "unmotivated." Now comes the tricky part. What is it about these children that causes you to give them such labels? What specific kinds of behaviors did you think about when you evaluated motivation? How fast the child completes assigned work? Previous work habits? Attitude? How would you construct a test to measure motivation? Would it be capable of measuring motivation in every situation and circumstance? Could it tell you if a child would be motivated in both math and reading?

Obviously, constructing a test to measure a concept such as motivation is a difficult task. Not everyone will agree on the best method for measuring motivation. At the outset, we wish to reinforce Cronbach's (1970) assertion that we cannot ask the general question, "Is this a valid test?" Instead, the question should be rephrased: "Is this a valid test for the purpose for which it is intended?" A test that has been validated for assessing intelligence may be totally useless when used to diagnose neurological problems even though neurological functioning and intelligence may both utilize cognitive processes.

In 1974, a joint committee of the American Psychological Association, the American Educational Research Association, and the National Council on Measurement in Education met to grapple with some of these issues and identified three separate methods for evaluating the validity of a test: content validity, criterion-related validity, and construct validity.

Content Validity

A test is said to have content validity to the extent that it is an adequate sample of the attribute, trait, or skill being assessed. The process of content validation consists of the test developer's decision that the items on the test are representative of a specified skill or ability domain. Obviously, an item requesting students to calculate the speed of the moon would be inappropriate on a test of third-grade math ability. A third-grade math test with good content validity should include a representative sample of the types of problems that third-grade children normally encounter. Thus, if a test contains too few items, omits some important aspects of math functioning (for example, no word problems), or contains subject matter irrelevant to math functioning, its content validity would be reduced. Most of the commercially available achievement tests are reviewed by experts in the particular subjects areas of the tests to determine if their content validity is adequate. Still, each user must determine if the test appropriately measures content for each particular use. If a skill is omitted on a test that is important in a particular situation, then the test may not be valid in that instance.

For some tests, such as the BRIGANCE Inventory of Basic Skills, content validity was a major objective in designing the test (Brigance, 1977). Such criterion-referenced tests are designed to assess major skills within a content area. Table 5.4 illustrates the various skills measured by the BRIGANCE.

Cronbach (1970) suggested that "the most general maxim to ensure content validity is this: *no irrelevant difficulty*" (p. 147, italics in original). For example, a student may be perfectly capable of computing the math problems on a test but fail certain items because they are embedded in lengthy paragraphs. Such a test might be more a measure of reading comprehension than computational skill. Test users should be alert to such instances in which irrelevant difficulties may unnecessarily influence test results.

Test users cannot rely on the test name to guide them in selecting an instrument that is valid for their purposes. Three problems that arise in using the test name to judge content validity are called the "jingle fallacy," the "jangle fallacy," and the "jungle fallacy" (Kelly, 1927; Messick, 1984). Test users fall victim to the jingle fallacy when they assume two tests with the same name are measuring similar things. A case in point is the Illinois Test of Psycholinguistic Ability (ITPA) (Kirk, McCarthy, & Kirk, 1968), which is assumed to measure something called "psycholinguistic ability," or, more simply, language functioning. However, as Carroll (1972) pointed out in his analysis of the ITPA,

> it requires some stretching of the meaning to call the ITPA a measure of "psycholinguistic abilities." The title is a misnomer, and users should be cautioned to look carefully at the true nature of the test, which might less misleadingly have been named the "Illinois Diagnostic Test of Cognitive Functioning." From the present title, a potential user might feel justified in expecting it to cover such language skills as reading, writing, and spelling. Actually, tests of these skills were deliberately excluded. (p. 442)

A second example of the jingle fallacy involves two tests that contain measures of spelling ability: the Wide Range Achievement Test–Revised (WRAT–R) (Jastak & Wilkinson, 1984) and the Peabody Individual Achievement Test (PIAT) (Dunn & Markwardt, 1970). The WRAT–R spelling test consists of dictating a word and requiring the examinee to write the word from memory. In contrast, the spelling subtest of the PIAT requires the child to select the correctly spelled word from four choices. If the technical characteristics of these tests were equal, teachers wishing to predict how well a child will actually spell would choose the WRAT–R because in reality children seldomly encounter a multiple-choice spelling situation. Thus even though the two tests purport to measure spelling achievement, they do not measure the same skills.

A companion to the jingle fallacy is the jangle fallacy, which causes a test user to assume incorrectly that two tests with different names are measuring different things. Close examination of the Devereux Child Behavior Rating Scale (McDaniel, 1973), which purports to measure child behavior, and the

Table 5.4 Detailed Range of Skills Assessed by the BRIGANCE® Inventory of Basic Skills

I. Readiness

Test	Title	Test	Title	Test	Title
1	Color recognition	9	Fine motor skills	17	Numeral recognition
2	Visual discrimination	10	Verbal fluency	18	Number comprehension
3	Visual-motor skills	11	Verbal directions	19	Recognition of lower case letters
4	Visual memory	12	Articulation of sounds	20	Recognition of upper case letters
5	Body image	13	Personal data response	21	Writing name
6	Gross motor coordination	14	Sentence memory	22	Numbers in sequence
7	Identification of body parts	15	Counting	23	Lower case letters by dictation
8	Directional/positional skills	16	Alphabet	24	Upper case letters by dictation

II. Reading

Test	Title	Test	Title	Test	Title
A. Word recognition		C-2	Initial consonant sounds auditorily	C-14	Common endings of rhyming words
A-1	Word recognition grade level	C-3	Initial consonant sounds visually	C-15	Suffixes
A-2	Basic sight vocabulary	C-4	Substitution of initial consonant sounds	C-16	Prefixes
A-3	Direction words	C-5	Ending sounds auditorily	C-17	Meaning of prefixes
A-4	Abbreviations	C-6	Vowels	C-18	Number of syllables auditorily
A-5	Contractions	C-7	Short vowel sounds	C-19	Syllabication concepts
A-6	Common signs	C-8	Long vowel sounds	**D. Vocabulary**	
B. Reading		C-9	Initial clusters auditorily	D-1	Context clues
B-1	Oral reading level	C-10	Initial clusters visually	D-2	Classification
B-2	Reading comprehension level	C-11	Substitution of initial cluster sounds	D-3	Analogies
B-3	Oral reading rate	C-12	Digraphs and diphthongs	D-4	Antonyms
C. Word analysis		C-13	Phonetic irregularities	D-5	Homonyms
C-1	Auditory discrimination				

Adapted from *BRIGANCE® Diagnostic Inventory of Basic Skills* by A. Brigance, 1977, Curriculum Associates, North Billerica, MA 01862.

Note: BRIGANCE® is a registered trademark of Curriculum Associates.

Inferred Self-Concept Scale (Spivack & Seift, 1967), which is supposed to reflect self-concept, will illustrate this fallacy. Both instruments ask someone familiar with the child to rate that child's behavior. In addition, both contain a list of behaviors that the rater is to check if applicable to the child being examined. Even though these tests have different names, their content is very similar, and in fact the Inferred Self-Concept Scale appears to be more a measure of overt behavior than self-concept.

The jungle fallacy is one to which many test developers fall victim. In this fallacy, two tests that are supposed to measure different things are found to be highly statistically correlated. The correlation is taken as evidence that the two tests are measuring the same thing. The fallacy is in not distinguishing between what is being measured and the instruments used for measuring. Thus, even though a test of self-concept and a test of intelligence may be highly correlated, this should not be seen as proof that they are both measuring intelligence or self-concept. Although either of these possibilities *may* be true, a third explanation is that both tests are measuring still another construct, such as social acceptability. When asked to define the concept of intelligence, some individuals have responded that it is what intelligence tests measure. We must draw a distinction between the test, the name of the test, and that which the test is supposed to measure. If the test has construct validity, it defines that construct, although the test developer names it.

Criterion-Related Validity

For a test to have criterion-related validity, it must be highly correlated with some other measure or event (that is, future or concurrent criterion). For example, when tests are given to candidates for medical school admission, there should be a high correlation between test scores and the criterion of success in medical school because predicting such success is the reason for the test. The criterion validity of such a test would be assessed by computing correlations between the applicants' scores with their actual grades in medical school a year or two later or with another criterion of medical school success.

Most intelligence tests are designed to have good criterion-related validity. With intelligence tests given to children, the most frequent goal is to predict success in school. Jensen (1980) has reported that correlations between intelligence tests and measures of school achievement are generally in the range of .50 to .70, which is relatively high for a single test predicting a complex set of skills.

A criterion measure may be available at the time the test is taken, but administering the test is more efficient than measuring the criterion behavior directly. For example, a behavioral measure of neurological dysfunction may not be nearly as accurate as examining the brain directly through a CAT scan, but it is much more time and cost efficient. If the behavioral test and other factors suggest some organic problem, additional testing may be warranted. In such situations, the test serves to predict a criterion (in this case, brain functioning) that is not readily and directly observed.

How successfully do tests predict behavior? In the field of special education, one does not have to look very far to find a very capable individual who was misdiagnosed, on the basis of tests, as someone who would never be a success in school. Predictive validity is not easy to establish; tests that are used to predict behavior are sometimes wrong, just as predictions of the stock market, longevity, and athletic game results are sometimes wrong. Tests with good predictive validity only help to improve accuracy, not to ensure it.

Construct Validity

Construct validity reflects the extent to which a test is capable of measuring a hypothetical trait, or construct. Tests have been designed to measure a number of constructs, including intelligence, motivation, anxiety, and self-concept. These traits are considered hypothetical because they do not represent observable behaviors that can be seen or measured directly.

To determine if a test has construct validity, we must rely on the theory behind the construct or statistical analyses of test scores. For example, psychological theory holds that there is a strong relationship between anxiety and scores on college exams. This theory predicts that people with a moderate level of anxiety perform best; extremely low levels of anxiety apparently do not provide motivation sufficient to perform well, and high levels of anxiety can interfere with test performance. Tests measuring anxiety could be validated against this prediction if students with high, medium, and low levels of anxiety should perform in the hypothesized ways on college tests.

The problem with a test lacking construct validity is that it may not be measuring the underlying trait. The Peabody Picture Vocabulary Test–R (Dunn & Dunn, 1981), for example, was once used to yield IQ scores. However, since the test measured only receptive vocabulary, we would not be too surprised if people who scored high IQs on the test did not perform as theory says those with high intelligence should perform, because the construct of intelligence is defined narrowly.

Normative Procedures

The third major factor we will consider in the evaluation of tests is the procedures for establishing test norms. Recall that in Chapter 3 we used percentiles, *z*-scores, and stanines to compare one person's score with those of others who had taken the same test, which is necessary because the interpretation of any score on a norm-referenced test requires some means of comparing it with an established point of reference. Test manuals facilitate such interpretation by providing a set of *norms* for use in comparing an individual's scores with those of a representative sample. Tables usually allow a raw score to be converted to one derived in reference to the norm group. A norm table from the Wide Range Achievement Test–Revised is displayed in Figure 5.3. From the table

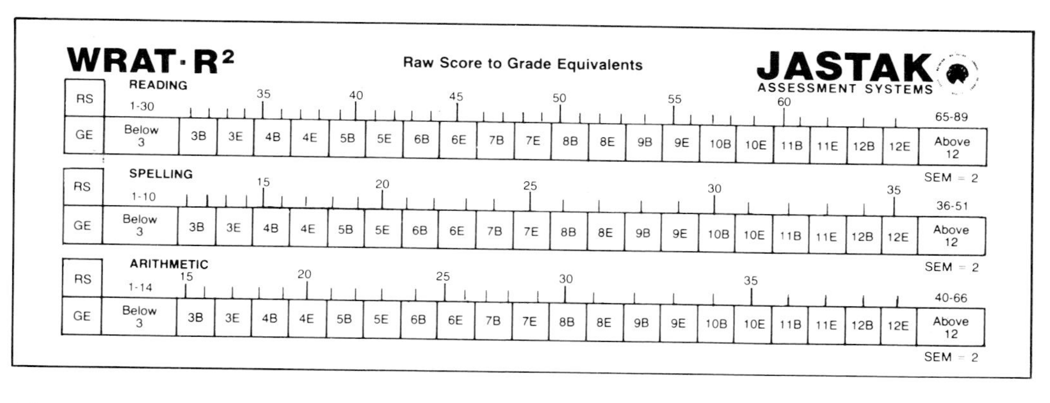

Figure 5.3 Normative table for translating raw score (RS) to grade-equivalent score (GR) from the manual of the Wide Range Achievement Test–Revised. To use the table an examiner enters with a child's RS and determines grade-level score. (From *Wide Range Achievement Test* by S. Jastak and G. Wilkinson, 1984, Wilmington, DE: Jastak Associates. Copyright 1984 by Jastak Associates, Inc. Reprinted by permission.)

it can be determined that a raw score of 45 on the reading subtest is consistent with the performance of a sixth-grader. People discussing this score would probably say that the student is reading at the sixth-grade level since reporting a score of 45 will have little meaning to most people. Because the scores from the norm group are the ones reported most frequently, the characteristics of the normative sample are extremely important in evaluating a test for possible use.

Criteria for Evaluating the Normative Sample

To evaluate the representativeness of the normative sample, one should first determine that the individuals in the norm group are reasonably comparable to those being tested. According to Hills (1976),

> the best clue for [someone] . . . who does not know a lot about sampling procedures is to look for a clear statement of the population, some description of how samples were drawn from the population, and a description of how closely the sample fits the characteristics of the population. If all these things are provided, the user is reasonably safe in assuming that the norms adequately represent the population and were obtained from sound sampling procedures. If the publisher does not give details of how the sample was drawn, how well it fits the population, and so on, but merely speaks of the size of the sample or gives a vague description perhaps based on equating this test through another test, etc., be careful. If the results seem strange it may be because the norms are not sound. (p. 130)

Table 5.5 WISC–R Standardization Sample by Age, Geographic Region, and Race. N = 200 for Each Age Group

	Percent in each age group by region and race														
	Northeast			North Central			South			West			All regions		
Age group	*White*	*Non-white*	*Total*	*White*	*Non-white*	*Total*	*White*	*Non-white*	*Total*	*White*	*Non-white*	*Total*	*White*	*Non-white*	*Total*
6½	18.5	3.5	22.0	25.5	3.0	28.5	24.0	7.0	31.0	17.0	1.5	18.5	85.0	15.0	100.0
7½	19.0	2.5	21.5	26.5	2.5	29.0	22.5	9.5	32.0	16.5	1.0	17.5	84.5	15.5	100.0
8½	21.5	1.5	23.0	24.5	4.0	28.5	23.5	8.5	32.0	15.5	1.0	16.5	85.0	15.0	100.0
9½	18.0	2.0	20.0	27.5	3.0	30.5	24.0	9.0	33.0	15.0	1.5	16.5	84.5	15.5	100.0
10½	19.5	2.5	22.0	27.5	3.5	31.0	24.0	7.5	31.5	14.0	1.5	15.5	85.0	15.0	100.0
11½	19.5	2.5	22.0	26.5	2.5	29.0	24.5	7.5	32.0	15.5	1.5	17.0	86.0	14.0	100.0
12½	19.0	3.0	22.0	25.5	3.0	28.5	24.5	8.0	32.5	15.5	1.5	17.0	84.5	15.5	100.0
13½	17.0	4.5	21.5	26.5	2.5	29.0	25.5	4.5	30.0	16.0	3.5	19.5	85.0	15.0	100.0
14½	17.5	3.0	20.5	25.0	3.5	28.5	24.5	7.5	32.0	17.0	2.0	19.0	84.0	16.0	100.0
15½	19.5	2.5	22.0	26.5	3.0	29.5	24.0	7.0	31.0	16.0	1.5	17.5	86.0	14.0	100.0
16½	19.5	3.0	22.5	26.0	2.5	28.5	23.5	7.5	31.0	16.5	1.5	18.0	85.5	14.5	100.0
Total sample (N = 2200)	19.0	2.8	21.8	26.1	3.0	29.1	24.0	7.6	31.6	15.9	1.6	17.5	85.0	15.0	100.0
Percent in U.S. population[a]	20.3	2.6	22.9	25.7	2.9	28.6	23.7	7.6	31.3	15.3	1.9	17.2	85.0	15.0	100.0

From the Wechsler Intelligence Scale for Children–Revised by D. Wechsler, 1974, New York: Psychological Corporation.

[a]These data were obtained from Table 56, U.S. Bureau of the Census, Census of Population: 1970, *General Population Characteristics*, Final Report PC(1)-B1 United States Summary, U.S. Government Printing Office, Washington, D.C., 1972. The reference group used to determine the "Percent in U.S. Population" consists of children aged 6 through 16 years.

This means that information given in the test manual should be quite specific. For example, over six pages of the Wechsler Intelligence Scale for Children–Revised (WISC–R) manual describe the normative sample alone. Table 5.5 is from this manual and represents the type of detailed information to which Hills was referring. Contrast this level of specificity with the Jordan Left-Right Reversal Test (Jordan, 1980), which contains only the statement that the standardization sample included children from "rural and urban areas, public and private schools, all socioeconomic levels," with little documentation of the precise characteristics of the sample, such as the number of children tested from rural and urban schools.

The representativeness of the sample can be inferred by noting the number of people in each of the following categories: sex, age, community size, geographic location, acculturation, primary language, and socioeconomic status. Certainly, it would affect the interpretation of a test of learning abilities if the norm group consisted only of Nashville children or only of learning disabled children. A common limitation is the failure to report the ages of the sample. For example, a test may be designed for children from two to ten years of age. However, the test authors may have been unable to test any two-year-olds. In this situation it is possible to extrapolate statistically how two-year-olds *might* have scored, although this is a much less accurate method of predicting performance.

In addition to being representative, the normative sample must also be *recent*. The decline of SAT scores of the last decade shows why it is necessary to review and reinterpret norm-referenced scores. When tests are revised or translated into a new language, new norms must be gathered. Since our culture is changing at a rapid pace, we would expect the way in which people respond to tests would also change.

Should you make comparisons even if the sample is probably unrepresentative? After all, isn't it better to use a poorly normed test than to make decisions without *any* comparative information? Salvia and Ysseldyke (1978) suggest that the answer is a resounding *NO!*

> It is occasionally argued that inadequate norms are better than no norms at all. This argument is analagous to the argument that even a broken clock is correct twice a day. With 86,400 seconds in a day, remarking that a clock is right twice a day is an overly optimistic way of saying that the clock is wrong 99.99 percent of the time. Inadequate norms do not allow meaningful and accurate inferences about the population. If poor norms are used, misinterpretation follows. (p. 122)

Cronbach (1970) suggests that norms are unimportant only if one is concerned simply with identifying individual differences within a group or a person's absolute performance. Thus, if the goal is to select the three students in each class most in need of remedial reading, national norms are not needed, for the purpose here is to choose those with the lowest absolute performances.

Alternatives to National Norms

As an alternative to national norms, some test users have developed local norms when the situation dictates the use of a particular test but the norms for that test are not representative of the locale or population being tested. Instances in which a local group is not adequately represented by national norms are not uncommon. Individuals familiar with school districts are aware that even *within* a particular district, the achievement levels of students vary from school to school. Local norms may be helpful when there is a reason to believe national norms should not be applied to a local group. The interested reader is referred to an article by Elliott and Bretzing (1980) for information on the procedures to use in constructing local norms.

Grade-Equivalent Scores

One of the most popular methods of using norms is to translate a person's score into a grade-equivalent. This popularity stems from the fact that grade-equivalent scores seem to be simple and easily interpreted by persons unfamiliar with tests. If we say that Tim scored at the third-grade level on a particular test of reading comprehension, people understand our words very quickly but may not have much real understanding. There are numerous such disadvantages to the use of grade-equivalent scores that mitigate against their use. In fact, in June 1980 the Board of Directors of the International Reading Association recommended that test authors and publishers eliminate grade-equivalent scores from their tests.

Critics of grade-equivalent scores have identified three major limitations to their use. First, these scores do not provide equal units of measurement (that is, they are ordinal rather than interval level measurements). This means that an increase in reading achievement from grade 5.0 to grade 6.0 on a particular test is probably not the same amount of growth as an increase from grade of 2.0 to grade 3.0 on the same test. On the Test of Written Language, for example, raw scores on the handwriting subtest range from 0 to 10. A student who earns a raw score of 5 obtains a grade-equivalent score of 4.6. If that test were given one month later and that same student were to earn *one* additional point, the grade-equivalent score for a raw score of 6 would be 7.2. Such a result would give the superficial impression that the student had made nearly three years growth in handwriting ability in only one month!

The second problem with grade-equivalent scores is that the same score may not have the same meaning for students of different ages. For example, a first-grade student and a seventh-grade student who have a grade score of 4.0 may not be equivalent in reading ability. Perhaps the test required only the ability to recognize words. If the task had been reading comprehension, the seventh-grade student, who may have a richer variety of experiences, may be able to comprehend the material at a higher level and thus out-perform the first-grade student on the more complex task.

Another problem with grade-equivalent scores is that they are misrepresented by critics of education (Mehrens & Lehmann, 1978). For example, a local school board candidate may alarm parents by indicating that fully 50 percent of the children in the district are functioning below grade level. The truth is that *by definition* 50 percent of the students *should* be below grade level. A score of 5.0 is used to describe the *average* fifth grader. On a national basis, about 50 percent of the students will be below average and about half will be above average. Some local districts may have a larger percentage above or below average depending on the composition of their student populations.

Sources of Information to Aid in Test Selection

The bulk of this chapter has been devoted to the three most important characteristics to consider when selecting a test: reliability, validity, and norms. Careful attention to these characteristics should increase the likelihood of selecting a good test. In addition to analyzing a test yourself, it is possible to obtain information from other sources.

Without any question the most highly regarded source when evaluating tests is the *Buros Mental Measurements Yearbook*. The *Yearbook* functions as a *Consumer Reports* for the testing industry. When selecting a stereo or automobile, many individuals do the best they can in evaluating the potential purchase but then, to be completely sure, they consult experts, who can determine the advisability of the choice by application of their advanced knowledge. This information is often already available in the form of such publications as *Consumer Reports*, which annually assigns experts to evaluate a large number of products. The *Buros Mental Measurements Yearbook*, a more technical and much more highly specialized version of *Consumer Reports*, contains experts' reviews of virtually every test marketed in the English-speaking world. The *Yearbook* series, which was initiated by Oscar Buros in 1938, has three primary objectives:

1. To provide comprehensive and up-to-date bibliographies of recent tests published in all English-speaking countries.
2. To provide comprehensive and accurate bibliographies of references on the construction, validation, use, and limitations of specific tests.
3. To provide frankly critical test reviews, written by persons of outstanding ability representing various viewpoints, which will help test users to make more discriminating selections of the standardized tests that will best meet their needs.

Yearbook test reviews are indeed "frankly critical," as can be seen in the Focus on Practice. The quality of the reviews is extremely high for two primary reasons. First and foremost, only specialists and scholars of the highest caliber are selected to write the reviews. Second, each review is carefully edited, and every fact is checked before it is published. Statements made by reviewers for or against a test are carefully evaluated.

FOCUS ON PRACTICE
Sample Review from Mental Measurements Yearbook

Borman-Sanders Science Test

CARL J. OLSON, *Assistant Professor of Medical Education, University of Illinois at the Medical Center, Chicago, Illinois.*

This test, containing 75 multiple choice and 25 matching items, allegedly measures the achievement of "elementary principles and facts of physical science with which the elementary school pupil should be familiar."

Despite the catalog claims, the Borman-Sanders is a prime example of a test that measures practically nothing of consequence but does it with high reliability. The failure of the test authors to provide important technical information — such as the distribution of the norming population, the methods used in computing reliabilities, and substantiating evidence to support claims of validity — is important, but it becomes secondary when one reviews the test content.

While the format is awkward and difficult to read, it may be the best feature of the test. It certainly helps to conceal the fact that most of the test items suffer from the molehill-out-of-the-mountain syndrome, asking for what may be the least important information about significant science concepts. In addition to being obsolete, the remainder of the test items are *insignificant* (e.g., "Inflate a balloon and release it, open end toward you. The principle it exemplifies was worked out by: 1. Sir Isaac Newton 2. Henri Becquerel 3. Alexander Graham Bell 4. J. Bjerknes"), *provincial* (e.g., "A wild flower sometimes called the 'Kansas Gay Feather' is really a: 1. sunflower 2. smartweed 3. spiked blazing star 4. snow on the mountain"), and *trivial* (e.g., "The space capsule of the Redstone rocket that carried the United State's [*sic*] second astronaut was named: 1. Monarch 2. Angel 3. Liberty Bell 4. Trieste").

In all fairness, it must be noted that the multiple choice items as exemplified above are superior to the matching section of the test.

There is not a single item that requires student cognition above the level of recall or which appears to be relevant to modern science curricula. If the Borman-Sanders has any use, it is as a convenient compendium for instructors of measurement courses. In it they will find examples of nearly every error in test development and construction that it is possible to commit, all arranged in one convenient unattractive package.

In addition to the reviews, the *Yearbook* also lists virtually every article that investigates the technical qualities of a particular test. For some of the more widely used tests, this can amount to several hundred references. The *Yearbook* can also be used as a catalog to locate various types of tests and their cost. One drawback is that the *Yearbook* is not really a *year*book and in fact is only published every five to seven years. This can mean that a newly published test is not reviewed until several years after it appears. This problem has been partially corrected by putting all test reviews on a national computer network so that they can be obtained through a computer terminal and a telephone hookup at most university libraries.

Reviews of tests are also available in other sources, particularly professional journals such as the *Journal of Educational Measurement*, *Measurement and Evaluation in Guidance*, *Journal of Educational Research*, and *Journal of School Psychology*. In choosing a test, one should not rely solely on the advice of experts. Rather, expert advice is most useful concerning the technical adequacy of a test. Whether the test is relevant and valid for the intended purpose can only be decided by the test user.

Summary

Beginning students in a testing course are often surprised to learn about the shortcomings of commercially available tests. The lesson is similar to learning that many car manufacturers are more often concerned with efficiency than with quality. It is a particularly bitter lesson that tests that are designed to help children are often developed by individuals who seem committed more to making money than to helping children. The solution, of course, is for the consumer to be prepared to evaluate the quality of tests rather than relying upon the claims of test publishers or the opinions of those who may be less than objective.

A very important lesson of this chapter is that the entire assessment process contains various degrees of error that may be based in the examiner, the test, the examinee, the teacher observations, the parent reports, and the thinking of the people who use the tests to make decisions. It is the wise student who takes from this chapter a sense of humility born of an awareness of the insufficiency of knowledge.

Chapter 6

Computer-Based Assessment and Test Interpretation

Learning Objectives

1. Distinguish between computer-based assessment and computer-based test interpretation.
2. Describe some of the concerns associated with computer-assisted testing.
3. Discuss expert systems and describe their potential applications to education.
4. List some of the concerns associated with the review and validation of computer-based test interpretation programs.
5. Describe approaches for protecting consumers from poorly developed computer-based test interpretation programs.

Audrey recently moved into the Livingston County school system. She is about to enter the second grade; however, her parents have expressed some concern about Audrey's ability "to learn as fast as the other children." Therefore they referred her for a comprehensive psychoeducational evaluation to assess her academic strengths and weaknesses as well as to help determine an appropriate educational program. Although only two weeks remain before the beginning of the school year, the school system has agreed to have a complete evaluation and feedback session prior to the first day of school. The speed with which the district has agreed to evaluate Audrey both pleases and amazes her parents, especially since her previous school had placed her on a waiting list for almost four months.

On the day of the scheduled testing, Audrey and her mother traveled to the Testing and Evaluation Center of the Livingston County school system. Following a conversation with the district's school psychologist, Audrey was led to a large room containing a number of microcomputers. Audrey had had almost no experience with computers, but the psychologist explained that this would not be a problem, for the psychologist would give Audrey a brief, introductory lesson to learn how to respond to the computer's questions; in addition, a psychological assistant would be present at all times to assist Audrey with any questions that she might have.

During the next four hours (with a number of bathroom, water, and exercise breaks), Audrey was "tested" by the computer. She completed a general test of cognitive ability (intelligence) and an achievement battery. In addition, she took a series of academic tests in reading, spelling, and arithmetic that were specifically tailored for her. That is, based on her responses to the standardized tests, the computer was programed to select specific items for administration. (This process is referred to as "adaptive testing," and is discussed in detail later in the chapter.)

Two days after the test, Audrey's parents returned to the Testing and Evaluation Center to confer with the school psychologist and two teachers (a second-grade teacher and a learning disability specialist) from Audrey's new school. Her mother was astonished to learn not only that Audrey was tested at a computer terminal but also that the computer was programed to analyze her results and print a long, interpretive report of her performance. Her scores were analyzed, the results summarized, and all the information carefully checked and reviewed by the school psychologist and the two teachers. According to the computer-generated report, Audrey met the federal, state, and local guidelines for assignment to a learning disability classroom. The school psychologist summarized the results and said that since the computer had done its work, she, Audrey's parents, and the teachers must discuss possible educational alternatives and plans for Audrey. It was decided that she would attend a classroom with other learning disabled children, and specific educational goals and objectives for Audrey for the next year were identified.

Introduction and Background

Does the situation described above—in which a computer was programed to test, analyze, and generate an interpretive report with specific educational recommendations and a school system's psychologist and teachers function primarily to check and evaluate the computer's print-outs and to convey the results to parents—sound far-fetched, ludicrous, improbable? Although the school system described exists only in our imagination, all the activities and procedures described do exist and occur in educational and clinical settings across the country every day. We know of no school system in which psychologists and teachers function only to check or review the computer's efforts, nor do we advocate such a system, but the possibility is not as unlikely as it may seem. To some, the activities described seem impressive. Others will be alarmed at the extent to which the computer can supplant the professional judgment of skilled educators and psychologists. In any case, we are about to explore the potential benefits that computer technology has to offer as well as the potential problems brought forward by this technological revolution.

As in many other areas in which the introduction of the computer has changed modern life, computer technology has the potential to alter significantly the practice of psychoeducational assessment. During the last few years the use of computers in education and psychology has become a very important and pressing topic (Moreland, 1985). Entire issues of professional journals have been devoted to computer-based assessment (see, e.g., Kramer & Mitchell, 1985), computers in school psychology (McCullough & Wenck, 1984), and computer applications in counseling (Sampson, 1986). Advertisements for new computer-based assessment and test interpretation products abound. This hoopla has occurred at the same time that many professionals have decried the fact that many computer-related products are inappropriately developed and used by unqualified personnel (e.g., Matarazzo, 1983). This chapter will examine some of the ways that computer technology has been applied to educational and psychological assessment and the controversy that has grown around the application of this technology. Finally, possible outcomes and solutions are discussed.

Issues and Basic Concepts

Although we might legitimately argue with Mitchell's (1984) assertion that computer-based test interpretation is the most important problem facing psychology in the next decade, there can be little doubt that there are real problems with this new technology. Many of the specific concerns regarding the development and current status of the computer in psychoeducational assessment have been detailed elsewhere (e.g., Kramer, 1985). We examine some of these issues with an eye toward future developments in the field of computer-based testing and their implications for the assessment of children.

To date, two types of computer systems have typically been used for assessment purposes: microcomputers (personal computers) and mainframes (very large computers such as those universities use to keep records, analyze experimental data, connect faculty and staff to a central computer system, and the like). Most professionals are likely to have access to microcomputers and the software developed for these systems; however, today many companies offer professionals access to mainframes to assist in the analysis of test results (at a price, of course!).

The computer itself (micro or mainframe) is referred to as the "hardware" of the system. "Software," usually contained on a floppy disk, refers to the programs that individuals develop to tell the computer how to handle information that is entered into the computer. These programs may be written in a variety of computer languages. Throughout this chapter we will make statements such as, "On the basis of these results the computer determines," or "The computer then decides," or "The computer analyzes." It would be more accurate to say that the computer has been told (i.e., programed) how to determine, or to decide, or to analyze based on a series of rules (the computer "program") that someone has developed and subsequently fed into the computer.

Much software has been developed to test, score, and interpret assessment data, and the use of these products has generated many questions about the role of computer-based products in the assessment process. Currently, there is a great deal of variability in the functions that assessment-related software perform. Some programs simply administer and score tests, others perform these functions and also interpret the test reports, generate interpretive educational and psychological reports, relate the results to the research literature, and integrate data from a variety of different tests into a comprehensive report. Although the technology has generated a great deal of controversy, there can be little doubt that it is here to stay.

Computer-Based Testing

As we have already noted, during the past few years much attention has been devoted to the use of the computer in educational and mental health settings. Much of the attention focused on the use of the computer has centered around its application to the diagnostic process and the use of computer programs in interpreting assessment results. Although less emphasis has been placed on the role of the computer in the initial assessment process, practitioners and researchers have recently begun to examine the use of the computer in assessment as well as interpretation (e.g., Kramer & Mitchell, 1985).

Computer-Assisted Testing

Computer-assisted testing (CAT) is the label applied to situations in which the traditional paper-and-pencil format of test administration is replaced with a computer and a monitor. The child sits in front of a computer keyboard, reads questions from the monitor, and responds by pressing a designated key. The computer has been programed to present items in a specific manner, and responses are stored in the computer's memory for subsequent analysis.

One of the most persistent questions in the area of computer-assisted testing is what happens when a standardized paper-and-pencil test of cognitive or academic skills is transferred to the computer? Do its reliability and validity remain appropriate? Do the original norms developed under standardized testing conditions adequately represent the group taking the test on the computer?

There are a number of reasons why conventional test administration and computer-assisted test administration might differ. First, the manner in which the computer presents items may differ dramatically from the way they are presented in the original test. For example, on some achievement batteries and personality tests, individuals are allowed to move through the test without regard to the order in which they answer items. In contrast, the computer can present only a few items at a time. Some subjects may also react negatively to forced interaction with the computer. Alternatively, a person may actually prefer to respond to a computer and to reveal sensitive information to this inanimate object. Moreland (1985) has examined factors that might influence performance on computer-assisted tests and concluded that although differences in individual performances sometimes occur when conventional tests are adapted to the computer, the differences are small enough to be of little consequence. Moreland also cautions that this conclusion is based on preliminary research (e.g., Hofer & Green, 1985) and that much work remains to be completed.

Test Scoring

There is little disagreement with the assertion that the computer is able to process more variables and to handle them more efficiently than even the most capable of people. One area in which these attributes of the computer have been extensively utilized is test scoring. It is clear that the computer can be very efficient in adding correct responses to yield a raw score as well as converting raw scores to standard scores, percentiles, grade equivalents, stanines, and the like, based on the normative data provided by the test publisher.

In situations in which practitioners are called upon to administer a large number of standardized tests (as in many school settings), the use of computerized scoring frees professionals from the monotonous, computational procedures associated with test scoring. Furthermore, this savings in time and effort may allow the professional to become involved in other activities. Computerized test scoring has generated less controversy than any other procedure associated with computer-based assessment and test interpretation. There is little doubt that it is possible to design test scoring programs for the computer that would be more reliable than most human scorers.

Adaptive Testing

Adaptive testing refers to the process of individualizing a test based on each subject's previous responses. If programed appropriately, the computer is capable of immediately analyzing an individual's responses and altering the sequence of subsequent items accordingly. Thus all individuals may begin at the same point in a test of, for example, academic achievement; however, subsequent items presented are based on the child's prior performance. Adaptive testing appears to be especially suited to tests that increase in difficulty as they progress and those in which specific answers result in the presentation or elimination of other items.

In the case of Audrey cited at the beginning of the chapter, the computer analyzed her performance on a number of norm-referenced measures of cognitive ability and academic achievement. Using this analysis, a pool of items was selected for further testing to obtain specific diagnostic information regarding Audrey's academic strengths and weaknesses. Based on her responses, the computer "decided" which items were to be administered next. For example, the computer quickly "realized" that Audrey was capable of completing one- and two-column addition problems with no renaming (e.g., 4 + 5 = ; 34 + 22 =) because of her correct answers to four questions of this type. However, in three attempts Audrey was unable to answer any of the one-column addition problems with renaming (e.g., 4 + 7 = ; 9 + 16 =); thus no two-column addition problems with renaming were administered. Had Audrey answered the renaming problems differently, however, the computer program would have selected different items to administer.

In summary, the objective of adaptive testing is to present subjects with the least redundant set of items possible by analyzing an individual's previous responses to test items. There is the potential for each subject to be administered a different set of test items based on their unique skills and abilities. In this manner irrelevant items are omitted and testing efficiency is increased.

Behavioral Assessment

Although much of the interest in computer applications in assessment has focused on testing, individuals interested in behavioral assessment have developed a number of microcomputer applications in the behavioral field, including interviewing, modifications of traditional assessment, psychophysiological assessment, self-monitoring, and direct observation (see Kratochwill, Doll, & Dickson, 1985, for a comprehensive review of such applications).

One example of a program using behavioral data is the Behavior Manager program (Tomlinson, Acker, & Mathieu, 1984), although no data are currently available regarding its efficacy. This program is designed to serve as a consultant to teachers experiencing behavior problems with their students. A teacher sits at the computer and types in information about the classroom routine, the target child, and her disciplinary procedures. The teacher then reviews a series of descriptors and is asked to identify those that describe the target child. The teacher responds to a series of forced-choice questions aimed at further delineating the problem. Ultimately the program provides a potential plan of action (as well as follow-up routines) based on the information and observations provided by the teacher. This program incorporates many features of expert systems programs described in the following section and is but one example of the potential benefits to be realized by utilizing the computer in behavioral assessment.

Computer-Based Test Interpretation

Software programs developed to interpret psychological tests were originally designed for adult clinical populations, most notably to interpret the Minne-

Table 6.1 Popular Tests with Computerized Scoring or Interpretation Programs

Test/publisher	Computer product/publisher
Wechsler Intelligence Scale for Children-Revised (WISC-R)/Psychological Corporation	WISC-R Microcomputer Assisted Interpretative Report/Psychological Corporation
	The Kaufman Method of WISC-R Hypothesis Generation/Wiley
	The Explorer/Academic Therapy
	Analysis of Interaction of WISC-R Variables/MADA Computer Programs for Psychologists
	WISC-R Analysis Program/HAPP Electronics
Woodcock Reading Mastery/American Guidance Service (AGS)	Woodcock ASSIST/AGS
Kaufman-Assessment Battery for Children/AGS	K-ABC ASSIST/AGS
American Association of Mental Deficiency Adaptive Behavior Scale/Publishers Test Service	ABSOFT/Publishers Test Service
Woodcock-Johnson Psychoeducational Test Battery/DLM Teaching Resources	COMPUSCORE for the WJPEB/DLM Teaching Resources
Luria-Nebraska Neuropsychological Services	Western Psychological Corporation Test Report: Luria-Nebraska/Western Psychological Services
Devereux Elementary School Behavior Rating Scale II (DESBII)/Devereux Foundation	DESBII Computer Program/Devereux Foundation

sota Multiphasic Personality Inventory, a comprehensive personality test. Computer-based test interpretation (CBTI) programs for use with children in educational settings have been more slowly developed but are now available for a wide range of tests (see Table 6.1 for a partial list of tests with computerized scoring or interpretation programs).

Clinical versus Actuarial Models of Prediction

The clinical versus actuarial distinction refers to the difference between models of prediction that are based on the research, hypotheses, and experience of skilled clinicians (clinical prediction) and those in which the computer output is determined by consistencies between that output and the input data (actuarial prediction) (Meehl, 1954). According to McDermott (1982), "a more simplistic way of explaining actuarial assessment would be to say that it is the process of making decisions about people on the basis of statistical probability" (p. 248).

Many of the systems available today for the interpretation of test scores clearly fall into the former (i.e., clinical) category. A CBTI program using clinical prediction will analyze the results obtained from a particular test (for example, the Wechsler Intelligence Scale for Children-Revised [WISC-R]) in a particular fashion. The rules that guide the program as it "interprets" the test data are based on the clinician's analysis of the available research and beliefs about appropriate methods of test interpretation.

One exception to the preponderance of clinical CBTI systems is the McDermott Multidimensional Assessment of Children (M-MAC) program (McDermott & Watkins, 1985). Based on the research of Paul McDermott and his colleagues (e.g., McDermott, 1980, 1981; McDermott & Hale, 1982; McDermott & Watkins, 1979), M-MAC is an attempt to develop an actuarially based system for the differential diagnosis and classification of school-age children (see Focus on Practice). The M-MAC program has had a great deal of publicity; however, its long-term impact remains to be seen.

The *process* of actuarial assessment, however, offers hope that psychologists and educators will be able to improve the reliability of classification decisions. With actuarial assessment a variety of statistical procedures are used to determine the factors (such as test scores, background information, and observational data) related to the assignment of children to specific groups (for example, mentally retarded versus learning disabled). These factors are then analyzed and translated into *decision rules*, which are used to determine whether new children qualify for inclusion in one group or another. The process of actuarial assessment ultimately results in the development of consistent rules that can be used for classification purposes. Much controversy has been generated about the efficacy and desirability of classification. However, if schools are going to group children on the basis of various factors, the process of grouping should be undertaken on the basis of clearly specified rules. Proponents of actuarial assessment claim that this process is a step in that direction and that the computer can facilitate the calculation of the complex decision rules involved in classification decisions.

Expert Systems

We have placed expert systems under the heading of computer-based test interpretations, although some might argue that this topic belongs with computer-based assessment or that these computer-based systems are a unique category that should be considered separately. Originally an outgrowth of the artificial intelligence field, expert systems (or knowledge-based systems) are computer programs that are designed to match the ability of a human expert in a particular problem area. These programs are an attempt to guide individuals in a step-by-step, common sense manner that makes it possible to diag-

FOCUS ON PRACTICE
McDermott Multidimensional Assessment of Children

According to advertisements, the McDermott Multidimensional Assessment of Children, or M-MAC (McDermott & Watkins, 1985) is "a microcomputer system for the objective assessment of children." It is designed to accomplish two major goals: classification and program design. M-MAC materials include seven computer disks and a manual of instructions and technical data. The current version is appropriate for use with Apple II computers.

The M-MAC system is based on extensive work done by Paul McDermott and his associates on the development and validation of an actuarial system for classification of childhood problems (e.g., McDermott, 1981, 1982; McDermott & Hale, 1982; McDermott & Watkins, 1979). They have gone to great lengths to determine the factors that tend to characterize individuals who belong to certain groups such as the mentally retarded, emotionally disturbed, and attention-deficit disordered. McDermott has used this information to develop a computer program that, when provided with information about a particular child, predicts the relative likelihood that the child belongs to a specific group. While others have criticized the classification process as being of little utility, McDermott believes that classification inevitably will be a part of the educational process and should thus be done as precisely as possible.

Exactly how does M-MAC work? First, M-MAC is not an interactive system. That is, the individual being assessed does not sit down and directly interact with the computer. Instead, the program asks for identifying information, including the child's name, age, sex, educational placement, and current date. Next, different types of background data are requested, including those related to sensory and general handicaps, general health, exceptional talents, linguistic features, cultural characteristics, environmental conditions, and educational background.

From here the computer program begins to inquire about specific assessment data. M-MAC is able to accept information from thirty-three different instruments related to intellectual, academic, adaptive, and social-emotional development. After these data are entered, the computer generates classifications as well as program objectives. The interpretive report ranges from four to sixteen pages. There is extensive evidence to indicate that the M-MAC program does lead to consistent decision making and that experts tend to agree more with the classification decisions of M-MAC than with each other (McDermott & Hale, 1982). However, the value of the educational and behavioral objectives generated by M-MAC remains to be seen. When one considers that there are 1,111 behavioral performance objectives available in the M-MAC system, it is apparent that the validation process will be no small task.

Table 6.2 Expert Systems Programs for Educational Applications

Area/Source	Description
Reading assessment/Colbourne & McLeod (1983)	This program guides users through reading diagnosis from initial problem to design of remedial programing. This expert system suggests the type of information to be collected. For example, it may ask for a particular standardized test to be administered or for background information on a student's academic history. After data have been entered and analyzed, the program suggests the next step. A report of diagnostic findings is the final step.
Math assessment/Roid (1986)	These computer programs (named DEBUGGY and IDEBUGGY) are designed to identify the "bugs," or problems, that a student has with subtraction. The program attempts to determine not only the student's "bugs," but also whether that student will incorrectly answer a particular problem and what that answer will be. The current version of this program (IDEBUGGY) is designed to interact with the student.
Maladaptive behavior/Tomlinson (1985)	This program (Behavior Manager) is designed to aid classroom teachers in identifying and remedying classroom behavior problems (see description in text).
Maladaptive behavior/Hasselbring (1985)	The author (with colleagues) is developing a program to assist users in the selection of instrumentation for assessing social behavior, development of a treatment plan, and selection of strategies for evaluation of the treatment.

Based on "Computer-Based Assessment in the Schools: Expert Systems Applications" by T. S. Hasselbring, 1985, American Psychological Association Annual Meeting. Los Angeles, CA.

nose, design treatments, solve problems, or offer advice in ways that are as accurate as current knowledge allows. The basic assumption with expert systems is that "knowledge is power" (Hasselbring, 1985, p. 8).

To date, expert systems have found their greatest application in the field of medicine (e.g., Van Melle, 1977), although these programs are not limited to a restricted range of problems (see Table 6.2). The potential educational applications for these systems seems extensive. Expert systems programs aimed at facilitating the ability of classroom teachers and diagnosticians to assess learning problems have received some attention in the literature (Colbourne & McLeod, 1982; Hasselbring, 1984) and are perhaps the most obvious application of this technology within education.

In his description of expert systems applications in education, Hasselbring (1985) points out that the

> expert system does not test the student directly, nor does it manage testing activities. Rather, at each step of the diagnosis, the system advises the user as to what to collect. The teacher or diagnostician performs the suggested task and enters the resulting information into the system. After these new data have been entered, the system analyzes the information and proposes the next step in the assessment process. When a sufficient amount of information has been gathered and entered, the system provides a report of its diagnostic findings. The teacher can then plan a remedial program based upon the system's findings. An obvious extension of this system is to have the system prescribe appropriate remedial strategies and instructional techniques based upon the diagnostic findings. (pp. 13–14)

As with any new and powerful tool, expert systems have the potential for doing harm as well as good. Roid (1985) points out that we must be careful not to assign the label of "expert system" too quickly to inefficient or harmful computer programs. It is inevitable that many so-called expert systems will fail to live up to their advanced billing. The potential benefits of careful application of these programs, however, appears extensive.

Review and Validation of CBTI Systems

One way to insure that consumers are protected from the use of inadequate CBTI programs is to make sure that professionals offer informed reviews of such systems. But in attempting to accomplish this goal, reviewers often face major problems not encountered when reviewing conventional tests. First, the decision rules, or instructions, that guide a CBTI program are hidden within the program itself, making it impossible for the reviewer to know how the program was constructed. This problem of inaccessibility of information is compounded by the fact that many CBTI companies are reluctant to release any information regarding how their software has been developed, fearing others will misuse or copy this information for their own benefit.

Moreland (1985) suggests that the consumer wanting information about a particular CBTI program should take at least three steps to judge the value of the system. First, find out who wrote the CBTI program and investigate the author's qualifications. Does the developer have a record of scholarship with the instrument in question or any credentials that indicate special expertise as a practitioner? If the answer to these questions is no, the consumer would be wise to look elsewhere. Next, it is important to examine the published documentation for the system. Specific information about decision rules for CBTI programs is rare; however, the general interpretive approach is usually documented. That is, one is usually told that the interpretation to the WISC-R is based on the work of Kaufman (1979), Sattler (1984), or whomever. Very often, the test publisher will also make available a series of references documenting the use of the CBTI system. Where do these references appear, in refereed journals or in-house reports? Are validity data available and how completely are they described? Finally, the consumer should see if there are any published reviews of the system. A number of professional journals (such as the *Journal of School Psychology*, *Journal of Psychoeducational Assessment*, and *Computers in Human Behavior*) routinely publish reviews of assessment-related software. Although the investigative activities described above might seem beyond the scope of a teacher's or psychologist's normal routine, someone must attempt to review CBTI programs in just as thorough a manner as one would review any test before recommending that it be administered to children.

CBTI: Concluding Thoughts and Needed Policies

As with the advent of any new, powerful technology, CBTI has generated enthusiasm as well as concern. If we are to maximize its potential, we must make "a sober assessment of its advantages and its problems and an effort to chart a course that will assure the latter and limit or avoid the latter" (Mitchell, 1984, p. 1).

Regarding the advantages of CBTI, it is obvious that the computer can apply decision rules more consistently than even extremely accurate people and that this capability results in more accurate decision making (Goldberg, 1970; Kleinmuntz, 1963). Further, the computer is capable of analyzing information much more quickly than a person can. An additional advantage of CBTI programs is their capacity to store enormous amounts of information. Between 1938 and 1978, the *Mental Measurements Yearbook* series contained some 57,846 research references to more than one thousand tests (Buros, 1978). To remain current on the relevant research for even one test is often difficult; however, keeping track of all relevant assessment research is clearly beyond the scope of human memory. By having this information, along with frequent updates, available on a CBTI program, clinical and educational psychologists can be better able to remain current and to provide efficient services. Finally, CBTI takes advantage of the computer with its penchant for speed, accuracy, and storing large amounts of information. As a result, efficient use of CBTI programs may result in an incredible savings in time and effort for professionals.

However, there are numerous problems with CBTI systems, some of

FOCUS ON RESEARCH
Man versus Model of Man

More than two decades ago Kleinmuntz (1963) undertook an innovative investigation of how the computer and the clinician might interact to evaluate human behavior more efficiently.

Ten experienced clinicians were provided with Minnesota Multiphasic Personality Inventory (MMPI) test protocols from 126 students exhibiting varying degrees of adjustment. The students' level of adjustment was determined by a variety of factors, including the ratings of counselors and fellow students. The clinicians were required to rate each individual on a continuum ranging from well adjusted to poorly adjusted. The clinician who most accurately classified the students was asked to examine a small subsample of the 126 subjects and to verbalize his thoughts as he examined each protocol.

Following this task, Kleinmuntz translated the data that the clinician had provided into decision rules (the rules the clinician had used to make judgments). He then used this information to develop a computer program that would perform an analysis similar to that of the ten clinicians. The program was then used to classify each of the 126 individuals according to the original adjusted/maladjusted criteria.

Not surprisingly, the computer program was more effective than the nine clinicians who were rated as less efficient than the "model" clinician. However, it is rather surprising to learn that the program outperformed even the clinician on whom it had been modeled!

Similar results have been obtained by others (e.g., Goldberg, 1970; Colbourne & McLeod, 1983), and, in general, it appears that the computerized statistical model based on the expert clinician outperforms the clinician. The model of man thus outperforms the man.

How can this be? Even the most expert, the strongest, the hardest working clinicians occasionally tire. Everyone sometimes takes shortcuts in the hope of accomplishing a goal without expending all of one's energy. The computer, however, is not smart enough to try to get by with less effort—it can only do what it has been told to do. Thus when a program is based on an expert model, the computer will use this model every time it is asked. The computer is dependent on us, but we are no match for its dependability and reliability.

which we have already enumerated (for example, professional review and validation). Furthermore, CBTI systems seem to have substantial potential for validating Buros's (1961) statement that "at present, no matter how poor a test may be, if it is nicely packaged and if it promises to do all sorts of things which no test can do, the test will find many gullible buyers" (p. xxiii). Although Buros was speaking of tests rather than CBTI, the statement still applies. As has been pointed out, the problem is even worse with CBTI in that much of the evidence that would substantiate (or refute) the claims of the CBTI publisher remains inaccessible to the general consumer.

The problems associated with the development of CBTI have recently been addressed by organizations such as the American Psychological Association (APA, 1985, 1986). According to Mitchell (1984), what is needed to protect professionals as well as consumers is a well-differentiated system of information dissemination for every CBTI system that provides data on at least three levels:

- Level 1: Complete disclosure for professional reviewers, including all information about program development and the decision rules that guide the program.
- Level 2: Basic and coherent information for the CBTI user. Publishers must provide the rationale for program development as well as more than just a general notion of how interpretive statements are generated. For example, an appendix could be provided for those wanting to learn more.
- Level 3: Information for the test taker. These individuals need to be removed from the realm of computer myth and mystery and receive a general perspective of how the system works as well as of its weaknesses and strengths.

It would appear that this type of differentiated system offers a good deal of protection to both the CBTI publisher and consumer.

Summary

Before concluding our examination of computer-based testing and test interpretation, we would like to return to an idea that has been discussed in a number of previous chapters: treatment validity. As you may recall, treatment validity refers to the extent to which a factor, such as test result, declarative statement, or problem-solving process, results in more efficient "treatment." Do our CBTI programs help us to design more effective programs and better treatment plans? Can we teach more quickly as a result of the information provided in the interpretive report?

To date, there is little evidence that the currently available CBTI programs facilitate program development and implementation. Why should there even be such evidence? Many of the most popular programs are based on tests for which treatment validity appears to be scarce or nonexistent (see Witt & Gresham, 1985). The data accumulated to date lack convincing proof that the results of these tests can be reliably translated into instructional strategies or educational goals.

However, this lack of evidence has not deterred individuals from developing CBTI programs based on test results (see Table 6.1). There appear to be few people connected with educational diagnosis who have not subjected the obtained results of various norm-referenced, general measures of cognitive or academic ability to the computer's wizardry. As we wait, the computer analyzes a bewildering array of scores and in the end prints an interpretive report summarizing the relationship among the scores and detailing the child's strengths and weaknesses. In some cases we may even receive a research summary for our subsequent analysis. It is truly amazing that the scores can be so quickly and completely analyzed, but should we not be concerned about the failure of previous researchers to document the treatment validity of the original test scores for which the CBTI program has generated a summary report? Should we not ask how the CBTI program can make something out of nothing? Have we forgotten the research showing that a scatter of intelligence test scores is rather normal (Kaufman, 1976a) and relatively meaningless in the design of educational programs (Kramer, Henning-Stout, Ullman, & Schellenberg, 1987)?

Although we have some concern about the current status of CBTI in psychoeducational assessment, there is hope. The work of Hasselbring (1984, 1985) and others on expert systems (see Table 6.2) as well as in areas such as adaptive testing appears to offer a great deal of promise.

Finally, we should say that it is clear that the computer will continue to increase in importance in psychological and educational assessment. Gradually, we will be able to use it to solve more and more complex problems. The widespread demonstration of computer-based programs with treatment validity awaits the talents of the skilled programer armed with sufficient ammunition. The process is ongoing. An incredible potential exists, but there are no guarantees that we will not misapply the technology. The best example of misapplication would be for us to continue to use the computer to analyze tests that are void of treatment validity.

Part Three

The Practice of School-Based Assessment

Teachers have numerous behavioral and academic expectations for children. Consequently, an array of assessment techniques has been developed to measure the many types of behaviors and abilities exhibited by children. In Part Three we examine ten major behavior domains, evaluate frequently used tests and assessment techniques for each domain, and discuss the linking of assessment information to classroom interventions. Five of the ten chapters in this section cover the traditional areas of cognitive ability (intelligence), academic achievement, reading, math, and language. Four of the remaining chapters cover topics of burgeoning interest to educators and psychologists alike: preschool screening and academic readiness, behavior and adjustment problems, adaptive behavior, and low-incidence handicapping conditions. Also included is a chapter on the assessment of perceptual-motor skills. Tests for this domain have been conceptually and technically limited, but because of its persistent popularity, we believe an enlightened examination of this assessment practice is in order.

Given the number of tests available, only the most frequently used or most reliable are reviewed. Many of the most commonly used tests, however, are inadequate and should never have been published. We discuss why such tests are conceputally, technically, or functionally flawed and constructively suggest alternatives. We have worked hard in selecting tests for discussion and have developed several extensive tables that directly compare tests on critical indexes. By the time you complete Part Three you should have an appreciation for the relationships among the development of children's behavior, the process of identifying and testing important skills and abilities, and the planning of instructional interventions for children.

Chapter 7

Preschool Screening and Educational Readiness

Learning Objectives

1. Describe the typical course of cognitive, motor, and social-emotional development during early childhood.
2. List typical expected learner outcomes for kindergarten students.
3. Identify at least five major preschool screening measures.
4. Discuss preschool screening procedures and identify at least two target behaviors in each of five major areas of development.
5. Cite and discuss three major concerns in the assessment of preschool children.

If you want to teach someone, does it matter whether the person is two or eight years old? Of course it does. Even if you have not had much firsthand experience with young children, you know that they differ in many ways that influence how they learn and how they are taught. For example, given normal development, we expect two- and eight-year-olds to differ significantly in language and other cognitive skills, motor performance, and social-emotional functioning. Developmental differences in such skill domains influence when children are *ready* to learn, or when their skills best match the instructional expectations or demands of formal educational systems.

In this chapter, we explore the concept of educational readiness, the burgeoning area of preschool screening, and the use of tests to make decisions about young children. Such a study is needed because a substantial number of young children are struggling and even failing in school. Some of these children are physically or cognitively handicapped, others have come from impoverished environments that did not facilitate their growth, and still others simply started school too early. This chapter will focus on three topics: (a) early childhood development and typical entry expectations of schools, (b) issues in preschool screening, and (c) methods for assessing young children's development and readiness for school. These topics have a rich and extensive history, particularly in the disciplines of education and developmental psychology (Biber, 1984; Bruner, 1960; Kelley & Surbeck, 1983).

Early Childhood Development and Educational Readiness

Early childhood, which we rather arbitrarily consider to occur between the ages of two and six, is typically a period of rapid physical, cognitive, and emotional growth. For example, during this time, children usually acquire the ability to ride tricycles and bicycles, draw pictures, print their names, speak in complete sentences, feed and toilet themselves, and play "appropriately" with other children. The abilities or skills underlying such tasks are the result of a complex interaction of a child's inherited and acquired characteristics with the environment. Jean Piaget has provided a viable model for understanding the development of many important cognitive and emotional attributes and has significantly influenced the concept of readiness. A brief examination of his work provides the theoretical background for conceptualizing human development and some benchmarks of normalcy.

Piaget's Theory of Cognitive Development

Piaget (1954, 1963, 1970) developed an interactive model to describe the process by which human beings go about making sense of their world. According to his model, people are adaptive, information-seeking beings with an internal set of principles that are used to organize knowledge about their environment. Piaget believed that from birth a person begins to look for ways to adapt to the environment. Two basic processes hypothesized to be involved in this adaption are *assimilation* and *accommodation*. *Assimilation* is the process of relating new information to existing ways of thinking. *Accommodation* is the process of modifying existing cognitive structures so that new information can be understood. It is imperative to think of assimilation and accommodation as occurring together. Consider the following example. A three-year-old is on a ride in the countryside with her parents and sees a cow for the first time. She promptly points toward the cow and says, "Big doggy!" Her mother, however, politely corrects her by saying, "That's a cow, honey, not a dog." In this brief example, the little girl has taken new information (seeing a cow) and assimilated it into her scheme for a dog. For this assimilation to occur, however, the dog scheme requires some modification (accommodation). By repeatedly seeing a cow and hearing it called a cow, she will differentiate her dog scheme into dog and cow schemes, thus allowing for rapid, accurate assimilation of both dogs and cows in future interactions with such animals.

Piaget believed humans strive for balance, or *equilibrium*, between assimilation and accommodation. Obviously, if we always assimilated information, we would end up with a few, very large schemes and thus have difficulty detecting differences in things. Conversely, if we always accommodated information, we would end up with a huge number of schemes and then have difficulty detecting similarities in the things we perceive. The desire for equilibrium is an overriding principle of mental growth that allows us to develop more and more complex but stable schemes.

Piaget hypothesized that equilibration (the act of searching for balance between assimilation and accommodation) was the major process of cognitive development. He identified the forces causing equilibration as biological maturation, activity with the physical environment, and experience with the social environment. Although the process of equilibration or cognitive development was theorized to take place throughout a person's life, the most significant growth was believed to occur between birth and fifteen or sixteen years of age. According to Piaget, the major changes in cognitive development could best be characterized by a sequential model of four stages: the sensorimotor, preoperational, concrete operational, and formal operational stages. Table 7.1 identifies the approximate ages and major characteristics associated with each stage. Since this chapter focuses on children between the ages of two and six, we will be interested primarily in the preoperational stage. A brief overview of the stages coming immediately before and after preoperations, however, is necessary for a more complete understanding of early childhood developmental changes.

Sensorimotor stage. This first major stage of cognitive development earns its name from the fact that infants gain information from their senses and their actions or body movements. An important acquisition during the first two years of life is the realization that objects in the environment are permanent, or in other words, stable and separate from the infant. This knowledge, referred to as object permanence by Piaget, arises from repeated activities and observations in which objects and people appear, disappear, and reappear.

A second major accomplishment during this initial period of development is the beginning of logical goal-directed actions. Through repeated trial-and-error interactions, infants begin to organize their behavior to manipulate toys and other objects successfully. Random, uncoordinated interactions with familiar objects diminish in number as they are replaced by more systematic, intentional motor actions.

Preoperational stage. This stage spans the period commonly referred to as early childhood and generally is characterized by tremendous growth in the internalization of operations. According to Piaget, operations are actions that

Table 7.1 Piaget's Stages of Cognitive Development

Stage	Approximate age	Characteristics
Sensorimotor	0–2 years	Begins to make use of imitation, memory, and thought Begins to recognize that objects do not cease to exist when they are hidden Moves from reflex actions to goal-directed activity
Preoperational	2–7 years	Gradual language development and ability to think in symbolic form Able to think operations through logically in one direction Has difficulties seeing another person's point of view
Concrete operational	7–11 years	Able to solve concrete (hands-on) problems in logical fashion Understands laws of conservation and is able to classify and seriate Understands reversibility
Formal operational	11–15 years	Able to solve abstract problems in logical fashion Thinking becomes more scientific Develops concerns about social issues, identity

From *Piaget's Theory of Cognitive Development: An Introduction for Students of Psychology and Education* (p. 45), 2nd ed., by Barry J. Wadsworth, 1979. New York: Longman.

are first carried out mentally rather than physically. To internalize actions, it is hypothesized that symbols representative of objects are used. For adults, written and spoken language provides the primary set of symbols. Preoperational children, however, have just begun to acquire language. In fact, language acquisition, which begins with physically mimicking others' actions and progresses to speaking in complete subject-verb expressions, is the most important development in the preoperational stage. Language provides the symbolic basis for internalizing thoughts and actions, thus allowing the child to interact with the surroundings in many ways that foster the equilibration process.

Piaget found that even though preoperational children are able to internalize actions using symbols, they are unable to reverse an operation. That is, they are able to model an action or image in the fashion shown, but cannot work consistently backward or in a reverse process from that shown. Reversible thinking requires the ability to keep an entire action in mind and to grasp the concept of conservation, or the understanding that the amount of something (for example, clay and water) remains the same even if its appearance is changed, as long as nothing is actually added or taken away. Piaget developed several simple tasks to assess conservation. He concluded that the ability to understand conservation is a complex task that few children younger than seven can consistently accomplish.

In addition to being unable to reverse their thinking and being confused by changes in appearance, preoperational children are very egocentric. This does not mean that they think a lot of themselves but rather that they are not able to see the world from a perspective other than their own. Egocentrism is predominant in preoperational children because of their inability to mentally manipulate their environment and their general lack of experience with the world.

In sum, the preoperational child is grappling with the ability to internalize actions. Language development provides a symbolic medium for this internalization, yet the child's cognitive skills are not developed sufficiently to permit mental reversibility or conservation of objects. An egocentric window on the world can be expected given the relative paucity of experiences and attention allocated to the task of language acquisition. Guidelines for successfully working with children in the preoperational stage include:

1. Make instructions relatively short (in two parts) and use actions accompanied by words to model the instructions.
2. Use concrete props and visual aids whenever possible to illustrate desired actions.
3. Do not expect the children to see the world from someone else's perspective easily.
4. Allow children much practice with facts and skills so they establish fundamental building blocks for later development.

Concrete operational stage. The basic characteristics of this stage, which spans the ages of approximately seven to eleven years, are that children recognize that (a) the physical world is logically stable, (b) elements can be changed or transformed and still retain many of their original characteristics, and (c) these changes are reversible. Probably the most basic of all concrete operational skills is the ability to conserve quantity. The reasoning skills underlying this ability are typically referred to as identity, compensation, and reversibility. Identity is the concept that if nothing is added or taken away, the material is unchanged. Compensation is the concept that an apparent change in one direction can be compensated or counterbalanced by a change in another direction. Finally, reversibility is the concept that a change that has been made can be mentally canceled. The combination of these three concepts allows the concrete operational child to master the two-way thinking unavailable to the preoperational child.

Two other important operations typically mastered in this stage of cognitive development are classification and seriation. Classification requires a child to assess and compare details of objects so they can be grouped according to similarities. Seriation is the process of orderly arranging objects according to size or quantity. With the ability to conserve, classify, and seriate, a child has developed a rather sophisticated system of thinking that allows for many varied interactions with the environment. The ability to deal with complex abstract problems and to think scientifically remains to be developed in Piaget's fourth and final development stage, formal operations.

As a means of reviewing many of the important cognitive developments of children, Table 7.2 summarizes the relationship between cognitive concepts and readiness to complete mathematical operations in children from two to seven years old. This table also highlights the practical impact of Piaget's work on early childhood education.

Despite much theoretical and empirical support, Piaget's theories of cognitive development have received criticism. Perhaps the most serious criticisms have been offered by neo-Piagetians such as Case (1974), who depart from Piaget's theory in assuming that stage transition takes place by a set of processes oriented toward problem solving. Thus, the neo-Piagetians seem to represent a middle position between information-processing theorists and Piagetian developmentalists. In brief, the neo-Piagetians readily acknowledge that knowledge is a critical factor in cognitive development, yet they perceive mental processes such as short-term memory to be more important. To date, the impact of this viewpoint primarily has been theoretical. Regardless of one's emphasis on cognitive processes, however, the stages of intellectual development described by Piaget have stood the rigorous test of time and still prevail today.

With this review of the highlights of Piaget's work and brief discussion of the neo-Piagetian position on early childhood cognitive development, we are ready to focus on nine areas of development traditionally assessed in a preschool evaluation.

Areas of Development Targeted for Assessment

Many different sets of developmental categories or skills have been identified as important targets of assessment. However, none of the sets is ideal because it is difficult to separate abilities into nonoverlapping categories. Lichtenstein and Ireton (1984) proposed an appealing taxonomy of nine broad areas: perceptual processing, cognitive, language, speech/articulation, gross motor, fine motor, self-help, social-emotional, and school readiness. In the remainder of this section, we define and discuss behaviors typically observed in each of these categories.

Perceptual Processing

A normal child develops the ability to perceive and act upon increasingly complex perceptual stimuli over several years. Visual and auditory information from the environment is received by the child's sensory system and must be neurologically transmitted and interpreted. Such processing of information requires a well-coordinated, intact neurological system. The typical preschool child will not have fully developed information processing capacities and thus may have difficulty copying simple shapes (e.g., triangle, squares, diamonds), distinguishing left and right consistently, discriminating between letter symbols, or blending sounds together to form words.

Perceptual processing difficulties are not easily distinguished from other developmental areas because the perception process is prerequisite to the functioning of virtually all behavior. Clearly, auditory perceptual processes are central to receptive language, and visual-motor processes are essential to fine motor and gross motor functioning.

In most cases, poor perceptual processing results from developmental immaturity and limited stimulation. A very small percentage of preschoolers, however, have some fundamental dysfunction in their neurological system and do not benefit from increased stimulation experiences.

Cognitive

In general, cognition encompasses a wide range of mental abilities that are often referred to as intelligence. In practice subsets of cognitive abilities, namely attention, memory, comprehension, and reasoning, are of primary concern to educators and psychologists. Activities such as classifying objects according to color, shape, or size, identifying similarities and differences, repeating phrases or sets of numbers, and naming letters and numbers are examples of tasks requiring basic cognitive skills.

Language

Language and cognitive abilities are interrelated and thus illustrate overlapping categories. Nevertheless, certain tasks, such as defining words, supplying words to complete a sentence, and labeling an object, place greater emphasis on language than other cognitive abilities.

Language abilities can be divided into receptive language and expressive language. Receptive language involves the ability to understand what is said, and is often assessed in young children by observing motor responses such as nodding or pointing. Expressive language requires speaking, and involves knowledge of syntax and grammar. It is assessed by analyzing language samples on dimensions of sentence length and complexity, word use, and grammatical features. In general, oral expressive language abilities develop later than receptive language; children thus often understand the meaning of a word long before they say that word.

Table 7.2 Mathematical Readiness According to Piaget's Preoperational Stage of Cognitive Development (Children from Two to Seven Years Old)

	Readiness of child	
Cognitive concept	*Stage I (2 to 5 years)*	*Stage II (5 to 7 years)*
Spatial relations		
The ability to perceive and compare spatial forms and patterns accurately.	Can discriminate between similar objects, if distinction is obvious.	Can discriminate difference in pattern if shape is similar.
The ability to visualize size, depth, and distance.		
Object permanence	Well established.	Well established.
Size	Can distinguish differences.	Can begin to discriminate using two characteristics. Can recall differences from own experiences.
Distance	Knows distance within own experience.	Can think about distance using concrete experiences.
Time	Remembers what comes first. Can wait according to own daily activities. Understands: today, tomorrow, morning, afternoon.	Can anticipate and plan on the basis of own experiences. Understands relative length of "minute," "hour," "day." Realizes birthdays are repeated, and how old will be on next birthday. Can tell time to hour.
Classification		
The ability to group objects according to certain defined characteristics.	Most often cannot classify because child forgets the characteristic to identify the class.	Can classify using some definite property, i.e., redness, but cannot put into more general category because does not understand the concept of inclusion: i.e., bananas, apples, and oranges are all fruit.

One-to-one correspondence		
The child's ability to understand that one object is *one*, regardless of its characteristics and that the number concept of *one* child is the same as *one* apple. The ability to count meaningfully is related to this concept.	Rarely understands. Can count by rote, but is usually reciting a memorized list of words and will skip items or "count" when no object is present.	Can do with some assistance. Spatial concepts are not well developed, so child will have tendency to assume that other characteristics influence numerosity. Has difficulty with such games as Musical Chairs.
Seriation		
The ability to order objects in relation to one or more of the characteristics, i.e., length, weight, or volume.	Cannot do, because cannot consider all the characteristics of an object.	Can do with objects that are equally separate from each other, i.e., line up sticks that are one inch, two inches, three inches, etc., but has more difficulty with such items as stones that are of random shapes and weights.
Reversability		
The ability to recognize that objects, when changed and rearranged can return to their original condition.	Cannot do.	Cannot do. Can perform an experiment such as pouring water from two beakers back into one larger one to prove the same amount of water is present, but does not understand concept.
Conservation		
The ability to recognize that number, size, weight, and volume remain the same regardless of the arrangement or shape of the object or objects.	Cannot do. Concentrates on only characteristics and centers on how object "looks."	Can do with some help. If shown that there are equal number of cups to saucers, will remember even when they are separated and rearranged. Understands conservation of quantity.
Language		
The ability to use words describing the concepts of number, comparing, contrasting, and problem solving.	Uses names for size, although there is some confusion, i.e., "big" for "tall" or "larger."	Uses words correctly to describe size, weight, depth, distance. Increasing vocabulary to correspond to increasing ability to classify. Can easily identify and label "biggest," "littlest."

From *Informal Assessment in Education* (pp. 260–261) by Gilbert R. Guerin and Arlee S. Maier, 1983, Palo Alto, CA: Mayfield Publishing Company.

Speech/Articulation

Although speech and language are highly related, they are distinct aspects of verbal communication. Speech involves the generation of sound in a coherent pattern. It is the process of using language. Important components of speech are articulation (formation of sounds), voice (pitch and intensity of vocal production), and rhythm (integration of sounds in a comprehensible manner).

In the preschool years, the assessment of speech is at a basic level. For example, are the child's verbalizations intelligible? Minor articulation errors are common. The most active period of speech-sound development is from eighteen months to four years, by which time all the vowel sounds and many consonant sounds are mastered by normal children. Acquisition of vowel sounds is normally completed by age three, while all consonant sounds often are not accomplished until age eight (Lamberts, 1979).

Gross Motor

The years from two to six are considered the "golden years" for motor development. During this period, most children acquire a basic repertoire of manipulative and locomotor skills, develop goal-directed motor behaviors, and learn to connect two or three movement sequences (Cratty, 1970). The major gross motor skills to develop during these years are body projection, body manipulation, and object manipulation (Williams, 1983). Typical body projection skills include running, jumping, hopping, skipping, and sliding. All require coordination among large muscle masses to move one's total body. Body manipulation skills, on the other hand, involve moving one's body or body parts in a well-defined but small area. Typical body manipulation skills include stretching, curling, rolling, bending, and balancing. Object manipulations universally observed in young children include throwing, catching, striking, kicking, and ball bouncing (De Oreo, 1980). It is not uncommon for this array of gross motor skills to be developed unevenly in preschoolers.

Fine Motor

Fine motor skills involve control over fine muscles. In regard to school functioning, these skills primarily involve eye-hand coordination. This is readily apparent in tasks such as drawing, coloring, cutting, and manipulating small objects. The skills required to accomplish these tasks successfully range from fundamental to more complex visual-spatial or perceptual-motor abilities, which in turn are important indicators of readiness for reading and writing. In Chapter 13 we will discuss perceptual-motor skills and assessment in detail, but we have provided Table 7.3 to illustrate a typical pattern of perceptual-fine motor skill development during the period from two to seven years.

Self-Help

Feeding, toileting, washing, and dressing are examples of basic self-help skills expected of preschoolers. They are commonly thought of as adaptive behaviors (see Chapter 15 for details) and are clearly prerequisites for entry to a mainstream school setting. Attitudes of independence from adults and control over one's environment accompany the development of self-help skills in preschoolers.

Social-Emotional

By two years of age most children display a unique personality. They exhibit emotions and are becoming increasingly social with peers and adults. The ability to separate from a parent without anxiety, follow rules and develop a sense of right and wrong, and relate to others are important social-emotional developments for preschoolers. Of all the areas of development, this one is possibly characterized by the greatest number of individual differences and thus is the hardest to describe in terms of a "normal" pattern.

The identification of social-emotional problems in young children is particularly difficult because it is normal for children to demonstrate some problems (such as temper tantrums, withdrawal from people, crying, and a high activity level) some of the time. The differences between children with serious social-emotional problems and normal children are often differences in the frequency, intensity, and duration of an undesirable behavior.

School Readiness

Technically, school readiness is not an area of development but rather subsumes a wide range of skills and behavior related to success in school. School readiness primarily cuts across areas of cognitive, language, and fine motor development. Skills or behaviors typically considered important to school readiness include copying shapes and figures, identifying numbers and letters, knowing left and right orientation, and understanding basic concepts such as same-different, top-bottom, first-last, and before-after. Most educators believe attentional abilities and interpersonal characteristics such as working and playing cooperatively and following teachers' directions are also very important prerequisites for success in school.

The concept of readiness has been an important issue for developmental psychologists for years and is a major concern of early childhood educators. Its essence is the match between the skills or abilities of a child and the skill demands of the tasks required at school. When these two variables match, learning is expected to advance more easily, meaningfully, and with less negative affect. Today there are nearly 100 tests and assessment procedures designed specifically to chart early childhood development and make decisions about school readiness. A sample of such tests is examined in the next section.

Table 7.3 Typical Perceptual-Fine Motor Development in Children from Two to Seven Years Old

2 years

Rotates forearm (supinates), turns knobs
Turns pages singly
Strings several beads
Unwraps piece of candy
Imitates vertical stroke
Crudely imitates circular stroke
Imitates a V stroke
Aligns 2 or more blocks for a train
Makes 6–7 block tower
Can match 2 or more simple shapes
Places blocks on formboard separately with demonstration

2J* years

Grasps too strongly with overextension
Places blocks in formboard with no demonstration
May imitate H in drawing
Imitates horizontal line
Holds crayon with fingers
Builds 8-block tower
Adds 1-block chimney to block train
Matches 1 color form
Dries own hands

3 years

Good rotation of wrist
Builds 9–10 block tower
Imitates cross
Copies circle from a model
Cuts with scissors
Matches 3 color forms
Puts on socks and shoes
Unbuttons medium shirt buttons
Places 10 pellets in bottle in 30 sec (1 at a time)

3J* years

Traces a diamond
Builds 3-block bridge from model
Washes and dries hands and face
Feeds self well
Matches simple colors

4 years

Throws overhand
Cuts with scissors
Copies cross from a model
Draws crude pictures of familiar things
Builds with large blocks

Developmental and Preschool Screening Instruments

The development and use of tests for preschoolers has rapidly increased during the past ten years. Much of this increase can be attributed to federal legislation directed at improving early childhood education, especially for "at risk" and handicapped children (see the Focus on Law). However, simply having a large number of tests does not guarantee that good tests exist nor that they are appropriately used. Our goal is to provide a rather extensive list of basic indexes of many tests and a detailed critique of three screening instruments. Readers interested in more comprehensive test reviews are referred to Lichtenstein and Ireton's (1984) book on preschool screening or Paget and Bracken's (1983) work on psychoeducational assessment.

Although nearly 100 tests are available for preschool screening, the viable alternatives can be readily reduced to a manageable few when selection criteria include adequate coverage of a specific domain of behavior and empirical evidence of reliability and validity. For our discussion we have selected individ-

Table 7.3, *continued*

4 years (*cont.*)

Copies a diagonal line
Buttons large buttons
Knows front from back on clothes
Brushes teeth
Places 10 pellets into bottle in 25 sec
Performs serial opposition of thumb to fingers

4J* years

Copies a square
Draws a person with several body parts
Draws pictures of familiar objects
Identifies simple objects by feeling, such as ball, block, or crayon
Catches a bounched ball
May name several colors

5 years

Prehends precisely and releases well
Tries to color within lines
May copy an *X*
May copy a triangle
Enjoys coloring, cutting, and pasting
Laces shoes without tying
Can dress and undress alone except for small buttons and bows
Draws a house with windows and doors
Draws a man with arms, legs, feet, and facial features

6 years

Ties shoelaces loosely in a bow
Throws ball with follow-through
Can print some letters and numbers (may be reversed)
Draws person with detailed body parts and some clothing
Imitates inverted triangle
May imitate horizontal diamond
Buttons small buttons on shirt or blouse
May know right and left on self
May have stable hand preference

7 years

Copies a Maltese cross
Cuts with knife
No longer has *b–d* confusion
Draws human figure with clearly represented clothing

*J means the skill/behavior is *just* beginning to appear.

From "Assessment of Perceptual-Motor and Fine Motor Functioning" by Zona R. Weeks and Barbara Ewer-Jones, 1983, in Kathleen D. Paget and Bruce A. Bracken (Eds.), *The Psychoeducational Assessment of Preschool Children* (pp. 268–269), New York: Grune & Stratton.

ually administered tests appropriate for children between the ages of two and six, and have categorized tests as multidimensional, language, speech/articulation, perceptual-motor, social-emotional, or observational.

Multidimensional Tests

Instruments covering multiple areas of functioning, such as cognition, language, and perceptual-motor skills, are traditionally referred to as a multidimensional tests. Lichtenstein and Ireton (1984) compiled a list of thirty-two tests that they considered multidimensional preschool measures. Many of these are identified in Table 7.4, along with basic selection information about their age range, administration time, nature, developmental areas covered, and availability of technical data.

FOCUS ON LAW
Federal Legislation and Preschoolers

Federal legislation beginning in the 1960s served as the impetus for widespread preschool programing. This government involvement was fueled by the belief that early intervention programs could offset the negative effects of cultural deprivation. As a result, several major pieces of legislation have been passed during the past twenty years. These include the Handicapped Children's Early Education Assistance Act of 1968, P.L. 90-538; the Early and Periodic Screening, Diagnosis and Treatment Program of 1968; the Education Amendments of 1974, P.L. 93-380; and P.L. 94-142, the Education for All Handicapped Children Act of 1975.

The Handicapped Children's Early Education Assistance Act called for the development of experimental programs for educating handicapped preschool children. Specifically, it facilitated the development and dissemination of model programs for handicapped preschoolers throughout the country.

The Early and Periodic Screening, Diagnosis and Treatment Program was designed to ensure that persons under twenty-one who are eligible for Medicaid would receive necessary medical services. This program was responsible for stimulating several new screening instruments and subsequent data on the incidence of handicaps among infants and preschoolers.

The Education Amendments of 1974, better known as P.L. 93-380, required the development of state plans for the provision of full educational opportunities to all handicapped children from birth to age twenty, with priority for handicapped preschoolers not receiving any services. This law was supportive of preschool education but did not mandate such programs. It was left to individual states to decide which programs were actually developed.

continued

Of all the multidimensional tests listed in Table 7.4, the Developmental Indicators for the Assessment of Learning or DIAL (Mardell & Goldenberg, 1975), the Denver Developmental Screening Test (Frankenburg & Dodds, 1967), and the Minnesota Preschool Inventory (Ireton & Thwing, 1979) are among the most popular, comprehensive, and psychometrically sound. Each will be examined in detail.

Developmental Indicators for the Assessment of Learning (DIAL)

The Developmental Indicators for the Assessment of Learning, or DIAL, grew out of the Learning Disabilities/Early Childhood Research Project funded by the State of Illinois and was designed to discriminate between children whose development appears satisfactory and those whose development seems seriously "delayed." The authors defined "delayed" as performing in the lowest 10 percent on an item compared to the normative sample of Illinois

FOCUS ON LAW *continued*

With the passage of the Education for All Handicapped Children Act (P.L. 94-142), the provision of educational services enacted under P.L. 93-380 was ensured. This act further defined program requirements, procedural safeguards, and due process requirements with regard to identification, placement, and continuing education services. However, the law did not mandate services to children up to three years of age and only required services be provided to children aged three to five years and eighteen to twenty-one years in states in which school attendance laws included these children.

In October 1986, the Education of the Handicapped Amendments to P.L. 94-142, Public Law 99-457, provided new federal incentives for the education of handicapped infants and young children. This bill has two major provisions: The first part requires states to provide special education services to eligible children aged three and older, and the second part establishes a grant program for the development of early intervention services for handicapped infants (from birth through two years). This law amends sections of P.L. 94-142 to include the term "developmentally delayed" for children aged three to five years, inclusive, in definitions of handicapped children. This term can thus be used to identify and serve preschool children without labeling them by disabililty. To serve these children, a multidisciplinary team must determine that the child has a "significant delay in one or more areas of development such as speech/language, cognition, motor, or social/emotional development."

Note: Readers interested in a more comprehensive coverage of laws and legislation that have affected services for preschool children are referred to David Prasse's chapter, "Legal Issues Underlying Preschool Assessment," which appeared in K. D. Paget and B. A. Bracken (Eds.), *The Psychoeducational Assessment of Preschool Children* (1983), New York: Grune & Stratton.

children tested. DIAL, intended for children between the ages of two and a half and five and a half, was constructed on the premise that six major areas of development are prerequisite to success in school: language, conceptual (cognitive), motor, social, affective, and sensory. The language, conceptual, and motor components are directly assessed through a standardized screening procedure, while data on social and affective functioning are collected through a behavior observation checklist. The use of vision and hearing screenings to collect sensory information is not actually part of the test but is recommended. Thus, although the authors of DIAL espouse a broad model of preschool screening, the language, conceptual, and motor areas are the primary focus of the instrument. At this writing, a revision of the DIAL, the DIAL-R, has been released. The content of the DIAL and DIAL-R are very similar.

Content. DIAL is divided into four sections, labeled gross motor, fine motor, concepts, and communications. Each is divided into seven subtests of multiple items for a total of over 150 items.

Table 7.4 Multidimensional Preschool Screening Instruments

Name of instrument	Age range	Administration time	T = Test	P = Parent record	E = Professional examiner	Cognitive	Language	Speech	Fine motor	Gross motor	Self-help	Social-emotional	Reliability data	Validity data	Normative data
ABC Inventory	3-6 to 6-6	10 min.	T			×			×				−	+	+
Brigance Diagnostic Inventory of Basic Skills	4-5 to 12-0	15 min.	T		E	×	×	×	×	×			−	−	−
Brigance Diagnostic Inventory of Early Development	0-1 to 6-0	30–45 min.	T	P	E	×	×	×	×	×	×		−	−	−
Comprehensive Identification Process	2-6 to 5-6	30 min.	T	P		×	×	×	×	×		×	−	−	−
Cooperative Preschool Inventory, Revised Edition	3-0 to 6-0	15–20 min.	T			×	×		×				+	+	+
Daberon: A Screening Device for School Readiness	4-0 to 6-0	20–40 min.	T			×	×		×	×			+	+	+
Dallas Preschool Screening Test	3-0 to 6-0	15 min.	T			×	×	×	×	×			+	+	+
Denver Developmental Screening Test	0-1 to 6-0	15–20 min.	T	P		×	×		×	×	×		+	+	+
Denver Prescreening Developmental Questionnaire	0-3 to 6-0	5 min.		P		×	×		×	×	×		−	+	+
Developmental Indicators for the Assessment of Learning (DIAL)	2-6 to 5-6	25–30 min.	T			×	×	×	×	×		×	+	+	+

Developmental Profile II (Developmental Profile)	0-0 to 9-0	30–40 min.		P		×	×		×	×	×	×	+	+	+
Developmental Tasks for Kindergarten Readiness	4-6 to 6-2	20–30 min.	T			×	×		×			×	+	+	+
Early Detection Inventory	3-6 to 7-6	15–30 min.	T	P		×	×	×	×	×		×	–	+	+
Early Screening Inventory (Eliot-Pearson Screening Inventory)	4-0 to 6-0	15 min.	T			×	×	×	×	×			+	+	+
Hannah-Gardner Test of Verbal and Nonverbal Language Functioning	3-6 to 5-6	25–35 min.	T			×	×	×					+	+	+
Kaufman Infant and Preschool Scale	0-1 to 4-0	25–30 min.	T	P		×	×						–	–	+
Kindergarten Questionnaire	4-0 to 6-0	20–30 min.	T	P		×	×		×	×		×	–	+	–
Lexington Developmental Scale, Short Form	0-3 to 6-0	30–45 min.	T			×	×		×	×		×	+	+	–
Lollipop Test: A Diagnostic Screening Test of School Readiness	4-0 to 6-0	15–20 min.	T		E	×	×		×				+	+	+
McCarthy Screening Test	4-0 to 6-5	20 min.	T			×	×		×	×			+	+	+
Minneapolis Preschool Screening Instrument	3-7 to 5-4	10–15 min.	T			×	×	×	×	×			+	+	+
Minnesota Preschool Inventory	4-8 to 5-7	15 min.		P		×	×	×	×	×	×	×	–	+	+
Preschool Attainment Record, Research Edition	0-6 to 7-0	20–30 min.		P	E	×	×		×	×	×	×	–	–	–
Preschool Screening Instrument	4-0 to 5-0	5–10 min.	T	P		×	×	×	×	×	×	×	+	+	–
Preschool Screening System (PSS Field Trial Edition)	2-6 to 5-9	15–20 min.	T	P		×	×	×	×	×	×	×	+	+	+
Riley Preschool Developmental Screening Inventory	3-0 to 6-0	5–10 min.	T			×			×				–	–	+
School Readiness Checklist — Ready or Not?	4-0 to 7-0	10–15 min.		P		×	×		×	×	×	×	–	+	+
School Readiness Survey	4-0 to 6-0	25–35 min.	T	P		×	×						+	+	+
Slosson Intelligence Test	0-1 to adult	10–20 min.	T			×	×						–	+	+

From *Preschool Screening: Identifying Young Children with Developmental and Educational Problems* (pp. 126–129) by Robert Lichtenstein and Harry Ireton, 1984, New York: Grune & Stratton. Copyright © 1984 Grune & Stratton, Inc. Adapted by permission.

The items for the test were selected as examples of school behaviors expected of children in a regular classroom. The authors successfully met this criterion of ecological and content validity. However, they provide no evidence in the test manual for construct validity. Instead DIAL's authors reported that an examination of test items indicated that a vast majority seemed appropriate and reflective of the developmental domain in which they were placed.

Administration. DIAL is designed as a mass screening device whereby each of the five or more members of a team administers a portion of the test at four separate work stations. The manual provides a detailed plan for how stations should be set up around a large, open room and how children should rotate through the stations. Administration time is estimated at approximately thirty minutes per child, but about four children could be evaluated in one thirty-minute period given the use of four assessment stations. All test materials are provided except for an instant camera and a balance beam.

The manual states that either professionals or paraprofessionals can administer the test. Based on our examination, however, it seems that considerable preparation could be required for a paraprofessional to administer subtests reliably and accurately. The gross motor and some of the fine motor subtests are particularly demanding (the examiner must read instructions word-for-word from the dense text of the manual and simultaneously demonstrate motor tasks for limitation by subjects). Scoring is largely objective, but again the gross and fine motor subtests require some subjective ratings, which adds to administration problems. In sum, we recommend that only professionals or carefully trained and monitored paraprofessionals administer this test.

The team administration format appears to have the advantages of time and efficiency; however, we have several concerns with such an arrangement, including interrater reliability across test stations and the impact of such a format on shy and distractible children.

Standardization and scoring. DIAL was standardized on 4,356 Illinois children stratified according to sex, race, demographic setting, and socioeconomic status. The sample was not representative of the national population since 30 percent were black and 65 percent were of a low status; however, it may represent those children most likely to have difficulty in school.

Scoring a child's performances on DIAL is rather straightforward and results in a decision of "OK," "reDIAL," or "follow-up." The number of items per subtest varies, but all responses are translated into a scale score of 0, 1, 2, or 3. With each area containing seven subtests, a child can achieve a total score of 0 to 21 points. Cutoff scores based upon age and sex (with lower cutoffs for boys) are applied to each area total. Scores above the cutoff score are characterized as "OK." Scores below the cutoff score in communications or in all three of the other areas (gross motor, fine motor, and concepts) receive a "follow-up" classification. Finally, scores below the cutoff score in two areas other than communications are given a "reDIAL" designation.

Reliability and validity. The DIAL authors report interrater reliabilities consistently over .80. This is adequate for a screening test because other evidence will accumulate later, but it does suggest problems in the instructions for administration or scoring or both. No actual test-retest data are provided, although the authors reported "high test-retest reliability, even after a full year" (Mardell & Goldenberg, 1975, p. 56).

Several pages in the test manual are allocated to the validity studies of the authors and others. However, in general the validity data is too meager to permit an accurate assessment of the validity of DIAL. For example, the authors report correlations from a concurrent validity study with the Peabody Picture Vocabulary Test (PPVT) in which PPVT scores and DIAL summed-scale scores for three-, four-, and five-year-olds were .64, .63, and .37, respectively.

In sum, the DIAL is one of the more comprehensive screening measures of school readiness. A recent report by Mardell-Czudnowski and Goldenberg (1984) indicated that the DIAL-R was psychometrically a vast improvement of the DIAL. Specifically, a national sample of 2,447 white and black children ranging in age from 2-0 to 6-0 were tested. Test-retest reliability was reported to be .87 and internal consistency via Cronbach's Alpha was .96. The results of this DIAL restandardization effort appear to have secured it a place among the leading tests for screening preschoolers.

Denver Developmental Screening Test (DDST)

The Denver Developmental Screening Test, or DDST (Frankenburg & Dodds, 1967), is an individually administered test designed for the early identification of developmental and behavioral problems in infants and children up to six years of age. It was intended for use by physicians and nurses with no background in psychological testing, yet many educators and psychologists have used it. Since the publication of the original version, there have been some revisions and variations of the DDST. Presently, there is a Spanish-language edition and a brief parent report form entitled the Denver Prescreening Developmental Questionnaire (Frankenburg, van Doorninck, Liddell, & Dick, 1976), although they will not be examined here.

Content. The DDST consists of 105 items standardized on 1,036 boys and girls from Denver ranging in age from two weeks to six years. The items are clustered into four areas: gross motor, language, fine motor, and personal-social. The item content varies with age, as might be expected in a test covering a period of such rapid development. A preponderance of items (75, or over 70 percent) are associated with development from birth to age two; this reflects the original intent of the DDST: to alert pediatricians to serious developmental deviations or medical problems.

Administration. The DDST was designed for easy administration in a short time (approximately twenty minutes). According to the manual, only those items at or below a child's chronological age are to be administered. It is even acceptable, according to the manual, to score many items without direct assessment if a parent reports observing the required behavior. This test is widely used because it is easily and quickly administered and scored.

Scoring and interpretation. Each item on the DDST is represented by a bar that spans several months. The left end of the bar represents the age at which 25 percent of the Denver sample passed the item. The right end of the bar represents the age at which 90 percent of the sample passed the item. A child who fails an item that 90 percent of younger children passed is considered to exhibit "delayed" development. The test manual provides classification criteria (abnormal, questionable, normal, and untestable) based on the number of delays in each area and the specific areas of delayed development.

Reliability and validity. Several reliability and validity studies of the DDST have been published during its twenty-year history. Most researchers have concluded the DDST has adequate interrater reliability (approximate mean $r = .96$), test-retest reliability (approximate mean $r = .78$), and content and concurrent validity.

Lindquist (1982) investigated the predictive validity of the DDST with respect to reading achievement in first, second, and third grades. The DDST was administered in the spring prior to kindergarten, and the Gates-MacGinite Reading Test was given as a measure of reading achievement. A statistically significant correlation of .46 was found between prekindergarten DDST results and reading achievement in first grade. However, an examination of the total sample of 351 children revealed that of 55 children characterized as "at risk" by the DDST results, only 26 were actually below the twenty-fifth percentile in reading. This study indicates the DDST may have limited use in preschool screening decisions. Rather, its strengths are in the assessment of developmentally delayed children between the ages of two weeks and three and a half years.

The development of multidimensional tests such as DIAL and its revision, the DIAL-R, seem to be replacing the DDST in preschool screening work. The DDST will likely continue to be popular in medical settings and in assessing severely handicapped toddlers.

Minnesota Preschool Inventory (MPI)

The Minnesota Preschool Inventory, or MPI (Ireton & Thwing, 1979), is a standardized form used for inventorying a parent's observations about a child's kindergarten readiness skills and development. The MPI thus quantifies an important perspective, parent observations, in the assessment of school readiness.

Content. The MPI consists of two parts, 87 statements about developmental behaviors of children aged two to six and 63 statements about adjustment problems and symptoms of children this age. The developmental items were taken directly from the Minnesota Child Development Inventory (Ireton & Thwing, 1974), while the adjustment items were derived primarily from research on elementary school children by Quay and Werry (1972). The 87 developmental items are grouped into seven scales: self-help (21 items), fine motor (17 items), expressive language (18 items), comprehension (34 items), memory (15 items), letter recognition (7 items), and number comprehension (9 items). In practice, memory, letter recognition, and number comprehension are all part of the comprehension scale. The 63 adjustment problem and symptom items are grouped into four adjustment problem scales — immaturity (18 items), hyperactivity (8 items), behavior problems (20 items), and emotional problems (11 items) — and four symptom scales — motor (4 items), language (5 items), somatic (4 items), and sensory (2 items). Item groups were derived clinically rather than empirically through factor or item analyses.

The normative sample for this inventory consisted of 360 white children and their mothers in a suburb of Minneapolis. The children ranged in ages from 4–8 to 5–7 years. The parents' socioeconomic status can best be characterized as upper middle class. Such a standardization sample is quite restrictive and meets only minimal standards, even for a screening test.

Administration and scoring. When the MPI is administered, a parent is instructed to complete all items, first, reporting any problems or handicaps they observe in their child, and second, simply marking "yes" or "no" to indicate if certain statements describe their child. Most parents complete this brief inventory in less than fifteen minutes.

The parents' responses are easily scored and transformed to a score profile sheet that converts raw scores to percentiles for each of the developmental and adjustment subscales. Items within the four symptom clusters are ordered from mild to severe and rather broadly ascribed to either the zero–fifth percentile, fifth–tenth percentile, or above the tenth percentile. All percentiles are based on the normative sample of 360 white middle-class children. Because they serve as normative comparisons, children falling below the fifth and tenth percentiles are considered to be "at risk" of severe developmental delays or maladjustment.

The test authors wisely recommend that users construct local norms to accompany those derived from the Minneapolis standardization sample. Little interpretative information or advice is provided for users. The successful use of this inventory depends upon a parent's ability to observe and accurately report observations of a child. (See the Focus on Research for more information on parents' ratings of children's behavior.)

Reliability and validity. To date, no reliability studies and only one validity study (Ireton, Lun, & Kampen, 1981) have been published on the MPI. The one validity study reported positive agreement between the prekindergarten

FOCUS ON RESEARCH
Parents' Predictions of Their Children's Preschool Performance

Parent report measures, such as the Minnesota Preschool Inventory, have appeared increasingly attractive as a cost-effective means of obtaining a broad range of relevant developmental screening information. Concerns, however, are raised frequently about the objectivity and accuracy of parent reports. For example, how comparable are judgments by different parents, given that some are better observers than others and that most have a limited sample of children against which to measure their own child? Do parents tend to be biased in reporting on their children due to their own personal needs?

Researchers have shown that structured interviews or questionnaires addressing *current* and *observable* behaviors that involve *low inferences* yield more reliable data. The validity of using parent-reported information to supplement or replace direct testing and other preschool screening measures, however, has not been demonstrated.

Lichtenstein (1984) recently investigated how well parent reports about their preschool children predicted school performance. Parents of 391 preschoolers between the ages of forty-nine and sixty-four months completed a brief developmental inventory as part of the screening program of an urban school district. The twenty-eight-item inventory assessed adaptive behavior and language development. In addition, the children were administered the Minneapolis Preschool Screening Instrument. Teacher ratings of their kindergarten performance the following year provided criteria to validate the screening measures. Correlations with the overall teacher ratings (the mean of 9 ratings) were .40 for the adaptive behavior scale and .57 for the language scale. Validity figures for the developmental inventory were significantly higher for children with low socioeconomic status than for those with high status, for older children (57 to 64 months) than for younger children (49 to 56 months), and for first-borns than for younger siblings. No effects were found by sex. While a positive relationship between parent reports of developmental functioning and early school performance was clearly established, validity levels did not justify the use of parent information as a sole source of preschool screening information.

From "Predicting School Performance of Preschool Children from Parent Reports" by Robert Lichtenstein, 1984, *Journal of Abnormal Child Psychology, 12*, pp. 79–94.

MPI scores of 287 children and their teachers' ratings at the end of kindergarten. Specifically, the comprehension, letter recognition, and memory subscales were the best predictors of kindergarten performance. When the final classifications of "developmentally delayed" or "normal" based on the prekindergarten MPI results were tested against reality, only 9 (or 3%) of the 287 were "mislabeled." Such a correlation is very good for a parent rating scale; however, one must remember that work in first grade rather than kindergarten will provide a better test of the predictive strength of the MPI.

In sum, the MPI can be a valuable supplement to a battery of preschool screening instruments. It involves a parent in the assessment process and provides a general picture of a child's current development. The normative data for the instrument, however, should be complemented by the construction of local norms.

Selected Other Tests

As noted, preschool developmental tests can be categorized in several ways. We elected to focus on multidimensional tests in this chapter because of their popularity in preschool screening programs and because areas such as language, perceptual-motor, and speech/articulation are covered in detail in other chapters. We have, however, compiled a list of tests in these and other developmental areas appropriate for use with young children, along with basic selection indexes (see Table 7.5).

Issues in Preschool Assessment

Preschoolers can be difficult to assess. They often do not have well-developed verbal skills, are not likely to sit attentively for twenty minutes, and are not very concerned about compliance with an examiner's directives. The rapid development of abilities and skills during the preschool years can result in assessment data of questionable value when it is based on only one brief time or cross-sectional sampling of a child's behavior. Finally, the relative paucity of psychometrically sound tests places a premium on direct, repeated observations of a child across settings and learning situations. Placement decisions should never be based on results of screening tests alone. In the final section of this chapter, we examine several practical issues central to preschool assessment and educational readiness.

Assessing Young Children

Assessing young children demands excellent test administration skills, foresight, and ability to communicate effectively. Not everyone is good at dealing with young, active children or severely handicapped children. There is no substitute for supervised experience combined with a basic concern for the testing environment, skill in establishing rapport, and sensitivity to a child's needs.

Ideally, testing should occur in a quiet, well-lighted, distraction-free room equipped with a table and chairs appropriate for small children. The child's comfort is more important than the examiner's comfort.

Whenever possible, assess a child without the parents present. This is often difficult with children younger than two years, and magnifies the importance of the examiner's rapport-building skills. To set a child at ease and to

Table 7.5 Selected Unidimensional Preschool Screening Measures

Name of instrument	Age range	Administration time	T = Test	P = Parent report	E = Professional examiner	Reliability data	Validity data	Normative data
Language and vocabulary measures								
Assessment of Children's Language Comprehension[a]	3-0 to 6-6	10–20 min.	T		E	–	–	+
Bankson Language Screening Test[c]	4-1 to 8-0	25 min.	T			+	+	+
Del Rio Language Screening Test[c]	3-0 to 6-11		T			–	+	+
Peabody Picture Vocabulary Test–Revised[a]	2-6 to adult	10–20 min.	T		E	+	+	+
Pictorial Test of Bilingualism and Language Development[b]	4-0 to 8-0	15 min.	T			+	+	–
Preschool Language Assessment Instrument[c]	3-0 to 6-0	20 min.	T			+	–	+
Screening Test for Auditory Comprehension of Language[a]	3-0 to 6-0	5–10 min.	T		E	+	–	+
Test of Early Language Development[c]	3-0 to 7-11	15–20 min.	T			+	+	+
Verbal Language Development Scale[c]	0-1 to 16-0	20 min.		P	E	+	+	–

Social-emotional measures								
Burks' Behavior Rating Scales: Preschool and Kindergarten	3-0 to 6-11	10 min.		P	E	+	–	–
Child Behavior Rating Scale	4-0 to 9-0	10 min.		P		+	+	+
Children's Self-Social Construct Tests: Preschool Form	3-6 to 10-0	10–15 min.	T			–	–	–
Joseph Preschool and Primary Self Concept Screening Test	3-6 to 9-11	5–7 min.	T			+	+	+
Speech/articulation measures								
Denver Articulation Screening Test	2-6 to 7-0	5 min.	T			+	+	+
Photo Articulation	3-0 to 12-0	5 min.	T		E	+	+	+
Perceptual-motor measures								
Developmental Test of Visual-Motor Integration	2-0 to 15-0	5–10 min.	T			+	+	+
Riley Motor Problems Inventory	4-0 to 9-0	10 min.	T		E	+	+	–
Tree/Bee Test of Auditory Discrimination	3-0 to adult	10–15 min.	T			+	+	+
Observational instruments for classroom use								
Basic School Skills Inventory–Screen	4-0 to 6-11	5–10 min.				+	+	+
Preschool Behavior Rating Scale	3-0 to 5-11	5–10 min.				+	+	+
Classroom Behavior Inventory, Preschool Form	2-0 to 6-0	10–15 min.				–	+	–

From *Preschool Screening: Identifying Young Children with Developmental and Educational Problems* (pp. 132–136, 138–139) by Robert Lichtenstein and Harry Ireton, 1984, New York: Grune & Stratton. Copyright © 1984 Grune & Stratton, Inc. Adapted by permission.

[a]Measures receptive language only.

[b]Measures expressive language only.

[c]Measures both expressive and receptive language.

encourage cooperation, the examiner should portray a warm, friendly, and reassuring demeanor. The use of a well-recognized and familiar toy of a character such as Big Bird or Mickey Mouse may facilitate a child's transition to a strange room and unfamiliar adult. Novice examiners often make the mistake of being too playful or cute, and consequently create a situation in which testing is difficult.

Sensitivity to signs of boredom, fatigue, or distress in a child are very important if an optimal testing situation is to be maintained. As a rule, young children are not intrinsically motivated to achieve in a new testing situation. Rather, it seems the responses of the examiner are frequently more important in determining success. Therefore, we encourage examiners to praise children's *work efforts* such as attention, persistence, and cooperation.

In sum, the test administration skills and interpersonal style of an examiner are critical influences on the test performance of a young child. A well-organized, time-efficient evaluation plan is likewise very important given the behavioral characteristics of preschoolers. When such an evaluation is accomplished, the personal rewards and job satisfaction are great.

Developmental Scores

Many tests, particularly those designed to assess young children, transform raw scores into age or grade equivalents. These scores are commonly referred to as developmental scores, for they provide comparisons to easily understood developmental landmarks. For example, an *age equivalent* of 4-2 means a child's raw score is the average (or mean) score for children four years and two months old who participated in the standardization of the test. Similarly, a *grade equivalent* of 1-5 is a test performance equal to that of the average child in the fifth month of first grade who participated in the standardization of the test.

Although conceptually meaningful, developmental scores are inferior to standard scores and subject to several problems. First, they tend to be ordinal rather than interval. Thus, when plotting the number of items correct by ages or grades, the result is generally a curved prediction line for young children with a flattening of the line for higher ages or grades. Second, the developmental scores of many tests are only estimates. In other words, children at all age or grade increments did not actually participate in the standardization of the test, and thus scores were interpolated or extrapolated based on those who did take part. Consequently, a child could earn an age equivalent of 4-1 when in fact no individual of that age even participated in the standardization of the test. Finally, perhaps the most common problem with developmental scores concerns developmental comparisons. When a four-year-old and a six-year-old both earn an age score of 5-0, for example, it only means they both correctly answered the same number of questions as the average of the children exactly five years old. The two children did not necessarily attack the questions identically, nor did they necessarily function like the average 5-0 child. In summary, the interpretation of age and grade equivalents requires caution. Whenever possible, it is wise to report standard scores along with developmental scores.

School Readiness

Throughout this chapter, we have interchangeably discussed school readiness and developmental instruments as if they were synonymous. However, although they are similar, as they both often focus on basic areas of development, they have at least two main distinctions: the purposes of the user and the scope of assessment. With school readiness tests, the user wants to predict whether a child's functioning is adequate for success in school. Thus, the major outcome of an assessment of school readiness is a "go" or "no go" decision. Developmental instruments, on the other hand, are not intended for use in placement or instructional decisions. Rather, they provide a normative standard of behavior in basic areas of development to which a child is compared. In essence, school readiness tests are best conceptualized as criterion-referenced, while developmental screening instruments are best viewed as norm-referenced.

The second distinction, the scope of assessment, is more pragmatic than the first. School readiness tests generally are designed to assess a narrower skill level or difficulty range than developmental instruments. To ensure good predictive validity, skills measured on a school readiness test should be drawn from kindergarten and early first-grade curricula. Skills assessed by developmental screening instruments necessarily are more diverse because they represent a greater span of development. Consequently, the point between being "ready" or "not ready" for school is at a much higher level of functioning than the point distinguishing between being "at risk" or "not at risk" for developmental problems.

The conceptual and pragmatic distinctions between school readiness and developmental instruments when selecting tests are not always obvious for a variety of reasons, such as the publisher's advertising and the name of the test. Regardless of the reason for ambiguity, one should always consult teachers familiar with the curriculum and demands of the potential receiving educational institution. In many cases, the teachers' reviews of the test content will provide valuable information about the extent of overlap between what is tested and what is taught.

Preschool Screening

Throughout this book, we repeatedly note that the primary purpose of assessment is to determine if a problem exists and how it should be solved. In other words, assessment is only a means to an end. In theory, preschool screening should aim to recognize early problem warning signs in order to make a comprehensive assessment for purposes of identification and treatment. The utility of preschool screening, however, is contingent on several factors, including the accuracy of screening procedures, provision of follow-up services, timing of screening, and involvement of parents.

FOCUS ON PRACTICE
Kindergarten ELOs

A common trend among school districts is to establish expected learner outcomes (ELOs) for each primary grade. Part of the basic competency movement in education, ELOs are used to communicate a school district's learning expectations to parents, teachers, and students. Well-written ELOs list curriculum-referenced cognitive and behavior objectives that can be empirically assessed.

Many school districts use their ELOs in making decisions about school entry and grade retentions. Ideally, preschool screening tests should be highly congruent with a school's kindergarten ELOs. Thus, when selecting preschool screening measures, you can assess their content validity by systematically comparing them to the ELOs developed by the schools the children will attend.

A representative set of kindergarten ELOs for reading, writing, and mathematics follows:

Kindergarten ELOs — Reading[a]

1. Identify common objects in the environment and pictures.
2. Identify these positions: above-below, behind-in front, top-bottom, and left-right.
3. Distinguish likenesses and differences.
4. Identify lowercase manuscript letters.
5. Identify uppercase manuscript letters.
6. Identify rhyming pictures.
7. Match upper- and lowercase manuscript letters.
8. Sequence pictures.
9. Select pictures that show story endings.
10. Recognize words that begin with the same sound.

continued

Accuracy of screening procedures. Inaccurate screening procedures pose serious problems because they result in identification and treatment errors. These errors include not identifying and treating a child who actually has a problem and, conversely, identifying and treating a child as if a problem exists but actually does not. Such errors, which cause inconvenience and anxiety for parents and children, occur in preschool screening because of a combination of factors. Specifically, screening procedures generally are administered in one setting during a rather brief interaction with children who lack experience with tests. In addition to setting demands and test-taking characteristics of children, most preschool screening measures are not refined psychometric instruments. Thus, some identification errors are to be expected. Hopefully, when errors do occur, they are in the direction of identifying more children as

FOCUS ON PRACTICE *continued*

Kindergarten ELOs — Writing[a]

1. Identify these positions: above-below, behind-in front, top-bottom, and left-right.
2. Distinguish likenesses and differences.
3. Identify lowercase manuscript letters.
4. Identify uppercase manuscript letters.
5. Match upper- and lowercase manuscript letters.
6. Sequence pictures.

Kindergarten ELOs — Mathematics[a]

1. Identify elements of a set.
2. Identify the smaller or larger object.
3. Identify these simple closed figures: circle, triangle, and square.
4. Compare the number of elements in two sets and indicate which is greater.
5. Classify objects or pictures according to color and shape.
6. Count concrete objects.
7. Count to ten by ones.
8. Identify one-half of a concrete object.
9. Identify these coins: penny, nickel, dime, and quarter.
10. Identify sets with an equal number of elements.
11. Identify the cardinal number of a set of not more than ten elements.
12. Identify the primary colors.

[a]Modeled after the New Orleans Public Schools' Kindergarten ELO, fall 1984.

"at risk" than really exist. Such identifications necessitate follow-up services that include direct, ongoing monitoring of the progress of the identified children.

Provision of follow-up services. Implementation of a screening program without the provision of follow-up assessment and treatment services is an irresponsible policy and poor educational practice. We believe the development of preschool screening procedures should be concurrently coordinated with a comprehensive assessment and treatment program. In fact, the instructional objectives of a treatment program provide the primary basis for determining the content validity of assessment procedures. Finally, as mentioned above, follow-up services that are coordinated with screening play a valuable role in confirming the identification of children as "at risk."

Timing of screening. The issue of timing of screening has two components: (a) the age of the child and (b) the time of year when screening is done. A guiding principle in all assessment activities is that the more recent an assessment, the more accurately it predicts behavior. This is particularly true with preschoolers because in a couple of months, a child may demonstrate quantitative and qualitative advances in development across several domains. A corollary principle of preschool assessment is that identification must be made soon enough to permit early intervention, especially for sensory problems and "disadvantaged" children. Thus, the critical question becomes: At what age can reliable and valid measures of skills and abilities that are relevant to successful performance in school first be obtained?

Generally, research indicates that by the ages of four and five, developmental gains in language, fine motor, and cognitive skills begin to stabilize and correlate significantly with school-age measures of achievement. Earlier assessments, except in cases of severe handicaps, generally do not have substantial predictive validity. Thus, the dilemma is wanting to intervene as early as possible but being confronted with the limitations of the reliability and validity of one's assessment tools.

Several schedules for preschool screening programs exist, including testing children (a) once in the spring or fall prior to school entry, (b) more than once during the years preceding school entry, or (c) once immediately before or during the first few weeks of kindergarten. Each schedule has its advantages and disadvantages. In general, periodic, repeated assessments offer several important advantages over a one-time, annual approach, for they have the potential for greater reliability and flexibility. Ideally, a combination of screening procedures whereby children are evaluated several times prior to and immediately upon school entry will be used to develop a flexible and comprehensive system.

Involvement of parents. Although parent involvement is the last topic discussed in this chapter, it is by no means the least important. In fact, parents play an instrumental role in the assessment and treatment of young, handicapped children and have been accordingly granted many rights and procedural safeguards by major special education legislation (i.e., P.L. 94-142 and P.L. 99-457). Working cooperatively with parents is thus not only the law but also good practice.

Summary

In this chapter, we have concentrated on the development and assessment of children between the ages of two and six years. Piagetian theory concerning cognitive development was briefly reviewed along with the development of perceptual and motor skills to establish some normative benchmarks. The major focus of the chapter was an examination of developmental and school readiness screening tests. Three tests were reviewed in detail: the Developmental

Indicators for the Assessment of Learning (DIAL and DIAL-R), the Denver Developmental Screening Test (DDST), and the Minnesota Preschool Inventory (MPI). Basic information on more than forty other tests was also provided in a summary fashion. The chapter concluded with an examination of four issues relevant to successful preschool screening. You should now be ready to complete the five learning objectives that guided the writing of this chapter. Are you also ready to make informed decisions about educational readiness?

Chapter 8

Cognitive Abilities

Learning Objectives

1. Discuss the major historical approaches to the measurement of intelligence.
2. Cite two reasons for the widespread use of intelligence tests.
3. Describe apropriate and inappropriate uses of intelligence tests in educational settings.
4. Explain different approaches to the measurement of bias in mental tests.
5. Discuss the strengths and weaknesses of major tests of cognitive ability.

A young school psychologist, Dr. Bailey, approaches a fifth-grade classroom. She knocks on the door and is greeted warmly by the teacher. The teacher turns toward her class and asks one of the students, Ted, to come to the door. Ted knows Dr. Bailey is there to see him. He worked with her last Wednesday, and she has come back to work with him again this week. During the next ninety minutes Ted and Dr. Bailey will be together in a quiet room adjoining the school library. During this time Ted is asked to answer a number of questions (for example, What is the capital of France? From what animal do we get veal? What is $6 \times 5 - 11$? How are concrete and asphalt alike?) and to complete a variety of timed tasks (for example, put these pictures in the correct order to tell a good story, copy these designs, tell me what important part is missing from this picture, put this puzzle together).

At the end of the testing session, Ted is tired. He has tried to do his best, and Dr. Bailey congratulates him for his effort. Ted knows that he answered some questions correctly and that he missed some of the harder ones. Dr. Bailey accompanies Ted back to his classroom, thanks him and his teacher, and then returns to her office to score Ted's responses. In approximately fifteen minutes she will have calculated Ted's IQ score according to the directions of the test developer.

Scenes similar to the one described occur many thousands of times across this country every year. Is the assessment of children's cognitive abilities by means of an IQ test a profitable exercise? Let's examine what some noted scholars have had to say about intelligence and IQ tests:

> The IQ test has also played an important part in the American school system — especially in assigning lower class and minority children to dead-end classes for the educable mentally retarded. (Kamin, 1981)

> A person's level of g [i.e., *general* intelligence] has ramifications for everyday life — in school, at work, and in personal matters. Because a standard IQ score is usually a good measure of g, it efficiently tells us something important. (Herrnstein, 1982)

> IQ is a questionable measure of general intelligence and a minor determination of success. (Robinson, 1973)

> IQ jointly with scholastic performance predicts more of the variance among persons in adult occupational status and income than any other known combination of variables, including race and social class or origin. (Jensen, 1981)

> If . . . the impression takes root that these tests really measure intelligence, that they constitute a sort of last judgment on the child's capacity, that they reveal "scientifically" his predestined ability, then it would be a thousand times better if all the intelligence testers and all their questionnaires were sunk without warning in the Sargasso Sea. (Lippmann, 1976)

> The outstanding success of scientific measurement of individual differences has been that of the general mental test. Despite occasional overenthusiasm and misconceptions and the fact that the established tests are rendered obsolescent by recent conceptual advances, the general mental test stands today as the most important technical contribution psychology has made to the practical guidance of human affairs. (Cronbach, 1970)

Who is correct? Should IQ tests be abolished or are they useful tools for understanding people? How can experts disagree so greatly? Obviously, the issues are complex, and there are no simple answers. The tests discussed in this chapter have sometimes been referred to as "mental tests," tests of "general ability" or "academic aptitude," "intelligence tests," or, more recently, "tests of cognitive abilities." Although these terms cannot always be used interchangeably, we have made no attempt to draw clear distinctions among them. As we proceed, it is anticipated that some of the confusion caused by the use of these different terms will be avoided not by an attempt to provide precise definitions but by a thorough presentation of the issues and research in the field. Toward that end we will examine the origins and current status of the mental testing movement, explore many of the issues surrounding the use of these tests in our society, discuss a number of the most widely used measures of intelligence, and conclude with a brief discussion of the future of cognitive ability testing.

Historical Approaches to the Definition and Measurement of Intelligence

Early Efforts

The study of intelligence can be clearly traced to nineteenth-century attempts to measure individual differences in a wide variety of human characteristics. It has been claimed that this testing movement was an essential part of the establishment of psychology as a separate discipline (see, e.g., Sattler, 1982). Three major contributors to these early efforts were Sir Francis Galton in England, Wilhelm Wundt in Germany, and J. McKeen Cattell in the United States. Galton developed psychophysical measurements such as strength of push and pull, breathing capacity, keenness of the senses, and mental imagery. His efforts in the study of individual differences led to the development of a psychometric laboratory at the International Exposition in England in 1884 and to his designation as the "father" of the testing movement (Shouksmith, 1970).

Wundt, who opened the first psychological testing laboratory in Leipzig, Germany, in 1879, utilized the early work of Galton and others but took a slightly different approach. He attempted to identify general laws governing behavior rather than to measure the extent of individual variation among humans. Cattell, who gave us the term "mental tests," imported these techniques to the United States. Procedures to measure factors such as sensory acuity, strength of grip, sensitivity to pain, and memory for dictated consonants characterized his efforts to assess individual differences and later to measure individual mental skills. The tests used by these pioneers did not predict academic achievement and seem primitive by today's standards. These early approaches did, however, serve as a foundation for future research and moved intellectual measurement out of the realm of speculation and clinical judgments and into the world of scientific measurement.

Early Twentieth-Century Approaches: The Search for Relevance

Around the turn of the century in France, Alfred Binet became interested in studying more complex mental processes. His findings also supported the notion that simple sensory discriminations and physical attributes had little relation to general mental functioning in schools. In 1905, at the request of the Minister of Public Instruction in France who wanted a test that would assist school personnel in determining which students were not capable of achieving in the regular classroom, Binet and his associate, Theodore Simon, developed and published the Binet-Simon Scale. Revised in 1908, the scale's major contributions were that it was pragmatic in development, used complex tasks as test items, ranked items in order of difficulty and grouped them according to age levels, measured general mental ability rather than separate mental faculties, included careful instructions for administration, and exhibited some concern with normative data. Further, student test scores were shown to be related to academic performance. The Binet-Simon Scale was designed to predict school achievement and did a fairly good job of it. Today, one of the primary reasons that tests like the Binet (or Stanford-Binet as it is often referred to today) continue to be so widely used is that they remain among the best (although imperfect) predictors of school achievement. Following the introduction of this scale in the United States, the testing movement began to flourish.

Although a significant advance over previous efforts, there were problems with the Binet-Simon Scale and its subsequent revisions. One of the most persistent criticisms was related to its age-scale format. That is, tests were selected for inclusion at various age levels based on the difficulty of the tests, and different tasks were included at different age levels. The result was a great deal of heterogeneity of item content (see Figure 8.1 for representative items across age levels). Thus, interpretation of an individual's performance on the Binet was difficult because of the varied item content and because measurements of individuals of different ages were not strictly comparable. (If all this talk about the structure and design of the Binet is a little fuzzy, don't be discouraged. This test has been confusing people for years).

Enter David Wechsler, who took a different approach to the development of an intelligence test. Wechsler wanted to find tasks that would measure various cognitive abilities and could be used across a wide range of age levels. He studied a variety of tests available and developed eleven subtests, which he used to form the Wechsler-Bellevue Intelligence Scale, designed for use with adults. This test led to the development of the Wechsler series of intelligence tests (Wechsler Primary and Preschool Scale of Intelligence [WPPSI], Wechsler Intelligence Scale for Children-Revised [WISC-R], Wechsler Adult Intelligence Scale-Revised [WAIS-R]), which today are the most widely used measures of cognitive functioning in educational and clinical settings. Later we will examine one of these instruments, the WISC-R, and the subtest format that Wechsler developed.

Recent Developments

Both Binet and Wechsler wanted to develop a test instrument that would be useful in the clinical and educational assessment of individuals. Although both men conceptualized intelligence as a very complex and multifaceted phenomenon, their tests yielded global intelligence scores that suggested a more uni-

Year III

Credit — 6 tests × 1 month or 4 tests × 1½ months

1. Stringing Beads — the examiner models the stringing of beads on a shoestring and the child is asked to "play this game."
2. Picture Vocabulary — naming pictures of common objects.
3. Block Building: Bridge — building a bridge of three blocks modeled by the examiner.
4. Picture Memories — finding animal pictures hidden by the examiner.
5. Copying a Circle — three trials of copying a circle.
6. Drawing a Vertical Line — one trial drawing a vertical line just like the one drawn by the examiner.

A. Repeating 3 Digits — repeating 3 digits in sequence.

Year VIII

Credit — 6 tests × 2 months or 4 tests × 3 months

1. Vocabulary — children are asked to provide the definitions of words.
2. Memory for Stories: The Wet Fall — children are asked a series of questions based on a story read by the examiner.
3. Verbal Absurdities I — a series of absurd or foolish situations are presented and the child asked to tell, "What's foolish about this?"
4. Similarities and Differences — describing the similarities and differences of two things.
5. Comprehension IV — a series of general comprehension questions to which the examinee must respond.
6. Naming the Days of the Week — naming the days of the week.

A. Problem Situation I — incomplete situations are presented, followed by questions which require the child to infer what is happening in the scene.

Superior Adult III

Credit — 6 tests × 6 months or 4 tests × 9 months

1. Vocabulary — providing definitions of words.
2. Proverbs III — explaining the meaning of words.
3. Opposite Analogies IV — analogies are provided with the final word in the analogy supplied by the subject.
4. Orientation: Direction III — analyzing distance and direction based on information provided by the examiner.
5. Reasoning II — individual is presented brief problem and given 5 minutes to solve it (without pencil and paper).
6. Passage II: Tests — repeating the main ideas of a brief passage read by the examiner.

A. Opposite Analogies — Same as above.

Figure 8.1 Stanford-Binet Intelligence Scale: representative year levels and subtests. (From *Stanford-Binet Intelligence Scale: 1973 Norms Edition* by L. M. Terman and M. A. Merrill, 1973, Boston: Houghton Mifflin. These Stanford-Binet materials are also included in the Fourth Edition, Copyright 1986 by the Riverside Publishing Company. Reproduced by permission of the publisher. Authors of this revision are Elizabeth Hagen, Jerome M. Sattler, and Robert L. Thorndike.)

fied view of intelligence. Many individuals lost sight of the fact that the Binet-Simon and Wechsler scales contained a variety of tasks tapping many different abilities, and instead focused on the comprehensive IQ scores these tests yielded. The question of whether intelligence is a single ability or a collection of multiple abilities has received the attention of theorists and researchers during the last fifty years.

The best known proponent of the former approach was Charles E. Spearman (1927), who set forth a two-factor theory of intelligence. He hypothesized that performance on intelligence tests resulted from a general factor *(g)* and a group of specific factors that varied from test to test. Spearman is sometimes viewed as a single-factor theorist due to his emphasis on the importance of *g*, which he said is involved in all problem solving and is especially important in complicated mental activities. Specific factors, on the other hand, are unique to a particular activity or test. A major implication of this theory was that although specific factors must be considered, the primary goal of intellectual measurement should be the construction of tests that measure *g*. Why? Because if we develop tests that are good measures of this general factor that influences performance on all tasks, we should be better able to predict how an individual will do on tasks in the future.

Louis L. Thurstone (1938) and J. P. Guilford (1967) have been more closely identified with the multifactor theory approach. Both believed that intelligence could not be reduced to a unitary factor such as *g*. Thurstone developed the Primary Mental Abilities Test to measure what he felt to be the primary mental abilities (such as verbal skills, perceptual speed, inductive reasoning, word fluency, and rote memory), and Guilford developed a three-dimensional Structure of Intellect Model (see Figure 8.2) that organized intellectual factors hierarchically. Both approaches assumed that a model of intellectual functioning must include a variety of fairly broad factors if it is to account for the complexity of mental activity.

Within the last decade, two other explanations of intelligence have gained increased attention. The first is based on the work of Alexsadr Luria, and has been expanded by J. P. Das and his colleagues (Das, Kirby, & Jarman, 1979; Jarman & Das, 1977). This model has been referred to as simultaneous/successive processing, and later in the chapter we look at a new test based, in large part, on this theoretical model. Simply stated, this model suggests that individuals process information primarily in one of two ways — simultaneously or successively. In the former, problem solving and decision making involve the simultaneous integration of a variety of stimuli. Information is processed in a holistic manner, as when people are asked to recognize faces, solve mazes, and complete puzzles. In the successive mode, stimuli are arranged in sequence and dealt with one at a time. Decisions are reached by processing information in an orderly, sequence-dependent fashion (for example, remembering a series of digits or words in the proper order). The usefulness of this model and its ability to increase our understanding of mental processes remain to be determined.

More recently, Sternberg (1984a) has postulated a "triarchic theory" of

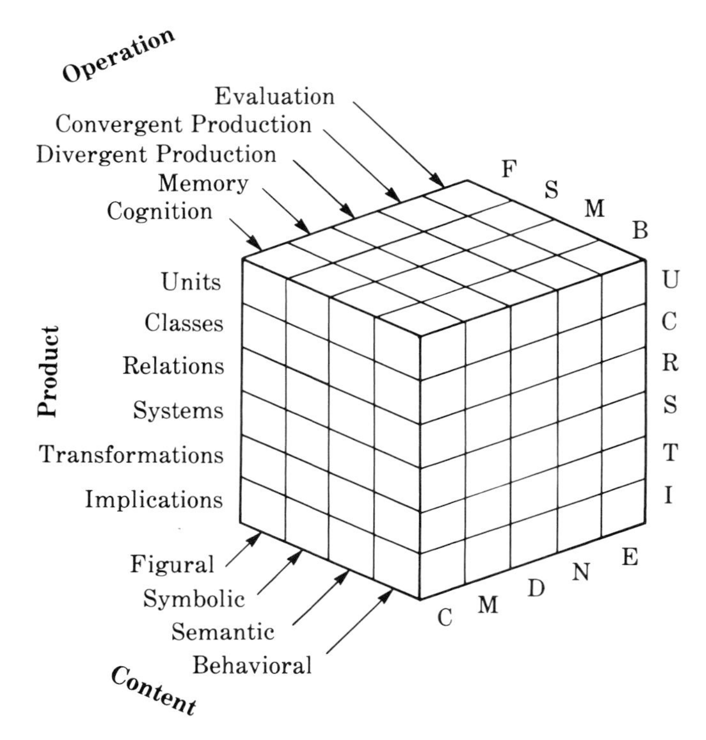

Figure 8.2 Guilford's three-dimensional structure of intellect model. (From *The Nature of Human Intelligence* by J. P. Guilford, 1967, New York: McGraw-Hill. Copyright © 1967 McGraw-Hill Book Company. Reproduced with permission.)

intelligence that is composed of three components. The first component emphasizes the ability of individuals to organize, plan, and carry out activities (these skills have sometimes been referred to as metacognitive abilities); the second component focuses on the individual's experience with novel, complex problems; and the third component concentrates on intelligence as it relates to the external world. Sternberg believes that conventional intelligence tests have worked as well as they have because the tasks represented on them involve a good deal of the abilities emphasized in his first two subtheories. He suggests, however, that intelligence tests are imprecise measures of these abilities and further, that we must take into account the ability of individuals to adapt to their particular environment to have a complete definition of intelligent behavior.

Summary

As we indicated at the beginning of this section, questions about the nature of intelligence have occupied the thoughts and research efforts of many people during the last century. We do not mean to imply that this concern began in the late nineteenth century, for the quest began long before. Furthermore, we have only touched upon the work of some of the most important contributors to this effort. Next we examine certain crucial issues related to the application of measures of cognitive ability by professionals in educational and mental health settings.

The Assessment of Cognitive Ability: Critical Issues and Concerns

Intelligence testing has gained widespread acceptance in the United States, among not only measurement experts, many psychologists, and educators but also the general public. Parents have become increasingly concerned with providing the optimal environment for their infants and preschoolers in order to maximize intellectual potential, and as children grow older teachers and parents want to know their IQ score. A trip to your favorite bookstore is likely to reveal a number of books concerned with "increasing your child's IQ" or "testing your own intelligence in fifteen minutes by asking yourself only four simple questions." This growing fascination with IQ measurement has not occurred without concern. Before analyzing the most widely used tests of cognitive ability, let's first explore a few of the most critical issues associated with the measurement of intelligence.

Stability of IQ

As a result of the popularization of intelligence tests and the intelligence testing movement, numerous misconceptions about the nature of intelligence developed and were fed by overzealous testers and a misinformed public. One of the most pervasive ideas, which became solidly entrenched, especially in public opinion, was the notion that an infant was born with a certain amount of "intelligence" that did not change as the child grew older. As with many myths, this one was supported with a grain or two of truth. In general, most research has suggested that IQ tests do *tend* to yield scores that are *fairly* stable. However, this same research indicates that IQs are more stable over shorter as opposed to longer periods and more stable for older children and adults than for children under six years of age. There is a good deal of evidence to indicate that IQ scores obtained before children enter kindergarten or first grade are not highly reliable. No one knows exactly to what extent intelligence scores can be altered through environmental manipulation. Although studies of the late 1960s and early 1970s (for example, the Milwaukee Project) reported that intensive early intervention in children's lives was capable of producing incredible increases in measured IQ, such studies have been severely criticized (see, e.g., Sommer & Sommer, 1983). Despite this criticism, most experts would agree that enriched environments are better than impoverished ones for fostering intellectual development.

Data on the relative stability of IQ can be deceiving and must be interpreted with care. When looking at the IQ scores of large groups of individuals, we can make the general statement that most of those within the group would receive similar scores if retested. However, it is not at all unusual for particular individuals to show a great deal of variability in their scores. Changes of 8, 10, 15, or even 30 IQ points are not unheard of, and each author of this text has tested children who exhibited these types of changes. This means that when examining test results, we must not assume that a child who obtained an IQ in a certain range of intelligence will always remain in that range.

Bias in Cognitive Ability Testing

No issue related to the assessment of cognitive abilities has generated as much nor as heated debate as the question of whether IQ tests are biased against individuals from minority cultures. Discussions in the popular press have vehemently assailed most aptitude and achievement tests as being unfair to children from backgrounds that are different from those of most middle-class white Americans (Herrnstein, 1982). Although we have no data other than our perceptions, we believe that most students enter our classes convinced that standardized tests are unfair, inaccurate indicators of the abilities of individuals from minority populations. Numerous researchers have investigated the issue of bias in mental tests, with the greatest amount of attention focused on the differences between the performance of blacks and whites (e.g., Jensen, 1981). Some have turned to the courts for help in determining whether IQ tests are biased and whether they should be used in the assessment of minority children, but the courts have not been consistent in their findings (*Larry P.* v. *Riles*, 1977; *PASE* v. *Hannon*, 1980).

Many different types of test bias have been identified, and these have been discussed at length by both proponents and opponents of cognitive ability testing. As Brown (1983) has indicated, although there is no universally accepted definition of bias, most definitions hold that

> a test can be considered biased if it differentiates between members of various groups (for example, between men and women or between blacks and whites) on bases other than the characteristic being measured. That is, a test is biased if its content, procedures, or use result in a systematic advantage or disadvantage to members of certain groups over other groups and if the basis of this differentiation is irrelevant to the test purpose. (p. 224)

Table 8.1 lists and defines the most common types of test bias that have been studied.

An examination of the research and writings related to bias in cognitive ability testing reveals that the issues are very complex, not easily resolved, and complicated by the emotional intensity with which individuals have ad-

Table 8.1 Types of Test Bias

Type	Definition
Mean differences	Average scores for various groups (such as black, white, and Hispanic or rich and poor) are different
Item/content bias	Portions of test content are biased in a manner that differentially affects the performance of certain groups (such as black and white, or men and women)
Factor analysis	The factors (for example, verbal abilities or attention) being measured are different for various racial, cultural, or economic groups
Predictive validity	Scores predict with varying levels of confidence for different groups
Social consequences	Tests are misused or misinterpreted to justify restrictive social policies
Selection ratios	Test results are used in ways that cause particular groups to be over- or underrepresented in special classes or certain diagnostic categories (for example, mentally retarded)

Adapted from "Concepts of Bias in Assessment and WISC-R Research with Minorities" by D. Reschly, 1980, in H. Vance and L. F. Wallbrown (Eds.), *WISC-R: Research and Interpretation* (pp. 87–94), Washington, DC: National Association of School Psychologists.

vanced their arguments in this area. Consider the factors listed below, and you will understand why testing bias has come to be such an emotional topic:

1. Our society has long discriminated against blacks through a variety of overt and covert mechanisms. Slavery, exclusionary voting laws, separate educational systems, racial slurs, and the like have all occupied a place in this abhorrent, unfortunate history. Although racial discrimination continues to exist at unacceptable levels, many public and private institutions have committed themselves to the establishment of equal opportunity for all.
2. Intelligence testing has been popular in this country since the introduction of the Binet scales. As a group, blacks have consistently obtained average scores that are approximately one standard deviation (15–16 IQ points) below the average score of whites. Some have used this information to argue for the existence of genetic differences between the races (e.g., Jensen, 1981), while others have suggested that environmental factors are more crucial (Kamin, 1981), but there is little disagreement with the fact that blacks average lower scores.
3. The most widely used tests of cognitive ability have been developed by whites, published by whites, and made money for whites, and are used to estimate and predict performance in a society that is dominated by the white culture. There is also a good deal of evidence indicating that white society has used the results of these tests to justify discriminatory laws and practices (McPherson, 1985).

Given society's attention to the issue of equality, the difference in black and white performances on IQ tests, and the fact that the history of these tests has been dominated by whites, it is not surprising that so many believe so strongly that these tests must be biased against blacks and in favor of whites.

In fact, there is little evidence to support this belief, at least as it relates to the tests themselves. First, although it is true that blacks average lower intelligence scores than whites, this is not enough information to conclude that the tests are biased, especially when socioeconomic status is considered. The tests may in fact be biased, but first we must determine if the differences in scores reflect true differences in the ability being measured. Tests are designed to discriminate — to tell good spellers from poor ones, to predict success or failure in graduate school or in a job as a bank teller, and to determine those who have learned the material in history class and those who have not. Simple differences in average scores alone do not prove that bias exists. Other factors must be studied to reach that conclusion. In the case of intelligence tests, we must investigate their content, construct, and predictive validity. That is, we have to examine whether the test items are biased in favor of one group, whether the test measures the same abilities for all groups, and whether the test predicts equally well for all groups.

The technical evidence overwhelmingly indicates that in fact the vast majority of items used on tests such as the WISC-R and Binet are not biased, that these tests tend to measure the same factors (verbal, perceptual, performance, quantitative, or the like) and predict success equally well for all racial groups (Reynolds, 1982). This last point is critical, for it is important to remember that IQ tests do not measure the amount of some innate, immutable ability that we all possess, but do provide a general measure of expected school achievement, just as they were designed to do in the early 1900s. The evidence on predictive validity suggests that whether someone is black, white, or Hispanic does not really matter: An individual with an IQ score of 60 from a reliable test is at risk of failing in most every public educational system, and an individual with a score of 140 is likely to do well in that same system. The research indicates that these tests, although not perfect predictors, are not biased and that race has nothing to do with the accuracy with which these tests predict. Therefore, when we say that the difference in the average IQ scores of blacks and whites is not due to test bias, we are not asserting that blacks are less intelligent but that they are more likely to experience problems in our educational system. Nor does the failure to find bias in these tests explain why one group obtains higher scores than another, and whether that difference is due to a biased school system, cultural deprivation (or advantages), or, as some have asserted, genetic differences. We only know that the tests do a fair job of what they were designed to do — predict school achievement.

Although we conclude that most intellectual or cognitive ability tests are not biased, these instruments have clearly not always been used in a nonbiased fashion. Many have argued that early immigration restrictions were in part based on the data showing that certain ethnic groups scored lower than others on IQ tests (McPherson, 1985). It is also apparent that some racial groups (such as blacks and Hispanics) are disproportionally represented in special education classes. Because the term "intelligence" has been misused by so many people and because there is such widespread misunderstanding of what these tests are designed to do, it has been easy for some individuals to use differences in the average scores of various racial groups as confirmation of racist ideology. Although it may be true that most intelligence tests are free of bias, it is also true that these tests have been used to discriminate. We must remain vigilant in our attempts to see that these tests are used fairly and judiciously. These tests must be frequently revised to make sure that they reflect the most advanced understanding of the nature of cognitive abilities and that they utilize appropriate methodologies for assessing cognitive skills. We believe that this is possible, that it can be done fairly, equitably, and that we should not abandon these tests simply because they have been misused by some in the past. There is no need to throw out the baby with the bath water!

Treatment Validity and Educational Applications

Our review of the measurement of cognitive abilities has uncovered a number of positive aspects of the testing instruments that have been developed. We have concluded that most measures of intellectual or cognitive ability yield reliable results, that they are reasonably good predictors of achievement levels, and that they are essentially free of bias. This last factor has been especially satisfying to those who have suggested that most of these tests validly estimate the cognitive abilities of minority populations.

We cannot help but wonder, however, if there is not a more subtle, more damaging problem in the manner in which these tests have been used in educational, clinical, and vocational settings (Witt & Gresham, 1985). We are specifically speaking of the question of *treatment validity*, of the ability of a test to lead to better treatments, such as more effective educational programs or better counseling or teaching strategies. Although many have tried, there simply is no clear evidence that test results yielded by general measures of cognitive ability can be directly translated into effective educational or clinical programs (Kramer, Henning-Stout, Ullman, & Schellenberg, 1987).

It is important to remember that although these types of tests were developed to provide educators with general predictions of success in the educational system, they were not designed to enable educators or psychologists to design effective remedial strategies for individual children. Although we can be relatively confident that children who score in the superior (or gifted) range of intelligence will do better in school than those who score in the retarded range, we cannot design individualized educational programs for either subset of children based on their particular pattern of scores or their overall intelligence test performance. The tests were not designed for that purpose, and attempts to make them into tools for specific instructional planning have failed miserably (Kramer et al., 1987). Throughout this book we have emphasized the need for more direct, effective, and unbiased approaches to the process of assessment and treatment validity. Tests of cognitive ability can be a valuable part of the assessment process because they allow for the observation of children in a structured situation and provide an additional sample of behavior for analysis. We must not abandon the use of measures of cognitive ability simply because they have been mishandled in the past, but we must keep in mind the purposes for which they have been developed and the practices for which they have been validated.

Measures of Cognitive Ability

What we have called "measures of cognitive ability" have typically been referred to as "tests of intelligence." Instruments developed early in the history of the testing movement (for example, the WISC-R) retain the term "intelligence" in their titles. Newer instruments are titled somewhat differently. Is this a reaction to all the controversy over intelligence tests and the true meaning of the term "intelligence," or the result of the realization that we must move beyond attempts to measure the hypothetical construct of intelligence? Both explanations are probably at least partly true, as is the realization by publishers that tests that do not mention "intelligence" in their title have a better chance of being effectively marketed. Whatever the reason, there are many, many different tests that purport to measure cognitive abilities: short tests, long tests; individual tests, group tests; comprehensive tests, specific tests; tests for infants, tests for children and adolescents, tests for adults, etc.

Wechsler Intelligence Scale for Children-Revised

Overview and purpose. Beyond a doubt, in recent years the most widely administered test of cognitive ability with school-age children has been the WISC-R (Wechsler, 1974). It was designed as a downward extension of the Wechsler Bellevue Intelligence Scale for children 6-0 to 16-11 years of age. Originally published in 1949 as the WISC, the test was revised in 1974, although the format and many items have remained the same for more than thirty-five years.

The WISC-R is individually administered by a qualified examiner (who is usually a psychologist with several advanced assessment courses and over five hundred hours of supervised experience) in sixty to ninety minutes. It is designed to provide a global measure of intelligence that "avoids singling out any ability, however esteemed (e.g., abstract reasoning), as crucial or overwhelmingly important" (Wechsler, 1974, p. 5). The test is comprised of twelve subtests, six in the Verbal Scale and six in the Performance Scale. All instructions are given orally, and all subtests on the Verbal Scale require oral responses.

Performance subtests have time limits, and in some cases bonus points are provided for quick, accurate responses. Let's examine the twelve subtests in more detail:

Verbal scale

1. Information — thirty questions requiring general knowledge of facts
2. Similarities — seventeen pairs of words requiring an indication of how the items are similar
3. Arithmetic — eighteen (timed) arithmetic problems requiring a response without the aid of paper and pencil
4. Vocabulary — thirty-two words, requiring definitions or synonyms
5. Comprehension — seventeen problem situations requiring practical problem-solving ability.
6. Digit Span — forward and backward repetition of digits

Performance scale (all timed tasks)

1. Picture Completion — twenty-six drawings of common objects, all of which require the identification of a missing, essential element
2. Picture Arrangement — twelve picture series (similar to cut-up comic strips) requiring placement in a logical sequence
3. Block Design — eleven abstract designs to be copied using two-colored blocks
4. Object Assembly — four jigsaw puzzles of common objects requiring assembly
5. Coding — symbols such as vertical lines and circles to be copied by matching them to numbers
6. Mazes — eight mazes requiring a child to mark the way out without being blocked

Verbal and Performance subtests are administered in alternating order. Mazes and Coding are considered supplemental tests and are not generally included in the calculation of the IQ scores, unless one of the regular subtests is omitted or "spoiled" because of improper administration or disruption.

Not all items on the WISC-R are administered to each subject. Each subtest has specific rules about where to begin and end, depending on the age or assumed ability of the subject. The specificity for administration and scoring provided in the manual are generally considered assets of the WISC-R. Wechsler originally divided the test into verbal and performance sections based on his conceptualization of intelligence, and he placed subtests that he believed involved primarily verbal or performance abilities into each domain. Many subsequent factor analytic studies (see, e.g., Kaufman, 1975) have generally supported this organization.

Standardization sample and norms. A decade after its revision, the WISC-R remains a model of standardization procedures. It was standardized on 2,200 children selected to be representative of the United States population based on the 1970 census data. The sample was stratified on the basis of geographic region, urban-rural residence, occupation of the head of the household, and race. Data were gathered in thirty-two states and the District of Columbia. Two hundred children (one hundred boys and one hundred girls) were tested at each of eleven different ages, and each child was tested within six weeks of the midyear between birthdays.

Data obtained. Raw scores on each subtest are first changed into normalized standard scores (scaled scores) with a mean of 10 and a standard deviation of 3. Tables of scaled scores and their raw score equivalents are provided for each four-month age interval (e.g., 10-0 to 10-3, 12-4 to 12-7). The scaled subtest scores are then added and converted into deviation IQs (standard scores) for the Verbal, Performance, and Full Scales. Verbal Scale IQ, Performance Scale IQ, and Full Scale IQ each has a mean of 100 and a standard deviation of 15. A child's "test-age" for each subtest can be obtained, and a mean or median test-age for each of the scales can be calculated.

Reliability and validity. Subtest reliabilities (split-half and test-retest) are very good, ranging from .70 to .86 and .65 to .88, respectively. Average Verbal Scale, Performance Scale, and Full Scale IQ split-half and test-retest reliabilities are .94, .90, .96, and .93, .90, .95, respectively. Retest coefficients (approximately one month test-retest interval) were obtained by testing 303 individuals from three different age groups. Average gains of 3.5 IQ points on the Verbal Scale, 9.5 points on the Performance Scale, and 7 points on the Full Scale were reported. The manual includes, for each age level, the standard error of measurement for each subtest as well as for the Verbal, Performance, and Full scales.

Little information related to validity is presented in the WISC-R manual. Mean correlations with the 1972 Stanford-Binet for the Verbal, Performance, and Full Scale IQ scores are reported as .71, .60, and .73, respectively. Correlations with the other tests in the Wechsler series (Wechsler Preschool and Primary Scale of Intelligence [WPPSI] and Wechsler Adult Intelligence Scale [WAIS]) are also reported for age ranges in which the tests overlap. Correlations for the Verbal Scale, Performance Scale, and Full Scale IQs are all reported to be greater than .80. Intercorrelations among the individual subtests and the correlations of each subtest with the IQ scores are also reported in the manual. Sattler (1982) provides a summary of a number of correlational studies that compares the WISC-R with a variety of intelligence, achievement, and special ability tests.

Summary. From a technical perspective, the WISC-R is a sound instrument. It continues to be widely used and to be moderately related to school achievement. It is the standard against which other measures of cognitive abilities have been judged for the last three decades. Revised and restandardized in 1974, the format and many items are unchanged from the original WISC pub-

FOCUS ON PRACTICE
Stanford-Binet—Past and Present

While the scales and most of the items in the 1986 edition of the Stanford-Binet are new, users will recognize some familiar items that have been revised to be in accord with current test standards and to improve testing procedures. For example, Figure 8.3 shows the evolution of two item types. The card used to measure the examinee's knowledge of parts of the body illustrates an increased sensitivity to issues of ethnicity and gender. The rosy-cheeked boy used in the 1937 edition wore a short red jacket, shorts, and black patent-leather shoes. The blue-eyed girl in the 1972 edition had blond hair tied with a pretty pink ribbon. By contrast, the child in the 1986 edition is drawn with facial features, dress, and hair that minimize gender and racial characteristics. The Bead Memory subtests, which also originated in the 1937 edition, required the examiner to create sample bead chains. The new test uses photographs as the stimuli, which eliminates the need for examiners to create sample chains and results in increased standardization of administrative conditions.

lished in 1949, although pictures and some items were updated and new norms were provided. Much has been learned about the nature of cognitive abilities in the last thirty years, and if the WISC-R is to continue to be a leader in the field, it will need to incorporate these findings.

Stanford-Binet Intelligence Scale

Overview and purpose. The original Binet-Simon Scale that was discussed earlier in the chapter has gone through a number of revisions during the last half century. Most practitioners were familiar with the 1973 edition of the test, the Stanford-Binet Intelligence Scale (SBIS), which served as the standard for intelligence testing for so many years (Terman & Merrill, 1973). Recently, the SBIS has undergone substantial modification and restandardization (Thorndike, Hagen, & Sattler, 1986). The Focus on Practice and Figure 8.3 detail certain ways that the test has been altered through the years. Although many item types that were present in previous editions have been retained, the current organization differs radically from previous editions. This difference is made more apparent by comparing the descriptions in the Focus on Practice and Figure 8.3 with Figure 8.1.

According to its authors (Thorndike, Hagen, & Sattler, 1986, p. 2), the SBIS is designed to meet the following objectives:

1. To help differentiate between students who are mentally retarded and those who have specific learning disabilities.
2. To help educators and psychologists understand why a particular student is having difficulty in school.

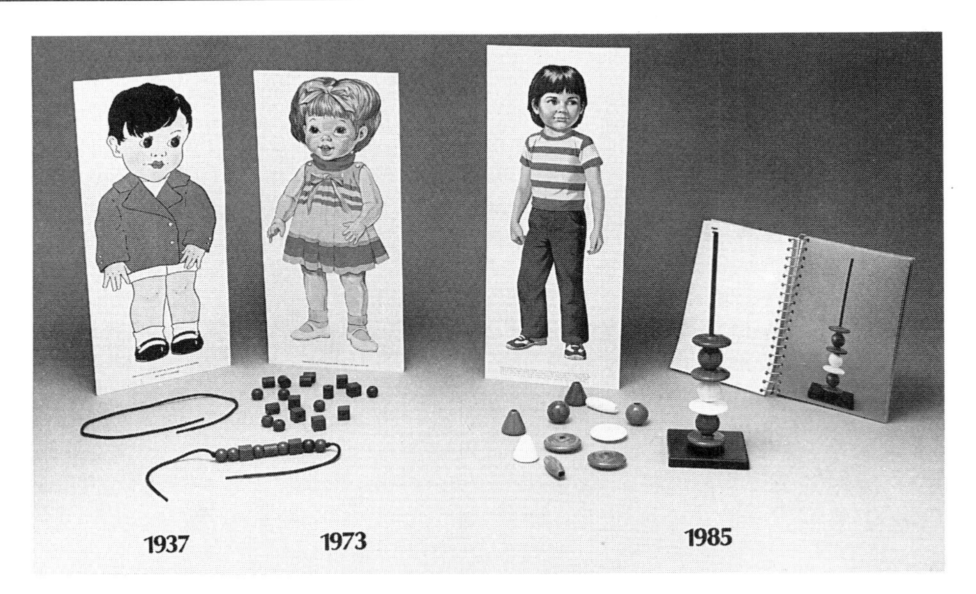

Figure 8.3 The development of two Stanford-Binet subtests. (From *Stanford-Binet Intelligence Scale*, 4th ed., by E. P. Hagen, J. M. Sattler, and R. L. Thorndike, 1986, Chicago: The Riverside Publishing Company. Copyright 1986 by the Riverside Publishing Company. Reproduced by permission of the publisher.)

3. To help identify gifted students.
4. To study the development of cognitive skills of individuals from ages two to adult.

The test is individually administered, covers ages two to adult, and includes items that are grouped into fifteen tests assessing four broad areas of cognitive functioning: Verbal Reasoning, Quantitative Reasoning, Abstract/Visual Reasoning, and Short-Term Memory. Descriptions of the subtests and their appropriate age ranges follow:

Verbal reasoning

1. Vocabulary (2-0 through adult) — forty-six items, the first fourteen being picture vocabulary with the remainder requiring oral responses
2. Comprehension (2-0 through adult) — forty-two items, the first six requiring the identification of various body parts on a picture card of a child (see Focus on Practice and Figure 8.3), with subsequent questions requiring verbal responses
3. Absurdities (2-0 through 17-11) — thirty-two items requiring the determination of what is wrong or silly in each picture
4. Verbal Relations (10-0 through adult) — eighteen items requiring a description of how the first three of four words are related, but different from the fourth word

Quantitative reasoning

1. Quantitative (2-0 through adult) — forty items assessing a broad range of arithmetic skills through tasks ranging from counting blocks to orally presented word problems
2. Number Series (5-0 through adult) — twenty-six items requiring the discovery of the "certain rule" according to which a number sequence is arranged and the naming of the numbers that come next
3. Equation Building (10-0 through adult) — eighteen items requiring rearranging numbers and arithmetic signs into a true equation

Abstract/visual reasoning

1. Pattern Analysis (2-0 through adult) — forty-two items requiring duplication of patterns presented via either a form board, an examiner's model, or pictured cube patterns
2. Copying (2-0 through 17-11) — twenty-eight items requiring the use of blocks to copy block designs or pencil and paper to copy line drawings
3. Matrices (5-0 through adult) — twenty-six items requiring the determination of an appropriate shape, design, letter, or the like to fill a blank spot in a matrix
4. Paper Folding and Cutting (10-0 through adult) — eighteen items requiring the study of pictures describing a paper-folding and cutting sequence to determine how a piece of paper would look after being folded and cut

Short-term memory

1. Bead Memory (2-0 through adult) — forty-two items requiring the identification of colored bead shapes exposed by the examiner for two seconds or the duplication of bead designs depicted on stimulus cards exposed for five seconds
2. Memory for Sentences (2-0 through adult) — forty-two items requiring the repetition of orally presented phrases or sentences or both
3. Memory for Digits (5-0 through adult) — twenty-six items requiring the repetition of a series of digits either as stated (14 items) or in reverse order (12 items)
4. Memory for Objects (5-0 through adult) — fourteen items in which examinees are shown a number of pictures of common objects, one at a time. Examinees are then shown a picture containing many different pictures and asked to identify the pictures shown previously, in the correct order.

As indicated above, not all items within a particular test nor all tests are administered to each individual. The starting point for each examinee is determined by the results of the vocabulary test, and all tests are to be administered in a prescribed order depending on the subject's age and ability.

Standardization sample and norms. The standardization sample was stratified on the basis of data from the 1980 United States census and included the following variables: geographic region, community size, ethnic group, age, and gender. The manual indicates that socioeconomic status was monitored through indexes of parental occupation and educational attainment. Approximately two hundred to three hundred (range of 194–460) individuals were tested within each of seventeen age groups.

Data obtained. Raw scores for each test are converted to Standard Age Scores (SAS), which have a mean of 50 and a standard deviation of 8. The SAS within each area are summed and an Area SAS derived. The Area SAS can be summed to determine a Composite SAS score. Both Area SAS and Composite SAS have a mean of 100 and a standard deviation of 16. If fewer than four areas are used to determine the Composite SAS, the examiner is cautioned to calculate a Partial Composite score.

Reliability and validity. Data related to internal consistency estimates and test-retest reliability are presented in the SBIS technical manual. Median KR-20 reliabilities for the individual tests range from .94 (Paper Folding and Cutting) to .73 (Memory for Objects). Standard error of estimate (SEM) figures generally range between 2 and 3 for each age group. Internal consistency estimates are usually lower for (a) younger children and (b) the Short-Term Memory tests. Reliability estimates for the Area SAS generally were above .80, with most above .90 (SEM 2.8–7.2). Composite score reliabilities were all above .95 (SEM 1.6–3.6). Two groups (five year olds and eight year olds), totaling 112 children, were retested within two to eight months of the original testing to determine test-retest reliability. Test-retest estimates for five year olds and eight year olds were as follows: individual tests: .56–.78 and .28–.86, respectively, Area SAS: .71–.91 and .51–.90, respectively, and Composite SAS: .91 and .90, respectively.

The only validity information presented with the SBIS is related to construct validity. Factor analytic studies tend to support the test as a measure of general cognitive ability. The rationale for the placement of each of the subtests within separate areas is sound, with the least amount of support for those within the Abstract/Visual Reasoning subtest. Correlations with other measures of cognitive ability also tend to support the construct validity of the SBIS (most correlation coefficients were above .60). The highest correlations were obtained with older samples (such as the Wechsler Adult Intelligence Scale-Revised [WAIS-R]) and the lowest generally with younger samples (such as the Wechsler Preschool and Primary Scale of Intelligence [WPPSI]). The manual suggests that the SBIS will not be a useful measure with two- and three-year-old children of below average abilities due to floor effects on a number of tests. Data from samples of exceptional children indicate that the SBIS does yield Composite SAS consistent with the children's identified areas of exceptionality (for example, high scores for gifted children). No information related to the use of the SBIS in educational planning or treatment is presented in the manual.

Summary. For many years the SBIS was synonymous with the very notion of intelligence testing in the United States (Boring, 1950). Although the current revision was long overdue, the extent to which it adequately measures cognitive abilities remains to be seen. The reasons given for the reorganization and the inclusion of specific tests are not substantial, and the descriptions of specific tests and the presumed abilities involved in each are inadequate. Although the authors do occasionally provide cautions regarding the limitations of the current SBIS, there is little evidence that it meets any of the four original objectives of the test. Much more study is required before its strengths and limitations can be adequately assessed.

Kaufman Assessment Battery for Children

Overview and purpose. The Kaufman Assessment Battery for Children, or K-ABC (Kaufman & Kaufman, 1983) is an individually administered, multisubtest battery designed to provide information on the intellectual and achievement abilities of preschool and elementary school children between the ages of two and a half and twelve and a half. Appropriate interpretation of the results requires an understanding of the Das/Luria theoretical perspective and extensive training and supervised experience. The K-ABC breaks intellectual functioning into two distinct styles of information processing: sequential and simultaneous. In the sequential (or successive) mode, stimuli are arranged in sequence, and decisions are reached by processing information in an orderly (that is, one at a time), sequence-dependent fashion. In the simultaneous mode, information is arranged in a simultaneous fashion, and the decision-making process proceeds in an integrated, holistic manner. The K-ABC, at least as it relates to mental processing, is not designed to measure what or how much a child knows but rather how that child goes about knowing. Stated differently, the K-ABC attempts to assess intellectual ability by asking questions about how a child approaches problem solving and information processing and places less importance on previously learned information. The K-ABC Mental Processing subtests (the Sequential and Simultaneous scales combined) were designed to minimize the importance of verbal skills to make the test as fair as possible for individuals from diverse cultural backgrounds. In fact, smaller black-white discrepancies in standard scores (3–8 points) have been reported for the K-ABC than for most popular intelligence tests.

The K-ABC is comprised of three scales (Sequential Processing, Simultaneous Processing, and Achievement) and sixteen subtests. The specific composition of each scale and the design and age range of each subtest is as follows:

Sequential processing scale

1. Hand Movements (2-6 through 12-5) — twenty-one items requiring the repetition of a series of hand movements in the correct order

2. Number Recall (2-6 through 12-5) — nineteen items requiring recall of numbers from 2 to 8 in sequence
3. Word Order (4-0 through 12-5) — twenty items requiring subjects to point to pictures of common objects in the same order as the objects were named by the examiner

Simultaneous processing scale

1. Magic Window (2-6 through 4-11) — fifteen pictures presented by rotating a wheel so that only a portion is visible at any one time. Children are required to name the object pictured
2. Face Recognition (2-6 through 4-11) — fifteen items requiring the identification of one or two faces from those in a group
3. Gestalt Closure (2-6 through 12-5) — twenty-five items requiring the identification of incomplete ink-blot drawings of common objects
4. Triangles (4-0 through 12-5) — eighteen items requiring the copying of abstract designs using several rubber triangles
5. Matrix Analogies (5-0 through 12-5) — twenty items requiring the selection of a picture or design that best completes an analogy
6. Spatial Memory (5-0 through 12-5) — twenty-one items requiring recall of the location of pictures on a page
7. Photo Series (6-0 through 12-5) — seventeen items asking subjects to organize an array of photographs illustrating an event and then to order the photographs in their proper time sequence

Achievement scale

1. Expressive Vocabulary (2-6 through 4-11) — fourteen pictures requiring identification
2. Faces and Places (3-0 through 12-5) — thirty-five pictures of famous persons, places, or fictional characters requiring identification
3. Arithmetic (3-0 through 12-5) — thirty-eight items requiring number identification, multiplication, division, and rounding
4. Riddles (3-0 through 12-5) — thirty-two items requiring the identification of the items or concepts referred to in riddles
5. Reading/Decoding (5-0 through 12-5) — thirty-eight items ranging from letter identification to word recognition
6. Reading/Understanding (7-0 through 12-5) — twenty-four items requiring the acting out of commands given in sentences

No child takes more than thirteen subtests, and not all items within a subtest are administered. Explicit instructions are provided to determine where to begin testing as well as the criteria for discontinuing a subtest.

Standardization sample and norms. Two thousand children, (one hundred for each six-month age group between the ages of two and a half and twelve and a half, were in the standardization group. Stratification variables included age, sex, geographic region, socioeconomic status (determined by parental education), race or ethnic group, community size, and educational placement (to insure adequate representation of handicapped children). In addition, to allow specific race and parental education comparisons, sociocultural norms were established by the additional testing of 496 black and 119 white children.

Data obtained. Raw scores on each subtest are first changed into normalized standard scores. Subtests on the Sequential and Simultaneous scales have a mean of 10 and a standard deviation of 3. Subtests on the Achievement Scale have a mean of 100 and a standard deviation of 15. The scores from the subtests on each scale are then totaled and transformed into a Sequential Processing Scale score, a Simultaneous Processing Scale score, a Mental Processing Composite score (Sequential plus Simultaneous scores), and an Achievement Scale score, each with a mean of 100 and a standard deviation of 15. A Nonverbal Scale score, with a mean of 100 and a standard deviation of 15, can be calculated as an estimate of the intellectual potential of individuals with language or communication problems. In addition to these scores, tables allow the examiner to generate information such as national percentile rank, sociocultural percentile rank, age equivalents, confidence intervals, and subtest (or scale) strengths and weaknesses for most of the subtest and scale scores.

Reliability and validity. Internal consistency reliablities (presented for both preschool and school-age children, respectively) for the subtests (.72–.89 and .71–.92, respectively) and global scales (Sequential: .90 and .89, respectively; Simultaneous: .86 and .93, respectively; Mental: .91 and .84, respectively; Achievement: .93 and .97, respectively; and Nonverbal: .87 and .93, respectively) are very good. Test-retest reliabilities were obtained by retesting a portion of the standardization sample at each of three different ages (2-6 to 4-11: $N = 84$; 5-0 to 8-11: $N = 92$; 9-0 to 12-5: $N = 70$) for the subtests (.62–.87; .61–.98; and .59–.94, respectively) and global scales (median coefficient = .88).

Extensive information, covering more than forty pages, related to construct, predictive, and concurrent validity accompanies the K-ABC. Evidence for construct validity is good, with factor analytic studies typically identifying two separate factors (interpreted as simultaneous and sequential factors). In addition, moderate correlations (.36–.76) between K-ABC standard scores and WISC-R Full Scale IQ scores have been obtained (with the K-ABC Achievement Scale — WISC-R Full Scale correlation generally the highest). Both predictive and concurrent validity studies suggest the relationship of the K-ABC with various achievement scales. Regardless of whether there was a delay of six to twelve months between the administrations of tests (predictive validity) or whether the tests were administered at the same time (concurrent validity), the results indicate moderate correlations between the Simultaneous, Sequential, and Nonverbal scales and achievement test scores (typically .30s–.50s); and slightly higher correlations when the Mental or Achievement scales were reported (.40s–.80s). Although no long-term predictive validity studies are currently available, they will be important in evaluating the test's usefulness. It will be especially interesting to see if the K-ABC predicts achievement equally well for blacks and whites in light of the small black-white differences in obtained test scores.

Summary. The K-ABC has received widespread attention since its introduction. Hailed by its publishers as the most innovative and useful entrant into the cognitive assessment arena in the last half-century, the test has not avoided substantial and pointed criticism (Bracken, 1985; Page, 1985). The K-ABC is psychometrically sound, has very good standardization, is attractively presented, and is relatively easy to learn and use. However, the major questions remain to be resolved over whether the theoretical model upon which the test is based is sound and whether the test ultimately aids in the treatment process (that is, treatment validity).

Columbia Mental Maturity Scale

Overview and purpose. The third edition of the Columbia Mental Maturity Scale, or CMMS (Burgemeister, Blum, & Lorge, 1972) was originally designed to estimate the "general reasoning ability" of physically handicapped and nonverbal children between the ages of three years, six months, and nine years, eleven months. The CMMS contains ninety-two items, each printed on a six-by-nineteen-inch card that features three to five color or black-and-white drawings of figural and pictoral symbols such as shapes, common objects, abstract designs, dots, and body parts. Children are asked to examine each card and identify the one image that does not relate to any of the others. Correct responses require the formulation of an explicit rationale for determining the relationships among the pictures. No time limit is imposed upon the child; however, the examiner is instructed to encourage a response after twenty to twenty-five seconds.

The CMMS is individually administered and takes approximately fifteen to twenty minutes to complete. It differs from the other individually administered instruments we have examined in that it assesses a very limited range of cognitive abilities: classifying, discriminating, and perhaps reasoning. However, since it requires only nonverbal, pointing responses, it has been useful in the assessment of children with a variety of handicaps.

Standardization sample and norms. The 1972 CMMS was standardized on 2,600 children from twenty-five states. The sampling procedure was designed to insure a representative national sample based on the 1960 census data, with the stratification variables including geographic region, race, parental occupation, age, and sex. The design and execution of the norming process for the CMMS is excellent.

Data obtained. An Age Deviation Score (ADS) with a mean of 100 and a standard deviation of 16 can be calculated for each child completing the CMMS. In addition, a Maturity Index, or mental age score, can be obtained by determining the age group in the standardization sample that most closely corresponds to a child's performance.

Reliability and validity. Test-rest reliability and internal consistency estimates (split-half reliability) are provided in the CMMS manual. Test-retest figures were calculated on a group of approximately one hundred children at each of three ages, and ranged from .84 to .86. Split-half estimates ranged from .85 to .91. The standard error of measurement is given as 5–6 ADS points (depending on the age group).

Validity for the CMMS was established by correlating scores with results from achievement and ability tests. Correlations with achievement scores ranged from .31 to .61 (Stanford Achievement Test) and with mental tests from .62 to .69 (Otis-Lennon Mental Ability Test) and .67 (SBIS).

Summary. As a test of cognitive abilities, the CMMS is limited because it does not sample a broad range of skills. The test, however, has traditionally been used to estimate the intellectual potential of individuals who have difficulty responding verbally, and it has proved to be an excellent adjunct when used in this manner. It is easily administered, simple to score, psychometrically sound, and a worthwhile addition to one's assessment repertoire.

McCarthy Scales of Children's Abilities

Overview and purpose. The McCarthy Scales of Children's Abilities, or MSCA (McCarthy, 1972) was developed to measure general intellectual development in children between the ages of two and a half and eight and a half. Before this test, psychologists and educators wanting to assess the abilities of this age group had been limited in their choices to the SBIS or the WPPSI. With the publication of the MSCA it was hoped that psychologists and educators would have a single instrument for measuring several aspects of cognitive and motor abilities in pre- and early elementary school children.

The MSCA is individually administered, like the WISC-R, SBIS, and K-ABC, and requires training and supervised experience for proper use. It has a wide variety of "gamelike and nonthreatening" tasks that are organized into eighteen subtests and six scales: Verbal, Perceptual-Performance, Quantitative, General Cognitive, Memory, and Motor.

1. *Verbal scale.* As on the WISC-R, this scale is designed to assess the ability of the subject to understand, process, remember, and problem solve with the English language. Subtests include Pictoral Memory, Word Knowledge, Verbal Memory, Verbal Fluency, and Opposite Analogies. In addition to measuring an individual's receptive and expressive language abilities, the Verbal Scale assesses attentional, short-term memory, and reasoning abilities.

2. *Perceptual-performance scale.* The seven subtests on this scale are designed to evaluate an individual's nonverbal problem-solving skills and visual-motor coordination. Subtests include Block Building, Puzzle Solving, Tapping Sequence, Right-Left Orientation (ages five and above), Draw-A-Design, Draw-A-Child, and Conceptual Grouping.
3. *Quantitative scale.* A unique feature of the MSCA is the Quantitative Scale, which is designed to provide an index of the ability to use and remember numerical symbols and concepts. Its subtests include Number Questions, Numerical Memory, and Counting and Sorting. In addition to math skills, the ability of children to attend, concentrate, and hold material in short-term memory are important on this scale.
4. *General cognitive index* (GCI). This index includes the fifteen subtests that are part of the Verbal, Perceptual-Performance, and Quantitative scales. Although not referred to as an IQ score, the GCI is defined as "a measure of the child's overall cognitive functioning" (McCarthy, 1972, p. 5).
5. *Memory scale.* This scale is composed of four subtests aimed at assessing auditory and visual short-term memory — Pictorial Memory, Tapping Sequence, Verbal Memory, and Numerical Memory — which all appear on other MSCA scales.
6. *Motor scale.* This scale includes five subtests designed to measure fine and gross motor skills: Leg Coordination, Arm Coordination, Imitative Action, Draw-A-Design, and Draw-A-Child (the last two also appear on the Perceptual-Performance Scale).

Standardization sample and norms. The standardization group was based on a national sample, stratified on the following variables: age, sex, color, geographic region, and father's occupation. Urban-rural residence was also included as an "informal selection variable." The standardization sample size at each of ten ages (each half-year from two and a half to seven and a half, plus eight and a half), ranged from 100 to 106, making a total of 1,032 cases. In general, the design and execution of the standardization process for the MSCA are considered excellent.

Data obtained. Standard scores (referred to as Indexes) are computed for each scale. The GCI has a mean of 100 and a standard deviation of 16. Each of the remaining scale indexes has a mean of 50 and a standard deviation of 10.

Reliability and validity. The manual provides internal consistency measures as well as stability coefficient and standard errors of measurement for each of the six scales (at all ten age levels in the standardization sample). Split-half reliability for the GCI ($r = .93$) and the other scales (.79–.88) is very good. The average standard error of measurement for the GCI is 4 points. Stability coefficients of the MSCA, with a thirty-day test-retest interval, are .90 for the GCI and range from .69 to .89 for the other scales.

Both concurrent and predictive validity are referred to in the manual. Concurrent validity was established by correlating the MSCA Scale Indexes with IQ scores obtained on the WPPSI and SBIS. Correlations ranged from .45 to .91 (median r = .75), if one excludes the scores from the Motor Scale Index (r ranged from .02 to .10). Predictive validity was established by comparing the MSCA scores of thirty-five children with their scores obtained four months later on the Metropolitan Achievement Test; correlations ranged from .34 to .54. A number of other validity studies have been published in recent years, and the concern has been raised that the MSCA seems to underestimate the intellectual abilities of children identified as learning disabled.

Summary. The MSCA is a well-designed, psychometrically sound instrument for assessing the cognitive abilities of young children. Most children find the test interesting and enjoyable. A good deal of evidence suggests that the MSCA yields lower scores for learning disabled and retarded children (Nagle, 1979) than do other frequently administered tests of cognitive ability. Perhaps a more significant concern is that the MSCA's design is based on a rather traditional conceptualization of intelligence (that is, verbal-performance) that has received close scrutiny in recent years.

Cognitive Abilities Test

Overview and purpose. The Cognitive Abilities Test (Thorndike & Hagen, 1982) differs from other tests examined in this chapter in that it is group administered. As with most group tests, the Cognitive Abilities Test is often used for general school administration planning for all children and as a screening device to help identify individuals who may need further diagnostic assessment (for example, to determine eligibility for educational programs). There are ten levels of the Cognitive Abilities Test, two in the Primary Battery (PB: Kindergarten–Grade 2) and eight in the Multilevel Edition (ME: Grades 3–12). Extensive training is not required to administer this test.

The PB yields a single score, is untimed, requires no reading, and is administered as a group test. Two levels of the PB are available to provide maximum discrimination among the skill levels of children in this age range. Subtests include Relational Concepts, Object Classification, Quantitative Concepts, and Oral Vocabulary. The eight levels of the ME are divided into tests that yield Verbal, Quantitative, and Nonverbal reasoning ability scores. Subtests on the ME include Verbal — Vocabulary, Sentence Completion, Verbal Classification, and Verbal Analogies; Quantitative — Quantitative Relations, Number Series, and Equation Building; and Nonverbal — Figure Analysis, Figure Classification, and Figure Synthesis. The nonverbal test is considered to be especially useful in the assessment of disadvantaged children and poor readers. No reading is required on the nonverbal test — all items involve either pictures or diagrams.

Standardization sample and norms. The Cognitive Abilities Test was standardized in 1977 and 1978 in conjunction with the Iowa Test of Basic Skills (ITBS) and the Tests of Achievement and Proficiency (TAPS) (all published by

Riverside Press). Stratification variables included the size of school district enrollment, geographic region, and community socioeconomic status. An attempt was also made to include representative samples of students from nonpublic schools and various racial and ethnic groups. Sample size ranged from 3,000 to 8,000 for the PB and 10,000 to 15,000 for the ME.

Data obtained. Raw scores are converted into scale scores, which can then be converted to any of the following: standard age scores (with a mean of 100 and a standard deviation of 16), percentile ranks for standard age scores, stanines corresponding to standard age scores, normal curve equivalents of standard age scores, percentile ranks for grades, and stanines by grade. As indicated, the PB yields a single score, while the ME results in three scores (Verbal, Quantitative, and Nonverbal). It is recommended that the three scores for the ME should *not* be averaged to yield an overall score.

Reliability and validity. Internal consistency estimates for the various levels of both the PB (.89–.92) and the ME (.91–.96) are provided. Retest reliabilities for the ME based on retesting with the same form after a six-month interval (the number of subjects is unknown) were .91 (Verbal), .86 (Quantitative), and .85 (Nonverbal).

Information related to content, criterion, and construct validity of the Cognitive Abilities Test is available in the manual. The description of its content validation is essentially a verbal explanation of the rationale for the inclusion of certain types of items. Criterion-related validity is assessed by correlating Cognitive Abilities Test scores with results from the ITBS (.58–.86), TAPS (.63–.85), and end-of-year grade point averages (.45–.60). Evidence of construct validity was provided through Cognitive Abilities Test correlations with the SBIS for 550 individuals (.65–.75).

Summary. The current version of the Cognitive Abilities Test is very similar to earlier forms. Among the several new features are shorter directions for administration and expanded information on the interpretation of scores. Although the Cognitive Abilities Test is psychometrically sound, results should only be used for general screening purposes. As with many group tests of cognitive abilities, this test is standardized on a very large sample, and standardization procedures were carefully executed.

Summary

What is this thing called intelligence? Is it a single ability that affects all cognitive activity? Is it something we all have to a greater or lesser extent? Or is it a collection of abilities and thus more appropriate for us to consider its re-

FOCUS ON RESEARCH
Defining Intelligence

There is an intuitive appeal to the method used by Robert Sternberg of Yale University in New Haven to define and describe intelligence. He began with the assumption that the usual definitions developed by and for experts were often "rarefied abstractions, unconnected with real people or real life. And formal IQ tests seem unfair or beside the point" (Sternberg, 1982, p. 30). His approach was simply to ask laypeople how they define intelligence or intelligent behavior.

Sternberg first asked people to list behaviors that were embodied in the terms "intelligence," "academic intelligence," "everyday intelligence," and "unintelligence." From the responses he developed a master list of 250 relatively unique behaviors that characterize either intelligent or unintelligent people. Next, Sternberg and his associates had another group of individuals rate each of the 250 behaviors on a 1-to-9 scale to indicate relative importance of each characteristic to an "ideally intelligent person." To determine whether laypeople differed from experts in their notions of intelligence, the behaviors were also rated by a number of university professors who specialized in the study of intelligence or intelligence testing.

Laypeople viewed intelligence as composed of three broad facets: practical problem-solving ability, verbal ability, and social competence. Surprisingly, the laypeople and the experts did not differ a great deal in their views of intelligence. There were, however, three areas of difference. First, laypeople tended to have a broader view of intelligence. What experts study in terms of intelligence and the content of IQ tests comprises only a portion of the broad array of characteristics that laypeople associate with the concept of intelligence. Second, laypeople tended to emphasize the importance of intelligence in *inter*personal relationships in a *social* situation, whereas the experts tended to stress *intra*personal competence in an *individual* context. For example, laypeople were more likely to associate "acts politely" with intelligence, and experts stressed behaviors such as "reasons logically and well." Third, the scientists considered motivation to be much more central to the concept of intelligence than did laypeople. Thus characteristics such as "displays dedication and motivation in chosen pursuits" were rated highly by the experts.

A remarkable aspect of this research was the use of the 250 behaviors as a measure of intelligence. The list of behaviors was used as a means for individuals to rate themselves. People were instructed to rate the degree to which each of the 250 behaviors was characteristic of themselves. The scoring was based upon how closely a person's responses resembled those of someone considered to be ideally intelligent. Thus, it was not possible to falsify the results by rating oneself high on the desirable characteristics. Results of the rating scale correlated about as well with IQs as other more traditional tests of intelligence, which suggests a kind of validity.

The appeal of this approach is that it allows society or the culture, not so-called experts or intelligence tests, to define intelligence. Obviously, Sternberg's method is but one of hundreds of approaches to defining and measuring intelligence.

FOCUS ON PRACTICE
How Useful Is the WISC-R?

A Review of the WISC-R by Joseph C. Witt and Frank M. Gresham

. . . With the wealth of information available about the WISC-R and the countless reviews which have preceded this one, it seems presumptuous to undertake another. However, this review is based upon the supposition that with respect to the WISC-R and the related research, there is less there than meets the eye. Although it is unfair (and untrue) to say the emperor has no clothes, we feel the emperor is wearing little beyond a g-string. These statements are premised on two primary lines of evidence: (a) that the WISC-R is outdated, and (b) that it lacks treatment validity.

Outdated. The WISC-R is an anachronistic albatross which hangs gamely around the necks of applied psychologists. Born in the time of traditional psychometrics when the precise measurement of hypothetical constructs (e.g., intelligence) reigned supreme, the WISC-R has remained virtually unchanged since its inception in 1949. The 1974 revision consisted primarily of cosmetic changes designed to appease women and minorities which in no way suggested that the author and the publisher made any serious attempt to revise the instrument such that it would reflect the monumental explosion of knowledge in the measurement of cognitive abilities. Developments in the fields of cognitive psychology and neuroscience have revolutionized our thinking about thinking, but the WISC-R remains the same. Using the WISC-R to assess intelligence in light of the surge of information in these fields is analogous to applying Newtonian formulae to modern physics problems.

Wechsler defined intelligence globally as the "overall capacity of an individual to understand and cope with the world around him." He further specified that this definition "avoids singling out any ability, however esteemed (e.g., abstract reasoning), as crucial or overwhelmingly important." Based upon the data now available in cognitive psychology, this statement is equivalent to suggesting the water boy, the person who sells soft drinks, and Kareem Abdul-Jabbar are all equally important contributors to the win/lose variance in Los Angeles Lakers basketball. Clearly, some cognitive abilities are more important than others and some of the most important are not even included in the WISC-R.

Cognitive science has especially emphasized the importance of abilities such as executive processes (Sternberg, 1984), planning and organizing functions (Das, 1980), and metacognitive skills (Flavell & Wellman, 1977). Although research has suggested that individuals who perform well on the WISC-R also perform well on tests of metacognitive skills (Kramer & Engle, 1981), it would be desirable to incorporate some direct measure of metacognitive ability into the instrument and test it directly. Developmental psychologists have told us repeatedly that children think in qualitatively different ways as they progress from one developmental stage to another, but the Wechsler series utilizes essentially identical tasks for individuals ranging in age from preschool to adult-

continued

FOCUS ON PRACTICE *continued*

hood. Similarly, the impressive developments in the area of neuroscience have not had any noticeable impact on the WISC-R. Even if one takes a more traditional view of intelligence such as that proposed by Guilford (1967), we find that the WISC-R is nowhere near a "global" measure of intelligence.

One final, blatant instance of datedness is the continued use of the term intelligence and the associated diagnostic categories by the author and publisher of the WISC-R. As suggested above, the WISC-R is nowhere close to a comprehensive test of intelligence and, in fact, omits many important characteristics and attributes of the "intelligent" person (Sternberg, 1984). Yet, Wechsler has not only retained the use of the term intelligence but also the antiquated labels such as "mentally deficient." Such a system is distasteful and stigmatizing to large groups of individuals. The McCarthy Scales of Children's Abilities and the Kaufman Assessment Battery for Children have managed to avoid the emotionally laden term of intelligence. Not only is the term objectionable but worse still is the implication that "mental deficiency" can be diagnosed solely on the basis of administering the WISC-R. In most instances such a classification would be contrary to existing law. Our clinical experience, however, suggests that psychological reports often contain such phrases as "Sam performed in the mentally defective range on the WISC-R." It is difficult to overestimate the power of these words on parents who may read the report. A term such as mentally defective reeks of an ancient medical model orientation which exemplifies popular stereotypical images of the psychology profession. Given the rapidity of changes in the WISC-R, we are surprised to find the terms moron, idiot, and imbecile have been abandoned.

Treatment Validity. . . . For a test to have treatment validity, it must lead to better treatments (i.e., better educational programs, teaching strategies, etc.). Many professionals are beginning to question the desirability of spending an hour and a half administering and scoring the WISC-R and ending up with only an IQ score. School psychologists, for example, find that teachers want to know specifically what to do for and with children. The WISC-R provides no such information. To partially salvage the information collected on the WISC-R, numerous schemes have been devised for making various neurological, psychological, and educational recommendations based on a particular pattern of scaled scores. However, most of these systems are highly dependent on an interpretation of inter-subtest scatter whereby a child who scores higher in Block Design than in Picture Arrangement should be remediated differently than someone for whom the reverse pattern is true. Kaufman's (1976) classic article on scatter in the normal population demonstrated that interpretation of scatter is at best fraught with difficulty and at worst totally inappropriate. However, there continues to exist a press to develop such systems because people who spend an hour and a half engaged in some endeavor want to (need to) believe that their labor has been productive. Similar to the initial experiment on cog-

continued

FOCUS ON PRACTICE *continued*

nitive dissonance, if you spend a period of time performing an exceedingly boring task with little promise of remuneration, you will judge that task as being interesting and important. This same phenomena may, in part, help to maintain the use of the WISC-R by applied psychologists in that spending the amount of time it takes to learn, administer, score, interpret, and write up the results of a WISC-R, given the payoff (which is miniscule in relation to the cost), creates cognitive dissonance. As a result, the WISC-R is judged to be a valuable and useful tool by most applied psychologists. Partly because of the time required to learn and use the WISC-R, it seems that the instrument is now viewed as appropriate for all manner and variety of problems regardless of whether it can provide any valuable information or not. In many school systems, nearly every child referred for diagnostic or special services is administered the WISC-R. Perhaps this confirms the old adage: If the only tool you have is a hammer, the entire world looks like a nail. . . .

Reviewer's References

Guilford, J. P. *The Nature of Human Intelligence*. New York: McGraw-Hill, 1967.

Kaufman, A. S. A new approach to the interpretation of test scatter on the WISC-R. *Journal of Learning Disabilities*, 1976, 9, 160–168.

Flavell, J. H., & Wellman, H. M. Metamemory. In R. V. Kail and J. W. Hagen (Eds.), *Perspectives on the Development of Memory and Cognition*. Hillsdale, NJ: Lawrence Erlbaum, 1977.

Reschly, D. J. Nonbiased assessment. In G. Phye & D. J. Reschly (Eds.), *School Psychology: Perspectives and Issues*. New York: Academic Press, 1979.

Das, J. P. Planning: Theoretical considerations and empirical evidence. *Psychological Research*, 1980, 41, 141–151.

Nelson, R. O. The use of intelligence tests within behavioral assessment. *Behavioral Assessment*, 1980, 2, 417–423.

Kramer, J. J., & Engle, R. W. Teaching awareness of strategic behavior in combination with strategy training. Effects on children's memory performance. *Journal of Experimental Child Psychology*, 1981, 32, 513–530.

Reynolds, C. R. The problem of bias in psychological assessment. In C. R. Reynolds & T. B. Gutkin (Eds.), *Handbook of School Psychology*, New York: John Wiley, 1982.

Sternberg, R. J. What cognitive psychology can (and cannot) do for test development. In B. S. Plake (Ed.), *Social and Technical Issues in Testing: Implications for Test Construction and Usage*. Hillsdale, NJ: Lawrence Erlbaum, 1984.

lationship to specific skills like verbal and performance abilities or simultaneous and successive processing? Or is it time for a new definition?

Sternberg (1979) argues that it is indeed time for a novel approach, some new ideas, a little fresh air. He suggests that we view intelligence as a prototype, an ideal model. This approach would argue that instead of formulating theories, developing tests to fit our theories, and testing individuals on our measures of cognitive ability (to confirm our theories!), we should move in a different, almost opposite direction. Sternberg would have us start by asking: What are the characteristics of intelligent people? How do they behave? How do they think? As we proceed, we would first answer the questions intuitively, based on our observations and experience (the intelligent person is a good planner and organizer, has excellent abstract reasoning skills, and is able to think logically), and only after we have developed some ideas about the intelligent person (our prototype) should we begin to research the nature of the abilities we have identified.

At this point Sternberg would have us ask: What is abstract reasoning? How do people demonstrate it? What are its components? What is the nature of logical thinking and what are the psychological mechanisms that underlie it? Are the types of people we have identified as intelligent really better planners, and if so, on what types of tasks? He would also have us ask how these skills relate to an individual's ability to adapt to the environment. Are the same skills important in all environmental settings, or are there important interactions between environment and ability of which we must remain aware? This approach has been referred to as componential analysis because it is designed to identify the critical components of intelligence that relate to performance as well as knowledge acquisition, transfer, and retention (Sternberg, 1985). This approach has received a great deal of attention and has been the focus of intensive research. Will componential analysis improve our ability to develop educational interventions for children? Will componential tests be the new tests of intelligence as we approach the twenty-first century? How will the psychologists of the next century view our efforts? Will our work seem as primitive to them as the efforts of Galton and Wundt seem to us? Stay tuned!

Chapter 9

Academic Achievement

Learning Objectives

1. Describe the differences between an achievement battery and an achievement test in reading, mathematics, or spelling.
2. Differentiate between survey and diagnostic tests and provide a rationale for the use of each.
3. Describe reasons for choosing either an individually or a group-administered achievement battery.
4. List and describe the various uses of achievement batteries.
5. Discuss the strengths and weaknesses of four of the achievement batteries examined in this chapter.

The scene is a familiar one. A teacher stands at the front of the classroom, a packet of test booklets held firmly in hand. In a few minutes she will break the seal on the packet of booklets and hand one to each student. She has placed a small clock on her desk so that students will be aware of how much time they have left on each section of the test. During the administration of the test she will also record the time remaining on the chalkboard. The students are sitting quietly, their pencils primed for action. They have been told that during the next few days they will be taking a number of different kinds of tests in reading, mathematics, and language arts. Although they may suspect that the test results will be reported to their parents, they are unaware of the many other uses for the results of standardized achievement batteries.

School districts all across the country set aside a certain number of days each year to administer achievement batteries. Indeed, many large school districts have separate departments that devote a great deal of time to the administration, interpretation, and dissemination of the results of such tests. Although these tests are given routinely, there is considerable misunderstanding about their appropriate use and the effective application of the data obtained from them.

Criticism of achievement tests has focused on their validity (Wright & Piersel, in press). A frequent complaint concerns their potential for underestimating the ability of individuals from minority populations such as blacks, Hispanics, and native Americans. These are important criticisms, which raise issues that are very similar to those voiced with regard to intelligence tests (see Chapter 8).

The manner in which achievement batteries have been used (and abused) has also come under close scrutiny. For example, suppose in the case cited above the teacher worked within a school district that in the past year had taken a good deal of criticism because the students' average test scores were the lowest in five years and were lower than those in most other districts in the state. Administrators, feeling the pressure to "do something," met behind closed doors to discuss two plans for raising the scores. One of the strategies is designed to elevate individual scores, while the other will eliminate some low scores, in both cases the score of the "average" student will go up. More specifically, the tactics include:

1. Coaching students in the weeks before the test. This coaching, or "teaching to the test," would involve using class time to practice answering items similar to those on the actual test. Although school officials do not know the exact items that will appear on the test, they do have a good idea of the types that will be sampled as a result of studying the publisher's objectives for the test.
2. Excluding special education students from the testing. The school officials argue that these students have already been extensively tested to qualify for special services and that there is little to be gained from further testing.

These strategies would most probably increase the average scores for each grade level, and thus the average score for the entire district would be higher than those from previous years. What is to be gained, however, if test scores are raised but no longer accurately reflect the knowledge level of a particular child nor the average performance of children within the district? Anastasi (1981) has examined some of the issues involved in coaching and concluded "that a test score is invalidated . . . when a particular experience raises the score without appreciably affecting the behavior domain that the test samples" (p. 1087). In the above example, the school officials would be raising scores without modifying students' knowledge, thus invalidating the test. Although such activities have taken place in some schools, they are certainly not standard practice. Achievement batteries can be valuable aids in the educational

FOCUS ON PRACTICE
The National Association of Test Directors

Although the above example of a fictional school district's approach to achievement batteries is not very flattering, most school districts do use data obtained from such tests in an appropriate fashion. The National Association of Test Directors (NATD) is a group of individuals (typically the coordinators of evaluation or assessment from large school districts) interested in learning the best ways to use tests within the public schools. They want to explore which tests have been found useful across the nation, the desirability of testing every student every year, and the most effective means of reporting scores to parents. During a recent meeting of the NATD, which took place at the annual meeting of the American Education Research Association, the agenda of items for future study included:

1. The desirability of developing a national, cooperative item bank for school systems designing their own achievement tests.
2. The effects of competency testing.
3. The merits of the national standardization of tests.
4. Methods of reporting district test results to the public.
5. Use of grade-equivalent scores by publishers, educators, and the public.
6. Strategies for test selection.
7. Methods of evaluating achievement in social studies and science.
8. Computer scoring of tests.
9. Use of standardized tests to determine school effectiveness, teacher effectiveness, and principal effectiveness.

Thus although our example focused on the misuse of testing practices, there are clearly individuals and groups, such as the NATD, working to improve their use in the schools.

process. In the sections that follow we examine the foundations of achievement batteries, methods of utilizing the data obtained from them, and a small sample of these tests. Although we cover domain-referenced achievement tests in other chapters (for example, reading and mathematics), the tests presented in this chapter are designed to measure more than one achievement area.

The Development and Use of Achievement Batteries

An achievement battery is a collection of tests from different subject areas that have been integrated into one test battery. Achievement batteries are often confused with aptitude tests, and both tests do measure, to some extent, prior learning. However, achievement tests differ from aptitude tests in two important ways (Anastasi, 1982). First, achievement tests typically are samples of rather well-defined knowledge domains such as elementary mathematics, geography, and American history before 1865, while aptitude tests have a much broader pool of information from which to choose. Second, achievement tests are intended to measure the result of *previous* instruction, while aptitude tests are designed to assess a student's potential to benefit from *future* instruction. It is important to remember, however, that both types of tests measure what an individual has learned. An aptitude test is not a test of innate ability but rather of how well someone will learn in the future.

The principles that guide the construction of achievement batteries are the same as those that guide the development of specific-subject tests (see Chapters 10–12). Selection of an appropriate instrument depends on careful analysis of (a) the purpose of the assessment, (b) the content and technical properties of the instruments being considered, and (c) the match between them. In other chapters we have emphasized the necessity of evaluating the technical adequacy of tests and the extent to which a variety of instruments meet this need. However, no understanding of reliability or validity will compensate for a failure to analyze carefully the purpose of the assessment. Questions related to the goals and objectives of a testing program must be answered before, not after, testing. For example, why is an achievement battery being considered? How will the results be used? Are you interested in receiving diagnostic information for students in special programs or only in reporting the results from a reliable, norm-referenced test to state and federal agencies? Do you want to know which subject areas in your curriculum are being successfully taught and which need improvement? Has the match between the content of the school district's curriculum and the content of the test been evaluated? This type of planning must be completed before one begins to consider specific instruments: No test is capable of correcting for insufficient or inadequate planning.

It is also important to note that the label a test author or publisher applies to an achievement battery (e.g., The All-Purpose Achievement Test) or a particular subtest (e.g., reading) is, in and of itself, not an indication of the validity of that test for measuring the variable indicated by the title. A thorough analysis of the content is the only sure method of determining whether a test really qualifies as "all-purpose," measures "reading," or meets your needs. Later in this chapter a number of achievement batteries are discussed, but we now turn to a closer examination of the specific issues that must be considered before beginning an evaluation of achievement batteries.

Survey versus Diagnostic Tests

Achievement batteries generally fall into one of two categories: screening or diagnostic tests. Many group tests designed for use with all students are used as screening tests in special education. Screening batteries are designed to provide a general estimate of current levels of academic achievement across a wide range of skill levels. Often, these tests contain a limited sample of problems from a particular content area. Survey tests typically are norm-referenced and administered to determine an individual's relative standing within a group. These tests are not generally designed to be aids in the development of specific educational programs. Instead, survey batteries provide a gross, overall picture of an individual's current level of achievement and as such are a reasonable first step in the assessment of academic skills.

Sometimes, as a result of prior testing or background information, an examiner may need more specific information about an individual's skills. Diagnostic achievement batteries are designed to identify specific strengths and weaknesses in a variety of academic skills, such as reading, arithmetic, and spelling. A particular content area (for example, reading) is typically subdivided into skill areas (in this case, word recognition, word analysis, and vocabulary). This process makes possible a more detailed interpretation of an individual's mastery of the basic skills in a certain area. Many diagnostic tests are criterion-referenced, although some also are norm-referenced. Diagnostic tests are intended to be useful in the development of specific educational programs.

Group versus Individual Administration

Achievement batteries can also be categorized as either group or individually administered. Group tests are typically given to entire classes at one time, making them an efficient tool for the cost-effective collection of a great deal of information in a relatively short period. In contrast, individual tests require one-to-one administration, but allow the examiner greater opportunity to observe the behavior of a particular individual. Group tests also require less training in administration techniques than do most individual tests. Although individual tests cannot routinely be given to groups, a group test may be administered to one student, provided that it is administered in the standardized fashion.

Individual administration is considered better than group administration for making placement and classification decisions about individual students because it allows for more direct observation of behavior and because one can select a group of tests that are directly related to an individual's situation (or problem). Some individual tests, however, are poorly constructed or sample only a limited amount of content (for example, the Wide Range Achievement Test-Revised [WRAT-R]), while some group tests have been meticulously developed (and normed) and sample from an extensive variety of academic areas (for example, the California Achievement Test [CAT] and Science Research Associates Achievement Series [SRA]). The importance of the information gathered from a well-constructed group test of achievement should not be overlooked. Anastasi (1982) has also suggested that an advantage of group achievement batteries that are administered on a regular basis (for example, each year) is that they permit both horizontal and vertical comparisons among large numbers of students. That is, a teacher can compare an individual's performance across academic areas (such as mathematics, reading, spelling, and social studies) in terms of a consistent standardization group (a horizontal comparison) and also evaluate the progress that the individual is making from year to year (a vertical comparison).

Potential Uses of Achievement Battery Data

As indicated earlier, we have sometimes lost sight of the fact that achievement batteries are designed to aid in the instructional process. School personnel may be concerned with getting the highest scores rather than the most representative. Or, in the rush to meet federal mandates for the assessment of handicapped children, educators have occasionally made sure that achievement test data are in the files of handicapped students without first examining all of the implications of the data. Luckily, such practices are less common today than they were only a few years ago. Two valuable ways of using the information collected from achievement batteries are in the evaluation of individuals and the evaluation of programs.

Evaluation of individuals. Achievement batteries often play an important role in the selection and placement of individuals in the educational system. For example, schools commonly conduct preschool screenings to determine a child's readiness for kindergarten. Sometimes these decisions are based on informal, locally constructed batteries, but in most cases professionals may choose to use commercially published tests. Data from achievement batteries may be used to make initial decisions about which children qualify for special programs (for example, for the gifted). In such cases, the results from the current year's district-wide group testing program (perhaps the Iowa Test of Basic Skills) will be examined, and all children with scores above the ninety-fifth percentile will be referred for individual testing to determine whether they qualify for placement in a program for talented and gifted students.

Achievement batteries also play an important role in the instructional planning process. Although we maintain that achievement tests may provide useful information about *all* students, special educators use the tests in planning for special needs students. Earlier we presented a model for a funnel approach to assessment (see Figure 1.1) that also illustrates how information from achievement batteries can be integrated with other assessment data to develop an educational program for handicapped as well as other children.

Finally, achievement batteries are receiving increased attention as educators, legislators, and the public become concerned with measuring "minimal competency," or the extent to which individuals have mastered the content of a particular area. Within the public schools, such attention has generally been focused on the testing of high school seniors and teachers, not to make a comprehensive assessment of their knowledge but rather to make sure that they have obtained a minimal level of competency to function in society or in the classroom. Achievement batteries will continue to play a part in this process.

FOCUS ON RESEARCH
The National Assessment of Educational Progress

How does student achievement today compare with that of previous generations, and what changes will occur during the next few decades? There appears to be as many answers to these queries as there are people to ask. In just the last few years numerous groups, such as the Carnegie Foundation National Commission on Excellence in Education, have filed reports on the current status of the American educational system. The National Assessment of Education Progress (NAEP) was also developed to monitor changes in the knowledge and skills of American schoolchildren (Ebel, 1966; Merwin, 1966; Tyler, 1966). In addition to written tests in ten areas (Literature, Science, Social Studies, Writing, Citizenship, Music, Mathematics, Reading, Art, and Vocational Education), interviews, observations, questionnaires, and performance items were included in the NAED project. The tests were to be administered at four age levels — nine, thirteen, seventeen, and twenty-three to thirty-five — and to be readministered to new groups periodically.

Over the last two decades the NAEP has undergone significant changes, and the future of this ambitious project is unknown (Frank B. Womer, personal communication, June 18, 1986). Currently the NAEP is funded by the Center for Educational Statistics and administered by the Educational Testing Service (ETS) of Princeton, New Jersey. During the past few years, the ETS has published thousands of pages detailing the results of previous NAEP testing. Although it is beyond the scope of this brief report to summarize those results, anyone desiring to examine the complete reports may write directly to the ETS.

Evaluation of programs. Given that two instructional programs for teaching mathematics cost the same, are equally well liked by students and teachers, and match the content objectives of the district, achievement batteries are one method of assessing their relative effectiveness. However, we must be aware of the many factors that may confound the results of such studies. When comparing instructional programs it would not be fair to claim that one was better than another if the "better" program was used in a school with students who were more completely prepared for learning (as in a suburban school with highly educated residents). Other factors such as cost and the satisfaction of students, parents, and teachers must also be assessed before making final decisions about the effectiveness of a particular program.

Representative Achievement Batteries

Many different achievement batteries are available for inspection and use. Some of the most widely used tests of achievement are discussed below, although options from which to choose are extensive and growing.

Diagnostic Inventory of Basic Skills

Overview and purpose. The Diagnostic Inventory of Basic Skills, or DIBS (Brigance, 1977), is one of a series of three individually administered, criterion-referenced diagnostic tests, including the Diagnostic Inventory of Early Development and the Diagnostic Inventory of Essential Skills originally developed by Albert H. Brigance. More recently, other tests have been added to this series (e.g., the Diagnostic Comprehensive Inventory of Basic Skills). The inventories are similar in purpose and format but differ in their assumptions about the performance level of the individual being assessed. Thus, the specific skills tested on each inventory differ, although there is some overlap. The DIBS is designed for students achieving in the kindergarten through sixth-grade levels, and its author has identified its five specific purposes:

1. to assess basic readiness and academic skills in key subject areas from the kindergarten to sixth-grade level;
2. to provide a systematic performance record, expressed in grade-level terms, for diagnosis and evaluation;
3. to define instructional objectives in precise terms to measure a student's performance in a given subject area;
4. to determine a student's level of achievement, readiness to advance, or need for improvement; and
5. to guide the teacher in designing an instructional program to meet the specific needs of the student (Brigance, 1977).

The DIBS assesses skills in four general areas: readiness, reading, language arts, and math. Each of these domains is broken into a number of skill (and subskill) areas, with the items arranged in order of difficulty. Table 9.1 presents the skill areas in the readiness and reading domains. As this table indicates, the DIBS attempts to provide comprehensive diagnostic information on a variety of skills.

The comprehensive nature of the DIBS has contributed to its widespread use, as has its ease and flexibility of administration. Directions are clear and are printed on each page of the examination material. Examiners are encouraged to modify the procedures in any manner they deem appropriate to determine whether students have mastered particular skills. Depending on the age, skill level, distractability of the child, and the amount of information desired, administration can take from ten minutes to a few hours spread across a couple of days. The DIBS can be used to supplement data obtained from other sources or to provide a comprehensive assessment of an individual's proficiency level in a number of academic skill areas.

Standardization sample and norms. The DIBS is criterion-referenced, and little normative data are reported in the manual.

Table 9.1 Readiness and Reading Skills Assessed in the BRIGANCE® Diagnostic Inventory of Basic Skills

Readiness

Color recognition
Visual discrimination
Visual-motor skills
Visual memory
Body image
Gross motor coordination
Identification of body parts
Directional/positional skills
Fine motor skills
Verbal fluency
Verbal directions
Articulation of sounds
Personal data response
Sentence memory
Counting
Alphabet
Numeral recognition
Number comprehension
Recognition of lowercase letters
Recognition of uppercase letters
Writing name
Numbers in sequence
Lower-case letters in sequence
Upper-case letters in sequence

Reading

Word recognition
Word recognition grade level
Basic sight vocabulary
Direction words
Abbreviations
Contractions
Common signs

Reading
Oral reading list
Reading comprehension level
Oral reading rate

Vocabulary
Context clues
Classifications
Analogies
Antonyms
Homonyms

Word analysis
Auditory discrimination
Initial consonant sounds auditorily
Initial consonant sounds visually
Substitution of initial consonant sounds
Ending sounds auditorily
Vowels
Short vowel sounds
Long vowel sounds
Initial clusters auditorily
Initial clusters visually
Substitution of initial cluster sounds
Digraphs and dipthongs
Phonetic irregularities
Common endings of rhyming words
Suffixes
Prefixes
Meaning of prefixes
Number of syllables auditorily
Syllabication concepts

From BRIGANCE® *Diagnostic Inventory of Basic Skills* (p. v), 1977, North Bielerica, MA: Curriculum Associates.

Data obtained. Based on their performance, individuals are considered to have either mastered or not mastered the skill assessed in each sequence. In addition, grade-level information is provided for many of the subtests based on the author's attempts to "text-reference" the DIBS. That is, many commonly used texts, word lists, developmental scales, and the like were examined to determine the level at which a particular skill is typically first introduced or expected. No summary or overall achievement level scores are provided.

Reliability and validity. No information related to the reliability and little validity data are reported in the test materials. Although the content validity of the DIBS appears excellent, specific details about its development and refinement are not included.

Summary. Perhaps the greatest disadvantage to the DIBS is the lack of specific information about the development of the scale and the author's failure to provide any reliability data. Beyond these shortcomings, the DIBS appears to be an excellent criterion-referenced achievement battery for teachers who are primarily concerned with what skill to teach next. The comprehensive sampling of content across the various domains assessed makes it easy to translate results from the DIBS into educational plans and programs.

California Achievement Tests

Overview and purpose. The California Achievement Tests, or CAT (CTB/McGraw-Hill, 1978), is one of a number of widely used and highly regarded group-administered, comprehensive achievement batteries currently available for use in public schools. (See Table 9.2 for others.)

The CAT (Forms C and D) is a series of comprehensive tests that measure skills in six areas: prereading, reading, spelling, language, mathematics, and the use of references. The CAT includes ten overlapping levels of Form C and seven overlapping levels of Form D for use in grades K through 12. The multiple levels of the test make it easy to assess children at their functional level rather than their assigned grade level. Brief, optional pretests are available for teachers who want to obtain an accurate reading of a particular child's functional level prior to the administration of a form of the CAT. Both norm-referenced (national and local) and criterioned-referenced (from a series of 98 category objectives) information is available with the CAT.

Standardization sample and norms. The CAT was standardized on a stratified national sample of approximately two hundred thousand students from 359 schools during the fall and spring of the 1976–77 school year. Stratification variables included type of school (public or Catholic), geographic region, socioeconomic status, and size of school district. An attempt was made to provide adequate representation of handicapped and minority populations.

Data obtained. The CAT may be hand scored or returned to the publisher for scoring. A variety of derived scores are available: grade equivalents, percentiles, normal curve equivalents, scale scores, anticipated achievement scores, and category objective scores. Information provided by the test publisher to assist in the interpretation of results is exemplary in its clarity, completeness, and accuracy.

Reliability and validity. Reliability estimates are provided for each subtest at each level. Extensive information is presented on the internal consistency (K-R 20) of the CAT, and these estimates appear to be excellent (median subtest = .84 and median total test = .93). Test-retest figures for the subtests range from .23 to .81 (median = .65) and for total scores from .52 to .94 (median = .93). Reliability estimates for the category objectives are also reported and range from .36 to .87 (median = .74).

Table 9.2 Widely Used and Highly Regarded Group-Administered Comprehensive Achievement Batteries

Battery	Grades	Subject areas assessed
Iowa Tests of Basic Skills (Forms 7 and 8) (Hieronymous et al., 1983)	K.1–1.5	Listening, Vocabulary, Word Analysis, Language, Mathematics
	K.8–1.9	Listening, Vocabulary, Word Analysis, Reading, Language, Mathematics
	1.7–2.6	Vocabulary, Word Analysis, Reading Comprehension, Spelling, Mathematics Skills, Listening, Language Skills, Work Study Skills
	2.7–3.5	Vocabulary, Word Analysis, Reading Comprehension, Spelling, Mathematics Skills, Listening, Language Skills, Work Study Skills
	3–9	Vocabulary, Reading, Spelling, Math, Capitalization, Punctuation, Usage, Visual Materials, Reference Materials
Iowa Tests of Educational Development (7th edition) (Iowa Tests of Educational Development, 1982)	9–12	Correctness and Appropriateness of Expression, Ability to do Quantitative Thinking, Social Studies, Natural Sciences, Literacy Materials, Vocabulary, Sources of Information Total, Reading Total
Metropolitan Achievement Tests (Survey Battery) (5th edition) (Balow, Farr, Hogan, and Prescott, 1978)	K.0–K.5 K.5–1.4	Reading, Mathematics, Language, Total
	1.5–2.4	Reading, Mathematics, Language, Total
		Reading, Mathematics, Language, Basics Total, Science, Social Studies, Complete Total
	2.5–3.4	Reading, Mathematics, Language, Basics Total, Science, Social Studies, Complete Total
	3.5–4.9	Reading, Mathematics, Language, Basics Total, Science, Social Studies, Complete Total
	5.0–6.9	Reading, Mathematics, Language, Basics Total, Science, Social Studies, Complete Total
	7.0–9.9	Reading, Mathematics, Language, Basics Total, Science, Social Studies, Complete Total
	10.0–12.9	Reading, Mathematics, Language Total

Table 9.2, *continued*

Battery	Grades	Subject areas assessed
Metropolitan Achievement Tests (Instructional Battery) (5th edition) (Balow, Farr, Hogan, and Prescott, 1978)	K.5–9.9	Reading, Language, Mathematics
SRA Achievement Series (Naslund, Thorpe, and Lefever, 1981)	K–1	Reading, Mathematics, Composite, Verbal, Nonverbal, Total
	1–2	Reading, Mathematics, Composite, Verbal, Nonverbal, Total
	2–3	Reading, Mathematics, Language Arts, Composite, Verbal, Nonverbal, Total
	3–4	Reading, Mathematics, Language Arts, Composite, Verbal, Nonverbal, Total
	4–6	Reading, Mathematics, Language Arts, Reference Materials, Social Studies, Science, Composite, Verbal, Nonverbal, Total
	6–8	Reading, Mathematics, Language Arts, Reference Materials, Social Studies, Science, Composite, Verbal, Nonverbal, Total
	8–9	Reading, Mathematics, Language Arts, Reference Materials, Social Studies, Science, Composite, Verbal, Nonverbal, Total
	9–12	Reading, Mathematics, Language Arts, Reference Materials, Social Studies, Science, Survey of Applied Skills, Composite, Verbal, Nonverbal, Total
Stanford Achievement Test (1982 edition) (Gardner, Rudman, Karlen, and Merwin, 1982)	1.5–2.9	Reading, Word Study Skills, Total, Mathematics, Listening, Spelling, Environment
	2.5–3.9	Reading, Word Study Skills, Total, Mathematics, Listening, Spelling, Environment
	3.5–4.9	Reading, Mathematics, Language, Listening, Science, Social Science, Using Information
	4.5–5.9	Reading, Mathematics, Language, Listening, Science, Social Science, Using Information

(continued)

Table 9.2, *continued*

Battery	Grades	Subject areas assessed
Stanford Achievement Test, *continued*	5.5–7.9	Reading, Mathematics, Language, Listening, Science, Social Science, Using Information
	7.0–9.9	Reading Comprehension, Mathematics, Language, Listening, Social Science, Science, Using Information
Stanford Test of Academic Skills (1982 edition) (Gardner, Callis, Merwin, and Rudman, 1982)	8.0–12.9	Reading Comprehension, Reading Vocabulary, Reading, Total, Spelling, English, English Total, Mathematics, Science, Social Science, Using Information
	9.0–13	Reading Comprehension, Reading Vocabulary, Reading, Total, Spelling, English, English Total, Mathematics, Science, Social Science, Using Information

Most validity data on the CAT are related to content validity. Objectives for the CAT were developed following a review of curriculum guides from various state departments of education and large cities as well as the objectives of other achievement tests. Test items were developed by professional item writers, and items were pretested during the fall of 1975. Care was taken to eliminate those items that appeared to be biased in any fashion.

Summary. The CAT is a well standardized, reliable achievement battery for testing school-age children. Its development began approximately a half-century ago, and this edition of the battery is an excellent example of a well-constructed group-administered test. Although billed as a comprehensive test, the CAT focuses on the evaluation of basic academic skills (reading, mathematics, and language arts). The adequacy of the test's category objectives has yet to be completely evaluated.

Kaufman Test of Educational Achievement (Comprehensive Form)

Overview and purpose. The Kaufman Test of Educational Achievement, or K-TEA (American Guidance Service, 1985) is a new entrant in the achievement battery field. The K-TEA is designed to measure school achievement of children from six years, zero months, to eighteen years, eleven months. It is individually administered and is available in two forms. The Brief Form assesses the global areas of reading, mathematics, and spelling; a Battery Composite score is also available. The Comprehensive Form assesses the areas of

Mathematics Applications, Reading Decoding, Spelling, Reading Comprehension, and Mathematics Computation; Reading Composite, Mathematics Composite, and Battery Composite scores are also available. Although there are a number of similarities between the two forms (for example, in how they are presented to subjects and the information in their manuals), the content does not overlap. Whether the Brief or the Comprehensive Form is used depends on the amount and type of information desired on an individual child (for example, screening versus diagnostic). The description and analysis that follow apply to the Comprehensive Form.

According to the K-TEA manual, the administration of the test takes from twenty to thirty minutes for first graders and from fifty-five to sixty-five minutes for eleventh and twelfth graders. The K-TEA may be administered by educational and psychological personnel skilled in testing as well as "technicians" and paraprofessionals with proper training, as described in the manual. It is suggested that the interpretation of the results requires more skill than does the administration and that interpretation should be the task of trained personnel.

The subtests on the Comprehensive Form include:

1. Mathematics Applications — sixty items presented orally and assessing a wide variety of concepts and applications of mathematical principles
2. Reading Decoding — sixty items involving identification of letters and pronunciation of words
3. Spelling — fifty items that the examiner reads aloud and uses in a sentence, with the student then writing the word
4. Reading Comprehension — fifty items requiring oral answers to questions related to paragraphs the subjects have read. Some items also require gestural or oral responses to printed sentences
5. Mathematics Computation — sixty written items ranging from simple addition and subtraction to algebraic computations

The Comprehensive Form allows for extensive error analysis of an individual's mistakes on any of the five subtests. For example, in Mathematics Computation, the subskill areas include Basic Addition, Regrouping Addition, Basic Subtraction, Regrouping Subtraction, Multiplication, Division, Fractions, Advanced Addition, Advanced Subtraction, Algebraic Equations, and Square Roots and Exponents. In Reading Comprehension there are two subskill areas, Literal Comprehension and Inferential Comprehension.

Standardization sample and norms. Standardization of the Comprehensive Form took place during two separate nationwide administrations in the spring and fall of 1983. Approximately 2,500 students (1,400 + in the spring and 1,000 + in the fall) participated in the standardization. An attempt was made to select a representative national sample based on United States Census Bureau data. The samples were stratified within each grade level (approximately one hundred per grade for both spring and fall) by race or ethnic group, sex, socioeconomic status (educational attainment of parents or other adults living in household), and geographic region. No systematic attempt to include special education students was made, although permission slips for participating in the standardization were given to special education students. That is, these students were provided an opportunity to participate, but no record was kept of the number returning permission slips.

Data obtained. The K-TEA provides standard scores, with a mean of 100 and a standard deviation of 15 (although there is some variability in the exact means and standard deviations on each subtest and composite at each grade), grade equivalents, age equivalents, percentile ranks, stanines, and normal curve equivalents.

Reliability and validity. Mean split-half reliability coefficients ranged from .90 (Mathematics Computation) to .95 (Reading Decoding) for the subtests and .94 (Mathematics Composite) to .98 (Battery Composite) for the composites. Test-retest reliability estimates (N = 172, retest interval of 1 to 35 days) are reported for grades one to six and seven to twelve. For the lower grades, estimates ranged from .83 (Mathematics Computation) to .95 (Spelling/Reading Decoding) for the subtests and .93 (Mathematics Composite) to .97 (Battery Composite) for the composites. For the higher grades, estimates ranged from .90 (Reading Comprehension) to .96 (Spelling) for the subtests and .94 (Reading Composite) to .97 (Battery Composite) for the composites.

Standard errors of measurement (SEM) are reported and generally range from about 2 standard score points for the Battery Composite to 3–5 points for the individual subtests. Reading Composite SEMs are generally about 3 points, while Mathematics Composite SEMs generally are 3–4 points.

Validation of the K-TEA was a sequential process, and is described in the manual under the headings of Content Validity, Item Selection, Construct Validity, and Concurrent Validity.

A content blueprint for the K-TEA was developed by its authors, members of the publisher's staff, and curriculum consultants. The large number of items originally considered were reduced through various types of analyses (both conventional as well as the Rasch-Wright item response techniques). After national samplings some items were eliminated either because they failed to fit the Rasch-Wright model or because of evidence of bias.

Evidence for construct validity is provided in that as children grow older and experience more schooling, their K-TEA scores tend to improve. Internal consistency estimates for the five subtests ranged from .77 to .85 (by grade level).

Evidence of concurrent validity is provided through correlations between the K-TEA scores of some of the standardization sample with either the Kaufman Assessment Battery for Children (K-ABC), Wide Range Achievement Test (WRAT), Peabody Individual Achievement Test (PIAT), or Peabody Picture Vocabulary Test-Revised (PPVT-R). Comparisons also were made between K-TEA scores and three group achievement batteries: Stanford Achievement Test, Metropolitan Achievement Tests, and Comprehensive Tests of Basic Skills. The large amount of information collected in these comparisons indicate that, in general, the K-TEA subtests and composites appear to measure the same abilities as similar subtests and composites on other academic tests.

Summary. The K-TEA appears to be a psychometrically sound achievement battery. The standardization process is exemplary in its attention to detail. The test provides both norm- and criterion-referenced information, which should prove to be a valuable aid in the assessment of children. The extent to which the K-TEA will be adopted as a measure of academic achievement remains to be seen, but it seems to have much promise.

Peabody Individual Achievement Test

Overview and purpose. The Peabody Individual Achievement Test, or PIAT (Dunn & Markwardt, 1970), is an individually administered, norm-referenced achievement battery. Designed as a screening measure, the PIAT provides an "overview of scholastic attainment" in four areas: Mathematics, Reading Recognition and Comprehension, Spelling, and General Information. The test takes thirty to forty minutes to administer and is normed for grades kindergarten through high school. The subtests are not timed, and examiners are encouraged not to rush examinees. The subtests include:

1. Mathematics — eighty-four items ranging from matching and visual discrimination at the lower levels to trigonometry at the upper levels
2. Reading Recognition — eighty-four items including matching letters, naming letters, and reading words in isolation
3. Reading Comprehension — sixty-six items requiring the subject to read a sentence silently and then pick the one of four different pictures on a page that best illustrates the meaning of the sentence
4. Spelling — eighty-four multiple-choice items requiring the identification of printed letters and the spelling of words read by the examiner
5. General Information — eighty-four items testing general knowledge in science, social studies, fine arts, and sports

The manual is clearly written, and the record booklet is easily used. The administration of the PIAT is generally easy to learn, although the Spelling and Reading Comprehension subtests do require some examiner practice.

Standardization sample and norms. The standardization group consisted of a national sample of 2,899 children attending regular public school classrooms. The children were selected from nine geographic regions and generally conformed to the 1967 census data. There were approximately two hundred children for each of the thirteen grade levels (kindergarten through twelfth grade) in the sample.

Data obtained. The PIAT provides grade equivalents, age equivalents, percentile ranks, and standard scores (with a mean of 100 and a standard deviation of 15) for each of the five subtests and the total test.

Reliability and validity. Median test-retest reliabilities (retest intervals of one month) are reported as .89 for the total test, .74 for Mathematics, .88 for Reading Recognition, .64 for Reading Comprehension, .65 for Spelling, and .76 for General Information. The median standard error of measurement for raw scores is reported as 12 points for the total test, and range from 3.06 to 6.51 for the subtests.

Two types of validity information are presented in the PIAT manual: content and concurrent. Content validity was established by having experts evaluate the extent to which the test material is representative of the curricula of various grade levels. Concurrent validity was based on correlations between PIAT and the PPVT (median coefficients across six grades range from .40 to .68 for the subtests and .68 for the total test) and the WRAT. For the latter Sitlington (1970) tested forty-six educable mentally retarded adolescents and compared the following scores: PIAT Reading Recognition with WRAT Reading (.95 correlation), PIAT Mathematics with WRAT Arithmetic (.58 correlation), and PIAT Spelling with WRAT Spelling (.85 correlation).

Summary. The PIAT has been widely used in screening a variety of academic skills. The multiple-choice format is especially useful for children with language or physical disabilities. The reliability and validity information presented in the manual is sketchy, although enough data have been collected over the last decade and a half to suggest that the test does what it purports to: provide a rough measure of academic competence across a number of important academic skill areas. The biggest drawback to the PIAT may well be its age: The test was standardized in 1969, and there have been a number of changes in the content of public school instructional programs since that time.

Wide Range Achievement Test-Revised

Overview and purpose. According to the authors of the Wide Range Achievement Test-Revised, or WRAT-R (Jastak & Wilkinson, 1984), this test is designed to measure the "codes" that are essential to learning basic skills in arithmetic, spelling, and reading. There are two levels (or forms) of the test. Level 1 is intended for subjects between the ages of 5-0 and 11-11 years, while Level 2 is for those from 12-0 years through adulthood. The specific number and type of items on each subtest vary between the levels. The test is designed to minimize the importance of comprehension skills in order to separate those whose problems are related to the "codes . . . necessary to acquire the skill" (p. 1) from those with comprehension problems. No definition of the term "codes" is provided. The subtests include:

1. Reading — naming and recognizing letters as well as reading words in isolation (i.e., word recognition)
2. Spelling — copying symbols, writing the subject's name, and spelling dictated words
3. Arithmetic — counting, reading numbers, and solving oral problems and written computations

Standardization sample and norms. The WRAT-R was standardized on 5,600 individuals, with 250 subjects tested in each of twenty-eight age groups between five years and seventy-four years, eleven months. The sample was stratified on the basis of five factors: age, sex, race, geographic region, and metropolitan/nonmetropolitan residence. Most handicapped populations were excluded from the standardization, although an attempt was made to include mentally retarded individuals (2 percent of the sample). Some difficulty in obtaining a representative adult sample was indicated.

Data obtained. Raw scores from the WRAT-R can be translated into standard scores, grade equivalents, and percentiles.

Reliability and validity. Reliability data is briefly presented on one page of the WRAT-R manual, and figures for test-retest (the retest interval is not specified) and standard errors of measurement are provided. Test-retest figures are: Level 1 ($N = 81$) — Reading (.96), Spelling (.97), Arithmetic (.94); Level 2 ($N = 67$) — Reading (.90), Spelling (.89), Arithmetic (.79). Standard error of measurement (SEM) calculations are provided at five points across the ability range. No details on the method of dividing the sample nor the number of subjects in any of the ability level groups are provided. Further, these calculations were made on the raw scores rather than any of the derived scores (e.g., standard scores). The range of raw score standard error of measurement figures for the WRAT-R are: Level 1 — Reading (1.55–2.55), Spelling (1.61–1.77), Arithmetic (1.22–1.89); Level 2 — Reading (1.96–2.52), Spelling (1.40–2.05), Arithmetic (1.92–2.12).

Information on content, construct, and concurrent validity is presented in the WRAT-R manual. According to its authors, the content validity of the WRAT-R "is apparent," although details are not provided. As evidence of construct validity the authors cite the fact that the test becomes easier as children get older and for concurrent validity the reader is referred to earlier studies with the WRAT. Although the authors should be congratulated for their desire to include data about the test's validity, the discussions are very minimal. It would be helpful to know, for example, how items were originally selected for inclusion on the WRAT-R. Were experts consulted? Were textbooks analyzed? Knowing that earlier editions of the WRAT yielded scores that were moderately correlated with other achievement tests is not sufficient evidence of the concurrent validity of the revised WRAT. The discussions of validity are often also difficult to follow, which appears to support Thorndike's (1972) comments about the description of validity procedures in an earlier edition of the WRAT: "The exact nature of the procedure is apparently known only to the authors and God, and He may have some uncertainty" (p. 68).

Summary. The WRAT-R has been a most durable achievement battery, probably because it is easily and quickly administered. First available in 1936, the standardization of its current version is an improvement over earlier editions with their many problems (see Thorndike, 1972). Indeed, the WRAT-R spelling test appears to be one of the most ecologically valid available. On this subtest the examiner says a word, reads a sentence using the word, and then repeats the word. Only then does the examinee attempt to write the word. However, a number of problems remain with the WRAT-R, among the most important of which is that it assesses a very narrow range of skills, by far the narrowest of any instrument examined in this chapter. To describe the word recognition task of the WRAT-R as reading is a misnomer, and the arithmetic test provides no sample applications of arithmetic skills. Except as a screening device or a supplement to other instruments, the WRAT-R cannot be recommended.

Woodcock-Johnson Psychoeducational Battery

Overview and purpose. The Woodcock-Johnson Psychoeducational Battery, or WJPEB (Woodcock, 1978), is a comprehensive, multiple-skill battery designed to assess cognitive skills, achievement, and interests. The WJPEB is individually administered to subjects from three to eighty years of age. The complete battery contains 27 subtests organized into three parts: Part I includes twelve subtests for evaluating cognitive ability and specific scholastic aptitudes; Part II contains ten subtests for assessing academic achievement; and Part III includes five subtests for measuring scholastic and other interests. The number of subtests administered to a particular individual is a function of the subject's age and the purpose of the assessment (for example, to measure academic skills, just cognitive abilities, or general interests).

Standardization sample and norms. The WJPEB was standardized on 4,732 subjects (the majority, or 3,935, were in school at the time) in forty-nine communities throughout the United States. The sample was stratified on the basis of the 1970 census data, with five variables used to guide subject selection: sex, race, occupational status, geographic region, and urban/nonurban community. Handicapped students were not included. During development of the WJPEB, extensive use was made of the Rasch-Wright item response theory model for analyzing data.

Data obtained. Although the WJPEB is organized into subtests, the basic units of analysis are the eighteen cluster scores, or scores earned on groups of subtests. The WJPEB yields a variety of derived scores including cluster scores, percentiles ranking, grade equivalents, age equivalents, and relative performance indexes (not included for the interest clusters).

Scoring the WJPEB may be the most difficult task associated with the test (see Figure 9.1). According to Cummings (1985),

> once the instrument has been administered, the process of obtaining derived scores is somewhat arduous. There are numerous score transformations and sums to be added. Consider the process of obtaining a percentile rank for a child's verbal ability cluster. The raw score is transformed to a part score, the part scores are totalled to obtain a cluster score, the average age score for the child's chronological age is found in a table and then subtracted from the obtained cluster score in order to arrive at the cluster difference score, and finally a table is consulted to determine the examinee's percentile rank. For Parts I and II of the battery, this procedure must be completed 13 times. (p. 1760)

Reliability and validity. Split-half reliabilities for subtest scores and cluster scores are reported and are generally excellent. Median reliabilities generally exceed .80 for subtests and exceed .85 for clusters, except for the perceptual cluster (.70). No test-retest comparisons are reported (except for speeded subtests, in which split-half estimates were inappropriate), and thus no evidence on the effects of stability over time is available.

Extensive concurrent and predictive validity data are reported in the manual. Correlations with a number of intellectual measures (for example, the Stanford-Binet Intelligence Scale [SBIS] and the Wechsler Intelligence Scale for Children-Revised [WISC-R]), achievement tests (for example, PIAT, WRAT-R), and questionnaires are reported. The WJPEB serves as an excellent model for the reporting of test validity data. A major shortcoming is that no specific information is presented to support the twelve uses that are recommended for the instrument. Although comparisons with the WISC-R have generally yielded satisfactory validity coefficients (around .80), there is evidence that, in at least some instances, the WJPEB yields scores about 12 points lower than the WISC-R (see, e.g., Woodcock, 1984). Evidence for validity of the cluster scores is minimal, so these should be used with considerable caution.

Summary. The WJPEB is a useful individually administered battery of tests. It is easy to administer, adequately standardized, reliable, and valid, but difficult to score. In a relatively short period it has had a significant impact on achievement testing and today is one of the most popular individually administered batteries with school-age populations. The inclusion of measures of cognitive ability, achievement, and interest within a single test is an innovative

PART I

SUMMARY OF SCORES: Do these test results provide a fair representation of the subject's present functioning? ☐Yes ☐No

If not, what is the reason for questioning the results? ____________

Subtest / CLUSTER	Raw Score	Part Score from Table A	CLUSTER SCORE	Grade Score	Age Score	AVERAGE CLUSTER SCORE ☐ Grade ☐ Age	CLUSTER DIFFERENCE SCORE	Percentile Rank at ☐ Grade ☐ Age	Percentile Rank Range	RPI at ☐ Grade ☐ Age	Functioning Level
BROAD COGNITIVE ABILITY											
1 Picture Vocab	___ (37)	___									
2 Spatial Rels	___ (74)	___									
3 Memory for Sents	___ (22)	___									
4 Vis-Aud Lrng (Stories 1-7)	___ (134)	___									
5 Blending	___ (25)	___									
6 Quant Concepts	___ (46)	___									
7 Vis Matching	___ (30)	___									
8 Ants-Syns	___ (49)	___									
9 Anl-Synth	___ (30)	___									
10 Nums Reversed	___ (21)	___									
11 Concept Form	___ (32)	___									
12 Analogies	___ (35)	___	a			b	a − b = c				
Full Scale Cluster Score			☐	___ TABLE B	___ TABLE B	− ☐ TABLE I OR J	= ☐ (+ OR −)	___ TABLE K OR R	___ to ___ TABLE K OR R	___ /90 TABLE Y	___ TABLE Y
1 Picture Vocab	___ (37)	___									
2 Spatial Rels	___ (74)	___									
3 Memory for Sents	___ (22)	___									
4 Vis-Aud Lrng (Stories 1-7)	___ (134)	___									
5 Blending	___ (25)	___									
6 Quant Concepts	___ (46)	___									
Preschool Scale Cluster Score			☐	___ TABLE C	___ TABLE C	− ☐ TABLE I OR J	= ☐ (+ OR −)	___ TABLE L OR S	___ to ___ TABLE L OR S	___ /90 TABLE Y	___ TABLE Y
6 Quant Concepts	___ (46)	___									
8 Ants-Syns	___ (49)	___									
Brief Scale Cluster Score			☐	___ TABLE D	___ TABLE D	− ☐ TABLE I OR J	= ☐ (+ OR −)	___ TABLE M OR T	___ to ___ TABLE M OR T	___ /90 TABLE Y	___ TABLE Y

SCHOLASTIC APTITUDE CLUSTERS	Raw Score	Part Score from Table A	CLUSTER SCORE	Expected Grade Score	RANGE OF EXPECTED GRADE SCORES 5 Percent are Below / 5 Percent are Above	Expected Achievement Cluster Score	AVERAGE CLUSTER SCORE	CLUSTER DIFFERENCE SCORE	Percentile Rank	Percentile Rank Range
4 Vis-Aud Lrng (Stories 1-7)	___ (134)	___								
5 Blending	___ (25)	___								
8 Ants-Syns	___ (49)	___								
12 Analogies	___ (35)	___	a				b	a − b = c		
Reading Apt Cluster Score			☐	___ TABLE E	___ to ___ TABLE E	___ TABLE E	− ☐ TABLE I OR J	= ☐ (+ OR −)	___ TABLE N OR U	___ to ___ TABLE N OR U
7 Vis Matching	___ (30)	___								
8 Ants-Syns	___ (49)	___								
9 Anl-Synth	___ (30)	___								
11 Concept Form	___ (32)	___								
Math Apt Cluster Score			☐	___ TABLE F	___ to ___ TABLE F	___ TABLE F	− ☐ TABLE I OR J	= ☐ (+ OR −)	___ TABLE O OR V	___ to ___ TABLE O OR V
6 Quant Concepts	___ (46)	___								
7 Vis Matching	___ (30)	___								
8 Ants-Syns	___ (49)	___								
10 Nums Reversed	___ (21)	___								
Written Lang Apt Cluster Score			☐	___ TABLE G	___ to ___ TABLE G	___ TABLE G	− ☐ TABLE I OR J	= ☐ (+ OR −)	___ TABLE P OR W	___ to ___ TABLE P OR W
3 Memory for Sents	___ (22)	___								
6 Quant Concepts	___ (46)	___								
8 Ants-Syns	___ (49)	___								
12 Analogies	___ (35)	___								
Knowledge Apt Cluster Score			☐	___ TABLE H	___ to ___ TABLE H	___ TABLE H	− ☐ TABLE I OR J	= ☐ (+ OR −)	___ TABLE Q OR X	___ to ___ TABLE Q OR X

Figure 9.1 Summary of scores: Woodcock-Johnson Psychoeducational Battery (Parts I and II). (From *Woodcock-Johnson Psychoeducational Battery* by R. W. Woodcock, 1977, Allen, TX: DLM/Teaching Resources. Copyright © 1977 DLM/Teaching Resources, Allen, TX 75002. Reprinted by permission.)

PART II

SUMMARY OF SCORES:

Do these test results provide a fair representation of the subject's present functioning? ☐Yes ☐No

If not, what is the reason for questioning the results? ____________

Subtest / CLUSTER	Raw Score	Part Score from Table A	CLUSTER SCORE	Grade Score	INSTRUCTIONAL RANGE Easy	Difficult	Age Score	AVERAGE CLUSTER SCORE ☐ Grade ☐ Age	CLUSTER DIFFERENCE SCORE	Percentile Rank at ☐ Grade ☐ Age	Percentile Rank Range	RPI at ☐ Grade ☐ Age	Functioning Level
ACHIEVEMENT CLUSTERS													
13. L-W Ident	___ (54)	___											
14. Word Attack	___ (26)	___											
15. Pass Comp	___ (26)	___	a					b	a − b = c				
Reading Cluster Score			☐	___ TABLE B	___ to	___ TABLE B	___ TABLE B	− ☐ TABLE G OR H	= ☐ (+ OR −)	___ TABLE I OR P	___ to ___ TABLE I OR P	___ /90 TABLE W	___ TABLE W
16. Calculation	___ (42)	___											
17. Appl Probs	___ (49)	___											
Mathematics Cluster Score			☐	___ TABLE C	___ to	___ TABLE C	___ TABLE C	− ☐ TABLE G OR H	= ☐ (+ OR −)	___ TABLE J OR Q	___ to ___ TABLE J OR Q	___ /90 TABLE W	___ TABLE W
18. Dictation	___ (40)	___											
19. Proofing	___ (29)	___											
Written Lang Cluster Score			☐	___ TABLE D	___ to	___ TABLE D	___ TABLE D	− ☐ TABLE G OR H	= ☐ (+ OR −)	___ TABLE K OR R	___ to ___ TABLE K OR R	___ /90 TABLE W	___ TABLE W
20. Science	___ (39)	___											
21. Soc Studies	___ (37)	___											
22. Humanities	___ (36)	___											
Knowledge Cluster Score			☐	___ TABLE E	___ to	___ TABLE E	___ TABLE E	− ☐ TABLE G OR H	= ☐ (+ OR −)	___ TABLE L OR S	___ to ___ TABLE L OR S	___ /90 TABLE W	___ TABLE W
Sum of the four Achievement Cluster Scores			___	*(To be plotted on the Subtest Profile)*									
13. L-W Ident	___ (54)	___											
17. Appl Probs	___ (49)	___											
18. Dictation	___ (40)	___											
Skills Cluster Score (Preschool)			☐	___ TABLE F	___ to	___ TABLE F	___ TABLE F	− ☐ TABLE G OR H	= ☐ (+ OR −)	___ TABLE M OR T	___ to ___ TABLE M OR T	___ /90 TABLE W	___ TABLE W
INTEREST LEVEL CLUSTERS													
23. Reading Interest	___ (25)	___											
24. Math Interest	___ (25)	___											
25. Wr Lang Interest	___ (25)	___											
Schol Interest Cluster Score			☐	....				− ☐ TABLE G OR H	= ☐ (+ TO −)	___ TABLE N OR U	___ to ___ TABLE N OR U		
26. Physical Interest	___ (35)	___											
27. Social Interest	___ (35)	___											
NonSchol Int Cluster Score			☐	....				− ☐ TABLE G OR H	= ☐ (+ TO −)	___ TABLE O OR V	___ to ___ TABLE O OR V		
Sum of the two Interest Cluster Scores			___	*(To be plotted on the Subtest Profile)*									

RESULTS FROM RELATED TESTS:

Test	*Date of Testing*	*Results*
___	___	___
___	___	___
___	___	___

RECOMMENDATIONS FOR FURTHER TESTING AND/OR PROGRAM PLANNING:

Figure 9.1, *continued*

and positive feature. Caution must be used when comparing WJPEB scores with other cognitive measures such as the WISC-R due to the tendency for the WJPEB to yield lower scores (Cummings & Moscato, 1984).

Summary

Earlier in the chapter we referred to certain issues involved in minimal competency testing. This area will continue to be an important one as schools and states attempt to develop evaluation programs to insure that students have learned and teachers are teaching. Achievement batteries will most certainly play a significant role in such evaluations, although many questions about their use have been raised. Many have even questioned whether *any* tests can measure competence. Debates will continue, but in the interim many states have already mandated that teachers and students must be tested to determine minimal competence.

Unfortunately, in the haste to develop programs to test minimal competence, many poor tests and testing practices have been used. One of the most persistent problems is how to establish the cutoff scores that determine who passes and who fails the test (Livingston & Zieky, 1982). In the past, three basic approaches have been used (Wise, 1985). The first is to adopt cutoff scores used at other locations for the same test. The second is to collect preliminary scores for a limited period and then to use them to establish a cutoff. The third approach is to form a panel of "experts" in the area you are evaluating (for example, teacher education) and have them systematically assess the test items to determine cutoff scores.

The first approach is clearly the simplest. However, this will not work if a test has been developed for local use, if others have not used the test, or if different cutoffs have been used in different places. Finally, this approach may cause legal problems if you cannot justify the score you have established. Imagine trying to justify your decision not to let students graduate from high school because their scores fell below a cutoff that was established in another state or part of the country!

In the second approach, local data could be used to establish the cutoff scores, although there remains the problem of establishing the number of individuals who should pass and fail. For example, it may be decided that the lowest 20 percent of the examinees will fail a given test. But what happens if the quality of the people passing and failing the test changes from year to year? In the first year you may be content that the lowest 20 percent failed, but in subsequent years you may feel that the 20 percent cutoff is discriminating against people who are truly competent or letting incompetent people slip through. In either case, how do you know what level of performance signifies competence?

In the third approach, the use of a panel of experts has the advantage of requiring panel members to directly judge the minimal level of basic skills required to pass certain test items. There is, however, no guarantee that the experts will arrive at an acceptable or useful cutoff.

The development of basic competency tests and the establishment of cutoff scores are thus not easy tasks. Can you think of other ways that cutoff scores might be determined? Although the answers are not simple, we can be assured that with the push for excellence in education, minimal competency tests will be with us for the foreseeable future. Achievement batteries have proved to be useful tools in the assessment of behavior, although they are not without the potential for abuse. In the future we will undoubtedly discover improved techniques for developing such tests and expand the number of uses for them.

Chapter 10

Reading

Learning Objectives

1. Describe the process of reading and identify major developmental milestones in the acquisition of reading skills.
2. Identify and discuss individual and environmental factors that influence reading performance.
3. Identify and select methods to assess decoding and comprehension skills.
4. Identify the types of reading errors a child could make.
5. Describe the salient features of an IRI and note the benefits of using IRIs to assess reading.

Notbeingabletoreadisafrustratingexperience. Being able to read but not understanding what you have read is also frustrating. The development of reading skills is a complex process that typically evolves over many years and is influenced by personal and environmental factors. Virtually everyone experiences some problems in learning to read and in learning from reading, and at least 25 percent of elementary school children experience moderate to severe difficulties that result in below grade-level performances (Gibson & Levin, 1975). In this chapter, we examine briefly the normal development of reading skills, identify typical reading problems, and then focus on the assessment of such problems.

What Is Reading?

Asking "What is reading?" may seem simplistic, but numerous definitions of reading have been proposed by experts (see, e.g., Chall, 1967; Gibson & Levin, 1975). For example: Reading is recognizing letters that make words; reading is sounding out a sequence of sounds to make words; reading is identifying words and understanding what the author is trying to say (Guerin & Maier, 1983). For our purposes, *reading is defined as a self-directed process of extracting information from written or printed symbols*. This definition is narrower than many and is influenced by the writings of Harris (1970) and Gibson and Levin (1975).

The Development of Reading

Learning to read occurs in three general stages labeled prereading, decoding, and comprehension. Each of these stages is characterized by the acquisition of several subskills that collectively contribute to efficient reading.

Prereading stage. Broadly defined, the prereading stage occurs between birth and the time a child can recognize and decode words. In normal children, the latter usually begins around five or six years of age. Sensory skills such as hand-eye coordination and sound discrimination are considered prerequisites to reading. A narrower and more practical approach to identifying prereading skills has been advocated by Venesky (1976), who suggested that the following five actions are involved in decoding:

1. attending to letter order
2. attending to letter orientation
3. attending to word detail
4. matching sounds
5. blending sounds

Once children master these skills, they should be able to recognize words and thus move developmentally into the decoding stage.

Decoding stage. This stage or period of reading development usually is the focus of reading instruction during the first three or four years of school. Often referred to as the "learning to read" stage, it primarily involves the refinement of sound blending skills and the acquisition of rules concerning word structure such as silent letter conventions, vowel conventions, and syllabification.

Current approaches to teaching decoding skills stress a combination of phonics and language experience methods. Phonics emphasizes letter-sound relationships, and the language experience approach emphasizes the relationship of decoding words to a child's general language experiences. Basal reading materials typically combine these two approaches to the task of teaching read-

Table 10.1 Curriculum Sequence Chart for a Typical Basal Reading Series

Grade	Skills acquired
Kindergarten	Identify sounds and pictures Express ideas in complete verbal sentences Understand meaning of words such as *above* and *far* Understand concepts of size, small, etc. Recognize and identify colors Organize objects into groups Match forms Understands beginning concepts of number
Grade 1	Recognize letters of alphabet; can write and give sound Auditory and visual perception and discrimination of initial and final consonants Observe left to right progression Recall what has been read Aware of medial consonants, consonant blends, digraphs Recognize long sound of vowels; root words; plural forms; verb endings *-s*, *-ed*, *-d*, *-ing*; opposites; pronouns *he*, *she* Understand concept of synonyms, homonyms, antonyms Understand simple compound words Copy simple sentences, fill-ins
Grade 2	Comprehension and analysis of what has been read Identify vowel digraphs Understand variant sounds of *y* Identify medial vowels Identify diphthongs Understand influence of *r* on preceding vowel Identify three-letter blends Understand use of suffix *-er* Understand verb endings (for example, *stop*, *stopped*)
Grade 3	Recognize multiple sounds of long *a* as in *ei*, *ay*, *ey* Understand silent *e* in *-le* endings Understand use of suffix *-est* Know how to change *y* to *i* before adding *er*, *est* Understand comparative and superlative forms of adjectives Understand possessive form using *s* Use contractions Identify syllabic breaks
Grade 4	Recognize main and subordinate parts Recognize unknown words using configuration and other word attack skills Identify various sounds of *ch* Recognize various phonetic values of *gh* Identify rounded *o* sound formed by *au*, *aw*, *al* Use and interpret diacritical markings Discriminate among multiple meaning of words

Table 10.1, *continued*

Grade	Skills acquired
Grade 5	Read critically to evaluate Identify diagraphs *gn, mb, bt* Recognize that *augh* and *ough* may have round *o* sound Recognize and pronounce muted vowels in *el, al, le* Recognize secondary and primary accents Use of apostrophe Understand suffixes *-al, -hand, -ship, -ist, -ling, -an, -ian, -dom, -ern* Understand use of figures of speech: metaphor, simile Ability to paraphrase main idea Know ways paragraphs are developed Outline using two or three main heads and subheadings Use graphic material
Grade 6	Develop ability for critical analysis Recognize and use Latin, Greek roots, such as *photo, tele, graph, geo, auto* Develop generalization that some suffixes can change part of speech, such as *-ure* changing an adjective to noun (*moist-moisture*) Understand meaning and pronunciation of homographs Develop awarenes of shifting accents

From *Informal Assessment in Education* (pp. 245–246), by Gilbert R. Guerin and Arlee S. Maier, 1983, Palo Alto, CA: Mayfield Publishing Company. Copyright © 1983 Mayfield Publishing Company. Reprinted by permission.

ing. Table 10.1 illustrates abbreviated instructional objectives by grade level for a typical basal reading series.

Comprehension stage. The ultimate goal of reading is comprehension, or extracting meaning from what is read. Thus, this last, broad stage of reading development is often referred to as the "learning from reading" stage. The reading skills and activities in this stage can be classified as literal or direct comprehension and inferential or indirect comprehension. Literal comprehension involves remembering written information. Inferential comprehension is much more complex and requires a reader to piece together information and go beyond what is written to make it meaningful. Both literal and inferential comprehension require good attention skills, memory ability, and some prior knowledge of a topic.

A Model of Reading

Understanding the reading process is essential to conducting meaningful assessments of children with reading problems. Just and Carpenter (1980), as well as several others (e.g., Carnine & Silbert, 1979; LaBerge & Samuels,

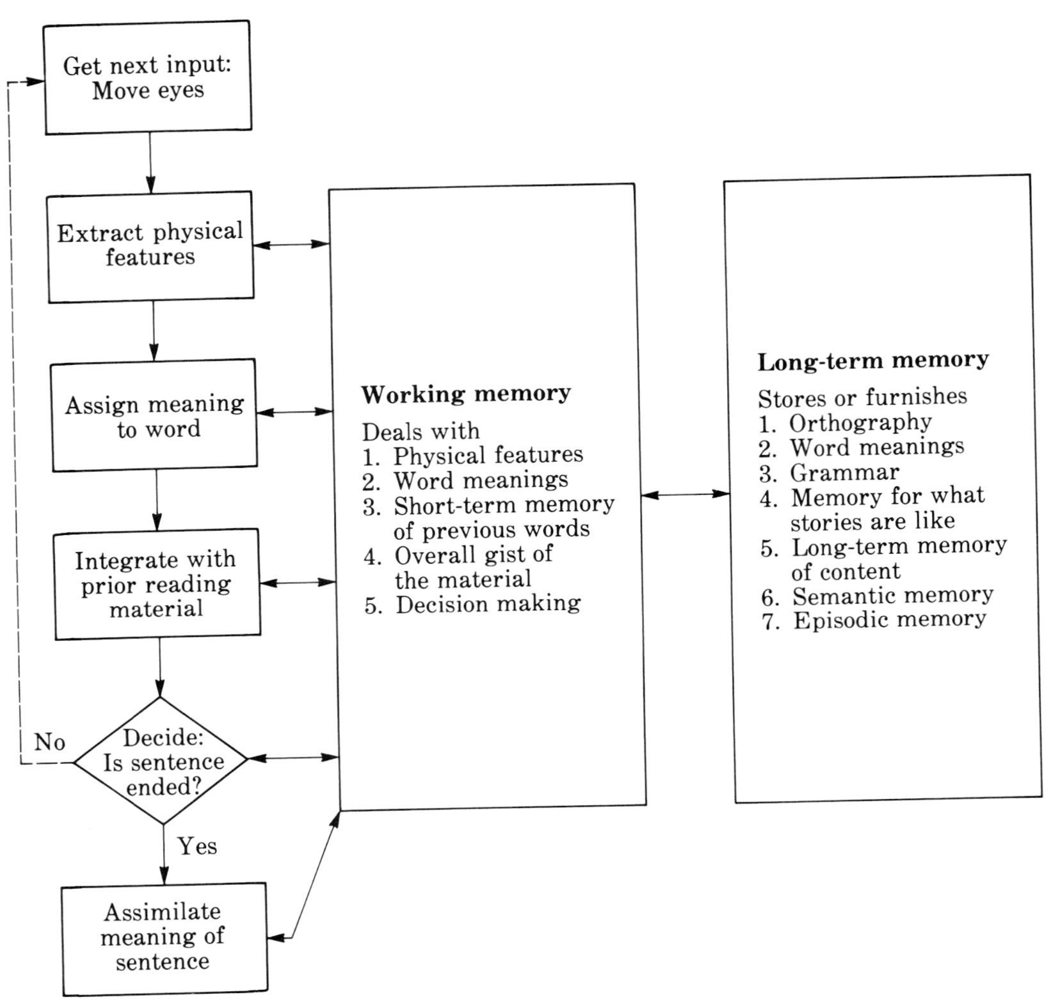

Figure 10.1 A cognitive model of the reading process. (From "A Theory of Reading: From Eye Fixations to Comprehension," by M. Just and P. Carpenter, 1980, *Psychological Review*, *87*, pp. 329–354. Copyright 1980 by the American Psychological Association. Adapted by permission of the authors.)

1974), have integrated information ranging from eye fixations to comprehension into a cognitive model of the reading process (see Figure 10.1). The Just and Carpenter model characterizes reading as a dynamic, interactive process whereby written stimuli are processed at several levels to extract meaning. As readers gain competence, most decoding skills become automatic, thus allowing for attention and memory to focus on comprehension.

Factors That Influence the Development of Reading

The research on reading indicates that numerous factors influence the development of reading. In this section, we identify and briefly review the effect of major noninstructional and instructional factors, both of which should be considered in any assessment of a reading problem.

Noninstructional factors. Noninstructional factors are those that cannot be controlled for by a teacher, including characteristics of the learner such as sex or auditory ability. A sex difference has historically been identified in reading achievement, with girls outperforming boys (Dwyer, 1973). Such assertions, however, are based on published reports at least twenty years old. Fry and Lagomarsino (1982), however, believe that the sex difference in reading achievement in regular classrooms is rather meager and is disappearing. More boys than girls may be labeled "reading disabled," but sex will not account for much of the difference in end of first-grade or third-grade reading achievement.

The relation between reading achievement and auditory acuity, however, is fairly strong. Deaf children rarely learn to read well (Gibson & Levin, 1975). Correctly identifying letters by name involves visual discrimination, and many researchers have found that a child's ability to recognize and name letters before or during kindergarten is a very good predictor of first-grade and primary reading achievement (see, e.g., deHirsch, Jansky, & Langford, 1966). On the other hand, intelligence, as typically measured, is a rather weak predictor of progress in learning to read.

Instructional factors. Time on task, classroom management, and size of reading group are all instructional factors that influence learning to read. Wyne and Stuck (1979) worked with second- and third-grade students who were reading below grade level. After an eight-week program to increase task-oriented behavior during reading, they found that reading achievement was positively influenced by the amount of time a student spent actively learning to read. Anderson, Evertson, and Brophy (1979) found that a teacher who can structure, maintain, and monitor classroom activities will facilitate higher reading performances. Good (1979) reported that small group instruction, compared to individualized programs, appears to yield higher reading achievement for first- and second-grade students.

Typical Reading Problems

Reading problems are usually manifested in children in three ways: (a) ineffective decoding or word attack strategies, (b) inconsistent comprehension, and (c) a negative attitude toward reading. Clearly, problems in any of these areas

FOCUS ON PRACTICE
Sight-Word Vocabulary

The English language is made up of thousands of words, yet, quite logically, beginning readers generally are exposed to a subset of 300 to 400 high-frequency words. Such a corpus of words is often referred to as a sight-word vocabulary. Regardless of the reading series and instructional approach used to teach reading, almost all young readers are exposed to words such as *to*, *we*, *up*, *big*, *dog*, and *girl*. Several published lists of high-frequency words from the first, second, and third grades exist, such as the Dolch Basic Sight Vocabulary List, the Brigance Basic Sight Vocabulary, and the Durrell Word Frequency List. Below are 50 words extracted from these lists:

to	that	like	father	run
the	are	did	come	name
in	up	her	from	over
and	they	baby	here	day
at	me	but	just	ride
we	go	with	if	where
see	mother	will	or	look
on	was	dog	make	home
not	box	what	blue	school
said	had	no	green	pets

For most children, the identification of these words requires practice and illustrative examples. By third grade these words should be read rapidly with very few errors. You might informally assess several young children to determine the development of their sight-word vocabulary.

will likely affect the others. Therefore, early and ongoing evaluation of reading progress is desirable.

Word attack problems often are evidenced by mispronunciations of letter sounds, omissions of syllables, and substitutions of sounds. Some of the most pervasive problems are the result of the failure to learn the long and short vowel sounds and the rules of word construction that provide cues to syllabification. In addition, efficient word attack ability requires a large sight-word vocabularly (e.g., *the*, *on*, *at*, *to*, *in*, *out*, *go*) and knowledge of prefixes (e.g., *pre-*, *post-*, *a-*, *re-*) and suffixes (e.g., *-ing*, *-ed*, *-ly*, *-ish*, *-ful*).

Difficulties with comprehension directly follow from flawed word attack skills. However, even when one can accurately read every word in a sentence, comprehension is not assured. Reading rate, memory, background knowledge, and perspective are all critical influences on reading comprehension. For young readers, among whom literal comprehension is usually stressed, reading rate and memory are probably the most salient. However, as readers mature, the importance of background knowledge and perspective increases. For example, read the following paragraph:

> Rocky slowly got up from the mat, planning his escape. He hesitated a moment and thought. Things were not going well. What bothered him most was being held, especially since the charge against him had been weak. He considered his present situation. The lock that held him was strong but he thought he could break it. He knew, however, that his timing would have to be perfect. Rocky was aware that it was because of his early roughness that he had been penalized so severely — much too severely from his point of view. The situation was becoming frustrating; the pressure had been grinding on him far too long. He was being ridden unmercifully. Rocky was getting angry now. He felt he was ready to make his move. He knew his success or failure would depend on what he did in the next few seconds. (Anderson, Reynolds, Schallert, & Goetz, 1977, p. 372)

Depending on your background and experience, you probably understood this passage to be about either a convict planning his escape or a wrestler plotting his moves to break a tough hold. A reader's background, which is largely measured through language proficiency and fund of words, thus plays an important role in comprehension. Obtaining such basic information is fundamental to administering and interpreting reading tests. Thus, if you believe you have a good command of this basic knowledge, you are ready to begin an examination of reading tests.

Reading Tests

Over 160 published reading tests were in circulation as of early 1982 (Reynolds & Elliott, 1983). Because it would be impossible to discuss each of these tests here, we have selected ten to examine in detail either because of their popularity or because they represented a particular type of test (such as group administered/individually administered, norm-referenced/criterion-referenced, and standardized/informal). We first document the various reading skills each test purports to measure and then discuss their technical adequacy.

Reading Skills and Selected Reading Tests

Carnine and Silbert (1979) developed a three-part model of reading instruction that is very useful for examining the content of reading tests. Specifically, they hypothesized that the important elements of reading could be described as units, skills, and knowledge base. Units form a hierarchy beginning with single words and continuing to entire passages. Skills begin with sounding out letters and increase in complexity to include inferential comprehension and evaluative

Table 10.2 Reading Skills Sampled by Selected Reading Tests

	Decoding																Comprehension																		
	Units						*Skills*							*Knowledge*			*Units*					*Skills*							*Knowledge*				
Test	*Letter sounds*	*Letters*	*Letter combination*	*Syllables*	*Words*	*Phrases*	*Sounding out*	*Sight reading*	*Breakdown of large words*	*Accuracy*	*Fluency*	*Oral reading*	*Silent reading*	*Oral language*	*Word familiarity*	*Syntax*	*Words*	*Phrases*	*Sentences*	*Paragraphs*	*Passages*	*Literal*	*Inferential*	*Sequencing*	*Summarization*	*Simplification*	*Critical reading*	*Study skills*	*Syntax*	*Semantics*	*Facts*	*Logic*	*Schema*
California Achievement Tests (CTB/McGraw-Hill, 1977)	×	×	×	×	×	×	×	×	×				×	×	×		×	×	×	×	×	×	×				×			×		×	
Metropolitan Achievement Tests (Farr, Prescott, Balow, & Hogan, 1978)																																	
Surveys	×	×	×		×	×	×	×					×	×	×		×	×	×	×	×	×	×		×					×		×	
Instructional	×	×	×	×	×	×	×	×	×					×	×	×	×	×	×	×	×	×	×		×	×		×		×		×	
Peabody Individual Achievement Tests (Dunn & Markwardt, 1970)		×			×			×		×		×	×	×	×		×	×	×			×								×			
Gates-McKillop-Horowitz Reading Diagnostic Tests (Gates & McKillop, 1962)	×	×	×	×	×	×	×	×	×	×	×	×		×	×	×																	
Diagnostic Reading Scales (Spache, 1972)	×	×	×	×	×	×	×	×		×	×	×	×	×	×	×	×	×	×	×	×	×	×							×			
Nelson-Denny Reading Test (Brown, Bennett, & Hanna, 1981)					×	×					×	×	×	×	×	×	×	×	×	×	×	×	×						×	×	×	×	
TERA: Test of Early Reading Ability (Reid, Hvesko, & Hammill, 1981)		×																															
Degrees of Reading Power (The College Board, 1981)																	×	×	×	×	×	×											
Woodcock Reading Mastery Tests (Woodcock, 1973)		×			×	×		×					×	×	×	×	×	×	×	×	×	×		×					×	×			
Gates-MacGinite Reading Tests (MacGinite, 1978)			×	×	×	×		×					×	×	×		×	×	×	×	×	×	×							×	×	×	

actions. The hierarchy for knowledge base begins with simple vocabulary and increases to sophisticated vocabulary. This three-part model can be used to describe and compare the content of the ten reading tests selected (see Table 10.2). Table 10.2 indicates that no single test *samples* all reading behaviors. For example, the California Achievement Tests (CTB/McGraw-Hill, 1979) and the Metropolitan Achievement Tests (Farr, Prescott, Balow, & Hogan, 1978) are both widely used group tests that cannot assess oral reading but rather sample a broad range of decoding and comprehension behaviors. Tests such as the Gates-McKillop-Horowitz Reading Diagnostic Tests (Gates, McKillop & Horowitz, 1981) and the Nelson-Denny Reading Test (Brown, Bennett & Hanna, 1981), which were developed for two very different age groups, are focused on decoding and comprehension, respectively.

The Technical Adequacy of Reading Tests

As emphasized in Chapter 5, reliability, validity, and norms are important indicators of the quality and utility of a test. However, Table 10.3 reveals that not one of our ten selected standardized reading tests provides data on all seven of the basic evaluative indexes. This should cause you to choose any reading test with caution, given that these ten are some of the best available. In all cases, users must consult a test's technical manual for details about its psychometric characteristics.

In the remainder of this section, we examine the content and outcomes of two tests, the Test of Early Reading and the Woodcock Reading Mastery Tests, which were selected because of their frequent use with young children with reading problems.

TERA: Test of Early Reading Ability

The TERA or the Test of Early Reading Ability is an individually administered test for assessing preschool children's prereading and beginning reading abilities. Items were constructed to assess children's efforts at (a) finding meaning in print, (b) learning the alphabet and its use, and (c) discovering conventions of reading and writing English. The TERA is most appropriate for English-speaking children who are between 4-0 and 7-11 years of age and can follow simple directions. Its authors recommend its use in identifying children who are significantly behind age peers in the development of basic reading skills, in research, and in instructional planning. Based on our examination of the TERA, use for instructional planning is questionable.

The TERA was standardized on performances of 1,184 children from eleven states and one Canadian province. This sample was reported to be representative of the United States population in 1979.

Content. The TERA is a 50-item test developed according to a three-factor conceptual model comprised of Meaning, Alphabet Knowledge, and Conven-

Table 10.3 Reliability, Validity, and Norms for Selected Reading Tests

	Reliability				Criterion validity	Norms	
Test*	*Test-retest*	*Parallel form*	*Internal consistency*	*Standard error of measurement*		*Sample*	*Representativeness*
California Achievement Tests	None	.54–.90	.76–.97	Yes		200,000: grades K–12; national representation	Excellent
Metropolitan Achievement Tests							
Survey	N/A	N/A	.85–.96	Yes	.55–.82	550,000: grades K–12; national representation	Excellent
Instructional	N/A	N/A	.88–.95	Yes	N/A		Excellent
Peabody Individual Achievement Tests	.61–.94	None	None	Yes	None	2,889: grades K–12; national representation	Adequate
Gates-McKillop-Horowitz Reading Diagnostic Tests	.94	None	None	No	.68–.96	600: grades 1–6	Inadequate
Diagnostic Reading Scales	.30–.96	None	.87–.96	Yes	.13–.77		
Nelson-Denny Reading Tests	None	.69–.92	None	Yes	None	25,000: grades 9–16	Excellent
Test of Early Reading Ability	.82–.94	None	.87–.96	Yes	.52–.66	1,184: ages 3–7; national representation	Excellent
Degrees of Reading Power	None	.86–.91	None	Yes	.70–.84	34,000: grades 4–12; national represention	Excellent
Woodcock Reading Mastery Tests	None	.16–.94	.02–.99	Yes	None	1,000: grades K–7	Adequate
Gates-MacGinitie Reading Tests	.77–.89	.77–.94	.88–.94	No	.88–.91	6,500: grades 1–12; national representation	Adequate

*For sources of tests see Table 10.2.

Note: "None" means the information is relevant and desired but not provided, whereas "N/A" means the information is not applicable.

tions of Written Language. Items measuring ability to construct meaning from print were of three types: (a) awareness of print in an environmental context, (b) knowledge of relations among vocabulary items, and (c) comprehension or awareness of print in connected discourse. To assess awareness of print in an environmental context, a child is asked to identify common signs, logos, or small words. To measure knowledge of relational vocabulary items, a child is required to select two words that relate to a stimulus word. To assess awareness of print in discourse, a child is told to retell a well-formed story or to supply missing words in a sentence during reading (cloze procedure). Items on Alphabet Knowledge include naming letters, reading short words, and proofreading. To assess the Conventions of Written Language factor, items tap book handling skills and responses to print conventions such as punctuation, left-right orientation, and spatial presentation of a story on a page. Our examination of item difficulties and discriminating power indicates that the TERA is most appropriate for five and six year olds.

Reliability and validity. The authors of the TERA provide basic information on its internal consistency and test-retest reliabilities. As noted in Table 10.3, the internal consistency reliabilities range from .87 to .96, depending on the age of the individuals. Such reliabilities are good and indicate consistent item content. The stability of the TERA over approximately two weeks was tested with a restricted subsample (N = 177, from the Dallas area only) of children varying in age. The test-retest reliability for this entire subsample was .97, although for some age levels within the small subsample the reliabilities were in the .82 to .85 range. Overall, the TERA has demonstrated very good stability, given that it is designed for use with young children.

The primary evidence for the validity of the TERA consists of correlational data with other reading tests and with tests of intelligence, language, and school readiness. Specifically, the authors reported correlations between TERA total scores and the Reading subtest of the Metropolitan Achievement Tests of .66 and the Test of Reading Comprehension of .52. These correlations were again based on a limited sample of children and are lower than desirable for the criterion validity of a diagnostic test. Evidence for the construct validity was sought by correlating TERA total scores with several tests, including the Slosson Intelligence Test (r = .66), the Test of Language Development (r = .62), and the Metropolitan Achievement Tests (Listening subtest) (r = .79). Although the authors have provided more information than most, the data are not particularly compelling because of the noticeable omission of validity evidence with other *reading* measures. From the present correlational data it seems that the TERA has a significant verbal ability emphasis. This, however, is only part of the development of early reading skills, as Venesky noted (1976). A final bit of validity evidence concerning group differentiation is discussed in the manual, although it cannot be seriously considered (and may even be misleading) since both the research methods and sample of children were limited.

Administration and scoring. According to the test manual, the TERA can be administered by anyone with basic competencies in the administration of individualized tests after the manual has been thoroughly reviewed. The TERA requires approximately twenty minutes to administer. The manual provides a specific procedural script for each item, but allows the examiner to improvise directions. Scoring the responses is a fairly objective task. Each of the 50 items is worth 1 point, and scoring criteria accompany the administrative scripts for each item. The basal point is where a child passes five consecutive items, and a ceiling is reached when five consecutive items are missed.

A child's performance on the TERA is reported in terms of three kinds of normative scores: the Reading Quotient (RQ), percentile, and Reading Age (RA). The RQ is a standard deviation score (with a mean of 100 and a standard deviation of 15) based on the cumulative frequency distributions of the raw scores of the standardization population. The Percentile is simply a conversion of raw scores with respect to the individual performances of the standardization sample. Finally, the RA was developed by plotting raw scores against ages in months. Because this score suffers from several statistical and interpretative problems, only the RQ and Percentile should be used.

Woodcock Reading Mastery Tests

The Woodcock Reading Mastery Tests (Woodcock, 1973) are a battery of five individually administered reading tests that are very useful for diagnostic assessment of basic reading problems in students in kindergarten through twelfth grade. Two alternate forms of the battery are available (Form A and Form B). As indicated in Table 10.3, the test manual provides most data needed to determine psychometric characteristics, and the test is well packaged and efficient to use.

Content. The items on the Woodcock were derived from a pool of 2,400 items that was reduced to 400 through the Rasch-Wright calibration procedure; small subsets of these items were administered to over 36,000 children from ninety-two schools in ten states and resulted in the two forms of the test, each with five subtests or scales that measure basic decoding and comprehension skills: Letter Identification (45 items), Word Attack (50 items), Word Identification (150 items), Word Comprehension (70 items), and Passage Comprehension (85 items).

Items representative of each subtest and the grades at which 50 percent and 90 percent mastery are expected are displayed in Table 10.4. The items on the Letter Identification subtest are single upper- and lower-case letters presented in various type styles, including the Roman, serif, cursive, and specialty faces. The letter items are arranged in order of difficulty, and subjects are required to simply name each letter. By fourth grade, most subjects receive a perfect score on Letter Identification. Items on the Word Identification subtest are single words ranging in difficulty from beginning school to twelfth-grade levels. Children are only required to name the word; no assumption is

Table 10.4 Representative Items of the Woodcock Reading Mastery Tests

Letter Identification Subtest		
Difficulty		Sample task
Grade scale		
50% mastery	90% mastery	
1.0^{28}	1.0	o
1.0^{31}	1.0	X
1.0^{41}	1.1	B
1.0^{49}	1.1	S
1.0	1.2	c
1.0	1.2	W
1.0	1.2	k
1.0	1.3	e
1.1	1.3	*f*
1.1	1.4	y
1.1	1.5	z
1.2	1.6	Q
1.2	1.6	j
1.3	1.7	*Q*
1.4	1.8	*t*
1.4	1.9	*n*

Word Identification Subtest		
Difficulty		Sample task
Grade scale		
50% mastery	90% mastery	
1.1	1.3	is
1.1	1.3	go
1.3	1.5	red
1.3	1.5	ball
1.3	1.5	look
1.4	1.6	dog
1.4	1.6	big
1.4	1.6	down
1.5	1.6	do
1.5	1.7	box
1.5	1.7	blue
1.5	1.7	black
1.6	1.8	two

Word Attack Subtest		
Difficulty		Sample task
Grade scale		
50% mastery	90% mastery	
1.7	2.6	dee
1.9	3.3	app
2.0	3.5	tat
2.1	3.9	tay
2.3	4.4	und
2.6	4.9	pied
2.8	5.6	fy
3.1	6.4	plad
3.4	7.5	keeting

(continued)

Table 10.4, *continued*

Word Comprehension Subtest		
Difficulty		Sample task
Grade scale		
50% mastery	90% mastery	
1.4	1.8	one—two three—(four)
1.5	1.9	he—she boy—(girl)
1.6	2.2	big—little up—(down)
1.7	2.4	father—mother brother—(sister)
1.8	2.6	walk—run slow—(fast)
1.9	2.9	job—work game—(play)
2.0	3.2	milk—drink apple—(eat)
2.2	3.6	up—down high—(low)
2.4	4.1	bed—sleep chair—(sit)
2.6	4.6	aunt—sister uncle—(brother)
2.8	5.3	day—light night—(dark)
3.1	6.3	duck—feathers dog—(fur)
3.4	7.1	table—wood dress—(cloth)
3.8	8.4	car—airplane drive—(fly)

Passage Comprehension Subtest		
Difficulty		Sample task
Grade scale		
50% mastery	90% mastery	
1.3	1.6	I have a ________. (puppy)
1.4	1.9	The boy has a cap on his ________. (head)
4.9	8.7	Remember that you are practicing drawing now, not making something to hang on the wall. Use cheap but strong paper that will not tear or crumble ________ you work. (as)
5.3	9.5	A tornado is a violent whirlwind that occurs frequently in the midwestern United States. As it spins, it sucks up dust and whatever happens to be in its ________ and moves over the land as a menacing funnel-shaped cloud. (path)

From *Woodcock Reading Mastery Tests (Technical Manual)* (pp. 117–121) by Richard W. Woodcock, 1973, Circle Pines, MN: American Guidance Service. Copyright 1973 by AGS. Reprinted by permission.

made about comprehension of its meaning. The Word Attack subtest measures a subject's ability to apply phonic and structural analysis skills. The use of nonsense words controls for prior exposure and the use of a whole-word approach to decoding. The nonsense words are not simply a random assortment of letters but rather have been constructed according to common English consonant and vowel combinations. This is a fun subtest for many children, for they seem to enjoy the sound of the "odd," new words. The Word Comprehension subtest is set up in analogy format. Each analogy consists of a double pair of words. The subject's task is to read silently the first pair, then read the first word of the second pair, and finally supply a word that appropriately completes the analogy (e.g., boy–girl, man–__?__). This task requires knowledge of word meanings as well as interrelationships. A subject could actually read and correctly define each of the three words in an item but still not provide a correct analogy. Thus, this is a very rigorous method for assessing word comprehension. The final subtest, Passage Comprehension, requires a student to read silently a short passage (one to two sentences) that has an important word missing and then suggest a word that correctly completes the passage. The easier items are also accompanied by a picture that facilitates understanding. This technique for assessing comprehension is referred to as a "modified cloze procedure" (Bormuth, 1969). For successful completion, a subject draws upon an array of word attack and comprehension skills. Consequently, Passage Comprehension can be considered an omnibus test of reading skills.

Reliability and validity. The overall reliability and validity of the Woodcock Reading Mastery Tests are summarized in Table 10.3, although its author also provided extensive details on each of the five subtests. Both split-half and test-retest reliability data are provided in the manual for samples of second and seventh graders. Most split-half reliabilities for these two samples were high (average $> .90$) and highly consistent for all subtests except Letter Identification, which has reliabilities of .79 (second grade) and .02 (seventh grade). The .02 for seventh grade is probably due to the fact that most fourth graders get a perfect or near perfect score on Letter Identification, resulting in a ceiling effect or increasing restriction of range above 4th grade.

A similar pattern of reliabilities was observed for a one-week test-retest using alternate forms of the Woodcock. Test-retest reliabilities for second and seventh graders were, respectively, .84 and .16 on Letter Identification, .90 and .85 on Word Attack, .94 and .93 on Word Identification, .90 and .68 on Word Comprehension, and .88 and .78 on Passage Comprehension.

The data to support the validity of the Woodcock Reading Mastery Tests are extensive. In addition to typical documentation that the content is reflective of actual reading tasks (content validity) there is evidence of convergent-discriminate and predictive validity. However, the data on convergent-discriminate validity is questionable, because alternate forms of the same test were used, which were assumed to reflect different methods. But this cannot be correct, for they cannot be both truly alternate forms and different methods. The predictive validity data are much more compelling and suggest that differential predictions of reading performance can be made from a score on the Woodcock Reading Mastery Tests.

Administration. Administration of the Woodcock, according to its author, does not require special training but simply familiarity with the materials. Although this may be technically true, this test can provide a person well versed in reading instruction rich data beyond merely the number of correct answers. For example, the strategies a child uses to decode the nonsense words on Word Attack cannot be portrayed quantitatively, but an expert examiner can derive much added information during the actual testing.

The test requires approximately thirty-five minutes to administer. It is nicely organized. The stimulus materials and examiner's instructions are arranged in an easel-like kit that can be positioned so a subject can see only the stimulus items while the examiner can see both the instructions and correct answers on one side and the stimulus items on the other.

The items on the test range in difficulty from first through twelfth grades. Given that items have been standardized with a large, developmentally diverse sample, they can be arranged from easiest to hardest with high confidence. Such an arrangement results in a power test and allows one to establish both basal and ceiling levels. By using Starting Point guidelines for each grade, the examiner administers the test items, page by page, until the subject has failed five consecutive items, thus establishing a ceiling. If during the testing the subject does not give five consecutive correct responses (a basal), the examiner returns to the starting point and tests downward until the subject achieves a basal.

Scoring and interpretation. Each item on the Woodcock is worth 1 raw score point. Therefore, during administration of the test, items are scored either 0 or 1 (that is, wrong or right). Items not given but preceding a basal are scored as correct; items above a ceiling are not scored. Thus, a total raw score is derived for each of the five subtests. The calculation of these raw scores is just the first step in interpreting a subject's performance on the Woodcock, which also reports grade scores, percentile ranks, and mastery scores. In fact, several of the test's interpretative scores, including the Mastery Score and the Reading Grade Score, are unique and require some explanation.

The Woodcock was designed as a set of equal interval scales, called Mastery Scales, which directly reflect changes in a subject's proficiency in a task. Any given difference between two mastery points (for example, 75 percent mastery to 90 percent mastery to 96 percent mastery) on the scale has the same meaning at any level and in any of the five skill areas. For example, a subject's change in proficiency from 75 percent mastery to 90 percent mastery is seen as a ten-point increase on the Mastery Scale.

Relative Mastery and the Reading Grade Score. By definition, Relative Mastery "is the predicted performance of a subject on tasks accomplished with 90 percent mastery by average students of the referenced grade level" (Woodcock, 1973, p. 31). The Reading Grade Score is thus the grade level at which the subject is predicted to perform at 90 percent mastery of the reading tasks on which average students at that grade level would also demonstrate 90 percent mastery. It follows that the Easy Reading Level is the grade level at which the subject is predicted to perform with 96 percent mastery of the reading tasks performed by average students at that grade with 90 percent mastery. Finally, the Failure Reading Level is the grade level at which the subject is predicted to perform with 75 percent mastery the tasks that are performed with 90 percent mastery by average students in the specified grade.

Several other scores may be calculated as interpretative aides for the Woodcock, although a detailed understanding of them requires the use of the many extensive score transformation tables in the test manual. The most important issue in interpreting the Woodcock, however, is that it provides both norm-referenced and criterion-referenced assessments.

Direct Assessment of Reading

The materials utilized in a direct assessment of reading include norm-referenced and criterion-referenced published tests; curriculum materials; and nonstandardized devices such as check lists, informal reading inventories, and behavior observation systems. A brief review of these nonstandardized devices and their uses follows.

Check Lists

Behavior check lists and rating scales are frequently used by psychologists and educators when working with children who exhibit problems. Such devices, many of which are commercially published, can help to define a problem objectively and to document the perceived strengths and weaknesses of a child. Although there are very few commercially published check lists dealing with reading problems (see, for example, the Checklist of Instructional Needs with the Durrell Analysis of Reading Difficulty [Durrell, 1955]), there is a plethora of informal check lists (Ingram, 1980; Miller, 1974; Potter & Rae, 1981), two examples of which are displayed in Tables 10.5 and 10.6. Note that these informal check lists do *not* define the terms used, provide administration directions, or indicate how to decide what constitutes a correct response.

The primary purposes of informal reading check lists are description and prescription. When description of an individual's current skill repertoire is the goal, any check list that adequately covers behaviors involved in reading may be helpful. For example, the check list in Table 10.5 could be used preceding or during an initial problem-solving consultation session with a teacher or parent to help operationalize a student's strengths and difficulties, thus allowing for a more focused, skill-oriented assessment.

A prescriptive check list goes beyond just describing by enumerating possible means for remediating an identified deficiency. Table 10.6 shows a portion

Table 10.5 Typical Informal Check List of Reading Difficulties

Name ______________________ Age __________ Date __________

School ______________________ Teacher ______________________

Oral reading

_____ Evidence of emotional tension
_____ Strained, high-pitched voice
_____ Monotonous tone
_____ Volume too loud or soft
_____ Poor enunciation
_____ Word by word reading
_____ Incorrect phrasing
_____ Eye-voice span too short
_____ Oral Accuracy Errors:
    _____ Hesitations
    _____ Refusals
    _____ Omissions
    _____ Repetitions
    _____ Mispronunciations
    _____ Ignore punctuation
    _____ Substitutions
    _____ Additions
_____ Inadequate oral comprehension
_____ Low oral reading rate

Silent reading

_____ Knowledge of letter names
_____ Use of context clues
_____ Phonic analysis
    _____ Single consonants
    _____ Consonant blends
    _____ Silent consonants
    _____ Short vowels
    _____ Vowel blends
    _____ Vowel diagraphs
    _____ Phonic rules
    _____ Sound blending ability
_____ Structural Analysis
    _____ Inflectional endings
    _____ Compounds
    _____ Common prefixes
    _____ Common suffixes
    _____ Roots
_____ Auditory-visual recognition of syllables
_____ Syllabication rules
_____ Use of Dictionary

Vocabulary development

_____ Inadequate sight vocabulary
_____ Inadequate meaning vocabulary

Comprehension skills

_____ Recall of factual detail
_____ Main idea of paragraphs
_____ Sequence of idea and events
_____ Following directions
_____ Making inferences
_____ Critical, evaluative reading

Reading rate

_____ Lack of flexibility in rate
_____ Low silent reading rate
_____ Scanning
_____ Skimming
_____ Finger pointing
_____ Head movements

Study skills

_____ Asks questions about readings
_____ Takes notes
_____ Reads maps and globes
_____ Reads charts, tables & graphs
_____ Uses the dictionary
_____ Uses the encyclopedia
_____ Uses other reference books
_____ Rereads difficult material
_____ Outlines difficult material

From "Direct Assessment of Reading Skills: An Approach Which Links Assessment to Intervention" by S. N. Elliott and W. C. Piersel, 1982, *School Psychology Review, 11*, p. 274.

Table 10.6 Selected Portions of a Check List for Planning Remedial Reading Interventions

Confusion in letter knowledge		
Behavior exhibited	*Possible cause*	*Possible remedies*
Reversals	Visual disability	Check auditory and visual acuity
Anxiety in writing and reading	Hearing disability (acuity-figure ground)	Auditory and visual discrimination training
Ineffective word analysis	Carelessness	Small group instruction at chalk board in initial teaching
Ineffective oral reading	Neurological development	Easily confused letters taught separately
Avoidance of writing	Inadequate instruction (improper pacing)	Appropriate training in phonics by use of error avoidance strategy for mastery
Poor spelling		Kinesthetic-tactile training

Difficulty in structural analysis		
Behavior exhibited	*Possible causes*	*Possible remedies*
Poor spelling	Auditory acuity and discrimination	Precise speech-separate words in spoken language
Inability in word perception	Lack of hearing precise speech	
Stagnate vocabulary	Inadequate instruction	Training in visual and auditory discrimination
Word guessing	Lack of understanding of what a syllable is	Differentiating between words similar sounds (minimal pairs — pen, pin)
	Teacher insecurity in personal knowledge resulting in avoidance	Recognition and synthesizing elements of word (phonemic, syllabic, morphemic)
		Building memory of word form
		Teach common affixes
		Adequate listening-speaking vocabulary
		Use of directed inquiry strategy in visual clues for syllabicating
		Provide sequential procedure in analyzing unfamiliar words

(continued)

Table 10.6, *continued*

Regressions in oral reading		
Behavior exhibited	*Possible causes*	*Possible remedies*
Poor oral reading	Inadequate sight vocabulary	Proper placement
Slow reading rate	Inadequate word analysis	Contextual clues
	Interruptions when reading orally	
	Inappropriate placement	Choral reading
	Inadequate listening-speaking vocabulary	Music (familiar tune, new words)
	Confusion in meaning	Read silently before orally
	Eye movement in tracking line	Build oral language facility
	Round robin reading	Build word analysis skills
		Self-evaluation of taped reading
		Do not interrupt when a word is mispronounced when reading

From "Direct Assessment of Reading Skills: An Approach Which Links Assessment to Intervention" by S. N. Elliott and W. C. Piersel, 1982, *School Psychology Review, 11*, p. 276. Copyright 1982 National Association of School Psychologists, Harrisonburg, VA. Reprinted by permission.

of a prescriptive check list developed by James Dunn (from Elliott & Piersel, 1982). We are skeptical of the direct remedial efficacy of such check lists, for the manner in which any given prescription is implemented would vary across instructors. In addition, there is little empirical evidence clarifying reading aptitude treatment interactions. Nevertheless, prescriptive checklists may function as *general guides* for brainstorming and designing alternative prescriptive interventions after assessment information has been collected and synthesized.

Informal Reading Inventories

An informal reading inventory (IRI) can be utilized to identify a student's skill level by observing reading performance on material of increasing difficulty. The most common form of an IRI is constructed by selecting short passages (60 to 200 words) from a set of graded materials that increase in difficulty. This is usually accomplished by drawing passages from each level of a basal reading series. To date, there have been several well-received attempts to "standardize" or package IRIs (McCracken, 1966; Silvaroli, 1965); however, we only discuss those made by school personnel for local use.

IRIs have been utilized in two major ways (Pikulski, 1974). First, they have been used by reading specialists and psychologists to identify children's independent, instructional, and frustration reading levels and to design plans for the remediation of any weaknesses. Second, IRIs have been used in the classroom for a rapid assessment of reading skills so students can be grouped more appropriately. In both cases, IRIs have been constructed from students' curriculum materials.

The strength of an IRI is not as a test instrument but as a means for studying and diagnosing a learner's reading behavior (Powell, 1971). According to Zintz (1975), IRIs have several advantages over other methods of reading assessment because they (a) are easy to construct and include material directly from a student's curriculum, (b) document reading errors in a context identical to a classroom task, and (c) provide an opportunity to observe reading behavior. Perhaps their most frequently cited advantage is that they can reveal several levels of reading skill: independent, instructional, and frustration (Learner, 1976; Robeck & Wilson, 1974). If used intelligently, issues of readability and interest can be controlled at least as well as with a standardized test. Readability is the grade-level difficulty attributed to a passage, which is based on factors such as word length and sentence complexity. Obviously, a subject's reading level will vary with the readability of a passage. A major goal of an informal assessment of reading is to establish the readability level of material with which a student achieves successes.

Betts (1946) is usually credited with suggesting that a child has three reading levels relative to curriculum materials. The *independent level* is the highest level of difficulty of a written material that a child can cope with independently and still maintain a nearly perfect reading performance (that is, the student has almost no difficulty with word identification, understands the passage, and can remember most of the contents as evidenced by answering questions. Quantitatively, the independent level has been defined by Lloyd (1979) as the highest level of material with which a child can sustain approximately 98 percent word recognition and answer nearly 100 percent of the comprehension questions asked. At the other end of the skill continuum is the *frustration level*, or the level at which material becomes so difficult a child cannot adequately cope because the word recognition demands or the comprehensibility of the material exceeds the skills of the reader. The frustration level is defined as the lowest level of reading material at which a child is able to recognize less than 90 percent of the words and can answer less than 50 percent of the comprehension questions. The *instructional level* lies between the independent and the frustration levels and is probably the level of greatest interest to teachers. This is the level of material on which a child encounters some reading difficulties, although these problems can be overcome with limited help. The instructional level is the highest level at which a child is able to recognize approximately 95 percent of the words and answer over 75 percent of the comprehension questions posed.

IRIs usually are individually administered and may be tape recorded so

Table 10.7 Typical Reading Behaviors Analyzed as Errors Using IRIs

Type of error	Scoring convention
External assistance needed (student is aided by another person after 5 seconds)	Underline words aided
Hesitations (student hesitates at a word but does not require help)	Check (√) above words
Insertions (student adds words not on page)	Write in word(s) or word part with caret (^)
Mispronunciation (student does not pronounce word accurately)	Write in the phonetic pronunciation above the word
Omissions (student skips a word and reads on)	Circle the omitted word(s)
Order reversals (student inverts word order)	Mark reversals with transpose symbol (∼)
Disregard of punctuation (student inserts or omits punctuation marks)	Circle marks omitted and insert and circle marks added
Regressions (student reads and then rereads a word or words)	Put a wavy line under the word(s) repeated
Self-corrections (student makes a mistake but corrects it spontaneously)	Write SC above word(s)
Substitutions (student reads a word as another word)	Cross out the omitted ~~word~~ and insert the substituted word above it

From "Direct Assessment of Reading Skills: An Approach Which Links Assessment to Intervention" by S. N. Elliott and W. C. Piersel, 1982, *School Psychology Review, 11*, p. 277. Copyright 1982 National Association of School Psychologists, Harrisonburg, VA. Reprinted by permission.

errors can be more accurately coded. A percentage score is then derived by dividing the number of errors by the total number of words in the passage and subtracting this from 100. Reading behaviors that commonly are scored by this form of error analysis include assistance needed, hesitations, insertions, mispronunciations, omissions, order reversals, regressions, self-corrections, substitutions, and disregard of punctuation. Conventions for describing and marking these ten behaviors are illustrated in Table 10.7.

A few words of caution about IRIs are in order. Because they are not constructed rigorously, they are prone to greater measurement error than most standardized reading tests. Therefore, the results from an IRI must be carefully interpreted and should not be the sole criterion for a diagnostic placement decision. IRIs are valuable sources of information for planning a teaching or remedial program for a student; however, the construction, administration, and interpretation of IRIs require considerable clinical and technical skills.

Behavioral Observation Systems

Assessing the prerequisite learning and basic reading skills of a student in a test is important; it is also critical to gather behavioral information in the classroom in conjunction with teacher behavior and an array of classroom stimuli.

Soli and Devine (1976), in a study of the behavioral correlation of third- and fourth-grade high and low achievers found that (a) the observation of classroom behavior was more critical for low achievers than high achievers and (b) the best predictors of achievement for the low achievers were absence of play, paying attention, absence of self-stimulation, and complying. Thus, these findings indirectly support the need to observe the prerequisite learning skills of children experiencing reading difficulties.

The Student-Level Observation of Beginning Reading (SOBR), developed and validated at the University of Pittsburgh's Learning Research and Development Center, is a classroom observation system designed for identifying and classifying both student and teacher behaviors (Leinhardt & Sewald, 1981). The SOBR has eight categories for the classification of student behaviors. Five of the categories are nonreading related: waiting for something or someone; engaged in an academic activity other than reading; engaged in a management activity; absent from school; and out of the room. Off-task is the sixth category and is divided into two subcategories, reading and nonreading, depending upon the situational demands. The two general reading categories are direct reading (oral and silent) and indirect reading (talking about reading and writing about reading).

The teacher observation includes four general categories: management, no student contact, other academic, and reading instruction. The reading instruction category is further divided into cognitive (cueing and monitoring) and cognitive explanation (presentation and feedback) components.

An examiner using the SOBR observes a target student for ten seconds, records observations for five seconds, observes another student (yoked or matched control student) for ten seconds, and again records observations for five seconds. Next, the examiner monitors the teacher's behavior. This student-to-teacher observation cycle is repeated several times. Leinhardt, Zigmond, and Cooley (1981) reported that interrater agreements on the SOBR ranged between 78 percent and 100 percent across nine trained observers over all students and categories during a one-hour classroom observation. In a generalizability study, both interobserver agreement and code stability coefficients were estimated to be above .95 (Lomax, 1980).

FOCUS ON RESEARCH
Dyslexia: A Confusing Term

The term "dyslexia" is commonly used to describe any reading disorder that is not the result of organic defect, low intelligence, emotional disturbance, or environmental deprivation. Knowing what dyslexia is *not*, however, is only half the story. Several researchers have described various subtypes of dyslexia characterized by deficits in word-analysis skills, configuration and orientation of letters and words, or a combination of these two problems. These difficulties are experienced by many developing readers and should not and cannot be reliably used to formulate a diagnosis of dyslexia because the research literature on dyslexia is replete with definitional problems. Researchers have simply chosen to define and measure dyslexia in so many different ways that the term has virtually lost a specific meaning. At best, the word "dyslexia" means a possible reading problem!

White and Miller's (1983) research supports our position about the construct of dyslexia. They investigated the use and meaning of the term "dyslexia" by examining 45 studies reported in the *Journal of Learning Disabilities*. They concluded that a major weakness in the studies was the inadequate definition of dyslexia, which ultimately negates the generalization and often the replication of the research. Those who consult such research should thus be cautioned that at this time, both research and practice concerning dyslexia should be questioned.

From "Dyslexia: A Term in Search of a Definition" by M. White and S. R. Miller, 1983, *Journal of Special Education*, *17*, pp. 5–10.

Linking Assessment to Intervention

The process of direct assessment, as described in this chapter, takes place primarily in the programing decision phase of assessment and leads directly to designing an individualized educational plan and subsequent remedial services for a student. This assessment paradigm does not reject standardized testing, nor does it hold up IRIs as the best means of testing a student's reading skills. Rather, in this paradigm tests of all varieties are considered as measures of behavior that vary in importance relative to the decision to be made (screening, diagnostic, or programing) and to the skills required for success in a given reading curriculum in a particular classroom. In the final section of this chapter, we focus on the direct measurement and remediation of comprehension problems, an area of primary importance to secondary-level educators. A major purpose of this section is to illustrate how direct assessment can aid in the development of interventions.

Assessment for Remediation of Comprehension Problems

The most popular method of measuring comprehension has been standardized reading comprehension tests. Usually, a student is given a passage to read and then asked a series of questions that require the selection of the main idea of the passage.

A basic problem exists with most reading comprehension tests, however, for it is not clear what they are measuring. In addition to comprehension, they may be measuring characteristics of the learner, such as attention, test-taking skills, motivation, and familiarity with the test, as well as other aspects of the reading process.

The lack of a basic understanding of the reading comprehension process makes it almost impossible to separate the above aspects of a student's functioning from reading comprehension ability. One way to remedy this problem is to develop better means of evaluating comprehension. However, before a refinement in test construction is undertaken, a framework of comprehension tasks is needed.

A Framework of Comprehension Tasks

What is reading comprehension? Farr (1970) compiled a list of subtests from reading tests designed to measure comprehension and believed they all attempted to measure comprehension as a "through-getting process," although how the tests achieved such a goal varied considerably.

Carroll (1972) classified the procedures for testing comprehension. A discussion of these procedures follows, organized according to the tasks required of an individual being tested.

Subjective reports. This category assumes the subject will attend to a task and honestly report what was not comprehended. According to Carroll, this method has been used in psycholinguistic research, but only infrequently. Such an approach could possibly be useful in an informal assessment of a subject's awareness of her reading problems. For example, it could reveal what elements of a message, such as particular words, clauses, or grammatical constructions, are causing a person difficulty in comprehension. Although subjective reports could yield false positive results when a subject believes comprehension exists when it actually does not, it seems unlikely they would yield false negative results. Thus subjective reports alone do not provide enough information about a subject's difficulties, but following a standardized measure of comprehension, they may provide valuable diagnostic insights.

Reports of truth, falsity, or equivalence. According to Carroll, this technique helps to measure pure comprehension because a correct response is directly dependent upon comprehension. The subject generally listens to or reads a passage and then responds to a question with a verbalization or by pointing to a picture referent. Another variant of this technique requires a subject to evaluate whether a message is equivalent in meaning to another message. This task, however, may place too great an emphasis on memory, as the subject must remember the first meaning before comparing it to a second meaning. If a subject is able to refer back to a text or have a message repeated, the memory load is diminished.

Following directions: Nonverbal responses to a message. Tests of a subject's ability to follow verbal or written directions provide reliable and convenient measures, although it may be memory more than comprehension that is assessed. Although this technique is not used widely in formal assessment, it is easily adapted to informal assessment. By itself, the ability to follow directions is not a good measure of comprehension; however, this skill is a prerequisite for successful learning and thus should not be ignored in the assessment of any learning difficulty.

Supplying missing elements in a message. This technique involves altering a passage of text by deleting words according to a rule, such as every fifth word or every other noun. A subject is then presented with the passage and asked to supply the missing words. Commonly referred to as the "cloze procedure," this method is employed in the Passage Comprehension subtest of the Woodcock Reading Mastery Tests.

Answering questions based on a message. On most standardized reading or listening comprehension tests, subjects are presented with a paragraph to read or listen to and then a set of multiple-choice questions to answer. According to Carroll, these questions are often not controlled for guessing. Tests designed so subjects are unable to answer questions without first reading or listening to a passage would seem to provide a reasonable test of skill at comprehending a message. The difficult task is to design tests that cover material relatively new to a broad population of subjects without using new vocabulary. As an informal, individual method of assessing comprehension, this approach is even more valid.

Recognizing a message on subsequent presentation. In this technique, which has been a traditional method of measuring learning and memory, a subject is presented with material to read and then given elements from the material along with new or modified elements and asked to identify which elements are from the original material. This approach has severe shortcomings, for the task can be successfully accomplished by memory alone without comprehension. Although the procedure may require some comprehension, it is difficult to separate the effects of comprehension from those of memory processes.

Reproducing a message. A variety of techniques for testing comprehension involve tasks requiring reproduction of a message. As with the previous technique, memory processes may also be involved, and thus the respective roles of comprehension and memory processes may be difficult to isolate.

A wide range of recall tasks have been used to measure a student's comprehension of sentences or passages. One method, however, that deserves special consideration is the paraphrasing task (Anderson, 1972), or the reproduction of a message in a subject's own words. Generally, this task must be performed without a subject being able to refer back to the original message, but the importance of memory processes can be reduced by allowing the subject to use the original message. If paraphrasing can be objectively and validly scored, this task may be useful for measuring comprehension.

This survey of Carroll's seven categories of techniques illustrates that no one method universally gives valid and reliable information about comprehension. Carroll (1972) concluded,

> It is seldom the case that success or failure in any of these tests can unequivocally be traced to success or failure in language comprehension since there are other factors of guessing, inference, memory, reliance on prior knowledge, etc. that are operating. (p. 24)

Informal Assessment of Comprehension Skills

Thus far we have attempted to show that comprehension (along with memory and perhaps other processes) can be measured in at least seven ways. Therefore, it is not surprising that constructors of reading tests have generally had difficulty in measuring comprehension. How can a diagnostician or teacher receive more complete information about a student's comprehension skills? An attractive alternative, which requires work and an experimental approach, is to design an informal measure of comprehension from instructional materials. In the remainder of this section, we will examine the feasibility of informally assessing comprehension.

Designing an Informal Assessment

Designing an informal test requires consideration of the (a) skills or behaviors to be assessed, (b) input and output modalities necessary for success, (c) types of questions to be asked, and (d) materials to be used in the test.

Skills. Six skills or behaviors important to the process of comprehension can be identified, and include two mental processes, memory and inference making, plus four means of interacting with a written or spoken message: identifying main ideas, following directions, paraphrasing, and using context.

Modalities. A student will be required to respond both orally and in writing.

Questions. A student would be required to respond to a wide variety of questions, most of which can be categorized either as open-ended or structured. Therefore, the student must both generate original responses and select the correct answers from several alternatives.

Materials. The characteristics of the materials used in the assessment of comprehension, such as readability, length, familiarity of subject, and in-text clues, play an important role in the quantity and quality of a student's response.

One would have to develop a test with hundreds of tasks to tap all possible combinations of the four dimensions listed above. Our intent is not to design a corpus of comprehension tasks but rather to outline important features that should be integrated into the construction of any comprehension tasks. To illustrate how a diagnostician or teacher can design a test of comprehension, we have developed two examples.

Example 1: Identifying the main idea. To assess a student's skill at identifying the main idea of reading material, one can extract five or six short passages of increasingly difficult readability from graded workbooks or classroom texts. A student is then requested to develop a one-sentence description of the main idea of each passage, plus three incorrect alternatives.

Remember that a student can and should give more than one answer for each passage. For example, have a student read a passage silently. Then, with the passage out of sight, ask (a) What is the main idea of this passage? (without the use of alternatives), (b) What would be a good title for this passage?, and (c) What is the main idea of this passage? (with the use of alternatives). If the student demonstrates comprehension of the main idea at any point, go on to the next passage. However, if the student is unable to give a satisfactory answer, reintroduce the passage and have the student read it aloud and attempt to answer the same questions with the passage present.

By using graded material and examining silent reading before oral reading, the initial emphasis is on memory (passage was taken away). Thus, the task is to be presented in the most mentally demanding form first, with a regression to a somewhat less difficult format. This design is efficient, because if a student can answer the most difficult question, one could assume he will also answer the easier questions correctly.

Example 2: Following directions. Tests of following directions can be used to assess attention and memory as well as comprehension. Attention and memory factors, however, can be minimized by varying testing situations. As before, materials in various formats can be used to help identify the strengths and weaknesses in a learner's comprehension skills.

Select a game or task with which the student is unfamiliar and write directions for it that are clear and understandable. Have the student read the directions and perform the task. Next, have the student describe the task and explain the role of each step. This allows subjects to act out and verbalize their understanding of a task. The comparison between doing something and describing how to do the same thing should provide insights into a student's verbal and comprehension skills. This is a very simple example and not specific to reading comprehension; however, it can provide important information about how a person learns and solves problems.

Conclusion

Educators and psychologists presently do not have sophisticated methods of accurately measuring reading comprehension, because it seems to involve so many cognitive skills. The best they can do to evaluate students' comprehension skills is to use tests, both formal and informal, that require subjects to behave as they do in typical learning situations and systematically to attempt to isolate skills and situations in which the students can and cannot succeed. Through a systematic, personalized assessment, the diagnostician can develop interventions to refine a learner's skills or change the instructional situation (that is, materials or teaching), or both.

Summary

You have been reading about reading for some time if you covered this entire chapter. We have tried to share with you the complexities of both the reading process and the accurate assessment of children's reading skills. Many tests have been developed to simplify the assessment of reading. Two individually administered tests, the Test of Early Reading Ability and the Woodcock Reading Mastery Tests, were examined in detail, along with a psychometric overview of eight other tests. Although good reading tests exist, we also strongly advocate that educators and psychologists become proficient at directly assessing reading skills. To this end, we reviewed the use of reading skills check lists, informal reading inventories, and classroom observations and provided examples of how comprehension can be directly assessed. We hope you have learned something about your own reading behavior as well as how to assess others. Now stop reading and start learning — assess your progress on each of the objectives that guided the development of this chapter.

Chapter 11

Math

Learning Objectives

1. Describe the uses of a scope and sequence chart.
2. Describe the use of learning hierarchies and list two differences between learning hierarchies and scope and sequence charts.
3. Describe the differences between diagnostic arithmetic testing using standardized tests and error analysis using informal assessment.
4. Explain why error analysis using standardized tests is usually inappropriate.
5. Conduct a simple error analysis with a sample of a student's work.

Louise had dyscalculia,[1] or at least that is what her parents had been told by her new teacher in a meeting at school on a day less than a week ago that was filled with bewilderment and sadness. However, her twelve-year-old brother, Todd, diagnosed her as normal in less than an hour and "cured" her even more quickly. And Todd was right!

Louise, a fifth grader, was never an outstanding student in any subject but had always "gotten by." In fifth grade she seemed to be falling behind the rest of her class and thus was referred to the school diagnostic team. The results of an evaluation indicated that she had average intelligence (that is, she

[1]*Dyscalculia* is a term that was originally used in medicine to indicate the virtual loss of mathematical ability after head trauma and was "borrowed" by some educators to describe basic arithmetic learning disorders.

$$\begin{array}{r} 3 \\ \times\ 2 \\ \hline 6 \end{array} \quad \begin{array}{r} 5 \\ \times\ 7 \\ \hline 35 \end{array} \quad \begin{array}{r} 6 \\ \times\ 6 \\ \hline 36 \end{array} \quad \begin{array}{r} 9 \\ \times\ 8 \\ \hline 72 \end{array}$$

$$\begin{array}{r} 12 \\ \times\ 2 \\ \hline 24 \end{array} \quad \begin{array}{r} 14 \\ \times\ 2 \\ \hline 48 \end{array} \quad \begin{array}{r} 42 \\ \times\ 3 \\ \hline 86 \end{array} \quad \begin{array}{r} 33 \\ \times\ 2 \\ \hline 96 \end{array}$$

Figure 11.1 Sample problems from Louise's arithmetic test.

achieved a Full Scale score of 103 on the Wechsler Intelligence Scale for Children-Revised) and that in reading and spelling she was performing at an average level (that is, at the fifty-first percentile). However, the testing in arithmetic suggested she was approximately two years below grade level, at the fourteenth percentile for her age. Based upon this information, the diagnostic team recommended that Louise be given special help for her problems in arithmetic. In an attempt to involve the parents in the evaluation of their child, the school had furnished them with a copy of the arithmetic quiz on which Louise had performed so poorly.

The quiz was a norm-referenced test on which each form was designed for a specific grade level (Louise took the fifth-grade form). One evening Todd picked up Louise's quiz and began to examine its content and her reponses. He noticed that many test items required multiplication (as would be expected for a test of fifth-grade mathematics) and that Louise had missed a large proportion of these items (not to mention the division items). Eight of the multiplication problems from the test are presented in Figure 11.1. From the first four problems on the test it was immediately obvious to Todd that his sister knew her multiplication facts. After all, she was capable of correctly multiplying 9 times 8. However, when she attempted to multiply anything but two one-digit numbers, she was almost always wrong.

Neither norm-referenced test scores nor the number of correct answers on a teacher-made quiz tell *why* an answer is right or wrong but only whether something *is* right or wrong. Todd, on the other hand, was a curious youngster who wanted to know what Louise was doing wrong. Maybe there was some pattern to her errors. Working under the assumption that she knew her multiplication facts, Todd decided that either she was careless or some problem existed with the *process* she was using to multiply. He soon discovered that there was, in fact, a problem with her process: She was multiplying digits within one factor. Thus to get an answer of 86 from the product of 42 times 3, Louise would first multiply 3 times 2 to get 6. Then, she would mistakenly multiply 4 times 2 to get 8. Her errors and her "dyscalculia" were related to this problem.

Todd quickly called Louise into the living room and instructed her in the appropriate process of multiplication. Later, her parents shared this information with her teacher and the evaluation team members. The problem was resolved without very much alteration in Louise's school routine.

This hypothetical example illustrates two important points relative to the assessment of arithmetic skills. First, it is important to go beyond test scores and examine the *content* of the test and the *processes* children use in responding to items. Second, arithmetical ability is not simply some general capacity that one has or does not have. Instead, it is composed of a series of clearly observable skills. A primary assumption of this chapter is that these skills are not only observable but they also fit into an orderly sequence. A major goal in mathematics assessment is to find exactly where in the sequence a child fails. This specific information is highly relevant, because instruction should logically be directed toward the next skill in the sequence.

The Sequence of Learning Arithmetic Skills as the Basis for Assessment

Learning arithmetic skills follows a logical and orderly sequence. A knowledge of this sequence of skills is essential for conducting assessments in arithmetic. We will discuss two approaches by which these skills have been described and organized: (a) scope and sequence charts, and (b) learning hierarchies.

Scope and Sequence Charts

Scope and sequence charts, such as the one presented in Table 11.1, list the skills students need to know (scope) along a timeline in the order according to which they are usually taught (sequence). Many teachers derive their weekly and even daily lesson plans by using scope and sequence charts to focus on specific aspects of major skills. Note that the same skills reappear at different levels for review or more sophisticated application.

Scope and sequence charts are useful in assessment in two ways. First, a norm-referenced test may suggest that a child is performing at a third-grade level, for example. By referring to a chart, it is possible to determine *in general* the types of skills that the child does or does not have. This information can be easily translated into instructional objectives. This whole process must be approached cautiously, because often there is not one-to-one correspondence among a test, a scope and sequence chart, and the actual curriculum being taught to a specific child.

Second, a scope and sequence chart can be used as a vehicle for informal assessment. Such charts provide abundant information about skill domains that should be assessed. One possible strategy would be to use a norm-referenced test to determine the approximate grade level at which a child is functioning and then consult a scope and sequence chart to discover the specific skills the child is expected to know. Informal tests of these skills could then be constructed to determine precisely what the child knows. Based upon what the child does know, recommendations for instruction would be to begin teaching with the next skill in the sequence.

Table 11.1 Scope and Sequence Chart for Mathematics

Grade	Skills acquired
Kindergarten	Rote counting to 10 Use whole numbers in serial order Begin cardinal numbers, ordinal numbers Begin reading numerals One-to-one matching Addition as joining of sets
Grade 1: First Half	Rote counting to 100 Read and write whole numbers through 50 Place value at tens place Equivalent/nonequivalent sets Know meaning of signs −, +, and = Addition and subtraction as inverse functions Solving missing addend problems Using 0 in subtraction
Grade 1: Second Half	Rote counting beyond 100 Counting by fives, twos, tens Odd and even numbers Signs (&) Read and write to 99 Begin fractions ½, ⅓, ¼ Addition combinations through 19 Addition of two-digit numbers with 2 or 3 addends through 99 (no carrying) Subtract two-digit numbers to minuends of 19 or less Multiples of 10 (2 tens = 20, 3 tens = 30)
Grade 2: First Half	Place value to hundredth place Addition two-digit numerals with 3 or 4 addends with sums less than 100 (no carrying) Subtract two-digit numerals (no borrowing) Understand division as separation of set into equivalent sets
Grade 2: Second Half	Count by ones, twos, fives, tens, hundreds, through 999 Odd-even numbers Read and write numerals through 999 Write numerals in expanded notation Introduce carrying (regrouping) Subtraction involving borrowing at the tens, hundreds places with numerals including 0 Begin combination of multiples of 2, 3, 4, and 5 with products of 0–25. Know meaning of x and y Begin division problem with same facts as above.

(continued)

Table 11.1, *continued*

Grade	Skills acquired
Grade 3: First Half	Count and write to 1,000 Place value for thousands Equivalent fractions for ½, ¼, ⅓ Roman numerals to XII Addition of three-digit numerals with carrying Subtraction facts with combinations of 0–19 Introduce $\sqrt{}$ for division
Grade 3: Second Half	Read and write numerals with dollars and cents Rounding of numbers Fractions ⅙, ⅛ Roman numerals through XXX Addition up to seven digits Begin addition of fractions with like denominators, with sums less than 1 Subtraction of 4–7 digits with borrowing Multiplication through 9 × 9 Multiplication of two- or three-digit factors by one factor with or without carrying Division with combination through 9 × 9
Grade 4: First Half	Read and write whole numbers to 9,999 Roman numerals through C Understand concepts of ½, ¼, ⅓ as equivalent sets of groups of objects, as well as congruent parts of a whole
Grade 4: Second Half	Read and write numerals to million Place value for million Learn names *numerator* and *denominator* Multiplication of two-digit numeral by two-digit multipliers Division with two-digit divisor Fractional parts, fifths, sevenths, ninths
Grade 5: First Half	Relationship between improper fractions and mixed fractions Write improper and mixed fractions Add three- and four-digit numbers of 2–6 addends Add fractions with like denominators Subtract like and mixed fractions with like denominators Multiply three-digit numbers by two-digit multipliers Two-digit divisors with 5–9 in one's place
Grade 5: Second Half	Decimals and place value Add decimal fractions Add fractions with unlike denominators Subtract five-digit numerals, fractional numbers, mixed numbers from whole numbers Multiplication with multiples of 100

Table 11.1, *continued*

Grade	Skills acquired
Grade 6: First Half	Learn to express numbers by using exponents Vocabulary: *power, squared, cubed* Add and subtract fractions with unlike denominators Multiplication with three-digit multipliers Multiplication of fractional numbers with proper fractions, whole numbers, and improper fractions Division of fractional numbers
Grade 6: Second Half	Relate percent to ratio, fractions, and decimals Add positive and negative numbers Multiplication with decimals and decimal fractions Division of decimal fractions

Learning Hierarchies

Learning hierarchies are a second approach to organizing skill sequences. Although both learning hierarchies and scope and sequence charts list skills in an ordered sequence, they differ in that (a) learning hierarchies are typically much more detailed and specific than scope and sequence charts, and (b) learning hierarchies specify a skill that a student will be required to learn and then list the *behaviors* the child must acquire before successfully performing the skill in question. Table 11.2 presents a series of objectives from a learning hierarchy that was used to teach the concept of number. Note the differences between the wording and specifications of these objectives versus those in the scope and sequence chart in Table 11.1.

Another difference between scope and sequence charts and learning hierarchies is that learning hierarchies do not specify the time periods for the acquisition of skills. This represents a philosophical as well as a practical difference. Scope and sequence charts are constructed in a manner consistent with many stage theories of child development in which children are thought to be ready to learn certain concepts at certain ages. On the other hand, learning hierarchies are derived from a behavioristic notion that children who have learned all the prerequisite skills for a specific learning objective are ready to learn the next objective regardless of age.

Whatever one's theoretical beliefs, learning hierarchies are an invaluable asset in the assessment of children's learning problems. A detailed discussion of the hierarchies is beyond the scope of this chapter, because to present a learning hierarchy that encompasses the same range of skills as the scope and

Table 11.2 Objectives of the Curriculum for Teaching the Concept of Number from a Learning Hierarchy

Units 1 and 2: Counting and one-to-one correspondence

A. The child can recite the numerals in order.
B. Given a set of moveable objects, the child can count the objects, moving them out of the set as he counts.
C. Given a fixed ordered set of objects, the child can count the objects.
D. Given a fixed unordered set of objects, the child can count the objects.
E. Given a numeral stated and a set of objects, the child can count out a subset of stated size.
F. Given a numeral stated and several sets of fixed objects, the child can select a set of size indicated by numeral.
G. Given two sets of objects, the child can pair objects and state whether the sets are equivalent.
H. Given two unequal sets of objects, the child can pair objects and state which set has more.
I. Given two unequal sets of objects, the child can pair objects and state which set has less.

Units 3 and 4: Numerals

A. Given two sets of numerals, the child can match the numerals.
B. Given a numeral stated and a set of printed numerals, the child can select the stated numeral.
C. Given a numeral (written), the child can read the numeral.
D. Given several sets of objects and several numerals, the child can match numerals with appropriate sets.
E. Given two numerals (written), the child can state which shows more (less).
F. Given a set of numerals, the child can place them in order.
G. Given numerals stated, the child can write the numeral.

Unit 5: Comparison of sets

A. Given two sets of objects, the child can count sets and state which has more objects or that sets have same number.
B. Given two sets of objects, the child can count sets and state which has less objects.
C. Given a set of objects and a numeral, the child can state which shows more (less).
D. Given a numeral and several sets of objects, the child can select sets which are more (less) than the numeral: given a set of objects and several numerals, the child can select numerals which show more (less) than the set of objects.
E. Given two rows of objects (not paired), the child can state which row has more regardless of arrangement.
F. Given three sets of objects, the child can count sets and state which has most (least).

Unit 6: Seriation and ordinal position

A. Given three objects of different sizes, the child can select the largest (smallest).
B. Given objects of graduated sizes, the child can seriate according to size.
C. Given several sets of objects, the child can seriate the sets according to size.
D. Given ordered set of objects, the child can name the ordinal position of the objects.

Table 11.2, *continued*

Unit 7: Addition and subtraction (sums to 10)

A. Given two numbers stated, set of objects, and directions to add, the child can add the numbers by counting out two subsets then combining and stating combined number as sum.
B. Given two numbers stated, set of objects, and directions to subtract, the child can count out smaller subset from larger and state remainder.
C. Given two numbers stated, number line, and directions to add, the child can use the number line to determine sum.
D. Given two numbers stated, number line, and directions to subtract, the child can use number line to subtract.
E. Given addition and subtraction word problems, the child can solve the problems.
F. Given written addition and subtraction problems in form: $\begin{array}{r} x \\ +y \\ \hline \end{array}$ or $\begin{array}{r} x \\ -y \\ \hline \end{array}$; the child can complete the problems.
G. Given addition and subtraction problems in form: $x + y = \square$, or $x - y = \square$; the child can complete the equations.

Unit 8: Addition and subtraction equations

A. Given equation of form $z = \square + \triangle$, the child can show several ways of completing the equation.
B. Given equation of form $x + y = \quad + \quad$, the child can complete the equation in several ways.
C. Given equations of forms $x + y = z + \quad$ and $x + y = \quad + z$, the child can complete the equations.
D. Given equations of forms $x + \square = y$ and $\square + x = y$, the child can complete the equations.
E. Given complete addition equation (e.g., $x + y = z$), the child can write equations using numerals and minus sign (e.g., $z - x = y$) and demonstrate relationship.
F. Given counting blocks and/or number line, the child can make up completed equations of various forms.

From "Task Analysis in Curriculum Design: A Hierarchically Sequenced Introductory Mathematics Curriculum" by L. B. Resnick, M. C. Wang, and J. Kaplan, 1973, *Journal of Applied Behavior Analysis, 6*, pp. 684–685, Table 1.

sequence chart presented in Table 11.1 could require several hundred pages. The interested reader is instead referred to an excellent little book entitled *The Analysis of Behavior in Planning Instruction* (Holland, Soloman, Doran, & Frezza, 1976).

Standardized Diagnostic Tests of Arithmetic

We will examine four diagnostic arithmetic tests from the many tests now available. An expanded list of these tests is presented in the skills-by-assessment-instrument-matrix in Table 11.3.

Table 11.3 Diagnostic Arithmetic Tests by Skills Assessed

Instrument	Operations						Application				Scores				Other	
	Add	*Subtract*	*Multiply*	*Divide*	*Fractions*	*Symbols*	*Money*	*Time*	*Measurement*	*Word problems*	*Grade equivalent*	*Age*	*Percentiles*	*Scaled scores*	*Administration time*	*Grade range of skills tested*
Buswell-John Diagnostic Test for Fundamental Process in Arithmetic (Buswell & John, N.D.)	×	×	×	×											15–20 min.	1–6
Diagnostic Mathematics Inventory (Gessell, 1977)	×	×	×	×												1-5–8-5
Diagnostic Test of Arithmetic Strategies (Ginsburg & Matthews, 1984)															80 min.	1–6
ENRIGHT Diagnostic Inventory of Basic Arithmetic Skills (Enright, 1983)	×	×	×	×	×						×				not stated	1–6
KeyMath Diagnostic Arithmetic Test (Connolly, Nachtman, & Pritchett, 1976)	×	×	×	×	×	×	×	×	×	×	×				30 min.	K–8
Stanford Diagnostic Mathematics Test (Beatty, Madden, Gardner, & Karlsen, 1976)	×	×	×	×	×	×	×	×	×	×	×		×	×	approx. 90 min.	1-5–12
Steenburgen Diagnostic-Prescriptive Math Program (Steenburgen, 1978)	×	×	×	×	×										10–20 min.	1–6
Test of Early Mathematics Ability (Ginsburg & Baroody, 1983)	×	×	×			×	×			×		×	×		20 min.	preschool 1–3
Test of Mathematical Abilities (Brown & McEntire, 1984)	×	×	×	×	×	×	×	×	×	×			×	×	1 hr., 45 min.	3–12

KeyMath Diagnostic Arithmetic Test

Overview and purpose. The KeyMath Diagnostic Arithmetic Test (Connolly, Nachtman, & Pritchett, 1976) is an individually administered instrument used with children in kindergarten through eighth grade. It contains fourteen subtests that are categorized into three major areas: Content, Operations, and Applications. The test is designed primarily for diagnosing difficulties in arithmetic.

The authors estimate that the instrument requires approximately thirty minutes to administer. The manual is well organized and provides detailed directions for administration. In addition to the manual and an easel kit containing the test, the other major component is a diagnostic record form that the test authors describe as a "simple" sheet that incorporates all data derived from the instrument. Although this record form is relatively simple to use once you become familiar with it, at first glance it appears extremely complex and may discourage some test users.

Standardization sample and norms. The technical procedures utilized in the standardization of the KeyMath are among the best of all the diagnostic arithmetic tests. It was normed on a sample of 1,222 children in kindergarten through seventh grade. This sample included both white and nonwhite children and was drawn from communities of varying size. The difficulty level of the items was established using a sophisticated latent trait model.

Data obtained. The KeyMath offers four diagnostic levels:

- *Level 1 — Total Test Performance.* At the most general level, the KeyMath provides a grade-equivalent score representing a child's overall test performance, which can be utilized for making placement decisions.
- *Level 2 — Area Performance.* Relative strengths and weaknesses among the test's three broad areas of Content, Operations, and Applications can be determined.
- *Level 3 — Subtest Performance.* The KeyMath provides a convenient system for profiling a subject's strengths and weaknesses across each of the fourteen subtests.
- *Level 4 — Item Performance.* As with most tests of arithmetic, it is possible to examine each individual item to ascertain the actual skills a student is lacking. However, a major asset of the KeyMath is its appendix, which states each item as a behavioral objective.

Administration. The KeyMath is constructed in an easel format. With the easel, a child is presented the test stimulus and the examiner is shown the test question. Administration procedures are quickly learned, and the authors state that the instrument can be administered by paraprofessionals who may lack formal training in testing. Obviously, the test must be interpreted by someone who is familiar with the mathematics curricula of elementary schools and who has some background in testing and measurement.

Reliability and validity. The only reliability data reported for the test were split-half coefficients. Reliability for the total test is satisfactory, ranging from .94 to .97 across all age levels. However, the reliability for some subtests, including some major ones such as fractions, addition, subtraction, and division, are well below minimal standards at some age levels. Comparisons across subtests must thus be made with caution.

A major weakness of the KeyMath is the lack of good validity data in the manual. Although the authors report correlations between this and other arithmetic tests, most correlations are based upon a previous version of the test and range from .38 to .69. This absence of data is partially compensated for by what we judge to be reasonably good content validity of the test. The procedures used to develop the test resulted in a comprehensive instrument that assesses a relatively wide range of arithmetic skills. However, the lack of other validity data is problematic.

Summary. The KeyMath is a well-organized test for the assessment of arithmetic skills in children in elementary and junior high school. Although some technical properties of the test are below minimal standards, it can provide useful information to teachers and other consumers.

Test of Mathematical Abilities

Overview and purpose. The Test of Mathematical Abilities, or TOMA (Brown & McEntire, 1984), is designed to assess skills in computations and story problems and to provide related information about attitudes toward math, math vocabulary, and general knowledge. The TOMA is distinguished in going beyond an assessment of the mastery of basic arithmetic skills to measure also factors that are thought to affect math performance, such as a child's attitude toward the subject. The instrument is designed for students who range in age from 8-6 to 18-11.

The TOMA has five subtests, which reflect various components of mathematical functioning and attitudes:

1. *Computation.* This test, which assesses students' mastery of arithmetical computations, consists of twenty-five problems ranging from addition (e.g., $5 + \_\_ = 8$) to simple algebra (e.g., $[x + y][x - y] = \_\_\_\_$).
2. *Story problems.* This subtest presents verbal descriptions of seventeen problems that require arithmetical solutions. For example: "Jack has a bird, a dog, and a cat. The dog is big and the bird is little. How many pets does Jack have?" The manual suggests these word problems assess a child's reading, syntax, ability to sort relevant from irrelevant information, and basic understanding of arithmetic processes.

3. *Attitude toward mathematics.* The subtest is composed of fifteen statements with which students must agree, disagree, or say they don't know. (For example: "I'd rather do math than any other kind of homework.")
4. *Vocabulary.* To assess knowledge of mathematics vocabulary, in this subtest students are asked to write definitions for words such as Celsius, coordinates, and probability.
5. *General information.* Although the items focus on mathematical concepts, this subtest is designed to assess a child's overall range of knowledge about the world. The test authors apparently assume that this subtest is roughly equivalent to a measure of general intelligence or, more specifically, the ability to learn, and indicates the rate at which a child could be expected to learn arithmetical concepts.

Very little specialized training is required to administer the TOMA. Directions for administration and scoring are clearly presented in the manual and can be followed by anyone reasonably familiar with educational and psychological tests. Each of the subtests requires from five to twenty-five minutes, with the total testing time ranging from forty-five minutes to one hour and forty-five minutes.

Standardization sample and norms. The TOMA was standardized on a sample of 1,560 students from Alabama, California, Washington, Wisconsin, and Vermont. Although this is not representative of the national population, the authors report a high degree of consistency between the standardization sample and the United States population with respect to important variables such as sex, race, and urban versus rural residence.

Data obtained. Norms are provided in terms of standard scores and percentiles for each of the five subtests, with separate norms for each of the thirteen age levels. Thus, users access the norm table for a particular child's age and determine percentiles or standard scores for each subtest. Because some subtests have a relatively small number of items and the subtests are not equal interval scales, passing or failing a single item can greatly change interpretation. For example, a ten year old with a raw score of three on the Computation subtests would be in the thirty-seventh percentile, but if the same child has one additional item correct (that is, a raw score of 4), the percentile equivalent would be 63. The difference in meaning between these two percentiles could be highly significant in making decisions about the child even though the practical significance of a raw score of 3 versus one of 4 is hardly worth noting. Intelligent users of this test will use the standard error of measurement to help correct for this unequal interval problem.

Reliability and validity. Two forms of reliability data, internal consistency and stability, are reported in the manual. Internal consistency coefficients are above .80 for all subtests, with many ranging into the high .90s. Figures for test-retest reliability were somewhat lower, with correlation coefficients ranging from .71 for story problems to .94 for general information.

The TOMA has moderate to low positive correlations with the KeyMath, the arithmetic portions of the Peabody Individual Achievement Test, and the Wide Range Achievement Test. Most of the correlations with these tests were in the .30s and .40s. The test authors infer construct validity because test scores are correlated highly with age and grade level. Missing was any mention of content validity. Thus, we must question whether the test samples adequately the broad content of most mathematics curricula. With only twenty-five items on such important subtests as Computation, it is highly unlikely that the TOMA has adequate content validity.

Summary. The major use of the TOMA is as a test of computational accuracy. In this role it is only mediocre. However, if math anxiety, vocabulary, or general knowledge about the world are thought to be influencing math performance, then the TOMA may be useful in determining whether one of these factors contributes to the problem. Scores from any of the subtests should be considered only as a rough screening because of very limited sampling of skills. Should the TOMA results suggest that a problem exists, additional testing will be required before specific problems are pinpointed and remediation strategies developed. For example, if a child scored poorly on the General Information subtest, additional testing with an intelligence test would be required before deciding that the child had a learning deficiency.

The TOMA is a multifaceted examination of mathematical abilities and attitudes toward math. It can be administered quickly and conveniently by teachers or educational diagnosticians for a general indication of a student's relative strengths and weaknesses. However, the instrument is not likely to be very useful for instructional planning because it lacks the specificity required to pinpoint problems and their causes.

Diagnostic Test of Arithmetic Strategies

Overview and purpose. One of the few math tests that takes advantage of the recent research pertaining to mathematical computation and thinking in children is the Diagnostic Test of Arithmetic Strategies, or DTAS (Ginsburg & Mathews, 1984). Unlike many other tests in this area, the focus of this test is on the identification of correct and incorrect strategies (that is, processes) rather than correct and incorrect answers to problems. Whereas a test such as the KeyMath may suggest that a child has a deficiency in, for example, subtraction, the DTAS is designed to provide reasons for that weakness.

Administration of the DTAS requires a different kind of thinking by the examiner than is needed for most formal tests. The primary difference is the degree to which the examiner must be flexible, as a passage from the manual:

> The identification of strategies and methods requires flexible questioning. The examiner should feel free at any time to ask questions designed to

> reveal how children solve particular problems. Questions like, "How did you get that answer?" or "How did you do it?" are always appropriate on the DTAS. Similarly, such techniques as telling the child, "Pretend that you are the teacher and tell me how to work the problem," may also be effective and should be encouraged. The examiner should feel free to improvise on the directions to some degree. (Ginsburg & Mathews, 1984, p. 10)

The authors suggest the test can be administered by anyone "reasonably experienced" in using tests in education, language, or psychology. We disagree. Much of the rich array of information that can be derived from the DTAS would be lost if it were administered by someone unfamiliar with testing in arithmetic. We believe that the test should be administered by a teacher, psychologist, or educational diagnostician.

The DTAS is designed for children experiencing difficulty with addition, subtraction, multiplication, or division. Thus, it is appropriate for most children in grades one through six and some older children who have deficiencies in basic arithmetic processes. The instrument is divided into four subtests, one for each basic arithmetic computational skill; each section requires approximately twenty minutes to administer. Generally, only one subtest is administered per session.

Standardization sample and norms. No data pertaining to the standardization sample or norms are provided with the DTAS, presumably because the purpose of the test is to identify processes, not to *compare* performances of children of the same age.

Data obtained. Each of the four subtests is scored in three major areas: (a) setting up the problem, (b) written calculation, and (c) informal skills. Detailed directions and assistance are provided for scoring each area.

Within each subtest, the section devoted to setting up the problem helps the examiner determine whether a child has mastered some of the mechanics of arithmetic. These mechanics include writing digits and aligning numbers appropriately for arithmetical operations. For example, if a child were told to add 84 plus 3, each of the numbers would have to be written correctly and the 4 in 84 would have to be aligned with the 3 on the bottom.

The written calculation section examines whether the child obtained the correct answer to each problem, whether some standard method or an idiosyncratic method was used to obtain the answers, whether there were number fact errors, and whether any "bugs" (incorrect processes) or "slips" (simple errors usually involving a lack of attention) were consistently used for computation. Scoring for "bugs" is a fascinating aspect of the test. Examiners are provided with a considerable amount of instruction for "bug hunting," as Table 11.4 shows.

The informal skills section assesses the specific type of strategy used by a child to obtain a particular answer. For example, a child who is asked to add

Table 11.4 Directions for Locating "Bugs"

The DTAS provides direct measures of key bugs. Problems 5 and 6 are designed to identify Bug A *addition like multiplication* as in the following:

$$\begin{array}{r} 32 \\ +\ \ 7 \\ \hline 109 \end{array} \qquad \begin{array}{r} 21 \\ +\ 6 \\ \hline 87 \end{array}$$

On problem 5 the child does: "2 + 7 = 9, and then 3 + 7 = 10 so that the answer is 109." On problem 6, the child does "6 + 1 = 7 and then 2 + 6 = 8, so the answer is 87."

Problems 7 and 8 are chiefly designed to test Bug B *zero makes zero* as in

$$\begin{array}{r} 26 \\ +20 \\ \hline 40 \end{array} \qquad \begin{array}{r} 30 \\ +42 \\ \hline 70 \end{array}$$

On problem 7 the child reasons: "6 + 0 = 0, 2 + 2 = 4, so the answer is 40." By the same logic, problem 8 gives an answer of 70.

Problems 9 and 10 are designed to identify Bug C *add from left to right*, which results in

$$\begin{array}{r} {}^{2} \\ 81 \\ +45 \\ \hline 18 \end{array} \quad \text{or} \quad \begin{array}{r} {}^{1} \\ 81 \\ +45 \\ \hline 27 \end{array}$$

$$\begin{array}{r} {}^{3} \\ 92 \\ +43 \\ \hline 18 \end{array} \quad \text{or} \quad \begin{array}{r} {}^{1} \\ 92 \\ +43 \\ \hline 36 \end{array}$$

Using this bug on problem 9 the child reasons: "8 + 4 is 12; put down the 1 and carry the 2: 2 + 1 + 5 is 8; so the answer is 18." Or on problem 9 the child may put down the 2, carry the 1, and get 27 as the answer. By the same logic, the answer to problem 10 will be 18 or 36. Of course this bug may be used on other problems.

From *Diagnostic Test of Arithmetic Strategies* (p. 34) by H. P. Ginsburg and S. C. Mathews, 1984, Austin, TX: PRO-ED.

4 plus 5 may use her fingers to count the correct answer, thus using the strategy of counting rather than the preferred strategy of long-term memory of addition facts.

The DTAS does not yield traditional scores such as percentiles or grade equivalents. Instead, the test describes a child's specific skills and the computational processes and strategies used. This type of information is highly relevant for instructional planning but is less useful for placement decisions.

Reliability and validity. Reliability data are not present in the manual, which is a serious omission and a cause for concern. The fact that the publisher suggests a flexible administration format may actually decrease reliability. In addition, scoring the test is a complex procedure, and one cannot know whether different examiners would reach the same conclusions about a particular child.

No validity data are provided. At the least, the authors should have incorporated a thorough analysis of content validity to demonstrate that the DTAS adequately samples all relevant computational processes.

Summary. Despite the lack of adequate standardization and validation data, the DTAS does hold promise for the diagnostician. Its primary advantage over virtually all other tests is the degree to which it assesses arithmetical *processes*. By assessing the strengths and weaknesses with such processes, it may be possible to determine why a child is failing. With reasons for the problem known, instructional remedies should not be far behind.

ENRIGHT Diagnostic Inventory of Basic Arithmetic Skills

Overview and purpose. The ENRIGHT Diagnostic Inventory of Basic Arithmetic Skills is described as an instrument that "thoroughly assesses, diagnoses, and analyzes 144 basic computation skills" (Enright, 1983, p. vii). The inventory has three basic functions: placement, skill assessment, and diagnosis. For placement, the ENRIGHT provides a starting point for assessing a student's needs, the steps within skill sequences that require additional testing, and the basic arithmetic skills that have and have not been acquired. A major portion of the test is devoted to measuring basic skills in addition, multiplication, subtraction, and division. Finally, the ENRIGHT can be used in error analysis for determining why computations were inaccurately completed.

Standardization sample and norms. The inventory is criterion-referenced and is based upon a task analysis of basic arithmetic computation skills. The student test booklet consists of over 125 pages of arithmetic problems, with each skill measured by at least five items. The instrument does yield grade-equivalent scores, but these are not derived from norms based upon a standardization sample. Instead, the grade levels are referred to as "text-referenced," because the grade levels were determined by examining five widely used basal mathematics series and identifying the level at which each of the 144 skills is supposed to be taught.

Data obtained. Essentially, the process of using the ENRIGHT involves moving from a very general assessment of arithmetic skills during placement testing to very specific assessment of strengths and weaknesses and finally to error analysis. The data obtained would include an approximate grade placement, arithmetic facts known and not known, computational process deficits (for example, regrouping with subtraction problems), and the reasons why the errors are made.

Reliability and validity. Data pertaining to reliability and validity are not provided.

Summary. The ENRIGHT offers a comprehensive assessment of basic computational skills. The large number of arithmetic problems provided would be an asset to individuals who frequently conduct arithmetic assessments. Unfortunately, the manual gives no information concerning the test's psychometric adequacy. The fact that it is criterion-referenced does not excuse the absence of such data. Because little is known about the reliability or validity of this instrument, it would not be used in placement decisions. However, the instrument may be quite valuable in the diagnosis of arithmetic problems.

Informal Assessment of Arithmetic

"It's not whether you win or lose, it's how you play the game." Although this statement is typically applied to competitive activities, it has a great deal of relevance to assessment in mathematics. Knowing how many problems a child completed correctly is only a small part of the assessment process in arithmetic. At least as important in designing instructional strategies is an examination of the *processes* that the student used to obtain correct and incorrect answers. According to Brown and Burton (1978),

> a common assumption among teachers is that students do not follow procedures very well and that erratic behavior is the primary cause of a student's inability to perform each step correctly. Our experience has been that students are remarkably competent procedure followers, but that they often follow *the wrong procedures*. (p. 157)

If Brown and Burton are correct, and they have large volumes of research to support their claim, the task of the diagnostician is to discover the incorrect procedures children are following. One possible means of examining arithmetic difficulties would be to give a norm-referenced test to all students to determine who is having difficulty. For children identified as having problems, follow-up criterion-referenced testing could be conducted to identify general areas of weakness. Informal testing and error analysis could then be applied to determine misconceptions about arithmetic problem solving. The heart of informal assessment in mathematics is error analysis.

Error Analysis

Virtually anyone can determine whether the answer to a particular mathematics problem is correct or incorrect by consulting a key. To go beyond, however, requires the motivation and skill to search carefully for the types of computational and conceptual problems a child is experiencing. Error analysis thus involves an attempt to determine what a child is thinking when various errors are made. This frequently requires a careful analysis of the actual computations completed by a child. Alternatively, it is occasionally necessary simply to ask the child, "How did you do this problem?" or "Can you do this problem for me again and tell me what you did?"

Some of the most common arithmetic errors are presented in Table 11.5. This list is by no means comprehensive but does illustrate the rich variety of error types. Certainly it cannot be used as a substitute for good problem-solving and detective work. Some may argue that such detective work is too time-consuming, but so is remediating children who maintain fundamental misconceptions about the process of computing arithmetic problems. If we assume that most errors are systematic (that is, not random), error analysis becomes a valuable tool.

Analyzing the errors that a child makes on a standardized arithmetic test is typically insufficient. Standardized tests, especially those that are individually administered and "wide range," usually provide only a small sample of each type of problem, making it impossible to detect patterns of errors. By using informal tests, which may be constructed through interaction with a child, it is possible to administer several problems of the same type.

Cawley (1978) has developed an excellent system that combines aspects of standardized testing, error analysis, and instructional programing. Called the Clinical Mathematics Interview, this procedure offers a process for linking assessment and instruction. Initially students are screened with the Mathematics Concept Inventory, and areas of strength and weakness are noted. Children with deficits are then administered the Clinical Mathematics Interview, which is "an intensive diagnostic procedure that integrates content, mode, and algorithm" (Cawley, 1978, p. 224).

The interview begins by having a student solve written problems. Following that, the student is asked to verbalize the process used for solving the problems. Through this process it is possible to identify the types of errors a student is making. The results of the interview are used to place a student within the Multiple Options Curriculum. Although the procedures were designed for high school students, the concept could be applied to elementary school children as well.

Summary

The most important ideas presented in this chapter focus on the *process* utilized in determining a student's arithmetical strengths and weaknesses. Knowing a child's grade-equivalent score or even which problems were right and wrong is not nearly as important as knowing why those problems were wrong. The situation is analogous to that of two football coaches who have different amounts of information about their opponents. One coach knows the scores of each of the opponents' games. The other has watched films of each game played by the opponents and made a detailed analysis of the strengths and weaknesses of each player on the opposing team. Which coach is better prepared for the meeting of the two teams?

Table 11.5 Common Arithmetic Errors

Analysis	Example
1. Lacks mastery of basic facts. a. Addition	3 2 +4 3 7 4
b. Multiplication	3 2 × 3 86
2. Subtracts incorrectly within the division algorithm.	3) 73 rem 1 70) 3⟌230 −21 10 −9 1
3. Does not complete addition: a. Does not write renamed number.	85 +43 28
b. Leaves out numbers in column addition.	4 8 2← + 3 15
4. Rewrites a numeral without computing.	→72 +15 →77 →32 × 3 →36
5. Does not complete subtraction.	582 − 35 47
6. Does not complete division because of incompleted subtraction.	1)41 40) 7⟌3 9 7 −2 8 0 7 7
7. Fails to complete division; stops at first partial quotient.	50 7⟌370 350

Table 11.5, *continued*

Analysis	Example
8. Fails to complete division; leaves remainder equal to or greater than divisor.	80 rem 9 9⟌729 720 — 9
9. Confuses role of zero in subtraction with role of zero in multiplication.	37 −20 — 10
10. Subtracts top digit from bottom digit whenever regrouping is involved with zero in minuend.	30 −18 — 28
11. Confuses role of zero in multiplication with multiplicative identity.	$7 \times 0 = 7$
12. Lacks facility with addition algorithm:	
a. Adds units to units *and* tens;	37 + 2 — 59
b. Adds tens to tens *and* hundreds;	342 + 36 — 678
c. Adds units to tens *and* hundreds;	132 + 6 — 798
d. Is unable to add horizontally: Thinks: 3 + 7 + 1 = 11; writes 1 4 + 3 = 7 (+ 1 carried) 5 = 5 May add zero to make sum greater than largest addend: 1850.	345 + 7 + 13 = 185 8 5 — 185
13. Does not regroup units to tens.	37 +25 — 52
14. When there are fewer digits in subtrahend: a. subtracts units from units *and* from tens (*and* hundreds);	783 − 2 — 561
b. subtracts tens from tens *and* hundreds.	783 − 23 — 560

(continued)

Table 11.5, *continued*

Analysis	Example
15. Does not rename tens digit after regrouping.	54 − 9 55
16. When there are two zeroes in minuend, renames hundreds twice but does not rename tens.	5 6 (crossed out) 1 1 700 (7 crossed out) −326 284
17. Decreases hundreds digit by one when unnecessary.	3 7 1 −1 3 4 1 3 7 (hundreds column circled)
18. Adds regrouped number to tens but does not multiply. * 7 × 5 = 35; 30 + 30 = 60	35 × 7 65*
19. Multiplies digits within one factor. *4 × 1 = 4; 1 × 30 = 30	31 × 4 34*
20. Multiplies by only one number.	457 × 12 914
21. "Carries" wrong number.	8 67 × 40 3220
22. Does not regroup; treats each column as separate addition example.	23 + 8 211
23. Subtracts smaller digit from larger at all times to avoid renaming.	273 −639 446

From *A Guide to the Diagnostic Teaching of Arithmetic* (pp. 270–276), 2nd ed., by F. K. Reisman, 1978, Columbus, OH: Charles E. Merrill.

FOCUS ON RESEARCH
Using BUGGY to Find Math Errors

Some of the work needed to analyze children's math errors has been reduced by research involving the computer. Below is an example of an interaction with a computer program developed to detect math errors, or "bugs."

WELCOME TO BUGGY.
I HAVE CHOSEN A BUG. HERE IS AN EXAMPLE OF THE BUG.

$$\begin{array}{r} 17 \\ +\ 5 \\ \hline 13 \end{array}$$

The system presents an example in which the student does not get the right answer. At present the initial examples are stored in the network linked to the buggy implementation.

NOW YOU CAN GIVE ME PROBLEMS TO DETERMINE THE BUG.

$$\begin{array}{r} 18 \\ +\ 6 \\ \hline 15 \end{array} \qquad \begin{array}{r} 43 \\ +79 \\ \hline 23 \end{array}$$

The team generates problems that are answered by the "student." Notice that the team's test problems are similar to the initial example generated by BUGGY. This is usually a poor diagnostic strategy as it may leave other symptoms of a bug undiscovered.

Got the bug!

The team forms an initial hypothesis and tells the system they have discovered the bug. The system now asks the team to describe the bug and then tests them on their understanding. Asking for a description forces the team to verbalize their sometimes fuzzy idea of what the bug is and often makes them realize how ill-defined or vague their idea actually is. In the present system, the descriptions are saved but no attempt is made by the system to understand them.

PLEASE DESCRIBE THE BUG.

Student adds the number to be carried into the last column worked in.

This cryptic description is typical of those we have observed. Describing bugs in English is surprisingly difficult. What the team is trying to say is that if a column adds to more than 9, the units digit and the carry digit are added together and the result is written as the answer. For example, in the first column of the example problem, when 7 and 5 are added, 1 (the carry) and 2 (the units digit) are added to get 3. The same with 8 + 6, 2 + 9, and 3 + 9. (This bug could easily arise if the student were using Method 2 from Fig. 1 and mistakenly wrote the carry under the same column.)

continued

FOCUS ON RESEARCH *continued*

The hypothesis does account for the observed behavior. Unfortunately, it is not the student's bug. Notice the possibly humorous, probably disastrous results that would have transpired if the team had stopped at this point and tried to tutor the student on the basis of their initial belief!

HERE ARE SOME PROBLEMS TO TEST YOUR THEORY ABOUT THE BUG. WHAT IS:

```
 21
+39
---
 51
```

To ensure that the team has found the correct bug, the system produces several problems for the team to solve. At present, BUGGY has a heuristic problem generation program that gives a broad range of "different" problems. (For examples in which the bug is very localized, such as requiring a 0 in the top number, a special problem generator can be linked to the bug and will be used instead.) These problems are then filtered to try to get three problems which cause symptoms and two that give correct answers. This simple routine does surprisingly well at producing critical problems. So well, in fact, that a more "intelligent" routine (which determined the set of bugs consistent with the student's data and then selected the test problems which split this set) was discarded as unnecessarily time-consuming. . . .

The team's hypothesis is revealed as incorrect by the first of the five test problems. BUGGY presents its answer and then allows the team to enter more problems.

THAT'S NOT THE BUG I HAVE.
USING MY BUG:

```
 21
+39
---
 15
```

TRY GIVING ME SOME MORE EXAMPLES.

```
   51     99    68
+1707    +99   + 9
-----    ---   ---
   21     36    23
```

After failing the test, the team gives a greater range of problems, specifically those using bigger numbers. How is it that 51 + 1707 can add up to 21? By broadening the scope of example problems they are able to reevaluate their initial hypothesis, dismiss it, and develop another one that is complete and consistent with respect to the new errors.

Got the Bug!

continued

FOCUS ON RESEARCH *continued*

PLEASE DESCRIBE THE BUG YOU THINK I HAVE.

The student is adding all the digits together.

HERE ARE SOME PROBLEMS TO TEST YOUR THEORY ABOUT THE BUG.
WHAT IS:

```
  33    1091      8     28     90
 +99   +  60    +34    +70    + 6
 ---   -----    ---    ---    ---
  24      17     15     17     15
```

This time the team's hypothesis passes the test and they are given the description of the bug stored in the procedural network.

VERY GOOD. MY DESCRIPTION OF THE BUG IS:
THE STUDENT ALWAYS SUMS UP ALL THE DIGITS WITH NO REGARD TO COLUMNS.

A variant of this game assigns a cost to each problem the user poses in the process of trying to discover the bug. At the same time, a much higher cost is assigned for claiming to have "discovered" the bug but then failing to pass criterion on the computer-generated test problems. A correctly structured cost algorithm encourages the user to think carefully about the diagnostic value of each problem he creates and not to jump to a conclusion too quickly or too slowly.

From "Diagnostic Models for Procedural Bugs in Basic Mathematical Skills" by J. S. Brown and R. R. Burton, 1978, *Cognitive Science, 2*, pp. 155–192.

Which teacher is better prepared for helping children — the one who knows the grade level at which each student is functioning or the one who knows exactly the types of errors made by each student and how to correct them? To those who have read and understood this chapter, it seems silly even to pose this question. Unfortunately, current math assessment practices lag far behind research, and most teachers are operating without road maps for improving math functioning.

Chapter 12

Language

Learning Objectives

1. Define language and identify major developmental milestones in the acquisition of spoken language.
2. Describe areas of language functioning and list methods for informally assessing each area.
3. Identify and discriminate language disorders from speech dysfunctions.
4. Name and evaluate five standardized tests of language functioning.
5. Conceptualize a comprehensive plan for assessing the language skills of children.

Language is the currency of learning. The ability to receive and send spoken messages is critical to academic and social success. Some children experience significant delays or deficits in language skills and often require special services to benefit from schooling. The purposes of this chapter are to review briefly language development and to document methods for assessing basic language abilities in schoolchildren. Two previous chapters, Preschool Screening and Educational Readiness and Reading, supplement coverage of early language skills. Interested readers are referred to sources such as Dale (1976) or Weiss and Lillywhite (1976) for more comprehensive treatments of language development and disorders.

Fundamentals of Language

Definitions of Language

The function of language is to communicate. The essence of communication is the ability to share one's thoughts, feelings, and experiences with other people. Thus, in any communication, there is a sender and receiver who are embedded in a physical and social context. As conceptualized here, characteristics of the sender, the receiver, and the communication context influence the meaningfulness of a communication. Nevertheless, the use and understanding of language are the main factors in successful communication. Language has been defined differently by numerous investigators. Two representative definitions are:

> Language is a system of signs and the possible relations among them which, together, allow for the representation of an individual's experience of the world of objects, events, and relations. (Bloom, 1975, p. 249)
>
> Languages are composed of speech sounds, syllables, and sentences, and meaning is largely conveyed by the properties and particular use of these units. (Menyuk, 1971, p. 15)

Bloom's definition emphasizes the *communication* aspect of language, while Menyuk's stresses the *structural* aspects of language. According to Lamberts (1979), these definitions have four components in common:

> 1. Language involves *symbols* which represent experiences; we must, therefore, obtain an estimate of the size of children's symbol sets (vocabulary).
> 2. Symbol combinations convey meaning; therefore, we must judge the child's knowledge of the *rules* for symbol combination (grammar).
> 3. . . . In the case of oral language, the symbols are made up of *vocal sounds;* we must, therefore, also assess the child's knowledge of the set of phonemes (speech sounds).
> 4. Communication has interpersonal dimensions that are not strictly related to knowledge of the linguistic code . . . ; [therefore] we must also assess the child's competence with regard to interpersonal *uses* of languages. (pp. 255–256)

Components of Language and Normative Development

Although numerous definitions of language exist, there is high agreement that language has four main components: *phonology*, *morphology*, *syntax*, and *semantics*.

Phonology is the sound system of language. The ability to perceive and reproduce sounds is the basis for speech. There are about 45 speech sounds, or phonemes, in English, which is why English sounds are significantly more diverse than the 26 letters in the alphabet. Children normally demonstrate mastery of the English sound system by the age of six or seven. As some guideposts, one can expect a child to master the phonemes *b*, *t*, *d*, *k*, *g*, and all vowels by age four, and *r*, *l*, *th*, *ar*, *bl*, *br*, and *pr* by age seven (Lillywhite, 1958). By about age three, children demonstrate knowledge of which sound combinations are typical of their language (Menyuk, 1972).

Words are composed of phonemes and form a second basic unit of language commonly referred to as *morphology*. Thus, words, or morphemes, are the smallest elements in language that have meaning. Inflection, root words, suffixes, and prefixes are all morphological components of words. Children use morphological clues in language to derive meaning. For example, *jump* indicates the action of a child, whereas *jumped* indicates both the action and that it already happened. A good command of morphology is invaluable in analyzing words and developing comprehension skills.

Another basic component of language is *syntax*, or the rules for joining words to form sentences. Children's language learning progresses from the establishment of simple, one-proposition sentences ("Mommy come.") through the gradual completion of the grammatical elements of a proposition ("Mommy is coming.") to the combination of two or more propositions ("Mommy is coming home and will play.") and finally to forming complex sentences ("Mommy is coming home and will play after she makes supper.") Most linguists agree that by age five children normally develop their basic oral syntactic ability.

We expect two-year-olds to verbalize approximately 150 words, to name familiar people, and to use verbs but not correctly with subjects. By the age of five, the normal child's vocabulary will have increased to approximately 1,600 words and will contain adverbs, adjectives, prepositions, and conjunctions used in sentences of six or more words.

A final component of language is *semantics*, or comprehension of the meanings and interrelationships of words as they are used in sentences and paragraphs. Besides learning a lexical, or dictionary, definition of a word, children must also learn how words derive meaning when used in a sentence. A solid understanding of syntax is essential to adequate semantic development, since the same word can often be used meaningfully as a noun, verb, and an adjective. For example, the word *swimming* can be used as follows:

1. *Swimming* (noun) is one of my favorite sports.
2. He is *swimming* (verb).
3. The *swimming* (adjective) club will have a meeting on Saturday.

Given such complexity, it should not be surprising that the development of semantics is a slow, error-filled process.

Development of the major components of language (phonology, morphology, syntax, and semantics), however, is not enough for successful communication. One must also learn how to use language appropriately within context, which is known as *pragmatics*. Van Hattum (1980) defined pragmatics as the "rules governing the use of language by an individual in context" (p. 300). In assessing the meaning of language within a social context, one must consider factors such as (a) the age and sex of the speaker and listener, (b) the relationship between the speaker and listener (for example, parent-to-child, sibling-to-sibling), (c) the prior knowledge or past experiences of the speaker and listener, (d) the physical setting of the communication, and, finally (e) the purpose of the message. Thus, a comprehensive evaluation of a child's language skills involves several linguistic and extralinguistic factors and provides educators and psychologists with a significant challenge. In the next sections, we identify typical language and speech problems in children and outline general considerations for conducting language assessments.

Language versus Speech Disorders

Central to competently assessing any domain of behavior is knowledge of desired behaviors. Guerin and Maier (1983) developed a Spoken Language Screening form that summarizes most language skills necessary for educational success (see Table 12.1). Close examination of this table shows that language functioning is characterized by three phases: receptive, inner, and expressive (see Figure 12.1). The assessment of language skills within each of these phases will be discussed in a later portion of this section. Let's now briefly examine speech problems that often accompany and occasionally confound a language assessment.

Speech disorders are commonly classifed as either articulation, voice, or fluency disorders. Individuals assessing children's language skills must be generally knowledgeable of speech problems so they recognize what is and is not a language problem and can make appropriate referrals to speech and language pathologists.

Articulation is the process of producing speech sounds. *Articulation* disorders, by far the most common speech problem, include the addition, substitution, omission, or distortion of speech sounds (see Table 12.2). Functional articulation disorders result from faulty learning, whereas organic disorders are due to abnormalities of the speech mechanism. Common organic articulation disorders in children are apraxia (deficits in performing voluntary moments of the speech mechanism) and dysarthria (impairment of both the reflexive and voluntary components of the speech mechanism).

Variations in pitch, loudness, or vocal quality may be considered *voice disorders*. These characteristics of voice are influenced by the speaker's age and sex. Descriptions of voice disorders are presented in Table 12.2.

Fluency disorders of speech are characterized by difficulties of sequence, duration, rate, and rhythm. Fluent speech is a smooth synthesis of sounds. Probably the most common and obvious fluency disorder is stuttering, which is characterized by sound repetitions, sound prolongations, and broken words. Other types of relatively rare fluency errors also are summarized in Table 12.2.

Table 12.1 Spoken Language Screening Form

Category	Above average 0	Average 1	Below average 2
I. Receptive Language			
1. Volume of voice	______	______	______
2. Understands gestures	______	______	______
3. Remembers directions	______	______	______
4. "Reads" picture stories	______	______	______
5. Response time to questions or direction	______	______	______
6. Listening vocabulary	______	______	______
7. Enjoys listening to books	______	______	______
8. Interprets anger or teasing from others	______	______	______
II. Inner Language			
9. Amount of general knowledge	______	______	______
10. Gets "point" of story or discussion	______	______	______
11. Understands directions or demonstrations	______	______	______
12. Sense of humor	______	______	______
13. Sticks to topic	______	______	______
14. Can predict what will happen next	______	______	______
15. Can summarize story	______	______	______
16. Can do simple mental arithmetic	______	______	______
III. Expressive Language			
17. Pronunciation	______	______	______
18. Speed of speech	______	______	______
19. Speaks in complete sentences	______	______	______
20. Uses words in correct order	______	______	______
21. Uses correct word in conversation	______	______	______
22. Ability to recall names for objects or people	______	______	______
23. Can repeat a story	______	______	______
24. Participates in class discussions	______	______	______

Score:

27 or less	Satisfactory performance.
28–35	Child should be watched and language abilities checked on a periodic basis.
36 or more	Thorough evaluation needed.

From *Informal Assessment in Education* (pp. 189–190) by G. R. Guerin and A. S. Maier, 1983, Palo Alto, CA: Mayfield Publishing Company.

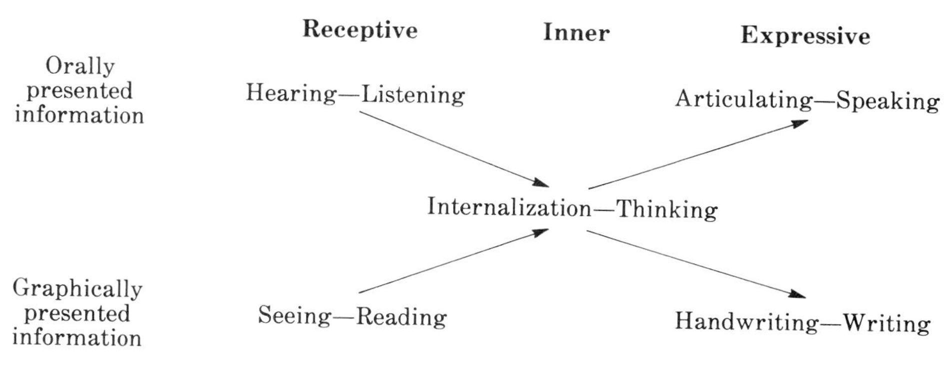

Figure 12.1 Phases of the language process.

Language Assessment Considerations

Formal Assessment

Both formal and informal assessment methods are available for screening the language skills of children; full speech and language examinations usually require the specialized knowledge of speech and language pathologists. Strategies for the formal assessment of language have evolved from tests of articulation and phonology to measures of language structure and content to the current emphasis on pragmatics.

Formal measures of language have typically used one or more of five types of tasks, which have been characterized by Bryen and Gallagher (1983) as:

1. elicited imitation (child repeats a list of phrases or sentences spoken by an examiner),
2. object manipulation (child moves objects as evidence of understanding a direction or a story),
3. picture identification (child points to the pictures that show a stimulus object or situation given by the examiner),
4. language completion (child supplies a missing word or otherwise finishes an incomplete linguistic structure), and
5. spontaneous language sample (child's spontaneous language is transcribed by an examiner).

An informal language assessment provides a rich source of data to supplement standardized tests and can utilize many of the above tasks.

An important issue in the formal assessment of language is the representativeness of language sampled. In many testing situations, it seems that language behavior is artificially separated from a meaningful context so it is distorted or represents a very small portion of a child's repertoire of linguistic

Table 12.2 Speech Disorders

Disorder	Type of errors	Description
Articulation	Addition	Adding a sound or sounds to a word, as in *rutin* for *ruin*.
	Substitution	Substituting a sound or sounds for a sound or sounds in a word, as in *tat* for *cat*.
	Omission	Omitting a sound or sounds from a word, as in *uck* for *truck*.
	Distortion	Distorting the sound or sounds in a word.
Voice	Hypernasality	Allowing excessive air to pass through the nasal cavity.
	Denasality	Allowing too little air to pass through the nasal cavity, so the student sounds as though he or she has a head cold.
	Hoarseness	Deep, harsh voice. Student sounds as though he or she has a cold.
	Intensity	Using the inappropriate loudness of speech. This varies with situations. For example, it is appropriate to be loud at a sporting event but not in a library.
	Frequency	Using the inappropriate pitch of speech. Appropriateness varies with a person's age and sex.
Fluency	Repetitions	Repeating sounds, syllables, or words, as in *my-my-my-my-my wagon*.
	Prolongations	Prolonging sounds in a word, as in *sssssssssssing*.
	Blocks	Pausing before or after a sound, as in *b . . . all*.
	Circumlocutions	Talking around feared words, as in "I live on the avenue between First and Third Avenues" for "I live on Second Avenue."
	Starters	Using various words or phrases to start sentences or phrases in hopes of avoiding stuttering. Examples include *and then*, *you know*, and *I mean*.

From *Assessment in Special Education: The Education Evaluation* (p. 145) by Linda J. Hargrove and James A. Poteet, 1984, Englewood Cliffs, NJ: Prentice-Hall. Copyright © 1984 by Prentice-Hall. Reprinted by permission of Prentice-Hall, Inc., Englewood Cliffs, New Jersey.

competence. When this occurs an inaccurate evaluation can result, and thus it is desirable to supplement any formal measure of language with direct observations, teacher/parent interviews, and spontaneous language samples (that is, informal assessment).

A second important consideration is the differentiation of receptive and expressive language. Clearly, language involves both the ability to receive messages and to express messages; however, during the assessment of a child's language skills, it is often desirable to focus on subskills such as reception and expression. Tasks that do not require a verbal response, such as picture identification or object manipulation, stress comprehension or receptive language, whereas elicited imitation and language completion tasks primarily are measures of expressive language. Of course, expressive skills require some foundation of receptive skills, but there is much controversy among linguists about the degree to which children's receptive language is more advanced than their expressive language (Ingram, 1974). We have set forth three pragmatic points that are relevant to the assessment of children's *receptive* and *expressive* language, regardless of the outcome of the theoretical controversy:

1. Assessment of language abilities should consider both receptive and expressive skills. Tasks in which a child is required to perform an action (for example, pointing to a picture) are tapping receptive abilities, whereas tasks in which the child describes something or repeats or completes a statement tap expressive abilities.
2. Many standardized language tests assess only receptive or only expressive abilities. Thus either multiple tests or informal methods should be used to achieve a balanced assessment of both types of skills.
3. Teachers often overestimate a child's linguistic abilities because of correct responses to instructions and classroom verbalizations. This occurs because the classroom provides a rather predictable context with many models and nonverbal cues that enhance some receptive skills; when removed from such a setting, the child's receptive skills may suffer. Therefore, in any assessment of receptive and expressive language, it is desirable to minimize extralinguistic cues such as teacher gestures or facial expressions, written instructions, and peer models.

Informal Assessment

Before reviewing several standardized tests of language, let us focus on some informal methods and tasks that can and should supplement any assessment of language competence. Approaches to informal language assessment can be divided into two categories: structured, nonstandardized tasks and spontaneous samples of language.

Structured, nonstandardized tasks. A wide variety of structured, nonstandardized tasks of informal assessment have grown out of research on language. These include tasks to assess (a) means-ends relations, (b) sentence imitation, (c) egocentric listening, (d) grammatical structures, and (e) comprehension of temporal relations, anomphoric pronouns, and questions. Leonard, Perozzi, Prutting, and Berkley (1978) outlined strategies by which informal assessment methods can be reliably developed with many such tasks. Bryen and Gallagher (1983) also provided excellent guidance to an examiner of young children's language. Samples of their work in developing structured, nonstandardized assessment procedures from the literature is illustrated in Table 12.3.

Table 12.3 Structured, Nonstandardized Assessment Procedures

Target language aspect	Materials needed	Response paradigm[a]	Procedures
Object use/play (Chappell & Johnson, 1976; Sinclair, 1970)	Common objects (e.g., cup, doll, pillow, hairbrush, ball, mirror, spoon, plastic phone)	OM	1. Place objects in groups of three in front of the child. Observe interaction. Does child interact with the object exploratively, functionally, or symbolically? 2. If child does not spontaneously interact with objects, hand the child one object at a time. Observe and note quality of interaction, as above. 3. Follow-up with verbal directives at a symbolic level (e.g., *Make dolly sleep on the pillow.*)
Early language comprehension (Bloom, 1973; Brown, 1973; Weiss & Lillywhite, 1976)	Contexts of commonly occurring activities	NC	1. Using commonly occurring activities, present simple sentences or words that relate to the context (e.g., at the door say, *bye-bye*). Observe and note child's response. 2. Use same procedure as in 1, but *not* in the context in which that activity typically occurs (e.g., at a table say, *Want to go bye-bye?*). Observe and note the influence of context on language comprehension.
Early language production (Bloom, 1973; Brown, 1973)	Familiar objects or toys	S & A	1. Place familiar toys/objects in front of child, one at a time. Engage child in play. Record any utterances child makes and the context. Analyze the semantic categories used by child (e.g., agent, action, location, recurrence). 2. If no spontaneous utterances, try eliciting utterances by asking early *wh-* questions (e.g., *What's this? What's the ball doing? Where's the ball?*).

Referent description/semantic features (Clark, 1973a; Katz & Fodor, 1963)	Common objects (e.g., nail, envelope, ball) and a list of words without a specific referent (e.g., *animal, toy, hungry, arithmetic*)	D	1. Ask the child to "tell you all about" the object presented. Probe, saying "Tell me more." 2. After using the referent words, ask child to tell you about the words without referents. Probe. 3. Record responses and analyze semantic features used to describe each word (function, name, attributes, class inclusion).
Semantic features at the sentence level (Clark, 1973a; Katz & Fodor, 1963)	List of sentences, some of which are anomalous (violate semantic categories): 1. *She is my brother.* 2. *My mother has no children.* 3. *The candy eats Carol.* 4. *My dog writes nice stories.* 5. *The liquid became an ordorless audience.* 6. *The sun danced lightly through the clouds.*	J.A.D.	1. After reading each sentence, ask whether sentence is a good (makes sense) or bad sentence; then ask why it is a good (or bad) sentence. Have child correct "bad" sentences. Record all responses. 2. Note what factors influenced child's judgments. Note child's explanations and ability to correct anomalous sentences. Note differences, if any, between tacit and explicit language knowledge.
Specific grammatical structures (Bliss et al., 1977; Menyuk, 1969; Potts et al., 1979)	Short stories, with or without accompanying pictures, which focus on particular grammatical structures Example 1 — copula and deletion of past tense marker in main verb: *Carol got a rag, and what she did next* ____ *(was wipe it up* versus *wiped it up)* (Potts et al., 1979, p. 33) Example 2 — count or mass nouns: *Look at this sandbox. There's lots of sand and lots of toys on it. Joe said, "There's no room for me in my sandbox, there's so many* ____ *(toys, things). And there's so much* ____ *(sand, junk)."* (Potts et al., 1979, p. 69)	SC	Construct or obtain short stories that tap structures of interest. Where appropriate, have pictures which provide needed content clues. Read each story, having the child complete it. Note the child's response for semantic relevance, correctness of syntactic structures, and awareness of the rules for dialogue.

(continued)

Table 12.3, *continued*

Target language aspect	Materials needed	Response paradigm[a]	Procedures
Comprehension of anophoric pronoun *it* (Chipman & deDardel, 1974)	Flattened cake of clay, one box containing 5 marbles, one with 20 marbles, one clear box (empty), one tray on which is displayed chocolate divided into demarcated squares on bar of plasticine	OM	Present appropriate materials saying: (1) *There is the clay. Give it to me.* (2) *There is a box with five marbles. Give it to me.* (3) *The chocolate is there. Give it to me.* Note the child's comprehension of the pronoun *it*.
Comprehension of temporal connectives *before*, *after*, *until* (Barrie-Blackey, 1973)	Dolls and dollhouse; sentences containing various subordinate clauses beginning with *before*, *after*, or *until* (e.g., *Daddy lies down after he comes in. Mommy sits down before Daddy comes in. Daddy stands up until Mommy sits down.*)	OM	Sentences are said to the child who acts them out using the toys.
Comprehension of connectives and propositional logical relations (Paris, 1973)	Paired pictures (e.g., Developmental Learning Materials (DLM), Sequential Picture Cards) related to accompanying sentences in four different truth forms: true-true, true-false, false-true, false-false. Compound sentences containing the following connectives: *and* (conjunction), *but* (conjunction), *both — and* (conjunction), *neither — or* (disjunction), *either — or* (disjunction), *if — then* (conditionality), *if — and only if then* (biconditionality)	A	Picture pairs are displayed and the descriptive sentence is read. The child must decide if the description was true or false (e.g., *The boy is riding the bicycle and the dog is lying down.*).
Comprehensions of *wh*-questions — *who*, *why*, *when*, and *how* (Cairns & Hsu, 1978)	Brief videotapes or films of family life, including a father, a mother, a teenage sister, a 6-year-old brother, and a dog. Questions of the following six types: *Who* subject (e.g., *Who bugged the*	A	After being introduced to each character by a photograph which remains on display, the child watches a taped segment and then is asked the six types of questions.

	Who object using progressive aspect (e.g., *Who was the Daddy feeding?*) *Who* object using *do* support (e.g., *Whom did the boy feed?*) *Why* (e.g., *Why did the dog eat the sandwich?*) *When* (e.g., *When did the girl feed the dog?*) *How* (e.g., *How did the girl feed the dog?*)		
Comprehending ongoing discourse (Glucksberg & Krauss, 1967)	Crayons and drawing paper or paste and cut-out construction paper of different sizes, colors, and shapes. A "make pretend" script of a fantasy story which the child will draw following your directions of the script or dictation of the script; or directions about the cut-out shapes that the child will follow to construct a design, mask, or scene. Script sentences should vary in complexity, have an ongoing coherent theme, and utilize, where appropriate, anophoric pronouns. Example 1: *Hi, I'm Mary Martian from Mars. As you know, I'm a little purple Martian with red, round eyes, a square head, and green pointed ears.* Example 2: *Through the window of my spaceship I can see your planet earth. It has a big round yellow sun and blue clouds. It has trees, flowers and birds.*	OM	Administer directions or the made-up scripts to the child in two or three sentences at a time. Encourage the child to make his picture story (or design) exactly like the story you tell. If possible, have child retell the story or design. Analyze child's picture to determine if he was able to accurately process elaborate ongoing language. This includes expanded NP's, anaphoric pronouns.

[a]Response paradigms: A, answers to stimulus questions; D, descriptions; J, judgments about grammaticality; NC, natural context; OM, object manipulations; PI, picture identification; S, spontaneous language; SC, story completion.

Spontaneous samples of language. Informal assessment through spontaneous samples of language involves transcribing and analyzing episodes of communication. This method has two advantages over more formalized, structured approaches to assessment, namely the availability of both a sizable body of normative data on spontaneous language production and more natural, less artificial, language samples (e.g., Kretschmer & Kretschmer, 1978). The potential features for analysis include phonological production, vocabulary, sentence length and structure, word uses, and pragmatics such as turn-taking, initiation of conversation, and listening skills. (For detailed systems for analyzing spontaneous language samples, see Engler, Hannah, & Longhurst, 1973; and Tyack & Gottsleben, 1974.) Engler, Hannah, and Longhurst provided a method for analyzing patterns of language used by children to determine linguistic constructions. This analysis determines deviant or absent linguistic structures and can be used to plan specific remedial interventions. Readers interested in a more comprehensive coverage of informal language assessment are referred to Bryen and Gallagher (1983) and Guerin and Maier (1983). We will now evaluate six commonly used standardized measures of language.

Standardized Language Tests

Fluharty Preschool and Language Screening Test

Overview and purpose. The Fluharty Preschool and Language Screening Test, or FPLST (Fluharty, 1978), is designed to identify preschool children (two-six years of age) in need of comprehensive speech and language evaluations. The test is individually administered and generally takes less than ten minutes to complete. Thirty-five items comprise the total test and are divided into three sections:

1. Section A, which requires the identification of fifteen common objects and is designed to assess vocabulary and articulation.
2. Section B, which measures receptive language abilities through nonverbal responses to ten sentences, and
3. Section C, which requires the oral repetition of ten short sentences and is an attempt to measure expressive language.

Standardization sample and norms. The FPLST was standardized on 2,147 children from four racial or ethnic backgrounds, three socioeconomic classes, and several geographic areas. More specific data on the exact composition of the standardization sample are included in the manual in tabular form, although no mention is made of its representativeness of the population at large.

Data obtained. Children receive four scores (identification, articulation, comprehension, and repetition). A child "fails" the test if any of the four scores falls below the cutoff scores, which, according to the manual, were determined by correlating scores from the FPLST with scores from the Peabody Picture Vocabulary Test (Dunn, 1965), the Goldman-Fristoe Test of Articulation (Goldman & Fristoe, 1972), and the Northwestern Syntax Screening Test (Lee, 1971). However, the derivation of the cutoff scores is not explained.

Reliability and validity. Test-retest reliability coefficients were obtained by retesting fifty of the children in the standardization sample six weeks after the initial testing. Pearson correlations ranged from .95 to .99 for the four scores. Five speech pathologists estimated interrater reliability. Ten children from the standardization sample were retested, and the five speech pathologists scored their responses. Interrater reliability (Pearson *r*) ranged from .87 to 1.00 for the four scores.

Validity is reported in the test manual by indicating the correlation between a child's performance on the FPLST (pass/fail) and the outcome of a more comprehensive speech evaluation (needs therapy/does not need therapy). A Pearson correlation was calculated on the basis of data from 211 children and equaled .90. At one level the validity data can be criticized, because the Pearson Product Moment correlation statistic is not the appropriate procedure for estimating the relationship between two dichotomous variables. More importantly, it is necessary to have the specific figures on the number of children who were correctly identified as needing therapy to evaluate the efficacy of the test as a screening measure. Finally, no information is provided on how the determination of whether a child needed speech therapy was made. (For example, what test was used and who made the determination?)

Summary. The FPLST is a simple screening instrument. Reliability and validity data are not known because the procedures used to determine them seem inappropriate. Thus, the ultimate value of the test can be questioned. In fact, other screening instruments provide more information with only a little extra commitment of time.

Goldman-Fristoe Test of Articulation

Overview and purpose. More than a decade after its development, the Goldman-Fristoe Test of Articulation, or GFTA (Goldman & Fristoe, 1972), remains very popular. Designed to evaluate a child's ability to articulate or produce the sounds of speech, the GFTA is divided into three sections: Sounds-in-Words, Sounds-in-Sentences, and Stimulability. Consonant sounds and blends are elicited in words and sentences (Sounds-in-Words and Sounds-in-Sentences), followed by an attempt to stimulate correct pronunciation of all misarticulated sounds (Stimulability). The first two sections of the GFTA help to determine the content of any remedial activity, while the final section aids in the assessment of a child's receptivity and ability to profit from instruction. The GFTA is individually administered and best used as a criterion-referenced measure of articulation skill.

Standardization sample and norms. No standardization data are reported.

Data obtained. Percentile ranks, based on the National Speech and Hearing Survey (Hull et al., 1971), are available for the Sounds-in-Words section. The most appropriate use of the GFTA, however, is as a criterion-referenced measure of children's ability to produce different sounds.

Reliability and validity. Reliability for the GFTA is reported as percentage of agreement. That is, six speech clinicians were asked to evaluate the test results, and reliability was reported as the number of times they agreed divided by the number of times they agreed plus the number of times they disagreed. Percentage of agreement for the presence or absence of an error was 92 percent, while the percentage of agreement for classification of the nature of the error was 80 percent. Interrater reliability was assessed by having the six clinicians rate the responses of four children. In this instance, the median agreement for the number and type of errors was 91 percent. This method of calculating interrater agreement tends to yield spuriously high percentages. Test-retest reliability (with a week between tests) was 94 percent for Sounds-in-Sentences and 95 percent for Sounds-in-Words.

No validity data are presented. For a criterion-referenced measure such as the GFTA, content validity is most critical. The test seems to include a thorough sampling of speech sounds, but documentation of content validity would be helpful.

Summary. The GFTA is a criterion-referenced measure of children's ability to articulate sounds in a variety of word positions and contexts (in words and sentences). Interrater reliability data appear adequate, and the test seems to sample thoroughly the content it purports to measure, although evidence in the manual for both reliability and validity is sketchy.

Peabody Picture Vocabulary Test-Revised

Overview and purpose. The Peabody Picture Vocabulary Test-Revised, or PPVT-R (Dunn & Dunn, 1981), is a revision of the original Peabody Picture Vocabulary Test. The PPVT-R is a measure of receptive vocabulary and, according to its authors, "it is not, however, a comprehensive test of general intelligence; instead, it measures only one important facet of general intelligence: vocabulary" (p. 2). This statement is important, because the original PPVT was described as a test of intellectual ability and yielded IQ scores. The PPVT-R is untimed and generally takes between 10 and 15 minutes to complete. There are two forms of the test (Form L and Form M), both containing 175 test and 5 training items. It can be administered to individuals between the ages of two and a half and forty. During administration, the examiner reads a stimulus word aloud, and subjects are required to pick the picture (from four choices) that best depicts that word. Minorities and women appear in nonstereotypical roles in the pictures of the PPVT-R (McCallum, 1985).

Standardization sample and norms. The PPVT-R was standardized on a national sample of 4,200 children and youths (ages two and a half to eighteen) and 828 adults (ages nineteen to forty). The sampling procedure was based on data from the 1970 United States census. Stratification variables for the younger sample included age, sex, geographic region, occupation of major household wage earner, ethnicity, and community size. Stratification variables for the older sample included age, sex, geographic region, and occupation. Although both of the standardization groups appear to be representative when compared to 1970 census data, the standardization for the younger group was clearly more comprehensive.

Data obtained. Raw scores (number correct between basal and ceiling) may be transformed to stanines, age equivalents, standard scores (with a mean of 100 and a standard deviation of 15), or percentile ranks.

Reliability and validity. Split-half, immediate test-retest with alternate forms, and delayed test-retest with alternate forms reliability data are presented in the test manual. Median split-half reliabilities of above .80 are reported for both forms. Median reliabilities during immediate retests ($N = 642$) are reported as .82 for raw scores and .79 for standard scores. Median delayed retest reliabilities ($N = 962$) equal .78 for raw scores and .77 for standard scores.

No data on the validity of the PPVT-R are included in the manual. Published data confirm that the alternate forms are equivalent and that the PPVT-R generally yields lower scores than did the original PPVT (see, e.g., Bracken & Prasse, 1981). The PPVT-R also tends to yield lower scores than frequently used measures of cognitive ability such as the Wechsler Intelligence Scale for Children-Revised (Bracken, Prasse, & McCallum, 1984; Davis & Kramer, 1985).

Summary. The PPVT-R is an easy-to-use, well-developed, and appropriately standardized test of receptive (or hearing) vocabulary. Reliability data suggest that it is appropriate for screening purposes, although this instrument does assess a narrow range of language skills. Furthermore, recent data indicate that the scores on the PPVT-R tend to be lower than those for either earlier versions of this test or commonly used measures of intellectual ability.

Test of Early Language Development

Overview and purpose. According to its manual, the Test of Early Language Development, or TELD (Hresko, Reid, & Hammill, 1981a), is a device for screening children with language problems. Administration of the test is simple and explained well in the manual. It has a total of thirty-eight items and is individually administered in approximately fifteen to twenty minutes. Children are required to repeat words and sentences, answer questions, and respond to a set of pictures.

Standardization sample and norms. The TELD was standardized on a sample of 1,184 children in eleven states and one Canadian province. The sample was stratified on the basis of age, sex, geographic region, race, rural versus urban residence, and occupation of parents. Data presented in the manual support the authors' contention that this sample compares favorably with national figures.

Data obtained. Raw scores (number correct) can be converted to percentiles, age equivalents (or language age), and language quotients (or standard scores; with a mean of 100 and a standard deviation of 15). The authors correctly caution users against an overreliance on age-equivalent scores due to the "shortcomings of age norms" (Hresko, Reid, & Hammill, 1981a, p. 9).

Reliability and validity. Reliability data are reported in terms of internal consistency and test-retest estimates. The median internal consistency figure (coefficient alpha) is .88. Median test-retest reliability ($N = 177$) over a two-week interval was .85.

Content, criterion-related, and construct validity of the TELD are discussed in the test manual. Data on item selection, sampling, and discrimination appear to support the claim of content validity for the TELD. Criterion-related validity was established by correlating TELD scores with those from similar language measures. These correlations ranged from .46 (with the Preschool Language Scale by Zimmerman, Steiner, & Evatt, 1970) to .80 (with the Test of Language Development by Newcomer & Hammill, 1981). Construct validity was established by correlating TELD scores with scores from tests of readiness, intelligence, and listening. These comparisons indicate that the TELD does appear to be more closely related to language measures than to other types of tests. These figures help substantiate the claims of criterion-related and construct validity for the TELD.

Summary. The TELD may be useful as a quick, easy-to-administer, overall measure of language ability in young children. The manual provides a clear and detailed explanation of the rationale and appropriate use of the test. Reliability data are adequate, and validity data appear to be fairly good.

Test of Written Language

Overview and purpose. The Test of Written Language, or TOWL (Hammill & Larsen, 1983), was designed to provide a comprehensive assessment of written language skills in children from seven to nineteen years of age. The test samples five areas thought to be involved in language: Mechanical, Productive, Conventional, Linguistic, and Cognitive. Each area is thoroughly explained in the manual. Subtests are Handwriting, Spelling, Style, Word Usage, Vocabulary, and Thematic Maturity. The TOWL is designed for either group or individual administration and can be completed in approximately 40 minutes. Administration and scoring are difficult but well explained in the manual. The results of the TOWL are described as appropriate for identifying students who perform below their peers, determining specific strengths and weaknesses, documenting progress, and conducting research.

Standardization sample and norms. The TOWL was standardized on 3,418 students. A comparison between the normative group and 1980 census data in terms of sex, rural versus urban residence, and geographic distribution is presented in the manual. The sample does appear representative in these areas. No mention is made of any attempt to control for socioeconomic status, educational level of parents, or the inclusion of handicapped children in the sample.

Data obtained. Raw scores on the TOWL may be transformed to percentile ranks or standard scores. Subtest standard scores have a mean of 10 and a standard deviation of 3, while the total test score (Written Language Quotient) has a mean of 100 and a standard deviation of 15. No grade or age equivalents are reported in the manual because "these scores promote misunderstanding of a student's abilities and lead to underreliance on other norm-referenced scores that are much less susceptible to misinterpretation and misunderstanding" (Hammill & Larsen, 1983, p. 13). Thus although the authors realize that educators often like to be able to report grade- or age-level scores, they feel the potential for misuse outweighs any benefits of these scores, a stand for which they should be commended.

Reliability and validity. Internal consistency, test-retest, interscorer, and standard error of measurement figures are reported. All measures of internal consistency (split-half) exceeded .80. Test-retest stability estimates (N = 116) over a two to four week interval indicate that the test composite score (.90) and most of the subtests, including Handwriting (.84), Style (.86), Word Usage (.73), and Spelling (.88), yielded stable scores. The reliability evidence for the Thematic Maturity (.77) and Vocabulary (.62) scores is less convincing, however. Fifteen teachers enrolled in graduate study were used to assess percentage of agreement in scoring the Thematic Maturity (93 percent), Handwriting (76 percent), and Vocabulary (98 percent) subtests. Average standard errors of measurement are reported as ranging from 1.2 to 1.8 for the subtests and as 4.7 for the composite score.

Information on content, criterion-related, and construct validity is reported in the test manual. Under content validity the manual thoroughly discusses the rationale for the test content and the manner in which it was selected. Correlations between the TOWL and a variety of other tests were used as an index of criterion-related and construct validity. These comparisons appear to support the authors' claim that the test does measure skills related to written language (Pollaway, 1985; Williams, 1985).

Summary. In our opinion, the TOWL ranks as the best instrument for the comprehensive assessment of written language skills. The test is difficult to learn to score, but the manual does provide thorough instructions. In fact, the manual serves as an excellent model in its description of what the test *does* and *does not* accomplish.

Woodcock Language Proficiency Battery

Overview and purpose. The Woodcock Language Proficiency Battery, or WLPB (Woodcock, 1980), assesses skills in three areas: oral language, reading, and writing language. There is also a Spanish-language version, the Bateria Woodcock de Proficiencia en el Idioma (Woodcock, 1981). The battery can be administered to individuals from three to eighty years of age, usually in less than an hour. The WLPB actually is a portion of the Woodcock-Johnson Psychoeducational Battery, WJPEB (Woodcock, 1978), that has been repackaged and distributed as a separate test of language ability. According to the manual, the WLPB can be used for individual assessment, selection and placement of students in special programs, individual program planning, guidance, evaluating gains in language development, program evaluation, and research.

Standardization sample and norms. The normative sample for the WLPB included 4,732 subjects stratified on the basis of sex, race, occupation, geographic location, and type of community. It should be noted that this is the sample that took the WJPEB and is not a separate norming the WLPB. As was indicated in the review of the WJPEB (see Chapter 9), the process of subject selection was excellent.

Data obtained. Raw scores on the WLPB may be converted into a number of other scores, including percentile ranks, age equivalents, standard scores, normal curve equivalents, relative performance equivalents, instructional ranges, and bilingual functioning levels (for individuals evaluated with both the English and Spanish versions).

Reliablity and validity. No reliability or validity data are presented in the WLPB manual. While it is true that this type of information is available in the WJPEB, it is the responsibility of the author and publisher to reproduce these data in each version of the test; it cannot be assumed that users of the WLPB

FOCUS ON PRACTICE

Assessment of Limited-English-Proficient Hispanic Children

As of 1980, over three million Hispanic students were enrolled in public schools in the United States, and with the increasing immigration of Hispanic families, the number of limited-English-proficient children will surely increase. A large portion of these youngsters will probably need some psychoeducational interventions to facilitate their academic progress. These interventions may range from bilingual, or English for Speakers of Other Languages (ESOL) programs to extensive special education services. In all cases, a Hispanic student functioning adequately in Spanish, but poorly in English is qualitatively different from a Hispanic student who is functioning poorly in both languages. The latter case is indicative of an actual language or communication disorder for which speech or language therapy is probably needed, whereas the former case suggests that ESOL services are more likely required.

Several English- and Spanish-language proficiency tests are available, including the Woodcock Language Proficiency Battery-English Form (Woodcock, 1980) and its Spanish version, the Bateria Woodcock de Proficiencia en el Idioma-Version en Espanol (Woodcock, 1981); the Expressive One-Word Picture Vocabulary Tests, in Spanish and English (Gardener, 1983); and the Test for Auditory Comprehension of Language, also in Spanish and English (Carrow-Woolfolk, 1973).

Readers interested in the development and assessment of English-language skills in Hispanic children are referred to comprehensive reviews by Cummins (1979) and Wilen and Sweeting (1986).

From "Linguistic Interdependence and the Educational Development of Bilingual Children" by J. Cummings, 1979, *Review of Educational Research, 49*, pp. 222–251, and "Assessment of Limited English Proficient Hispanic Students: Recommendations for School Psychology Practice" by D. K. Wilen and C. V. M. Sweeting, 1986, *School Psychology Review, 15*, pp. 59–75.

will have a copy of the WJPEB. Given the comprehensive nature of the WLPB manual, this omission is surprising. Further, the WJPEB provides no validity data to support the specific uses of the WLPB enumerated in the manual (and listed above).

Summary. The major value of the WLPB appears to be its comprehensiveness. Because a wide survey of skills are covered in a thorough manner, the test seems to have a great deal of promise for a wide range of application. The existence of a Spanish form of the battery, which allows for a direct comparison of proficiency in each language skill, is an important asset in an increasingly bilingual culture. Future editions of the WLPB should include all available reliability and validity data.

Summary

In this chapter, we have tried to convey both the complexity and richness of children's spoken language and the methods commonly used to assess it. Major points were that (a) components of spoken language targeted for assessment include phonology, morphology, syntax, semantics, and pragmatics, (b) both receptive and expressive phases of language should be assessed, and (c) both formal and informal approaches to the assessment of language are necessary to enhance the meaningfulness and representativeness of a language sample. Speech deficits and language proficiency (for example, in English versus Spanish) were noted as critical factors to consider when assessing a student's language performance.

Educators must keep abreast of advances in language research to be useful and dependable evaluators of children's language. We hope you are now better prepared to undertake a language assessment and acknowledge the need for involving speech and language pathologists when confronted with complex problems.

Chapter 13

Perceptual-Motor Skills and Abilities

Learning Objectives

1. Describe the relationship between selective attention and perception.
2. List and explain the principles of perceptual organization.
3. Explain the levels of inference problem.
4. Outline a process for directly assessing perceptual-motor skills.
5. Explain why tests of perceptual-motor skills continue to be in widespread use despite the lack of empirical support for them.

The assessment of perceptual-motor (PM) skills has been popular in educational settings because many psychologists and educators view perceptual-motor development as an important prerequisite to academic skills (Salvia & Ysseldyke, 1981). Children who perform poorly on tests of PM skills are often labeled as having a "perceptual-motor dysfunction" and are placed in specialized curricula to remediate these so-called dysfunctions. Many educators believe that learning problems such as reading and math difficulties are caused by deficits in PM development (Cratty, 1969). Many educational programs thus focus upon teaching or remediating PM rather than academic skills.

The practice of teaching PM skills, or what is called "perceptual-motor training," is questionable given that research has not shown that such training is effective in enhancing basic academic skills (Kavale & Mattison, 1982; Myers & Hammill, 1982). It appears from a careful review of the literature that improving a child's performance on PM tests may improve PM functioning but does not improve reading, arithmetic, or language skills. This holds true regardless of the child's characteristics (such as sex, race, and socioeconomic status), the types of PM programs used, the grade levels trained, or the quality of the research designed to investigate PM training programs (Kavale & Mattison, 1982).

If the research does not support the practice of assessing and training PM skills, why do we devote an entire chapter to this area? Our rationale is simple: *PM tests are among the most frequently used, abused, and misused measures in school settings.* Surveys have consistently shown that PM tests rank second only to intelligence tests in their frequency of use in the schools (see, e.g., Goh, Telzrow, & Fuller, 1981).

The purposes of this chapter are: (a) to provide an overview of PM development, (b) to review selected tests of PM skills, (c) to review briefly some research regarding PM training programs, and (d) to provide an alternative strategy for assessing PM skills.

Fundamentals of Perception

In this section we provide a context for understanding PM assessment and describe how this type of assessment came to prominence in the evaluation of children with learning problems. PM assessment, like most other forms of assessment, relies heavily on theoretical and conceptual underpinnings. Therefore, knowledge of these issues is a prerequisite for understanding PM assessment techniques.

Perception and Attention

The term *perception* has been used to refer to the active process of selective attention to certain sensory input and the interpretation of that information as a function of stored information and concepts and the current qualitative level of cognitive development (Wyne & O'Connor, 1979). A great deal of controversy rages, however, about what constitutes perception and how it may be separated from higher order cognitive processes, or cognition. One way to view perception is to see it as an intermediate step in information processing between sensation and cognition. At a very basic level, a breakdown or impairment of the senses can adversely influence perception, which in turn can affect cognition.

A critical aspect of perception is *selective attention*, or the capacity to select, from an array of competing stimuli, those that are relevant to the task at hand. Selective attention becomes particularly crucial in learning tasks since there are a variety of competing and often confusing stimuli in the typical classroom, such as noise from other classrooms, whispering, and sounds from the heating system. Obviously, if one could not ignore these distractions, it would be difficult to learn.

Attention is a complex concept, although teachers frequently refer to attention during instruction. When a teacher says, "Frank, pay attention!" because Frank is looking out of the window during reading instruction, how do we know that he is paying attention if he redirects his eyes to his book? The only way to know is to ask him a question regarding the task in which he is supposedly engaging. If he answers correctly, he must be paying attention. However, he could answer correctly because he had learned the answer earlier. Alternatively, Frank could answer incorrectly because the question was unclear or poorly asked. It should thus be apparent that attention is a complex, difficult construct because it describes a covert process that cannot be directly observed; it must be measured by observing changes in performance. Similarly, the only way we can measure perception is by the same process of direct observation of performance.

Perceptual Organization

The assessment of PM skills began in the early 1900s with the work of gestalt psychologists such as Max Wertheimer, Kurt Koffka, and Wolfgang Kohler (Salvia & Ysseldyke, 1981). The gestalt school of psychology can best be defined by the statement, "The whole is greater than the sum of its parts." That is, a perceived stimulus has greater meaning to an individual than its component parts. The basic assumptions of gestalt psychology are called the *principles of perceptual organization.* The three basic laws most relevant in the assessment of PM skills are (a) the law of proximity, (b) the law of similarity, and (c) the law of closure.

The *law of proximity* states that groups are formed by elements close to one another in space or time. For example, separate notes played in rapid succession comprise a melody in music. Similarly, separate printed stimuli on a page comprise words that in turn comprise sentences and paragraphs. Figure 13.1a depicts the law of proximity. The *law of similarity* states that similar items tend to be perceived in groups. Figure 13.1b illustrates this principle, with the filled circles and the open circles each being perceived as separate groups. Finally, the *law of closure* states that parts of a stimulus that are not presented will be filled in by the perceptual system. Figure 13.1c shows an example of this law using the word *boy.*

The Relationship Between Perceptual Impairments and Learning

The work of the gestalt psychologists set the stage for the clinical application of gestalt principles in the assessment of perceptual impairments. Kurt Goldstein (1939; 1948) was a pioneer in the assessment of brain-injured adults. Further application of these principles was evident in the work of Heinz Werner and Alfred Strauss who worked with mentally retarded, autistic, and brain-injured children in the 1940s (Strauss & Lehtinen, 1947). Central to Werner's

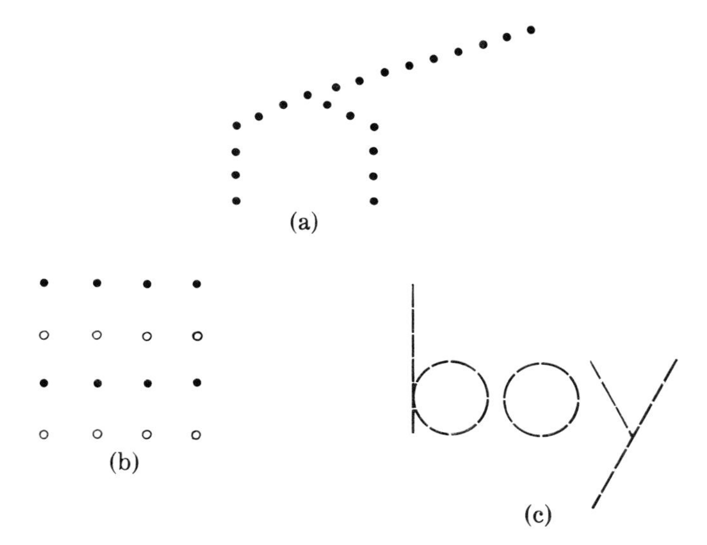

Figure 13.1 Examples of the Law of Proximity (a), the Law of Similarity (b), and the Law of Closure (c).

and Strauss's assumptions regarding learning problems were *perceptual disorders*, particulary figure-ground disturbances.

In the 1960s a new term was introduced to describe children who had no demonstrable sensory impairments and were not mentally retarded but still had great difficulty learning. Kirk (1963) labeled these children *learning disabled*, and many of their characteristics were similar to those first described in the 1940s by Werner and Strauss in discussing brain-injured children. Assessment procedures that focus upon the measurement of perceptual functioning were stimulated by and continue to be fueled by the concern for children with learning disabilities. However, most if not all of these tests are technically inadequate and do not yield information on which to base interventions.

Tests of Perceptual-Motor Skills

Our position, which is supported in the following test reviews, is that tests of PM skills should never be used to diagnose nor to develop remediation strategies for school-age children and youth. We believe that the data provided by these tests add little if any useful information concerning a child's learning difficulties in the classroom. The majority of tests of PM skills on the market do not merit review because of their psychometric inadequacy. The following discussion is limited to a small sample of commonly used tests of PM functioning. Table 13.1 presents a categorization system for such instruments. Most of

Table 13.1 Perceptual-Motor Tests According to Perceptual System and Perceptual Process

Perceptual process	Perceptual system	
	Visual	*Auditory*
Discrimination	Illinois Test of Psycholinguistic Ability (ITPA) — Visual Closure (Kirk, McCarthy, & Kirk, 1968)	ITPA — Auditory Discrimination Test (Kirk et al., 1968)
Memory	Revised Visual Retention Test (Benton, 1963)	ITPA — Auditory Sequential Memory (Kirk et al., 1968)
Integration	Bender Visual Motor Gestalt Test (Koppitz, 1975)	ITPA — Sound Blending (Kirk et al., 1968)

these tests involve the *visual perception system* and require *visual-motor integration*, such as copying geometric designs from a stimulus or memory.

Hammill and Bartel (1975) suggest that the following questions be asked before assessing PM skills in the schools:

1. Do I wish to assess perception, perceptual-motor integration, or both?
2. Am I interested in a particular perceptual skill (for example, discrimination, figure-ground, closure) or in overall perceptual ability?
3. Is the measure appropriate for the prospective sample (that is, are the children physically able to respond, and is the test too easy or too difficult)?
4. Is the measure reliable enough to be used for educational purposes (that is, as the basis for an educational classification decision)?
5. Are the data derived from the test worth the time and effort of administering and scoring the test?
6. Are there any data that support the relationship between performance on the test and academic performance in the classroom? If so, how strong is this relationship and to what extent can it be generalized across samples (that is, the external validity of the data)?
7. Are there more direct ways of assessing this skill (for example, through the use of curriculum-based assessment methods)?

These questions are important because many professionals unfortunately administer tests of PM skills more out of habit than out of thoughtful consideration of what is to be assessed and why. Table 13.2 presents summary data on selected tests of PM skills and demonstrates the psychometric inadequacy of the most commonly used tests of perceptual-motor skills. None of the tests in the table includes a representative standardization sample, and the reliabilities of these tests are too low to make diagnostic decisions for individuals.

Table 13.2 Technical Data of Selected Perceptual-Motor Tests

Test	Age range	Representative norms	N	Test-retest reliability	Internal consistency reliability	Interrater reliability
Auditory Discrimination Test (Wepman, 1973)	5–8	No	—[a]	.93	—[a]	—[a]
Bender Visual Motor Gestalt Test (Koppitz, 1975)	5–11	No	975	.71	—[a]	.90
Developmental Test of Visual Motor Integration (Berry & Buktenica, 1982)	2–15	No	1,039	.85	.93	.98
Goldman-Fristoe-Woodcock Test of Auditory Discrimination (Goldman, Fristoe, & Woodcock, 1970)	3–84	No	745	.94	.73	.91
Memory for Designs Test (Graham & Kendall, 1960)	8–70	No	825	.89	.92	.99
Motor-Free Test of Visual Perception (Colarusso & Hammill, 1972)	5–8	No	378	.80	.78	—[a]
Revised Visual Retention Test (Benton, 1963)	8–44	No	600	.85	—[a]	.95
Total	3–84	0%	709[b]	.85[b]	.83[b]	.95[b]

[a]Not reported

[b]Median

Bender Visual Motor Gestalt Test

Overview and purpose. The Bender Visual Motor Gestalt Test (Bender Gestalt) was developed by Loretta Bender, a physician, to differentiate brain-damaged from non–brain-damaged adults. Bender (1938) used nine geometric designs published by Wertheimer in 1923 to illustrate the principles of gestalt psychology. Each design is printed on a 4-by-6-inch white card and presented in a specified sequence to an examinee, who is asked to copy all nine designs on a sheet of 8½-by-11-inch white paper. The accuracy of the reproduced designs is evaluated by relatively objective scoring criteria.

According to Koppitz (1975), the Bender Gestalt is a test of *visual-motor integration* because it required the examinee to integrate what is perceived visually with the fine motor responses required to reproduce the designs. It should be noted that some persons may perform poorly on the Bender Gestalt yet not have a visual perception problem. For example, someone who has extremely poor fine motor coordination may be misdiagnosed as having difficulty in visual perception when the problem is simply one of fine motor coordination; Koppitz warns against such simple-minded misinterpretations. This is particularly problematic with cerebral palsied and developmentally delayed children.

Standardization sample and norms. The most frequently used normative sample and scoring system was developed by Koppitz (1975). The Bender Gestalt was originally standardized on 975 children between the ages of five and eleven. The sample was not geographically representative of the United States population since 83 percent were from the Northeast, 15 percent from the West, and only 2 percent from the South. Koppitz's standardization sample was somewhat more representative with respect to race, with 86 percent being white, 8.5 percent black, 4.5 percent Hispanic, and 1 percent Oriental. Koppitz did not attempt to stratify the sample according to socioeconomic status (SES) and suggests that SES may not be an important variable in performance on the Bender Gestalt. This claim, however, is not substantiated by other research, which suggests that Bender Gestalt performances do vary by SES level (Buckley, 1977).

Data obtained. In school settings, the most commonly used scoring is a relatively objective system known as the Koppitz Developmental Bender Scoring System (Koppitz, 1964). Four types of errors (see Koppitz, 1975) are scored with this system:

1. *Distortion of shape.* Distortion of the figure by drawing parts in disproportionate size or substituting angles for curves or circles or dashes for dots. Distortion of shape is scored for Figures A, 1, 3, 5, 6, 7, and 8 for a total of 10 points.
2. *Rotation.* Rotation of any part of the figure by forty-five degrees or more. Rotation errors are also scored if the subject draws the figure correctly but

rotates the stimulus card. Rotation errors are scored for Figures A, 1, 2, 3, 4, 5, and 8 for a total of 8 points.
3. *Integration.* The failure to connect two parts of a figure, the crossing of two lines at an incorrect place, the failure to cross two lines, or the omission or addition of rows or dots. Integration errors are scored for Figures A, 2, 3, 4, 5, 6, and 7 for a total of 9 points.
4. *Perseveration.* The increase, prolongation, or continuation of the number of units in the design. Perseveration is scored for Figures 1, 2, and 6 for a total of 3 points.

A total of thirty errors can be made on the nine designs. The total number of errors a child makes is compared to the appropriate age-level norms in the Koppitz (1975) manual. The error score is then converted into a percentile ranking, which can be used to interpret the child's test performance.

Reliability and validity. Koppitz (1975) reported both interrater agreement and test-retest reliability, or stability, for the Bender Gestalt. Interrater reliability studies reported in the manual ($N = 23$) show that reliabilities range from .79 to .99, with a median of .90. These high reliabilities suggest that raters agreed in the total number of errors they scored on the test. The objective scoring criteria listed above probably account for these high agreement estimates.

The manual reports nine test-retest reliability studies, with stability coefficients ranging from .50 to .90 and averaging .71. Unfortunately, over half of these studies were conducted with kindergarten children. Furthermore, the mean reliability of .71 suggests that the Bender Gestalt is not stable enough to use in making important decisions for children.

Convincing empirical evidence is not presented in the manual to support Koppitz's (1975) claim that the Bender Gestalt is a measure of visual-motor integration. In other words, there is little evidence for the construct validity of the test, although the manual does report the results of correlational studies between the Bender Gestalt and measures of achievement, intelligence, and visual perception.

Evidence for the test's criterion-related validity is presented in the manual, mostly in the form of correlations between the total score on the Bender Gestalt and measures of academic achievement. The manual lists fifty-four studies in which the Koppitz-scored Bender Gestalt has been compared with measures of school achievement. Fifty of these studies have been conducted with children in kindergarten through third grade. The validity coefficients in the fifty-four studies range from −.13 to −.58, with a median concurrent validity coefficient of −.23. The direction of these correlations is negative because the Koppitz scores are based upon the number of errors (that is, the lower the number of errors, the higher the academic achievement score). Based on the data presented in the manual, the Bender Gestalt is not a useful predictor of academic achievement; on the average, it accounts for only 5 percent of the variance in academic success.

The manual also presents the results of eight correlations between the Bender Gestalt and various measures of intelligence. Validity coefficients in these studies ranged from −.19 to −.62, with a median of −.22, which indicates generally poor prediction of intellectual functioning and thus directly contradicts Koppitz's (1975) claim that "the Bender Gestalt can be used with some degree of confidence as a short nonverbal intelligence test for young children" (p. 47). One is perplexed that Koppitz could even make such a statement in light of the data in her own manual: by definition a correlation of −.22 does not inspire a high degree of confidence and indicates that the Bender Gestalt (scored according to Koppitz) does not measure the construct of intelligence in even the broadest and most liberal interpretation of that concept. Put simply, if you wish to measure intelligence, use an intelligence test.

Summary. The Bender Gestalt is by far the most frequently used test of PM functioning, and, because of its simplicity and ease of administration, it is also one of the most frequently *misused* tests. The test's reliability and validity relative to those of similar tests have been the subject of much research. The reliability of the Bender Gestalt (Koppitz scored) is too low for making any kind of placement decision, yet the test is often inappropriately used to diagnose children as brain damaged, perceptually handicapped, or emotionally disturbed (Salvia & Ysseldyke, 1981). Validity of the Bender Gestalt is likewise not well established. It has not been demonstrated that the test measures the construct of "visual-motor integration" and has been found to be a very poor predictor of academic achievement and intelligence.

In summary, the Bender Gestalt is, in the words of Koppitz (1975), "one of the most overrated, most misunderstood, and most maligned tests currently in use" (p. 2).

Goldman-Fristoe-Woodcock Test of Auditory Discrimination

Overview and purpose. The Goldman-Fristoe-Woodcock Test of Auditory Discrimination, or GFW (Goldman, Fristoe, & Woodcock, 1970), was designed as a measure of speech-sound discrimination skills in persons aged four to adulthood. The GFW has two subtests: (a) Quiet Subtest and (b) Noise Subtest. Both are individually administered by tape recordings. A subject is presented with four pictures and must select the one that corresponds to the word spoken on the tape. Pictures depict items with names that have some sound similarity but at least one major sound difference.

Standardization sample and norms. The GFW was standardized on 745 subjects ranging from three to eighty-four years of age. The standardization sample was not geographically representative of the United States population, with the subjects coming from only three states (New Jersey, Minnesota, and Tennessee). The manual presents no information regarding their ethnicity, socioeconomic status, or other important demographic characteristics. In short, the GFW norms represent a restricted sample.

Data obtained. Scoring is straightforward and consists of counting the number of errors made by the examinee. Error scores are converted to T scores, which have a mean of 50 and a standard deviation of 10 for each subtest. The manual also reports a supplementary method of scoring that differentiates errors by certain kinds of words, such as voiced and unvoiced sounds. Separate norms using this method are not presented.

Reliability and validity. The manual reports internal consistency reliability coefficients of .79 for the Quiet Subtest and .68 for the Noise Subtest. Coefficients of this magnitude suggest some problem in internal consistency, which in turn suggests error rather than auditory discrimination is being measured. The manual indicates that these low coefficients are due to the relatively few number of items on each subtest. Although this is an explanation, statistically viable, it does not increase confidence in the test. Furthermore, the small number of items calls into question the adequacy of content sampling, which then leads one to question the content validity of the test. Validity evidence for the GFW reported in the manual show correlations of .60 (Quiet Subtest) and .52 (Noise Subtest) with the Stanford Binet Intelligence Scale, but lower correlations with measures of receptive language such as the Peabody Picture Vocabulary Test (.15 for the Quiet Subtest and .00 for the Noise Subtest). In our opinion, the GFW does not adequately discriminate individuals who have good or poor auditory discrimination abilities.

Summary. The GFW is a poorly standardized, technically inadequate test that was designed to measure auditory discrimination abilities under quiet and noisy background conditions. Although a noise subtest does represent a more ecologically valid condition for testing learning since most classrooms have some background noise at most times, the background noise for the GFW appears to have been a school cafeteria. The GFW should thus not be used to make classification or placement decisions because of its poor normative characteristics, low reliability, and dubious validity.

Illinois Test of Psycholinguistic Abilities

Overview and purpose. The Illinois Test of Psycholinguistic Abilities, ITPA (Kirk, McCarthy, & Kirk, 1968), is intended to measure the ability to understand, process, and produce verbal and nonverbal language in children between the ages of two years, four months, and ten years, three months. Although it was partially designed to represent a linguistic theoretical model, Carroll (1972) stated that "it requires some stretching of meaning to call the ITPA a measure of psycholinguistic abilities" (p. 442).

The ITPA is composed of ten regularly administered individual tests and two optional subtests. According to the technical manual (Paraskevopoulos & Kirk, 1969), the psycholinguistic model on which the test is based attempts to relate those functions whereby the intentions of one person are transmitted either verbally or nonverbally to another with functions whereby the environment or the intentions of another person are received and interpreted. Specifically, the ITPA was designed to measure an individual's ability to comprehend, remember, and express stimuli that are presented visually or auditorily. The twelve ITPA subtests and examples of items from each are provided in Table 13.3.

Standardization sample and norms. The ITPA was standardized on 962 children between the ages of two years, seven months, and ten years, one month. The standardization sample was not geographically representative of the United States as all subjects came from around Urbana, Illinois, and Madison, Wisconsin. The authors stated in the technical manual that children were primarily selected on the basis of "the practical requirements of accessibility and because of suitability to the requirements of being middle class communities" (Paraskevopoulos & Kirk, 1969, p. 57). This lack of representation is a serious problem because curriculum emphasis in local schools can easily affect ITPA scores, and research indicates that ITPA scores are clearly modified by instruction.

The standardization sample included only those children demonstrating "average intellectual functioning," "average school achievement," and "average characteristics of personal-social adjustment." This is perplexing, however, since the ITPA was designed as a diagnostic instrument primarily for children encountering learning difficulties. Yet because these children were systematically excluded from the sample, there are no scores in the sample with whom the scores of children with learning problems can be compared. Moreover, since only middle class children were included in the sample, the test is vulnerable to claims of bias for lower class and minority children.

In summary, the ITPA norms are based on a sample that is highly restrictive in terms of geographic region, socioeconomic status, minority group membership, and the inclusion of the full range of scores for comparison purposes, particularly of children with learning difficulties. Thus, the ITPA is a poorly standardized test.

Data obtained. Three types of derived scores can be obtained from the ITPA: (a) scale scores for each subtest, with a mean of 36 and a standard deviation of 6; (b) psycholinguistic ages (PLAs) for each subtest, which are similar to a mental age on certain intelligence tests (e.g., Stanford Binet); and (c) psycholinguistic quotients (PLQs), which are ratio scores (PLA/CA × 100), similar to an IQ score. There are a number of statistical problems with the use of PLAs and PLQs, including unequal standard deviations at each age group, which render scores incomparable from one age to another. For example, a PLQ of

Table 13.3 Description and Examples of the ITPA Subtests

Auditory reception: This test assesses the child's ability to derive meaning from verbally presented material. Since the receptive rather than the expressive process is being sampled, the response throughout is kept at the simple level of a "yes" or "no," either verbally or with a nod or shake of the head. The test contains 50 items.

Typical items
"Do dogs eat?"
"Do dials yawn?"
"Do carpenters kneel?"

Auditory association: This test taps the child's ability to relate concepts presented orally. In this test, the requirements of the auditory receptive process and the vocal expressive process are minimal, while the organizing process of manipulating linguistic symbols in a meaningful way is tested by verbal analogies of increasing difficulty. There are 42 orally presented sentence completion items.

Typical items
"I cut with a saw; I pound with a ———."
"A dog has hair; a fish has ———."

Visual association: The organizing process in this channel is tapped by a picture association test with which to assess the child's ability to relate concepts presented visually. The child is presented with a single stimulus picture surrounded by four optional pictures, one of which is associated with the stimulus picture. The child is asked, "What goes with this?" (pointing to the stimulus picture). "Which one of these?" (pointing to the four optional pictures). The test contains 20 items of the simpler form and 22 visual analogies.

Verbal expression: The purpose of this test is to assess the ability of the child to express his [*sic*] own concepts vocally. The child is shown four familiar objects, one at a time (a ball, a block, an envelope, and a button), and is asked, "Tell me all about this." The score is the number of discrete, relevant, and approximately factual concepts expressed.

Manual expression: This test taps the child's ability to express ideas manually. This ability is assessed by a gestural manipulation test. In this test, 15 pictures of common objects are shown to the child one at a time and he [*sic*] is asked to, "Show me what to do with a ———." The child is required to pantomime the appropriate action, such as dialing a telephone or playing a guitar.

Grammatic closure: This test assesses the child's ability to make use of the redundancies of oral language in acquiring automatic habits for handling syntax and grammatic inflections. There are 33 orally presented items accompanied by pictures which portray the content of the verbal expressions. The pictures are included to avoid contaminating the test with difficulty in the receptive process. Each verbal item consists of a complete statement followed by an incomplete statement to be finished by the child. The examiner points to the appropriate picture as he [*sic*] reads the given statements.

Typical items
"Here is a dog; here are two ———."
"This dog likes to bark; here he is ———."

Table 13.3, *continued*

Auditory closure: This is basically a test of the organizing process at the automatic level. It assesses the child's ability to fill in missing parts which were deleted in auditory presentation and to produce a complete word. There are 30 items ranging in difficulty from easy words to more difficult ones.

Typical items
"airpla / "
"ta / le / oon"
" / ype / iter"

Sound blending: This test provides another means of assessing the organizing process at the automatic level in the auditory-vocal channel. The sounds of a word are spoken singly at half-second intervals, and the child is asked to tell what the word is. At one end of the scale it has been made applicable to younger children by including pictures, thus making the task less open-ended. At the upper levels the test has been extended by including nonsense words.

Typical items
"type(pause)wri(pause)iter"
"ta(pause)ble"
"wa(pause)ter(pause)me(pause)llon"

Visual closure: This test assesses the child's ability to identify a common object from an incomplete visual presentation. There are four scenes, presented separately, each containing 14 or 15 examples of a specified object. The objects are seen in varying degrees of concealment. The child is asked to locate and point to all examples of a particular object within 30 seconds.

Typical items
"Find as many fish as you can."
"Find as many hammers and nails as you can."

Auditory sequential memory: This test assesses the child's ability to reproduce from memory sequences of digits increasing in length from two to eight digits. This test differs from the Digit Span subtest from the WISC-R in that the digits are presented at the rate of two per second instead of one per second. The more rapid presentation makes the task easier, which is necessary for two- and three-year-old children.

Typical items
"4-2"
"3-1-7"
"7-4-8-5-1-3-6-2"

Visual sequential memory: This test assesses the child's ability to reproduce sequences of nonmeaningful figures from memory. The child is shown each sequence of figures for five seconds and then is asked to put corresponding chips of figures in the same order. The sequences increase in length from two to eight figures.

Adapted from *The Development and Psychometric Characteristics of the Revised Illinois Test of Psycholinguistic Abilities* by J. N. Paraskevopoulos and S. A. Kirk, 1969, Urbana: University of Illinois Press.

99 at age four represents the 50th percentile whereas this same score at age ten years is at the 31st percentile.

The technical manual also provides tables for *intraindividual* comparisons in which performance on a given subtest can be compared to the median performance over all ITPA subtests. However, the reliabilities of the subtests are so low that it is unwise to make comparisons among or between them and the total score.

Reliability and validity. The manual extensively presents reliability data, including test-retest, internal consistency, and interscorer reliability. Table 13.4 shows the median internal consistency and five-month test-retest reliability coefficients across all age levels and for all subtests. As can be seen in this table, the stability of the majority of subtests for the scale are less than adequate. The internal consistency reliabilities are, for the most part, below acceptable standards, with Verbal Expression (r = .65), Visual Closure (r = .60), and Auditory Closure (r = .65) the least internally consistent subtests. In sum, the ITPA does not possess an adequate level of reliability on which to base either diagnostic or placement decisions for children. Most subtests are neither internally consistent nor sufficiently stable to ensure accurate measurement of the skills purportedly assessed by the scale.

The ITPA technical manual is virtually devoid of validity data. Thus little

Table 13.4 Median Internal Consistency and Five-Month Test-Retest Reliability Coefficients for ITPA Subtests[a]

Subtest	Internal consistency	Test-retest
Auditory Reception	.88	.46
Visual Reception	.80	.29
Auditory Association	.80	.67
Visual Association	.79	.45
Verbal Expression	.65	.47
Manual Expression	.76	.46
Grammatic Closure	.67	.61
Auditory Closure	.65	.44
Sound Blending	.85	.47
Visual Closure	.60	.63
Auditory Sequential Memory	.82	.74
Visual Sequential Memory	.74	.31
Composite	.90	.77

Adapted from *The Development and Psychometric Characteristics of the Revised Illinois Test of Psycholinguistic Abilities* by J. N. Paraskevopoulos and S. A. Kirk, 1969, Urbana: University of Illinois Press.

[a]Coefficients are collapsed across age levels and are not corrected for restriction in intelligence range.

evidence exists to support the statement that the test measures the construct of psycholinguistic abilities. As Carroll (1972) pointed out, almost half of the subtests could be completed by individuals who had never acquired *any* language system. Calling the ITPA a measure of psycholinguistic ability is a misnomer, since it measures only a small fraction of skills that might be considered linguistic. For example, reading, writing, and spelling are clearly language (linguistic) skills, but they were excluded from the ITPA on the premise that the scale was designed to measure basic cognitive skills not attained through schooling.

The technical manual presents no evidence for the criterion-related validity of the ITPA in predicting academic achievement. The ITPA has moderately positive correlations with Stanford Binet IQ scores, although these correlations may be depressed because of the restricted range of the sample tested.

Summary. The ITPA is a poorly standardized and questionable instrument for measuring the psycholinguistic abilities of children. The subtests have relatively low reliability, and the test's validity has not been clearly established. The nonrepresentative standardization sample creates a problem analogous to a situation in which one wishes to define shortness on the basis of a group of persons of average height. If you only measure persons who are of average height (relative to the general population), how can you define a person of average height as short? The answer is, of course, you cannot, unless you are willing to enter into the fallacious reasoning of stating that a person of average height is short relative to other persons who are in the range of average height. Thus, in our opinion, neither placement nor diagnostic decisions can be made on the basis of ITPA scores.

Perceptual-Motor Training

As mentioned at the beginning of this chapter, many educators and psychologists believe that there is a direct relationship between perceptual-motor development and academic achievement. Between 1936 and 1970, perceptual programing unquestionably became the most widely used method of assessing and teaching children with learning problems (Hallahan & Cruickshank, 1973). A spate of tests were developed to diagnose PM problems and to generate PM training programs to remediate these problems (see Wallace & Larsen, 1978).

A basic tenet of perceptual theory is that impairment in PM skills will significantly interfere with learning, especially learning to read. Underlying this assumption is the hypothesis that there is a strong relationship between measures of PM skills and academic achievement. In fact, however, there is *not* a strong relationship between PM skills as measured by tests of PM functioning and academic achievement as measured by tests of academic achievement (Wallace & Larsen, 1978).

Studies investigating the relationships between auditory perception skills

FOCUS ON RESEARCH
Recent Attempts at Ability Training

Special educators have experienced a great deal of difficulty in deciding how best to teach problem learners. Logic would appear to indicate that if one could identify the learner's strengths and weaknesses, one could teach to the strengths and avoid the weaknesses. Unfortunately, research has not supported this process.

Educators and psychologists attempting to identify learner strengths and weaknesses began to talk about underlying learning processes or abilities such as visual sequential memory, auditory discrimination, and visual closure. However, these and other, similar so-called abilities merely represent reifications of constructs. That is, these terms do not represent anything concrete but are merely abstractions. When used often enough, these abstractions begin to be discussed and used as if they were real entities (for example, "she is an auditory learner," or "he needs training to increase his auditory discrimination").

This approach to assessment and teaching is called the *ability training model*. It rests upon the assumptions that learning "abilities" exist, that they can be reliably measured, and that they can be enhanced by training. Extensive research over the past fifteen years, however, offers little support for these assumptions (Hammill & Larsen, 1974b; Myers & Hammill, 1982; Ysseldyke, 1973; Ysseldyke & Mirkin, 1982). First, there is little evidence that these so-called abilities even exist. Second, attempts to measure these "abilities" have resulted in some of the most psychometrically inadequate tests on the market today (see the test reviews in this chapter). Thus there is little proof that these "abilities," even if they do exist, can be reliably

continued

(Hammill & Larsen, 1974a), visual perception skills (Larsen & Hammill, 1975), and psycholinguistic processes (Hammill & Larsen, 1974b) with academic achievement have been extensively reviewed. Collectively, these studies provide little empirical data to support the assumption that perceptual ability is related to academic achievement (see Focus on Research).

Myers and Hammill (1976) reviewed 105 studies and found little support for the continued use of PM training to facilitate academic achievement of school-age children. We must therefore ask what problem is one trying to solve when PM tests are administered? We have no simple answer to this question, although we have several hypotheses. Perhaps the use of PM tests is promulgated by the testing industry. A basic principle of marketing is that as long as a product is kept before the public's eye, it will be consumed. A brief perusal of testing catalogues suggests that testing companies are not decreasing their marketing emphasis on PM tests.

Another hypothesis is that some individuals want to attribute learning difficulties to causes intrinsic to the person (for example, a perceptual-motor

FOCUS ON RESEARCH *continued*

measured. Finally, there is little evidence that training these "abilities" can improve school performance.

A basic assumption of the ability training model is the existence of *aptitude by treatment interactions* (ATIs) (Cronbach & Snow, 1969). ATI research has focused on the notion that individuals with certain aptitudes will behave differently in certain treatments (that is, teaching strategies) than in others. For example, the statement that a student is a "visual learner" is a statement about a student's aptitude. The statement that the child needs a "whole-word" reading program is a treatment statement. The statement that visual learners will learn more in a whole-word reading program than in a phonics-based program is a statement about an aptitude by treatment interaction.

In special education there is widespread popular belief in the presence of ATIs. Although logic would seem to indicate that ATIs exist, empirical research on teaching has not supported this. Cronbach and Snow (1969) comprehensively reviewed ATI research and concluded that there are no solidly established ATI relations. Thus the age-old adage applies here: "I am an empiricist because logic is only as strong as its assumptions." The assumptions on which ATIs are based are faulty. As such, teaching strategies based upon ATIs will necessarily be faulty as well.

It would be difficult to find a special educator or school psychologist who does not talk in terms of "aptitudes" or "abilities." The use of these terms is widespread to the point of being epidemic. Although this terminology is a convenient way to label behavior, the terms represent mentalistic fictions used as pseudoexplanations of a child's difficulty in learning academic materials.

dysfunction). Using this logic, one is able to assign a label to a problem that becomes an explanation for the existence of the problem. Thus if the inability of some children to read, compute, or use language appropriately is attributed to "perceptual-motor deficits" or "psycholinguistic processing dysfunctions," assessment of these children will focus upon perceptual and processing abilities that are the presumed "causes" of poor achievement. Perceptual-motor assessment therefore continues in spite of what we consider to be overwhelming empirical evidence to the contrary (for a review, see Myers & Hammill, 1976).

Finally, we believe many persons are simply unaware of the research findings regarding perceptual-motor and psycholinguistic training programs. The conceptual appeal of these programs coupled with the simplicity of assessing certain PM skills may lead many into pseudoexplanations of a child's poor achievement. In this sense, saying something (even though it is inaccurate) about the cause of Johnny's inability to read is less aversive than saying, "I don't know."

The Level of Inference Problem in Assessment

Our review of perceptual-motor assessment has been negative for what we consider to be obvious reasons that pertain to the poor normative samples of most PM tests, the relatively poor reliability and validity evidence for these measures, and the lack of a demonstrated relationship between PM skills and academic achievement. A major problem with all of these measures, in our view, is the high *level of inference* required to interpret performance on these instruments. Level of inference refers to the relationship between behavior actually observed and the interpretation of or meaning attributed to that behavior. The level of inference can vary from simple, straightforward, precise descriptions of what was seen or observed (no inference) to quite abstract and remote interpretations of the meaning of that behavior (high inference).

Figure 13.2 provides examples of the different levels of inference that might be used with Danny's copying of a design from the Bender Gestalt. Each of the interpretations has appeared in the literature on the Bender Gestalt or similar perceptual-motor assessment devices. The level of inference varies from a straightforward description, "Danny could not accurately copy these

Danny's Bender

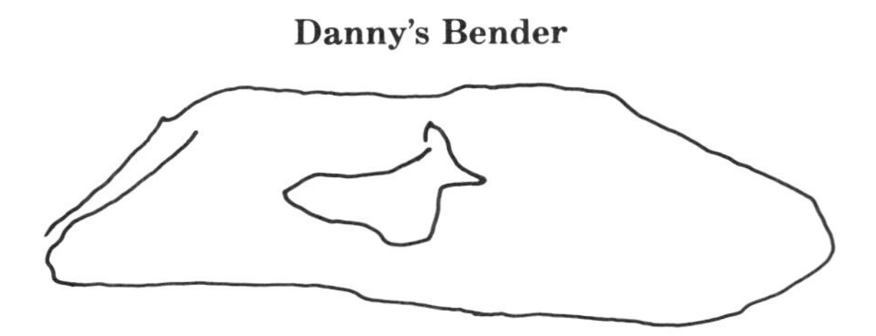

Level I:	**A straightforward description of behavior (e.g., "Danny could not accurately copy these geometric figures.")**
Level II:	**Naming the skill that presumably underlies the behavior (e.g., "Danny has poor visual-motor skills.")**
Level III:	**Suggestion of immaturity or developmental lag (e.g., "Danny's drawing appears to be immature, suggesting that his overall pattern of development is uneven.")**
Level IV:	**Conclusions about underlying neurological status (e.g., "Danny appears to have neurological dysfunction, particularly in the right parietal lobe of the brain.")**
Level V:	**Indication of underlying personality dynamics or conclusions about emotional status (e.g., "Danny's psychosexual stage of development appears to be rather primitive in view of his inability to correctly reproduce a relatively simple geometric figure which is believed to evoke information on psychosexual status or development.")**

Figure 13.2 Five levels of inference for Danny's Bender. (The authors wish to thank Dr. Daniel J. Reschly of Iowa State University, Ames, Iowa, for allowing us to use not only his Bender but also the interpretations derived therefrom.)

geometric figures" (Level I), to a suggestion of underlying personality dynamics or conclusions about emotional status, "Danny's psychosexual stage of development appears to be rather primitive . . ." (Level V).

There are a number of problems with highly inferential interpretations of performance on perceptual-motor tests. One, there are little empirical data to support the inferences made from such tests (Reschly, 1980). Two, the alleged variables involved (such as processing and perceptual dysfunctions) cannot be directly observed nor is there hard evidence that the alleged condition actually exists. Three, in virtually all instances there are no treatments or interventions that directly deal with underlying problems of academic deficiencies. We do not deny that individuals with severe neurological impairments may draw "poor" Bender designs, but we cannot find any clear-cut evidence that knowing about Bender errors helps one to teach a handicapped child.

Direct Assessment of Perceptual-Motor Skills

Given the conceptual as well as empirical problems with the use of highly inferential interpretations of performance on perceptual-motor tests, what alternatives are there to this type of assessment? Our recommendation is relatively simple and straightforward. We suggest the *direct assessment* of skills with stimuli or materials that the child must use in the classroom setting. We also suggest that the child's performance using these stimuli or materials be integrated using the Level I inference depicted in Figure 13.2. For example, we may be interested in whether Danny has adequate visual-motor ability. We could assess this in basically two ways. One, we could present geometric figures (for example, the Bender Gestalt designs) and ask him to copy them from cards. Two, we could present numerals or letters and ask Danny to copy them from the board or from a workbook. Which strategy would you think had the most direct relevance for classroom performance? We would obviously opt for the latter, since numerals and letters, not geometric designs, are the stimuli with which children must become proficient.

Another example might prove enlightening. We have all heard interpretations of perceptual-motor performance such as this: "Danny had difficulty in reproducing the Bender designs achieving a developmental age of only five years. His scale score of four on the Coding subtest of the WISC-R corroborates his poor visual-motor abilities. Taken together, these performances would suggest that Danny will have great difficulty in copying from the board and in performing written work at his desk such as reading and math skill sheets."

We consider this type of interpretation to be superfluous. If one wanted to make a prediction about Danny's ability to (a) copy from the board and (b) complete reading and math skill sheets, it would seem logical to assess these behaviors directly. To do this, we might take Danny into his classroom (after class or at recess), have him sit in his assigned seat, and ask him to copy from the board. We could also ask Danny's teacher for representative reading and math skill sheets and ask him to complete these tasks in his classroom. If Danny performed these tasks adequately, what would be the point of knowing his scores on the Bender Gestalt or the WISC-R Coding subtest? Our interest in Danny is not whether he can copy meaningless designs but whether he can perform the tasks required of him in the classroom.

Suppose that Danny could not copy from the board or complete the skill sheets. Does this mean that the Bender Gestalt and WISC-R performances support the conclusion that a visual-motor problem exists? *Not necessarily.* Our interpretation would be consistent with the Level I inference presented in Figure 13.2. That is, "Danny had difficulty in copying geometric designs, copying from the board, and completing reading and math skill sheets." Of course, one will never have to deal with the problem of inconsistencies in performances on perceptual-motor tests and direct assessment if one utilizes only one type of assessment strategy. We strongly prefer to use direct assessment of academic skills in the classroom setting, utilizing the stimuli and materials that the child confronts daily.

The potential of the informal assessment of so-called perceptual-motor skills is virtually limitless and depends upon the nature of the materials being used in the classroom for a particular child. The chief advantage of this form of assessment is that it has direct relevance for that child in the classroom. Some may argue that this type of informal assessment provides no basis for comparison to a normative sample. Although this is true, we should be more interested in what the child can or cannot do (criterion-referenced assessment) than in how the child compares to others. Moreover, we have already shown that the normative samples for virtually all perceptual-motor tests are inadequate for comparison purposes. We thus believe that the direct assessment of these skills is by far the most useful and relevant approach.

Summary

The available research strongly suggests that assessment based upon a traditional perceptual-motor model has neither high reliability nor validity and has little to do with diagnosing or remediating learning problems. Moreover, better methods of assessment have been developed to accomplish the same goals that perceptual-motor tests purportedly fulfill. This chapter has addressed the widespread use of tests of perceptual-motor functioning and the belief that direct assessment using lower inference techniques is preferable. While we recognize that perceptual-motor tests may be useful in well-designed research investigations, since this book is about using assessment to help solve problems for children, such tests have little to offer us.

Chapter 14

Behavior and Adjustment Problems

Learning Objectives

1. Compare and contrast the terms *emotional disturbance* and *behavior disorders*.
2. Compare and contrast the traditional approach to assessment with a behavioral approach.
3. Discuss each of the four major aspects of behavioral assessment: dimension, behavioral system, method, and quality.
4. Describe and discuss various definitions for behavior disorders.
5. Discuss the principles of behavioral assessment.

Phil is a behavior problem in Ms. Adams's fourth-grade classroom. His behavior disrupts the class and makes it difficult for Ms. Adams to teach and for the other children to learn. Phil is frequently out of his seat, he bothers other children during reading and math periods, he often gets into fights on the playground, and he is currently failing all of his academic subjects. Ms. Adams wants Phil out of her class because his behavior makes teaching a difficult if not impossible task.

Children like Phil are not uncommon. One child like Phil in a class of thirty children can interfere with the learning and academic performance of almost everyone in the class, not to mention the mental health and stress level of their teachers. What is Phil's problem? What makes him behave in this way? Is he emotionally disturbed? Most importantly, how do we assess Phil's problem so that we may help him (and Ms. Adams)?

Children like Phil exhibit behaviors that are variously termed "behavior problems," "adjustment problems," "emotional disturbances," or "behavior disorders." A valid assessment of these problems is essential given their potential to interfere with the learning and social development of a child and her peers. All school curricula assume that learners are "willing and receptive" consumers of academic instruction. Anyone who has ever set foot in a classroom knows differently. Some learners are receptive, others are indifferent, and still others seem intent on exhibiting any behavior that will make teaching, and hence learning, downright impossible.

When a student's behavior interferes with normal classroom functioning, teachers and school officials either ask or imply the following questions:

1. Why does this student behave this way?
2. What causes this problem behavior?
3. How can this student be made to stop this behavior?
4. Is this student emotionally disturbed?
5. Who can determine the seriousness of this student's problem?

In this chapter we will present and discuss a variety of strategies for assessing behavior problems in the classroom. It reviews specific assessment techniques and provides a critical appraisal of each with respect to several criteria, such as reliability, validity, and practical utility. An assessment model will be discussed to offer readers a guide to assessing *any* behavior problems that may occur in school settings. Implicit within the proposed procedures is a critical link between assessment and intervention strategies. Before discussing specific assessment procedures, we will define what it is we hope to assess.

Toward a Definition of Behavior Disorders

The process of identifying children and adolescents as "emotionally disturbed" is an ambiguous and vague area of psychology and special education. The vocabulary with which we describe different types of "emotional disturbance" lacks precision, and we know little about the causation, prevalence, and long-term outcomes of various types of emotional handicaps (Barlow, 1979).

Epstein, Cullinan, and Sabatino (1977) surveyed forty-nine state department of education definitions of emotional disturbance and found that most were phrased very generally and ambiguously. In fact, some were circular in nature (for example, "behaviorally disordered children are those who show emotional handicaps"). Clear definitions of any type of handicap (such as behavior disorders and learning disabilities) are essential to an adequate assessment technology. A more recent survey by Cullinan, Epstein, and McLinden (1986) showed that in many ways state definitions have remained constant over the past five years. There have been, however, several changes in these definitions. One, there has been an 11 percent increase in the use of the criterion of interpersonal (social skills) problems in state definitions. Two, there has been a 25 percent increase in the use of the criterion of learning/achievement problems. Finally, the largest shift in state is their increased similarity to the definition of "seriously emotionally disturbed" in the Education for All Handicapped Children Act of 1975, Public Law No. 94-142. According to Cullinan, Epstein, and McLinden (1986), between 1976 and 1982 there was a tenfold increase in the percentage of state definitions that are identical or nearly identical to the definition in P.L. 94-142.

Part of the reason for the ambiguity over the emotionally disturbed (ED) label has to do with the term itself. *Emotionally disturbed* implies that what is disturbed is one's emotions. However, the overwhelming majority of students classified as ED and placed into special education programs are so diagnosed on the basis of *disturbing behavior* rather than disturbed emotions (Algozzine, 1977). Children and youth whose behavior is disruptive, aggressive, situationally inappropriate, and has a *negative outward focus toward the environment* are prime candidates for the ED label. Many, if not most, ED children exhibit behavior that has been deemed unmanageable by teachers or parents.

The term now used in several states is *behavior disorders* (BD). This label reflects more than just a semantic change; it recognizes that the major reason these children are placed in special programs is primarily their disturbing *overt behavior* rather than covert emotions. The semantic difference between ED and BD might appear to be a minor point. However, the effects of these two labels may have substantial impact upon the conceptualization of behavior problems and the types of assessment information that is collected.

Many children and youth referred for ED or BD assessment are evaluated within what can be termed the *traditional assessment model*, which attempts to identify underlying traits as well as more observable problems such as academic skill deficits. Traditional assessment of this sort is based primarily upon the *medical model* described in Chapter 3 and views aberrant behavior as a sign of a broader or more encompassing emotional disorder. Such assessment procedures rely heavily upon *projective* and *objective* personality tests to diagnose the presence of ED, since responses to these measures are interpreted to be characteristic of some personality trait or disorder.

In contrast, in *behavioral assessment* deviant behavior is viewed as a sample of behavior that may or may not occur across situations, settings, or time. In behavioral assessment, inferences are not made about underlying traits; instead descriptions are made of specific behaviors and the situations and settings in which they occur. Behavioral assessment methods primarily involve systematic behavioral observations, behavioral interviews, and behavioral ratings by significant others.

The assessment model one adopts in assessing problem behavior bears a direct relationship to the quality and relevance of educational intervention strategies designed to help overcome such behavior. For example, a child who is labeled as ED on the basis of personality tests will, in all likelihood, be presumed to have an underlying pathological state (that is, disturbed emotions). The information yielded by traditional assessment methods provides little or no information to teachers or parents regarding which specific behaviors should be changed.

In contrast, behavioral assessment gives information about frequency, intensity, and duration of problem behaviors; the situations and settings in which these behaviors occur; and the antecedent, sequential, and consequent conditions surrounding such behaviors. With this data, intervention strategies can be more specifically focused and the effects of these interventions are more easily assessed than in the traditional assessment model. We thus utilize the term *behavioral disorders* rather than *emotionally disturbed* and rely upon a definition of the term which is derived from a behavioral framework.

Defining Behavior Disorders

The definition. As previously mentioned, most state definitions of ED or BD are vague, subjective, and do not specify the direction of change for given behavioral excesses or deficits. It thus appears advantageous to have a BD definition that includes the following seven components (see Gresham, 1985a):

1. specification of the excesses, deficits, or situational inappropriateness of the behavior;
2. specification of the objective features of the behavior and its multiple dimensions such as frequency, intensity, temporality, and permanent products;
3. specification of the behavior system or systems through which excesses, deficits, or situational inappropriateness are expressed;
4. demonstration of the occurrence of behavioral excesses, deficits, or situational inappropriateness over time;
5. occurrence of behavioral excesses or deficits across situations;
6. agreement upon the occurrence of excesses, deficits, or situational inappropriateness of the behavior using multiple methods of assessment; and
7. continuation of excesses, deficits, or situational inappropriateness of the behavior at unacceptable levels subsequent to school-based intervention.

The following definition is influenced by Ross (1980) and others operating out of a behavioral assessment model (Gresham, 1982a, 1985a; Mash & Terdal, 1981; Walker & Hops, 1976):

> A behavior disorder is said to be present when a child or adolescent exhibits behavioral excesses, deficits, or situational inappropriateness that authoritative adults judge to be too high or too low. These behaviors are considered to be atypical because their frequency, intensity, or duration deviates from a relative social norm. The excesses or deficits that constitute a behavior disorder can be expressed through one or all behavioral systems or repertoires (cognitive-verbal, overt-motoric, or physiological-

emotional) and occur across settings, situations, and time. No single assessment method is the primary basis for the diagnosis of a behavior disorder, but rather the diagnosis is based on the multifactored assessment information that agrees or converges both between and within assessment methods. In addition to the above considerations, a behavior disorder can only be said to be present when the excesses, deficits, or situational inappropriateness continue at an unacceptable level subsequent to a school-based intervention.

Explanation and implications. First, the focus of this definition is on behavior rather than on nebulous, unobservable constructs or traits. By defining a behavior disorder in terms of excesses or deficits, the direction of behavior change is specified. The definition also acknowledges that some behavior problems may not necessarily be excessive or deficient but rather are situationally inappropriate. Thus, while certain behaviors may be considered to be appropriate in some settings by some people, the same behavior may be viewed as inappropriate and hence a problem in other settings (e.g., the school) by authoritative adults (e.g., teachers or principals). The definition also implies that because a given behaviorally disordered child may have excessive, deficient, and situationally inappropriate behaviors, multiple targets of intervention can be identified.

A second aspect of this definition is that it stresses the importance of assessing objective features of behavior problems such as frequency, intensity, and duration. By focusing the assessment upon objective dimensions of behavior, one does not rely excessively upon subjective factors such as "unresolved emotional conflict," which are of questionable validity and have little practical explanatory value. Additionally, the definition suggests that these objective features of behavior can be expressed through one or all response systems or repertoires. For example, the class of behaviors that might be labeled as anxiety or fear could be expressed through the cognitive-verbal repertoire ("I am afraid" or "I feel nervous inside"), the overt-motoric repertoire (the child's avoidance of feared situations or settings), and/or the physiological-emotional repertoire (trembling, sweating, crying, vomiting, and the like). These behavioral channels or repertoires have been extensively discussed in the behavioral assessment literature (see Burns, 1980; Cone, 1978).

Third, the definition requires that the behavior problems be exhibited across settings, situations, and time. In short, this means that a given behavior problem must show *behavior-setting-time generalization* (Drabman, Hammer, & Rosenbaum, 1979).

A fourth requirement of the definition is that behavior problems be assessed using multifactored assessment procedures. While this is obviously consistent with the Protection in Evaluation Procedures requirement of P. L. 94-142, it takes these requirements a step further by insisting upon agreement both between and within assessment methods.

Finally, a unique and perhaps the most controversial aspect of this definition is the requirement that a school-based intervention be implemented *be-*

fore a classification decision is made. If, and only if, the problem continues to be exhibited at an unacceptable level subsequent to such an intervention can a classification of behavior disorders be made. School-based interventions refer to those initiated by school personnel (such as school psychologists and teachers), and focus upon problem behaviors occurring in the school setting. As such, this in no way rules out home-based interventions such as daily report cards, parent training, and the like as examples of school-based interventions.

The term *behavior disorder* simply refers to a socially unacceptable and intolerable pattern of behavior rather than an underlying disease process. Thus, the crucial determinant of the presence of a behavior disorder is that it exists at a level that is considered to be unacceptable in a particular setting or environment (for example, the regular classroom). If behavior does not come within tolerable limits following intervention, this would suggest that an alternative educational placement may be needed for a time to get the problem under control, with the eventual goal of reintegration into the regular classroom (mainstreaming).

Perhaps the most crucial aspect of this definition of BD is the requirement of an intervention *before* a classification is made. Although this appears to be a reasonably sound idea that seems relatively easy to implement, it does create potential problems in ensuring that the intervention is given a fair and equitable chance to work. That is, it assumes that the intervention will be implemented with *integrity*. Peterson, Homer, and Wonderlich (1982) have offered several suggestions for ensuring the integrity of intervention strategies. The most time- and cost-effective is to specify all the steps required for an intervention and subsequently spot-check its implementation. Thus, the integrity of the intervention is assessed much like the frequency, rate, or duration of target behaviors. Given the importance of an intervention for BD classification, assessment of the integrity and accuracy of intervention implementation is required.

Applying Behavioral Assessment

The foregoing discussion has primarily focused upon a conceptual approach to assessment rather than its application. In this section we present some specific rules or principles for translating assessment concepts into assessment practice.

The Principle of Problem Solving

The assessment of problem behaviors can be viewed as a problem-solving process much like the model of behavioral consultation provided by Bergan (1977) and his colleagues. Kratochwill (1982) has conceptualized behavioral assessment as a problem-solving process in which assessment data are directly related to an intervention program and are used to evaluate the effectiveness of interventions.

A useful problem-solving model is that of Bergan (1977) in which consultation is divided into the four stages of problem identification, problem analysis, plan implementation, and plan evaluation. Similarly, behavioral assessment can be conceptualized as these same four stages in which the purposes of assessment are to identify behavioral excesses or deficits, analyze the variables that are maintaining these excesses, deficits, or situational inappropriateness, implement an intervention plan to ameliorate these problems, and evaluate the effectiveness of the intervention plan (Gresham, 1984; Witt & Elliott, 1983). Bergan's problem-solving approach is very similar to the model of Gutkin and Curtis (1982) described in Chapter 1.

The Principle of Functional Analysis

Most school-based assessments are designed to make classification and placement decisions rather than to collect data for planning an intervention (Salvia & Ysseldyke, 1981). The focus of behavioral assessment is to obtain assessment information that is primarily useful in designing interventions for problem behaviors. A very helpful process for obtaining information with which to design interventions is the *functional analysis* of behavior (Bergan, 1977), which requires the identification of the antecedent, sequential, and consequent conditions surrounding behavior. For example, a functional analysis would be needed to determine that peer attention is causing (that is, that it is *functional*) the inappropriate outbursts of a referred student. An accurately conducted functional analysis allows for the development of interventions to change the frequency, intensity, and duration of problem behaviors, to increase the rate or quality of behavior deficits (for example, in social skills), and to identify those environmental events that result in situationally inappropriate behavior.

It should be noted that problem behaviors probably have multiple causes and that there are potentially a number of controlling variables, such as physical, cognitive, historical, and affective factors, that contribute to their occurrence (Mash & Terdal, 1981). However, there are a relatively limited number of variables that are amenable to manipulation by school personnel or parents. As such, the emphasis in behavioral assessment is upon those variables that can be controlled to change problem behaviors (that is, antecedent, sequential, and consequent events). Although nonmanipulable variables such as learning history, socioeconomic background, and neuropsychological status may contribute to our understanding of the child, they are not a useful class of factors from which to design interventions since they are not easily changed.

The most useful assessment techniques for conducting a functional analysis of behavior are behavioral interviews and direct observations of behavior (Gresham, 1985a). Self-monitoring has also been shown to be a potentially useful technique for obtaining information regarding the antecedents and consequences of behavior (Shapiro, 1984). All of these procedures have one thing in common: an emphasis upon the identification of environmental events that surround problem behavior (that is, a functional analysis). In-depth discussions and critical reviews of behavioral interviews, direct observations, and self-monitoring procedures can be found in other sources (Alessi & Kaye, 1983; Gresham, 1984; Shapiro, 1984).

Assessment procedures that enhance or lead to effective interventions are said to have *treatment validity* (Nelson & Hayes, 1979). An accurate, empirically based functional analysis of behavior has perhaps the most potential for treatment validity in the sense that variables that surround problem behaviors can be identified and changed. Thus, behavioral interviews, direct observations, and self-monitoring procedures have perhaps the most treatment validity because of their functional analysis potential and thus should guide assessment practice.

The Principle of Multiple Operationalism

Behavioral assessment demands that behavior problems be assessed from a variety of perspectives using a number of methods and information sources. What is therefore suggested for behavioral assessment is that the same excessive, deficient, or situationally inappropriate behaviors be multiply operationalized using several assessment methods.

In practice, the principle of multiple operationalism would require the assessment of problem behaviors using interviews, ratings by others, self-reports, direct observations, and so forth. By multiply operationalizing behavior problems in this way, assessors can evaluate the convergence or agreement of data from several sources. The lack of convergence or agreement between sources does not necessarily invalidate the data because disagreement between methods (for example, parent and teacher ratings or interviewers) could be merely due to the situational specificity (that is, behavior is different in different settings) of behavior (Kazdin, 1979). It is quite possible too that lack of agreement is the result of the lack of validity of some of the data, inaccurate reporting, or the unreliability of some of the instruments. The point is that the major reason for multiply operationalizing a behavior assessment is that the lack of agreement between methods should prompt a more in-depth assessment of those situational variables that may be functionally related to these behavioral differences (Nelson, 1983).

The Principle of Social Validity

Social validity refers to the determination of the clinical, applied, or social importance of exhibiting certain behaviors in particular situations (Kazdin, 1977). Social validity has become an important concept in the behavioral literature (Kazdin, 1977; Van Houten, 1979; Wolf, 1978) and has emerged as an important consideration in the special education literature (Kazdin & Matson, 1981; Witt & Elliott, 1985).

Wolf (1978) has suggested that social validation occurs on three levels: (a) determining the *social significance* of behavior, (b) determining the *social ac-*

ceptability of interventions to change behavior, and (c) evaluating the *social importance* of the effects of interventions. The notion of social validity, and particularly its concepts of *social significance* and *social importance*, are extremely important in the assessment of behavior disorders. Social acceptability is also crucial, although it is beyond the scope of this chapter (interested readers are referred to Witt and Elliott, 1985).

Social significance. Children are referred for behavior disorder assessment because authoritative adults in the environment (teachers or parents) have indicated that the child's problem behaviors are unacceptable or intolerable in a particular setting (such as the classroom). It is extremely important in such assessment that these behaviors represent a socially significant problem and that they deviate from the behaviors typically exhibited by the referred child's peers. Kazdin (1977) has discussed three general approaches to determining the social significance of problem behaviors: (a) social comparison, (b) subjective evaluation, and (c) combined social validation procedures.

Social comparison initially involves the identification of the referred child's peers who are similar in age and demographic variables but differ in the performance of problem behaviors. Next, the behavior of the referred child is compared to that of classmates to determine if it significantly departs from the norm. Walker and Hops (1976) present an excellent example of how social comparisons can be applied in classroom settings. This procedure is like establishing local "micronorms" against which to compare the observed behavior of the referred child (Nelson & Bowles, 1975).

Subjective evaluation consists of having persons familiar with the child in a particular setting (for example, school or home) rate the qualitative aspects of behavior. These global evaluations assess how well the child is functioning and provide an overall indication of performance (Kazdin, 1977). An example of subjective evaluation would be to have teachers and parents rate the referred child using standardized behavior rating scales. This represents more of a qualitative than a quantitative assessment in that most of these scales require raters to make a determination as to the typical behavior of the child.

Perhaps the most useful means of establishing the social significance of problem behaviors is to use *combined social validation procedures* incorporating both social comparisons and subjective evaluations. In this approach, behavior rates and intensities of referred children could be compared with those of nonreferred children, and the results could be compared to norms for behavior rating scales such as the Child Behavior Checklist (Achenbach & Edelbrock, 1983) or the Revised Behavior Problem Checklist (Quay, 1983). Behavior ratings of the referred child could also be compared with those of selected peers from the same classroom. Thus, the degree of deviance in the behavior of a child referred for behavior disorder assessment can be compared to (a) behavior rates of selected nonreferred children in the same classroom, (b) behavioral ratings for a normative sample, and (c) behavioral ratings of nonreferred peers in the same classroom.

Social importance. The definition of behavior disorders requires that a school-based intervention be attempted for a referred child before a classification decision is made. Recall that one criterion used to determine whether a behavior disorder existed was whether the behavior continued at an unacceptable level subsequent to this intervention. The concept of social importance addresses the question: *Does the quantity and quality of behavior change make a difference in the child's school functioning?* In other words, do the changes in problem behaviors made subsequent to an intervention bring these behaviors into tolerable or acceptable limits? The previously described social comparison, subjective evaluation, and combined social validation procedures can be used to determine the social importance of the effects of intervention. For example, if the rates of problem behavior are brought within the range of rates of nonreferred classmates after intervention, one could reasonably conclude that the intervention produced socially important effects.

The evaluation of social significance and social importance requires not only that an intervention be implemented but also that the changes in behavior be compared to socially acceptable standards. In schools, these standards should be the behavior of nonreferred peers, teacher evaluations of the behavior of referred versus nonreferred children, and comparisons to representative normative samples available from many behavior rating scales. This ensures that referral problems are evaluated for social importance. If the intervention does not produce socially important effects, a classification of behavior disorder can be seriously entertained.

Procedures in the Assessment of Behavior

We can now describe a model for the assessment of behavior disorders and detail procedures that will be useful in such assessments in educational settings. This model, unlike a traditional model that requires a psychologist to administer specialized testing, can be applied daily by a wide variety of professionals. The model is based upon a practical behavioral assessment framework and focuses upon the precise formulation of intervention goals, the specification of target behaviors in operational terms, the establishment of functional relationships between current environmental factors and target behaviors, and the evaluation of intervention outcomes. Perhaps the most salient difference between behavioral assessment and traditional assessment is the former's inseparable relationship between assessment and intervention. That is, behavioral assessment yields information that is directly related to the design, implementation, and evaluation of interventions for problem behaviors (Gresham, 1982a, 1985a).

A plethora of methods are used in behavioral assessment, many of which, including interviews, self-reports, and ratings by others, are also used in traditional assessment. At first glance, this might appear to nullify the distinctions between these two assessment models. However, recall that the major differences between the models concerns the *assumptions* each makes about the nature of behavior: Behavioral assessment assumes that behavior assessed at one point is merely a *sample* of behavior in a particular situation that may or may not be representative of behavior in other situations or times. In contrast, traditional assessment assumes that behavior is a *sign* of underlying personality traits that indexes the intrapsychic causes of the behavior.

Behavioral assessment methods can be ordered along a continuum of *directness* (see Table 14.1) based upon the extent to which the method measures the target behavior (a) of clinical or educational relevance and (b) at the time and place of its natural occurrence (Cone, 1978; Kratochwill, 1982).

Direct assessment methods include self-monitoring and naturalistic observations because they measure behavior at the time and place of its actual occurrence. *Indirect assessment* methods include interviews, self-reports, and ratings by others because these strategies actually are verbal representations of behavior that has taken place in the past and in some other place.

Gresham (1985a) categorized behavioral assessment methods by their purpose (see Table 14.2): (a) assessment for classification or selection and (b) assessment for intervention. Some assessment approaches are more useful for classifying than for yielding information for intervention purposes. For example, self-reports, ratings by others, and behavioral role playing are classification or selection methods since they identify, in a global sense, behavioral excesses or deficits to be targeted for remediation. Other assessment approaches are much more relevant for intervention because they assist in deriving a *functional analysis of behavior* (that is, they identify the antecedents and consequences of specific behaviors). Behavioral interviews, naturalistic observations, and self-monitoring represent assessment methods for intervention purposes because they yield data for a functional analysis.

Table 14.1 Classification of Behavioral Assessment Methods on a Directness Continuum[a]

Indirect methods
- Interviews
- Self-reports
- Ratings by others
- Behavioral role playing

Direct methods
- Naturalistic observations
- Self-monitoring

[a]Indirect assessment procedures are removed in time and place from the actual occurrence of the behavior. Direct assessment procedures measure behavior at the time and place of its actual occurrence.

Table 14.2 Classification of Behavioral Assessment Methods

Assessment for classification, diagnosis, or screening[a]
- Ratings by others
  - Teacher
  - Parent
  - Peer
- Self-reports
- Behavioral role playing
  - Analog
  - Naturalistic

Assessment for intervention or therapy
- Behavioral interviews
  - Teacher
  - Parent
  - Child
- Naturalistic observations
- Self-monitoring

[a]The difference between assessment methods for classification versus methods for intervention is the extent to which the assessment method yields data for a functional analysis of behavior.

Behavioral Assessment Methods

This section describes and reviews three commonly used behavioral assessment methods: (a) behavioral interviews, (b) direct observations, and (c) ratings by others.

Behavioral Interviews

Psychological interviews are perhaps the assessment method most frequently used in both clinical and school settings (Haynes & Jensen, 1979; Mash & Terdal, 1981). Behavioral interviews are conducted with parents or teachers or both to collect information regarding a child's academic and behavior problems in the home and school. Such interviews are designed to: (a) gather information about teacher or parent concerns, (b) identify factors that may be contributing to problem behaviors, (c) assess how teachers or parents are currently dealing with problem behaviors, and (d) evaluate the outcomes of interventions (Gresham, 1984).

Behavioral interviews can be differentiated from more traditional interviews by their underlying assumptions (Goldfried & Kent, 1972). Behavioral interviews focus on current environmental conditions (for example, antecedents and consequences), view behavior as a sample of responses in specific situations, and utilize interview data to plan, implement, and evaluate interventions.

Behavioral interviews have several advantages over other methods of behavioral assessment such as self-reports, direct observations, and naturalistic observations. One, the behavioral interview is flexible in that both general and specific information can be ascertained. The interviewer can clarify, modify, and extend the interviewee's verbal descriptions of behavioral and situational variables influencing the occurrence of behavior and thus broaden or narrow the assessment band depending upon the relevance and importance of the information. Other assessment methods lack this flexibility and as a result may fail to capture the target behavior of specific concern to teachers or parents. Second, behavioral interviews permit the assessment of teachers' and parents' receptivity to various intervention strategies. Those who find certain strategies unacceptable are less likely to implement them (Witt & Elliott, 1985). Third, with behavioral interviews one can often detect irrational beliefs or unrealistic expectations adults harbor about children, information that is not typically obtained through other assessment methods.

Bergan (1977) has discussed three types of interviews that are used in designing, implementing, and evaluating interventions: (a) the problem identification interview (PII), (b) the problem analysis interview (PAI), and (c) the problem evaluation interview (PEI). The primary purpose of the PII is to operationalize and define problem behaviors so they can be measured and modified (Witt & Elliott, 1983). The goals of the PAI are to conduct a functional analysis of behavior and to design an intervention plan for target behaviors. The purpose of the PEI is to evaluate the effectiveness of the intervention plan designed during the PAI. Table 14.3 outlines the goals and objectives of the PII, PAI, and PEI. A more in-depth discussion of behavioral interviewing can be found in Bergan (1977), Gresham (1982a, 1984), and Witt and Elliott (1983).

Direct Observations

There are literally an infinite number of behaviors that could be observed in a particular setting. In addition, there are a number of ways behavior can be defined for observational purposes. The first task in direct observation is thus to decide what behaviors to observe and to construct an *operational definition* of each. An operational definition precisely describes which behaviors will be counted as occurrences of the behavior in question. For example, the category labeled *appropriate behavior* might be operationally defined as: (a) sitting in seat, (b) looking at book or teacher, (c) raising hand before talking, and (d) writing on work sheets during independent work periods.

An efficient way of identifying target behaviors is through the use of behavior rating scales. Behaviors that are of most concern can be easily identified through ratings. This can be followed by a *problem identification interview* in which each behavior can be operationally defined for recording purposes.

A number of factors must be considered before conducting observational assessment, including: (a) the setting in which behavior will be observed, (b) who will conduct the observations, (c) the method of recording data, and (d)

Table 14.3 Objectives of Problem Identification, Problem Analysis, and Problem Evaluation Interviews

Type of interview	Objectives
Problem identification	Specification of the goals of intervention Objective description of behavior in operational terms Identification of environmental conditions surrounding behavior Estimation of the frequency, intensity, and/or duration of behavior Agreement on types of data collection procedures
Problem analysis	Validation of problem behavior and adequacy of base-line data Analysis and validation of environmental conditions surrounding behavior Design of intervention plan to remediate problem behavior
Problem evaluation	Determination of goal attainment Evaluation of effectiveness of intervention plan Decision on continuation, modification, or withdrawal of plan Follow-up and generalization of plan's effects

Adapted from *Behavioral consultation* by J. Bergan, 1977, Columbus, OH: Charles E. Merrill Publishing Co.

the reliability of the recording procedures. Each of these factors is briefly discussed below.

Setting in which behavior will be observed. An important consideration in behavioral observation is the setting in which the assessment will take place. Recall from Chapter 3 that one assumption in behavioral assessment is that behavior is situationally specific. This is also a factor in evaluating the quality of behavioral assessment from the perspective of the Generalizability Theory (Cronbach et al., 1972). Users of direct observation, however, are often interested in generalizing beyond the setting in which data are collected. For example, observations of a child's behavior collected in a resource room may not be generalizable to the same behaviors in the regular classroom. Similarly, observations on the playground may not be generalizable to the classroom. The solution to this problem is either to restrict observations to a single setting or to assess behavior in multiple settings. If determining the generality of behavior is the goal, observations must be collected in several settings.

Who will conduct the observations? Another important variable in direct observations is the person who collects the information. Teachers can easily track the frequency of many behaviors that occur in classroom settings, such as the number of math problems correctly solved or the number of times a child gets out of his seat. However, many behavior recording procedures are complex and time-consuming for teachers to use, especially when multiple behaviors are being tracked across several children. In these cases, observers must be trained to use the observation code.

Method of recording data. Earlier in this chapter we discussed several dimensions of behavior. Before deciding upon a specific method of recording behavior, one must decide which dimension of behavior is to be measured. For example, discrete behaviors, such as hitting others, using profanity, and leaving one's seat are more amenable to *frequency recording*. Other behaviors are more continuous and cannot be measured with frequency recording but rather with some form of *interval recording*, in which a period of observation is divided into smaller intervals and the occurrence or nonoccurrence of behavior in each is recorded. There are several types of interval recording: (a) *whole interval recording*, in which the behavior must occur throughout the interval for it to be scored as an occurrence, (b) *partial interval recording*, in which a behavior is scored as an occurrence if it occurs at any time during the interval, (c) *time sampling*, in which a behavior is scored as an occurrence if it occurs at the end of the interval, and (d) *sequential time sampling*, in which the behavior of several children is sequentially recorded at the end of each interval.

Interval recording can be used to measure almost any behavior. The length of the interval (for example, 10 seconds, 30 seconds, 1 minute) is based upon the frequency of the behavior. A general rule is that the more frequent the behavior, the shorter the interval (Barton & Ascione, 1984). The chief advantage of interval recording is that multiple behaviors across several children can be measured. We recommend using sequential time sampling because it provides "micronorms" against which to compare the behavior rates of a target child (Gresham, 1982a). Figure 14.1 and Table 14.4 present a sequential time

Interval	BB	AB	PB	BB	AB	PB	BB	AB	PB	BB	AB	PB	BB	AB	PB	BB	AB	PB
1 minute	O	O	X	O	X	O	O	X	X	O	O	O	O	O	X	O	O	X
2 minutes	O	X	X	O	X	X	O	O	X	O	O	X	O	O	X	O	O	X
3 minutes	O	O	X	O	O	X	O	O	X	O	O	X	O	O	O	O	O	O
4 minutes	O	O	O	O	O	O	O	X	X	O	O	O	O	O	O	O	O	X
5 minutes	O	X	X	O	O	O	O	O	O	O	X	X	O	X	O	O	O	O

Figure 14.1 Sequential time sampling for teacher-nominated best-behaved, average-behaved, and poorly behaved students. (The target behavior was disruptive behavior, including leaving one's seat, talking without permission, and hitting other children. BB = best behaved, AB = average-behaved, PB = poorly behaved, 0 = behavior occurred, × = behavior did not occur.)

Table 14.4 Sequential Time Sampling: Summary of Observational Data

Student	Total possible intervals	Number of intervals behavior occurred	Percentage disruptive
Best-behaved	30	0	0
Average-behaved	30	8	26.8
Poorly behaved	30	18	60

sampling procedure conducted with teacher-nominated best-behaved, average-behaved, and poorly behaved students. It should be remembered, however, that sequential time sampling is virtually impossible for teachers to use while teaching and thus must be conducted by others such as aides, school psychologists, and educational consultants.

A useful recording system for classroom settings that incorporates both frequency recording and time sampling is the State-Event Classroom Observation System, or SECOS (Saudargas & Lentz, 1986). The SECOS records important classroom variables such as student orientation to work, student behavior during teacher attention, child-child interactions, out-of-seat behavior, and student engagement in other activities.

A final direct observation strategy is to measure the *permanent products* of behavior, such as the number of chairs overturned, the amount of trash on the floor, and the number of work sheets correctly completed. The chief advantage of this type of recording is the ease with which data can be collected and the objectivity of having tangible products of behavior.

Reliability of recording procedures. An important consideration in using direct observation is the reliability of the recorded rates of behavior. The reliability that is most critical to observational data is *interobserver reliability*, which refers to the relative agreement between two observers who record the same behavior for the same person. In the Generalizability Theory (Cronbach, Glaser, Nanda & Rajaratman, 1972) this is called *scorer generality*, meaning the degree to which the agreement between any two scorers or observers can be generalized to all possible scorers or observers.

A number of formulas have been developed to estimate interobserver agreement for various recording procedures (for a comprehensive review, see Kent & Foster, 1977); several are presented in Table 14.5. As one might expect, the clearer and more specific the operational definitions of behavior, the higher the agreement between two observers. In many, if not most, applied settings, the reliability of observations is not assessed. Our recommendation regarding interobserver reliability is to collect this information whenever possible to enhance the believability of the data.

FOCUS ON RESEARCH
Classifying Children as Emotionally Disturbed

Efforts to classify childhood psychopathology have not been as successful as most researchers and practitioners would like. No single classification scheme for childhood psychopathology has been generally accepted as reliable and valid. Three major classification schemes have been advocated for school-age children and youth: (a) Public Law 94-142 criteria for Seriously Emotionally Disturbed (SED), (b) the *Diagnostic and Statistical Manual of Mental Disorders*, 3rd edition (DSM III) (American Psychiatric Association, 1980), and (c) the Child Behavior Checklist and Profile (CBCL) (Achenbach & Edelbrock, 1983).

The SED guidelines specified in P.L. 94-142 are used to determine whether children qualify for special education and related services because of the impact of their emotional problems on educational performance. The DSM III is the most frequently used system to classify children as disturbed in clinical outpatient and inpatient settings. The CBCL system is derived from multivariate statistical procedures and classifies children as having an Internalizing, Externalizing, or Mixed psychological disorder.

To date, no research has compared these three methods to assess the degree of agreement in classification using these three systems. A study by Tharinger, Laurent, and Best (1986) was designed to compare the classification rates of these three systems using a sample of thirty-eight males between the ages of six and eleven ($M = 7\frac{1}{2}$ years) who had been referred for suspected emotional disturbance.

Results indicated that the DSM III had poor interrater agreement (52 percent) on classifying children as emotionally disturbed. Using the P.L. 94-142 criteria, 92 percent of the subjects were classified as having a handicapping condition (SED = 53 percent, LD = 34 percent, and other health-impaired = 5 percent). Using the CBCL system, 66 percent of the subjects were classified as disturbed (Internalizing Disorder = 3%, Externalizing Disorder = 26 percent, Mixed Disorder = 37 percent).

A three-way comparison among the 94-142, DSM III, and CBCL systems showed that only 29 percent of the sample were classified as SED using all three systems. Combined three-way agreement among the systems was only 37 percent (14 of 38 cases).

Tharinger et al. indicated that the DSM III classified most of the subjects as disturbed (82 percent) followed by the CBCL (66 percent), and P.L. 94-142 systems (52 percent). These systems identified neither the same numbers of children as SED nor the same children as SED. Although eight cases is a very small sample, these findings clearly show a need for objective criteria for classification of "emotionally disturbed" children in schools.

FOCUS ON RESEARCH

How Do Learning Disabled Children Differ from "Normal" Children?

A number of researchers have attributed certain behavioral characteristics to learning disabled (LD) children and youth. For example, LD students have been said to possess attention deficits, poor concentration, distractability, impulsivity, and hyperactivity. These behaviors often result in differential teacher-student interactions in the classrooms, with LD students receiving more teacher criticism, warnings, and negative feedback than their nonhandicapped peers.

Slate and Saudargas (1986) recently conducted an interesting investigation into the classroom behaviors of average and LD elementary school students in the regular classroom. The purpose of this study was to compare the behaviors of average and LD students as well as teacher-student interactions. Subjects consisted of fourteen LD and fourteen average students in grades three, four, and five from twelve classrooms in five elementary schools. All subjects were observed in their regular classrooms for ten weeks, and observational data were collected in the morning while students were engaged in individual and group academic assignments. Each student was observed from four to six times, each observation period lasting 20 minutes.

Subjects were observed using the State-Event Classroom Observation System (SECOS), which is comprised of fourteen student and five teacher behaviors. The student behaviors included: (a) schoolwork, (b) looking around, (c) out-of-seat, (d) motor, (e) playing with objects, (f) social-interaction child, (g) other activity, (h) raise hand, (i) object aggression, (j) approach-child, (k) other-child approach, (l) call

continued

Ratings by Others

Teacher and parent ratings of problem behavior and social skills are a popular method of behavioral assessment, partly because of the relative ease of using these procedures. Rating measures have considerable variability in format. Some rating scales require a simple "yes" or "no" response from the rater regarding the occurrence or nonoccurrence of target behaviors. These measures are perhaps more accurately termed behavioral checklists rather than rating scales. Others require a more qualitative judgment concerning the occurrence of behavior (for example, "very true," "somewhat true," or "not true"), while still others use five- or seven-point Likert-type scaling formats (for example, 1 = Behavior Never Occurs to 5 = Behavior Occurs Very Frequently). Few scales ask the rater to specify how important the behavior is for classroom success or to what extent the behavior will be tolerated in a specific setting. An exception is the Importance Rating on the Social Skills Rating Scales (Gresham & Elliott, 1987), in which teachers rate the behavior's importance to classroom success.

Behavioral rating scales are designed to tap domains such as "personality,"

FOCUS ON RESEARCH *continued*

out, (m) out-of-seat (event), and (n) social interaction-teacher. The five teacher behaviors included: (a) teacher approach/student engaged in school work, (b) teacher approach/student engaged in other behavior, (c) direction, (d) approval, and (e) disapproval.

The results of this investigation revealed that LD students were found not to exhibit *keystone* or *marker* behaviors (that is, behaviors that were markedly different from average children). Learning disabled students were involved in academic assignments as much as average students, were in their seats as much as average children, looked around as much as average children, and were involved in as many social interactions as other children. In short, LD and average children did not differ in their observed rates of classroom behavior.

Large differences, however, were observed in teacher behaviors toward LD and average students. For example, LD students received more individual teacher contacts and directions even though they and their average peers were equally engaged in a particular activity. In short, teachers interact differently with LD students than average students although the observed classroom behaviors of LD students did not differ from those of average students.

Slate and Saudargas (1986) conclude that it is essential to observe teacher behaviors toward students in regular classrooms. Their study strongly suggests that regular classroom teachers behave differently toward LD students even though student behaviors do not differ from those of their average peers. Assessment specialists are well advised to assess not only student behaviors but also the context or ecology in which these behaviors occur.

"problem behavior," "psychopathology," "temperament," and "social-emotional functioning." Virtually all such scales measure several dimensions of problem behavior, although those dimensions have different meanings and names depending upon the scale selected. For example, the Revised Behavior Problem Checklist (Quay, 1983) measures six dimensions of problem behavior: (a) Conduct Disorder, (b) Socialized Aggression, (c) Attention Problems — Immaturity, (d) Anxiety-Withdrawal, (e) Psychotic Behavior, and (f) Motor Excess. In contrast, the Pittsburgh Adjustment Survey Scales (Ross, Lacey, & Parton, 1965) measures: (a) Withdrawn Behavior, (b) Aggressive Behavior, (c) Passive-Aggressive Behavior, and (d) Prosocial Behavior.

Some behavioral rating scales focus upon a single type of problem behavior rather than several dimensions. For example, the Connors Abbreviated Parent-Teacher Questionnaire, or Hyperkinesis Index (Conners, 1973), is designed to measure hyperactivity. Table 14.6 summarizes commonly used behavioral rating scales and the dimensions assessed by each scale.

Given the sheer number of behavioral rating scales and the number of dimensions assessed, how does one choose the most appropriate instrument? Perhaps the best guide to selection is what Mash and Terdal (1981) call the

Table 14.5 Formulas for Calculating Interobserver Agreement

Percentage agreement estimates for interval, time sampling, and sequential time sampling recording:

		Observer 1	
		Occurrence	Nonoccurrence
Observer 2	Occurrence	A	C
	Nonoccurrence	B	D

Agreement reliability (overall):

$$\frac{A + D}{A + B + C + D}$$

Occurrence reliability:

$$\frac{A^{a}}{A + B + C} \qquad \frac{(A + B)(A + C)^{b}}{A + B + C + D}$$

Nonoccurrence reliability:

$$\frac{D^{a}}{B + C + D} \qquad \frac{(B + A)(C + A)^{b}}{A + B + C + D}$$

Agreement calculation for frequency, rate, latency, duration, and interresponse time recording:[c]

$$\text{Agreement} = \frac{\text{smaller recorded frequency (duration, etc.)}}{\text{larger recorded frequency (duration, etc.)}} \times 100$$

[a]Uncorrected for change agreements

[b]Corrected for change agreements

[c]This formula estimates the overall level of agreement but does not indicate that observers agreed on specific occurrences of behavior.

Table 14.6 Behavioral Dimensions of Commonly Used Behavior Rating Scales

Child Behavior Checklist and Profile-Parent Version (Achenbach & Edelbrock, 1983)
- Internalizing Syndrome
  - Social Withdrawal
  - Depressed
  - Uncommunicative
  - Obsessive-Compulsive
  - Somatic Complaints
- Externalizing Syndrome
  - Hyperactive
  - Aggressive
  - Delinquent
  - Cruel
  - Sex Problems

Conners Teacher Rating Scale
- Hyperactivity
- Conduct Problem
- Inattentive-Passive
- Tension-Anxiety
- Sociability

Devereux Elementary School Behavior Rating Scale
- Classroom Disturbance
- Impatience
- Disrespect-Defiance
- External Blame
- Achievement-Anxiety
- External Reliance
- Comprehension
- Inattentive
- Creative
- Closeness to Teacher

Pittsburgh Adjustment Survey Scales
- Withdrawn Behavior
- Aggressive Behavior
- Passive-Aggressive Behavior
- Prosocial Behavior

Problem Checklist and Social Competence Scale
- Interest-Participation versus Apathy-Withdrawal
- Cooperation-Compliance versus Anger-Defiance

Revised Behavior Problem Checklist (Quay & Peterson, 1983)
- Conduct Disorder
- Socialized Aggression
- Attention Problems-Immaturity
- Anxiety-Withdrawal
- Psychotic Behavior
- Motor Excess

(continued)

Table 14.6, *continued*

Teacher-Child Rating Scale
Acting Out
Shy-Anxious
Learning
Frustration Tolerance
Assertive Social Skills
Task Orientation
Walker Problem Behavior Identification Checklist (Walker, 1976)
Acting Out
Withdrawal
Distractibility
Disturbed Peer Relations
Immaturity

functional-utilitarian view of behavioral assessment, according to which a scale is chosen on the basis of the information it provides to help professionals make informed judgments to improve child services. In short, use whatever works and not what is available or theoretically advised (Edelbrock, 1983). Thus, if the purpose of using the rating scale is to screen children for behavior problems, a multidimensional scale such as the Child Behavior Checklist (Achenbach & Edelbrock, 1983) or the Revised Behavioral Problem Checklist should be used. If the goal is to assess one dimension of problem behavior (for example, hyperactivity), a unidimensional scale such as the Hyperkinesis Index should be used. Finally, if the purpose of assessment is to measure specific behaviors as part of an intervention, one should construct an *informal* behavioral rating scale for the target behaviors specific to the child and setting in which the intervention takes place.

A number of technical aspects of formal behavioral rating scales should be considered before a selection is made. One consideration is the *types of items* on the scale. Some rating scales include items that do not functionally relate to the problem behavior being assessed (for example, "comes from a broken home" or "wears dirty clothing"). Others contain items that reflect the consequences of behavior rather than the behavior itself (for example, "is kept after school" or "is sent to the office for disruptive behavior"). Such items confuse and confound a behavioral description of the child. Before using a rating scale, the degree to which each item represents the specific areas of concern should thus be assessed by simply reviewing the item content and comparing it to the problem situation.

Another technical consideration is the scale's *level of analysis*, or the degree to which its items reflect global behavioral characteristics or specific behavioral units. Global items (for example, "behaves inappropriately") may provide reliable information, but ratings of such behaviors do not capture the components of the construct being rated. In contrast, overly specific items (for example, "drums fingers on desk") may be meaningless and trivial and be subject to a variety of interpretations. One should inspect all items on a rating scale to ensure that their level of analysis will provide the information most useful for assessment.

The *time frame* upon which the ratings are based represents another important but often ignored technical consideration. For example, the rater may simply not have sufficient exposure to the child's behavior to provide a well-informed behavioral description. For example, ratings obtained from teachers early in the school year are likely to be based upon an inadequate sampling of the child's behavior and may thus be misleading. Likewise, raters may report dated information that is no longer relevant to the child's behavioral status. Edelbrock (1983) suggests that two months are adequate for teachers to rate behaviors of children in classroom settings and six months for parents to rate their children.

A final technical consideration in using a behavioral rating scale is its *standardization sample*. Unfortunately, most scales are not norm-referenced, which represents a major inadequacy of this method of assessment. Those scales that do have norms typically have unrepresentative samples that are usually small. Norms are crucial because they allow for the comparison of problem behaviors with an appropriate sample. The Child Behavior Checklist (Achenbach & Edelbrock, 1983) is one of the few behavioral rating scales that is well standardized in terms of age and sex. This scale provides separate norms for age (4–5 years, 6–11 years, and 12–16 years) and sex. Norms were not stratified according to race and socioeconomic status because these variables accounted for relatively little variance in behavioral ratings. This scale, however, was not standardized on a geographically representative sample of children.

Although the rater is a critical element in the use of behavioral rating scales, many scales do not specify who that person should be. Many simply state that ratings should be completed by someone knowledgeable about the child's behavior. This causes a major problem in the potential accuracy of ratings since parents, teachers, mental health workers, and other professionals differ in the nature and amount of their contact with the child, the settings, and the situations in which they observe and interact with the child, and in their perspectives, biases, and expectations regarding child behavior (Edelbrock, 1983).

Few attempts have been made to design rating scales for specific raters. This oversight is perplexing since common sense would suggest that parents would be most qualified to report on behaviors that occur primarily at home, (such as sleep disturbances and eating problems,) whereas teachers would be more familiar with classroom behaviors, such as inattentiveness and poor academic performance. This ambiguity creates a problem in interpreting scores because the frequency and patterning of scores for specific behaviors changes as a function of who completes the scale. Thus, scores on scales standardized using parents as informants may not be comparable to scores obtained using a teacher as an informant. However, several behavior rating scales do specify the rater, including the Behavior Rating Profile (Brown & Hammill, 1978), the

Child Behavior Checklist (Achenbach & Edelbrock, 1983), and the Walker Problem Behavior Identification Checklist (Walker, 1976).

Review of Selected Behavior Rating Scales

We now review several behavior rating scales that are used frequently in school settings and represent a variety of rating formats and profiling methods for scores. In addition, these scales vary somewhat with respect to dimensions of behavior assessed, numbers of items, basic psychometric properties, and representativeness of standardization samples.

Walker Problem Behavior Identification Checklist

Overview and purpose. The Walker Problem Behavior Identification Checklist, or WPBIC, is designed to identify behavior problems in children in grades four, five, and six. It is composed of observable, operational statements about classroom behavior that were furnished by a representative sample of elementary school teachers. The WPBIC represents a supplemental tool in identifying problem behaviors rather than an instrument to classify children as behaviorally disordered. It can be useful in identifying children with behavior problems who should be referred for psychological evaluation and intervention.

The WPBIC tests five categories of problem behavior: (a) Acting-Out, (b) Withdrawal, (c) Distractibility, (d) Disturbed Peer Relations, and (e) Immaturity. A child receives a score on each of the five factors, which is then compared to the scores of a normative sample. Examples of behaviors for each category follow:

1. *Acting Out:* Child complains about unfairness and/or discrimination toward self, becomes upset when things don't go his way, and has temper tantrums.
2. *Withdrawal:* Child does not engage in group activities, has no friends, and does not initiate relationships with others.
3. *Distractibility:* Child is overactive and restless and continually shifts body position; continually seeks attention; and is easily distracted.
4. *Disturbed Peer Relations:* Child babbles to self; comments that nobody likes her; and refers to self as dumb, stupid, or incapable.
5. *Immaturity:* Child reacts to stressful situations with body, head, or stomach aches; has nervous tics; and weeps or cries without provocation.

Standardization sample and norms. The fifty checklist items were drawn from teacher descriptions of classroom behavior problems. A sample of thirty experienced teachers was randomly drawn from the fourth-, fifth-, and sixth-grade teachers in an Oregon school district. The teachers were asked to nominate their students who exhibited chronic behavior problems. Each teacher was interviewed and asked to give operational descriptions of the overt behaviors that concerned them; this yielded a pool of 300 items. Fifty of the most frequently mentioned behaviors were selected for inclusion on the WPBIC.

The WPBIC was given to a sample of twenty-one fourth-, fifth, and sixth-grade teachers, who evaluated all pupils in their classes after having observed them for approximately two months. This procedure yielded 534 children from the three grades. Since the WPBIC was normed on twenty-one teachers and 534 children from one school district in Oregon, it is not well standardized because of the unrepresentativeness of its standardization sample.

Data obtained. Each item on the WPBIC is assigned a score from 4 to 1 based upon five expert judges' ratings of the degree to which each behavior was thought to handicap the child's present adjustment. The interjudge reliability of ratings was .83, and the means of the five judges on all items were pooled and assigned as score weights for the items. The weighted raw scores were converted to a *T*-score distribution, which has a mean of 50 and a standard deviation of 10. Each scale or factor yields a *T*-score, and there are separate norms for males and females. A *T*-score of 60, which is 1 standard deviation above the mean, was established as the point for identifying those children who may require special services because of behavior problems.

Reliability and validity. The manual presents evidence for the internal consistency and test-retest reliability of the WPBIC. The split-half reliability of the total score was estimated to be .98, thus suggesting an internally consistent scale. No reliabilities are reported for the five factors of the WPBIC, which limited the interpretability of these scales. Test-retest reliabilities of the WPBIC range from .80 (over a three-week interval) to .89 (over a five-week interval). These data suggest that the total score on the WPBIC is relatively stable for up to one month.

The manual also reports evidence for contrasted-groups, criterion-related, and factorial validities. The WPBIC total score reliably differentiates behaviorally disordered from nondisordered children, as indicated by the behaviorally disordered group receiving higher total scores than the nondisordered group. Criterion-related validity was established by correlating total scores with three criteria: (a) whether the child had been examined by a psychologist or been referred to a clinical psychiatric facility, (b) whether the child was receiving special education programing, and (c) whether the child was receiving homebound instruction because of an inability to profit from classroom instruction due to behavior problems. The biserial correlation between total scores and the criteria was .68, suggesting that the WPBIC is predictive of behavioral disturbance in elementary school children. This correlation, however, was based on the scores of only seventy-six children in the standardization sample.

Factorial validity of the WPBIC was obtained by factor analyzing the fifty items on the scale. Five factors were obtained and have previously been discussed. The intercorrelations between the five factors range from .02 (Acting-Out and Withdrawal) to .67 (Acting-Out and Distractibility). The factor structure was based upon the 534 children in the standardization sample; the manual does not report data regarding replication of the factor structure on other samples.

Summary. The WPBIC is useful in identifying behavior problems in elementary school children. Its greatest drawback is that because it was not standardized on a representative normative sample of children, the scores may not be comparable to those of other samples. The scale appears to be reliable in terms of internal consistency and stability and seems to differentiate behaviorally disordered from nondisordered children. The unique features of the WPBIC lie in its development, for its items were selected from those generated by teachers. This process enhanced the scale's social validity because only those behaviors that were the most frequent sources of concern for teachers were included. In addition, the item weighting procedure, which was based upon expert judges' ratings of the degree to which each problem behavior interfered with school performance, represents a unique and socially valid method of item selection.

Child Behavior Checklist-Parent Version

Overview and purpose. The Child Behavior Checklist-Parent Version (CBCL; Achenbach & Edelbrock, 1983) consists of 113 problem behaviors rated by parents of children from four to sixteen years of age. The behaviors were selected from descriptions of problems common in the research and clinical literature. For the most part, these behaviors are observable operational statements of problems, although there are some exceptions, such as "feels guilty," "feels inferior," and "feels she needs to be perfect."

The CBCL has separate norms for boys and girls in three age ranges: (a) four to five years, (b) six to eleven years, and (c) eleven to sixteen years. According to the manual, it can be filled out by most parents whose reading skills are at a fifth-grade level or higher. The average time it takes to complete the scale is 15 to 17 minutes. The manual recommends that if a parent cannot read, an interviewer can read the CBCL aloud and enter the parent's responses.

The CBCL has two broad-band factors, Externalizing Syndrome and Internalizing Syndrome. Under each are a number of narrow-band, or more specific factors that vary for boys and girls and for the three age ranges. For example, under the Externalizing Syndrome are the narrow-band factors such as Aggressive, Delinquent, Hyperactive, and Cruel. Under the Internalizing Syndrome are clusters of behaviors such as Depressed, Social Withdrawal, Somatic Complaints, and Anxious. Scores on each of these narrow-band factors are profiled on the Revised Child Behavior Profile, which also gives norms for comparison purposes.

Standardization sample and norms. The CBCL was normed on 1,300 children between the ages of four and sixteen. All data were collected in randomly selected urban, suburban, and semirural homes in Washington, D.C., Maryland, and northern Virginia. Census data on socioeconomic, race, and age distributions were used to select blocks for the sample.

The normative sample was 80.5 percent white, 18.2 percent black, and 1.3 percent other; 13.5 percent were mothers and 3.4 percent were other relatives, foster parents, and the like. It appears that the CBCL has a relatively equal representation of socioeconomic groups. It should be noted, however, that it was *not* based upon a nationally representative sample.

Data obtained. Each behavior problem on the CBCL is scored on a three-point scale (0 = Behavior Not True of Child; 1 = Behavior Sometimes or Somewhat True of Child; and 2 = Behavior Very True or Often True of Child). For each item that describes the child at present or in the past six months, parents are asked to circle the appropriate number on the three-point scale. Each item is given equal weight in computing scores for each of the narrow-band factors.

Reliability and validity. The manual presents evidence for test-retest reliability and interparent agreement. The reliability of narrow-band factors across all ages and sexes ranged from .61 (Obsessive-Compulsive) to .96 (Hyperactive), with a median one-week test-retest reliability coefficient of .81. Five of the narrow-band factors had one-week stability coefficients over .90, three had coefficients over .80, two had coefficients over .70, and two had coefficients over .60. The broad-band factors had one-week stability coefficients of .82 and .91 for Internalizing Syndrome and Externalizing Syndrome, respectively. The total CBCL score had a stability coefficient of .91.

The agreement between mothers and fathers in CBCL ratings ranged from .26 (Sex Problems) to .78 (Delinquent), with a median reliability of .55. The interparent agreement for the Internalizing Syndrome, Externalizing Syndrome, and total scores was .59, .75, and .64, respectively. No data are presented in the manual regarding the internal consistency of the narrow-band factors for each sex or age range.

The CBCL manual presents a great deal of evidence for content, construct, and criterion-related validity. The content validity was established by obtaining descriptions of problem behaviors of children from case files, the research literature, and the reports of parents as well as professionals. The items on the CBCL include a wide spectrum of problems that are relevant to children's mental health referrals and cover a broad range of deviant behaviors that are developmentally appropriate for children of varying ages.

The construct validity of the CBCL was established through factor analysis, contrasted-groups research, and discriminant analysis. The manual presents a great deal of evidence attesting to the factorial validity of the CBCL as well as the fact that the scale reliably differentiates referred from nonreferred children.

The criterion-related validity of the CBCL was demonstrated by correlating the scores of the narrow-band and broad-band factors with the Conners

Parent Questionnaire Scale (Conners, 1973) and the Revised Behavior Problem Checklist (Quay & Peterson, 1983). The manual shows that the correlations between the CBCL and these scales are in the moderate to high range (.35 to .90).

Summary. The CBCL is a well-designed, well-constructed, and well-researched parent rating scale that is useful in identifying clusters of behavior problems in children. It is a relatively short scale, taking only about 15 minutes to complete, and should be used as part of the behavioral evaluation process to measure the cross-situationality of behavior (that is, at school and home). It is useful in identifying top-priority behaviors for intervention purposes as well as providing the generality of behavior problems.

One of the strengths of the instrument is its careful attention to psychometric detail. A major weakness is its lack of a nationally representative standardization sample. Future developments of the CBCL should include a national or otherwise more representative sample of children.

Revised Behavior Problem Checklist

Overview and purpose. The Revised Behavior Problem Checklist, or RBPC (Quay, 1983), is a behavior rating scale with eighty-nine items designed to identify behavior problems in children and adolescents. The RBPC represents a revision and extension of the original fifty-five item Behavior Problem Checklist (Quay & Peterson, 1979), which has been utilized in more than one hundred published studies with a variety of populations (for a comprehensive review see Quay, 1979). The scale is designed to be completed by adults familiar with a target child or adolescent and may include teachers, parents, or direct service child-care workers.

The RBPC is comprised of six factors or dimensions of problem behaviors: (a) Conduct Disorder, (b) Socialized Aggression, (c) Attention Problems-Immaturity, (d) Anxiety-Withdrawal, (e) Psychotic Behavior, and (f) Motor Excess. A child receives a raw score on each factor, which may then be compared to data derived from empirical investigations of the scale. Examples of behaviors for each dimension follow:

1. *Conduct Disorder:* Child is disruptive, annoys others, fights, and blames others.
2. *Socialized Aggression:* Child stays out late at night, has bad companions, and is loyal to delinquent friends.
3. *Attention Problems-Immaturity:* Child has a short attention span and poor concentration, is distractible, and has trouble following directions.
4. *Anxiety-Withdrawal:* Child feels inferior, self-conscious, fearful, and anxious.
5. *Psychotic Behavior:* Child uses repetitive speech, parrots others' speech, and expresses far-fetched ideas.
6. *Motor Excess:* Child is restless, hyperactive, squirms, fidgets, and unable to relax.

Standardization sample and norms. According to the manual, four samples were used to generate the item statistics and factor analyses of the RBPC. Sample 1 consisted of 276 cases in two private psychiatric residential facilities. This sample consisted of males (72 percent) and females (28 percent) between the ages of five years, five months, and twenty-two years, eleven months, with a mean of fifteen years and a standard deviation of three years. Sample 2 consisted of 198 cases who were rated by their parents (mostly mothers) at the time of their admission to either an inpatient or outpatient psychiatric facility. The ages ranged from three to twenty-one years, with an average of eleven years, six months, and a standard deviation of four years. Sample 3 included 172 students in a special school for children with developmental disabilities. No ages were reported for this sample. Sample 4 consisted of 114 students attending a private school for children with learning disabilities. They had a mean age of ten years with a standard deviation of two years.

In sum, the available standardization data were based upon 760 cases, which were exclusively "clinical" or pathological groups. The manual does provide some data from 566 "normal" children in public schools in New Jersey and South Carolina in grades one through five. This sample, however, is inadequately described in terms of raters, demographic characteristics, and other relevant criteria for standardized tests and rating scales. Further, the manual does not provide standard scores or percentile ranks, but instead relies upon unweighted raw scores. Given the nature of the standardization sample, the RBPC is inappropriately used as a norm-referenced instrument to identify behavior problems of the general school-age population.

Data obtained. Each item on the RBPC is scored on a three-point scale (0 = Not a Problem; 1 = A Mild Problem; and 2 = A Severe Problem). The maximum score on any scale is twice the number of items on that scale, whereas the minimum score is zero. For example, the Conduct Disorder scale, with twenty-two items, has a maximum weighted raw score of 44 and a minimum score of zero. The Motor Excess Scale, with five items, has a maximum weighted raw score of 10 and a minimum score of zero. All scores on the RBPC are weighted raw scores that are summed for each scale or factor. Standard scores cannot be derived from the RBPC in its current form.

Reliability and validity. The manual provides evidence for internal consistency and interrater reliability. The coefficient alphas for each of the six scales are as follows: (a) Conduct Disorder = .94, (b) Socialized Aggression = .84, (c) Attention Problems-Immaturity = .92, (d) Anxiety-Withdrawal = .82, (e) Psychotic Behavior = .72, and (f) Motor Excess = .75. The only interrater reliability evidence was based upon staff members in residential facilities and ranged from .85 (Conduct Disorder) to .52 (Anxiety-Withdrawal), with a median interrater reliability coefficient of .58. No data concerning test-retest reliability are reported.

Quay (1983) states that "it is, of course, reasonable to assume that much of the concurrent, predictive, and construct validity already established for the Behavior Problem Checklist [Quay & Peterson, 1979] can be generalized to the RBPC" (p. 247). However, this is not necessarily true, since the RBPC represents a new scale and as such must establish reliability and validity in its own right. The only validity evidence provided for the RBPC is factorial validity and group differentiation in which "normal" children were differentiated from "clinical" samples. To date, the RBPC has a paucity of validity data to support its use.

Summary. The RBPC is a poorly standardized behavior rating scale that has limited evidence for reliability and validity. The fact that the original Behavior Problem Checklist has extensive reliability and validity evidence does not necessarily ensure that the RBPC will assume the same psychometric features. However, the RBPC can be used to identify teachers' behavioral concerns for individual students, particularly from a criterion-referenced framework. In addition, teachers may be asked to rate several students in their classroom, and these ratings can be compared.

Putting It Together

The following sample case report (see Focus on Practice) elucidates the principles of good assessment practice for behavior problems in the classroom. Read this report carefully and try to find each of the seven components of behavior disorder assessment listed in the beginning of this chapter.

Summary

What should be the guiding force behind the assessment of behavior and adjustment problems? The answer to this question may be easily lost in the large array of conceptual and technical issues that surround assessment in this important area. However, the answer is quite simple: Assessment should be driven by the need to answer specific questions about a particular child. It has been the focus of this chapter, indeed of this entire text, that assessment that leads only to classification and placement outside the regular classroom for the maximum time allowed by the Least Restrictive Alternative rule may solve problems for the regular classroom teacher but not for the child.

Knowing that a child is hyperactive contributes very little to our ability to help that child. However, knowing that a child is hyperactive *in specific situations and under certain circumstances* can be invaluable in designing an intervention to help the child. It is important to remember the basic reasons for assessment so we can plan our assessment with full consideration of the unique problems of the child to be assessed.

FOCUS ON PRACTICE
Psychoeducational Evaluation

Name: Henry E.
Date of Birth: 1-24-75
Age: 11-3
Grade: 5

Date of Report: 4-25-86
School: Athens Elementary School
Teacher: Mrs. G. Adams
School Psychologist: Frank M. Gresham

Reason for Referral

Henry E. was referred by Mrs. G. Adams, his fifth-grade teacher at Athens Elementary School, because of his disruptive, noncompliant, and aggressive behavior in her classroom. According to Mrs. Adams, Henry was academically able to succeed in the fifth-grade curriculum, but his disruptive and aggressive behavior prevented him from performing on grade level. This report represents a complete psychoeducational evaluation to determine the severity of Henry's problem behaviors and to design, implement, and evaluate a school-based intervention to facilitate his adjustment at school.

Assessment Procedures

Permanent records
Behavioral interviews
Behavior rating scales
School-based direct observations

Results of Assessment Procedures

Permanent Records. An inspection of Henry's permanent records on file at the school showed that he had not been reported as experiencing any particular difficulty in his previous four years at the school. His grades in those years were all satisfactory, and teacher comments were generally positive. He had no record of suspensions or expulsions or of having been sent to the principal's office for disciplinary action. In fourth grade, Henry performed at approximately the 55th percentile on the Stanford Achievement Test. In sum, there was nothing in his permanent records to suggest that he had experienced school adjustment difficulties.

Behavioral Interviews. An interview was conducted with Mrs. Adams to determine the specific nature of Henry's problem behaviors and to estimate their severity. According to Mrs. Adams, Henry would disrupt the class by getting out of his seat, wandering around the room, pulling papers off of other children's desks, and hitting others. She indicated that these behaviors seemed to occur more frequently during times of independent seat work and after lunch. She had responded to Henry's behavior by telling him to sit down and by threatening to send him to the principal's office. She had also moved his seat to the front of the class in an attempt to monitor his behavior more closely. These techniques were apparently not effective in decreasing Henry's disruptive behaviors. Mrs. Adams also indicated that Henry would

continued

FOCUS ON PRACTICE *continued*

typically hit other children after he had pulled papers off their desks. This frequently occurred when the others told him to stop bothering them. Mrs. Adams was not able to identify any specific children Henry hit more often than others. She estimated the frequency of his disruptive behaviors at approximately five times per day.

A problem identification interview was also conducted with Mrs. Jones, Henry's art teacher, to determine whether these same disruptive behaviors occurred in her class. According to Mrs. Jones, they did not. Although he was not the best-behaved child in her class, she indicated that his behavior was comparable to that of most other children.

Another interview was conducted with Henry's mother to determine if he exhibited problem behaviors in the home. According to Mrs. E., Henry had become somewhat noncompliant with her requests in the home — not completing homework when asked, not cleaning his room, and not coming in from play at the desired time. She indicated that this behavior had become more of a problem this school year. Mrs. E. stated that her response to such behaviors was typically to nag or even to scream at Henry. In addition, she indicated that Henry did not exhibit noncompliance as often with his father as with her. Henry's father, however, was frequently out of town and apparently did not have to deal with his son's noncompliance on a daily basis. No other problem behaviors were identified by Mrs. E.

Behavior Rating Scales. The Walker Problem Behavior Identification Checklist (WPBIC) was completed by Mrs. Adams and Mrs. Jones to assess their perceptions of Henry's behavior. Mrs. Adams rated Henry's behaviors high on the Acting-Out and Disturbed Peer Relations scales of the WPBIC (in the 99th and 98th percentiles, respectively). Specifically, she rated Henry as exhibiting behaviors such as arguing, having temper tantrums, not obeying, and displaying physical aggression toward others. These ratings are consistent with her problem identification interview. In contrast, the art teacher did not rate Henry as having any particular problems in her class, which was also consistent with her interview.

Henry's mother completed the Child Behavior Checklist (CBCL) to assess her perceptions of Henry's behavior. According to Mrs. E., he exhibited behaviors such as disobedience, stubbornness, and sulking. Again, these behaviors are fairly consistent with those identified in Mrs. E.'s interview.

School-Based Direct Observations. To establish the frequency of Henry's problem behaviors in Mrs. Adams's classroom, a series of direct observations were conducted over six days. Three behaviors were observed by using a *frequency recording* procedure: (a) leaving his seat, (b) pulling papers off others' desks, and (c) hitting others. These observations were noted between 1:00 and 1:30 each day. As a basis of comparison, Mrs. Adams was asked to nominate a well-behaved and an average-behaved child from her class. Data on these three behaviors were also taken on these

continued

FOCUS ON PRACTICE *continued*

two children as well. Results showed that, on the average, Henry was out of his seat four times per observation session, pulled papers off others' desks two times per session, and hit others once per session. The comparison children had no instances of these behaviors over the six-day observation period.

Integration of Assessment Data

Based upon the assessment procedures, the following problem behaviors were identified for Henry:

Behavioral Excesses

Disruptive Classroom Behaviors. Henry exhibited relatively high frequencies of leaving his seat, pulling papers off others' desks, and hitting others. These behaviors were identified by Mrs. Adams in a problem identification interview using a behavior rating scale and were corroborated with direct classroom observations. These behaviors, however, were not observed in Mrs. Jones's art class, nor did Mrs. Jones report their occurrence in her interview.

Noncompliance in the Home. A problem identification interview and behavior rating scale completed by Henry's mother indicated that Henry was often noncompliant with Mrs. E.'s requests, particularly when his father was not present.

Behavioral Deficits

Poor Grades. Henry's academic performance has declined from previous years. His grades are all in the unsatisfactory range and appear to be related to his excessive disruptive behavior in Mrs. Adams's class.

Situational Inappropriateness of Behavior

Henry's disruptive behavior seems to be specific to Mrs. Adams's class and his home, because his art teacher does not indicate that he is disruptive in her class. In the home, Henry does appear to exhibit noncompliant behavior, specifically in his interactions with his mother.

School-Based Intervention

To decrease Henry's rates of disruptive classroom behaviors, a classroom-based intervention, developed in conjunction with the school psychologist, was implemented by Mrs. Adams. This intervention consisted of a *response cost procedure* combined with a school-home note system, or "daily report card." The response cost procedure involved the teacher's deducting three minutes of recess for each time Henry left his seat, pulled papers off others' desks, or hit others. In addition, Henry could earn ten minutes of *extra* recess time on Friday if he went the entire week (five days) without an instance of disruptive behavior. A report card, which simply had the

continued

FOCUS ON PRACTICE *continued*

number and type of disruptive behaviors noted and was signed and dated by the teacher, was sent home with Henry each day. For each occurrence of disruptive behavior at school that day, Henry lost thirty minutes of television time that night. If he had no instances of disruptive behavior for the week, he could go to a movie of his choice on Saturday. It was specified that Henry's father would take him to the movie to increase the frequency of positive interaction between father and son. If Henry failed to bring home his daily report card, he lost access to the television for the night.

The results of this intervention demonstrated that Henry's rates of disruptive behavior were drastically reduced by the response cost and daily report card procedures. During the first week, his average rate of disruptive behavior decreased from seven times per observation period to only three times. In the second week, Henry's disruptive behavior rates even decreased further, to an average of only once per session. The teacher considered this to be within acceptable limits, and the intervention will be continued for the rest of the semester. Henry's mother also reported that his rate of noncompliance had decreased in the home and that his father seemed to be spending more time with Henry than before the intervention.

Summary

In summary, Henry E. was referred for a behavior disorder assessment by Mrs. Adams, his fifth-grade teacher. The assessment procedures revealed that his behavior in school was restricted to Mrs. Adams's class and did not appear to occur in Mrs. Jones's art class. The interview, rating scale, and observational data were in agreement that Henry had relatively high rates of disruptive behavior in Mrs. Adams's class. In addition, the interview and rating scale data obtained from Henry's mother agreed that he displayed noncompliance.

Collectively, the assessment data did not indicate the presence of a behavior disorder because the problems were limited to one classroom. Moreover, the frequency of Henry's disruptive behavior was reduced drastically by a school-based intervention implemented in Mrs. Adams's classroom.

Frank M. Gresham, Ph.D.
School Psychologist

Chapter 15

Adaptive Behavior

Learning Objectives

1. Define adaptive behavior.
2. Give two major reasons why the assessment of adaptive behavior has become so widespread.
3. Describe the strengths and weaknesses of at least two major adaptive behavior assessment instruments.
4. Explain the problem of declassification and propose some solutions.
5. Discuss the relationship between adaptive behavior and intelligence.

The community of Guadalupe is located on the outskirts of Phoenix and Tempe in central Arizona. It is inhabited almost exclusively by Yaqui Indians who migrated from Mexico. For the most part, the residents live in abject poverty — many live in huts with dirt floors and have neither water nor electricity. Children growing up in Guadalupe often speak a mixture of Yaqui, Spanish, and English. Their cultural values encourage cooperation over competition and quality of work over speed of work. Because of economic pressures, many children drop out of school at the legal minimum age and begin working.

The culture and values of the residents of Guadalupe are quite different from those of the officials of the Tempe school district, in which Guadalupe is located. Not unlike many other suburban school systems, in the Tempe schools value is placed on achievement, timely completion of work, and preparation for college. Many middle-class children come to school knowing their English alphabet and numbers; many Guadalupe children lack these skills. Many of those who teach children from Guadalupe have white middle-class values and white middle-class expectations for their students. When children deviate markedly from these expectations, there is a good chance they will be referred for psychological and educational evaluation.

In the early 1970s large numbers of Guadalupe children were failing in the Tempe classrooms, and referrals for special education were occurring at an alarming rate. Many of these children were diagnosed after taking standardized intelligence tests administered in English. These tests often contained items that require good facility with the English language or are timed. On the basis of the teachers' referral and the testing, many of the children were diagnosed as mentally retarded and placed in special education classrooms *even though many were reported to function quite normally in their home environment.* Upon learning of this, a group of concerned citizens in Guadalupe filed suit in federal court (*Guadalupe Organization* v. *Tempe Elementary School District*, 1972) and successfully barred the school district from continuing these practices. Numerous similar suits were filed in other parts of the country because children, primarily those from minority cultures, who functioned well outside of school were labeled as mentally retarded because of poor performance in school. One result of these suits was a broadening of the criteria used in schools for classifying mental retardation. Instead of relying solely on in-school behavior and performance on an intelligence test, it was mandated that the evaluation of mental retardation include an assessment of out-of-school behavior as well. This out-of-school behavior has been referred to as *adaptive behavior*.

What Is Adaptive Behavior?

Although the term applies to the behavior of children with a variety of handicaps (especially behavior disorders), adaptive behavior is best understood within the context of defining mental retardation. The most commonly used definitions are those developed by the American Association of Mental Deficiency (AAMD). Prior to the establishment of guidelines by the AAMD, which were formalized in 1959, mental retardation was defined almost exclusively in terms of a score on an intelligence test. Individuals who scored significantly below average were labeled mentally retarded. The AAMD definition of mental retardation has gradually changed since first appearing in 1961 (Grossman, 1973, 1977, 1981; Heber, 1961), primarily in the use of a wider range of criteria for defining the condition. The 1961 definition broadened the previous definition based on testing. "Mental retardation refers to subaverage general intellectual functioning which originates during the developmental period and is associated with impairment in adaptive behavior" (Heber, 1961, p. 3). A subtle change in wording occurred in 1973: "Mental retardation refers to significantly subaverage general intellectual functioning existing concurrently with deficits in adaptive behavior, and manifested during the developmental period" (Grossman, 1973, p. 11). Although adaptive behavior is mentioned in both definitions, the latter made it quite clear that adaptive behavior must *coexist*. The current AAMD definition (Grossman, 1981) suggests that mental retardation should be defined by means of a clinical process in which not only IQ but also adaptive behavior, social and developmental history, and current functioning in a variety of settings are considered. Adaptive behavior has thus become an integral component of the definition of mental retardation.

But exactly what is adaptive behavior? Several definitions have been offered, but perhaps the most widely accepted is the one advanced by the AAMD:

> Adaptive behavior is defined as the effectiveness or degree with which an individual meets the standards of personal independence and social responsibility expected for age and cultural group.
>
> Since these expectations of adaptive behavior vary for different age groups, deficits in adaptive behavior will vary at different ages. These may be reflected in the following areas:
>
> During infancy and early childhood in:
>
> 1. Sensory-motor skills development
> 2. Communication skills (including speech and language)
> 3. Self-help skills
> 4. Socialization (development of ability to interact with others); and
>
> During childhood and early adolescence in:
>
> 5. Application of basic academic skills in daily life activities
> 6. Application of appropriate reasoning and judgment in mastery of environment
> 7. Social skills (participation in group activities and interpersonal relationships); and
>
> During late adolescence and adult life in:
>
> 8. Vocational and social responsibilities and performances.
>
> The skills required for adaptation during childhood and early adolescence involve complex learning processes. This involves the process by which knowledge is acquired and retained as a function of the experiences of the individual. Difficulties in learning are usually manifested in the academic situation but in evaluation of adaptive behavior, attention should focus not only on the basic academic skills and their use, but also on skills essential to cope with the environment, including concepts of time and money, self-directed behaviors, social responsiveness, and interactive skills. (Grossman, 1977, pp. 11–14)

There are two important components to this definition. First, it suggests that adaptive behavior must be evaluated relative to the social context in which it occurs. Thus, such behavior is not an immutable property of the individual, but instead differs from culture to culture. Second, an individual who behaves adaptively must exhibit skills consistent with his or her age. In younger children this requires the development of skills necessary for independent functioning (for example, self-help and communication skills). Older children and adults must assume personal and social responsibility and maintain themselves independently, especially in an economic sense.

Reasons for Assessing Adaptive Behavior

Although now a routine part of school evaluation of children who may be mentally retarded, the assessment of adaptive behavior was uncommon in public schools twenty years ago. There are a number of reasons for this, and we will begin with the most important.

The Law Requires the Assessment of Adaptive Behavior

The delivery of services to handicapped children has been significantly influenced by legislation and the courts. The area of adaptive behavior is no exception. The most obvious reason for the increase in adaptive behavior assessments is the numerous lawsuits filed on behalf of children who were diagnosed as mentally retarded even though they functioned adequately outside of the classroom. Certainly, the assessment of adaptive behavior is warranted on other grounds, but without the force of law, such assessment would be far less common today. It would be easy to assume that court intervention in the educational system is an unwarranted intrusion and that educators know best how to assess and educate handicapped children. However, in many instances, court decisions have taken what was simply good educational practice and made it the law.

The *Guadalupe* case provides an illustration. The apparent practice in the Tempe schools in the early 1970s was to administer highly verbal intelligence tests in English to children whose primary language was not English. The scores derived from these tests were a major determinant in whether the child was diagnosed as mentally retarded, even if that child seemed normal to people in his community.

The plaintiffs in *Guadalupe* argued that school assessment practices were inappropriate. The court agreed and required the assessment of adaptive behavior outside of school as well. Further, the court stipulated that results of intelligence tests could not be the sole basis for classifying children as mentally retarded. From the perspective of a professional psychologist or educator, it is difficult to disagree with the court's ruling because it is consistent with good practice!

As cases similar to *Guadalupe* became more numerous, the assessment of adaptive behavior was incorporated into more and more federal and state legislation governing the education of handicapped children. Perhaps the most important of these developments was the incorporation in 1975 of the following clause into the Education for All Handicapped Children Act of 1975, Public Law 94-142:

> "Mentally retarded" means significantly subaverage general intellectual functioning existing concurrently with deficits in adaptive behavior and manifested during the developmental period, which adversely affects a child's educational performance. (§300.5[3]).

Reduction of Bias in Assessment Processes

It is incumbent on professionals who collect and utilize test data to be as fair as possible in identifying retarded children. The problems are compounded when evaluating a child from a minority culture. In many cases the content of some tests is especially difficult for such children, even though, as we have stated, the tests are unbiased. Often language problems, cultural differences, and economic factors contribute to differences among racial and ethnic groups. Including a measure of adaptive behavior in the assessment process can help differentiate children whose cultural differences account for low IQ scores. Adaptive behavior is, by definition, the ability to perform in line with *cultural* expectations. *Every* normally functioning six-year-old can reasonably be expected to take care of his or her self-care needs. However, whether the same child knows which animal gives milk or what skis are is dependent on a number of sociocultural factors.

Assessment Provides Information on What Skills Need to Be Taught

Intelligence tests can be used for classification and diagnostic decisions, but they are much less useful in providing a parent or teacher with information about *what* to teach. On the other hand, most adaptive behavior scales are composed of check lists or ratings, and respondents indicate whether a child can or cannot perform or how well she performs a particular skill. A typical item might assess the extent to which a child is capable of getting dressed without assistance. Perhaps the child can put the clothing on but cannot button buttons or snap snaps. Logically, performing these skills will be appropriate educational goals.

A slightly different approach is to view the age-appropriate skills on a measure of adaptive behavior as goals that must be accomplished before a child can be integrated into the community at a level consistent with societal expectations. Some measures of adaptive behavior provide lists of directly teachable behaviors.

Measures of Adaptive Behavior

The selection of an adaptive behavior assessment instrument that is appropriate for a given child in a specific situation requires careful study. However, few of the scales measure all components of adaptive behavior and some are appropriate only for certain ages. Well over a hundred such instruments are available. We will describe a small sample of what we consider to be the most important. A slightly wider selection is profiled in Table 15.1.

AAMD Adaptive Behavior Scale-School Edition

Overview and purpose. Of all the instruments available for the assessment of adaptive behvior, perhaps the most widely known and used is the AAMD Adaptive Behavior Scale-School Edition, or ABS-SE (Lambert & Windmiller, 1981). Its widespread use is due to three factors. First, the ABS-SE is one of the oldest measures of adaptive behavior, with the present version representing a revision of the ABS-SE published in 1974. Second, sponsorship by the AAMD, which has assumed leadership in the development of definitions of both mental retardation and adaptive behavior, has added to its visibility. Third, the ABS-SE is technically superior to most other measures in its standardization procedures and the degree to which it comprehensively assesses a broad range of competencies and skills.

The comprehensive nature of the ABS-SE is illustrated in Table 15.2. Note that the instrument is divided into two parts. Part One consists of nine domains considered important to the development of personal independence in daily living. Part Two assesses a wide array of behaviors generally considered to be inappropriate and unacceptable. The behaviors assessed in Part One are those most commonly associated with traditional definitions of "social maturity" and adaptive behavior, such as self-help skills and language. The personality and behavior disorders assessed in Part Two, which are not usually included on such instruments, offer a way to measure those behaviors that may actually *interfere* with successful adaptive functioning.

To simplify understanding and interpreting the ABS-SE, the test's domains were categorized into five clusters (see Figure 15.1). These clusters were derived by evaluating statistically* whether certain domains were highly interrelated. It turned out, for example, that several items in Domains 4 and 5 were highly related to each other and that each of those items seemed to be measuring some aspect of *Community Self-Sufficiency*. Because the statistical procedure used to determine these clusters of interrelated items is called factor analysis, the clusters are referred to as factors. In communicating information about a particular child it is much easier to interpret only the five factors than to refer to each of the ninety-five test items or even the twenty-one domains.

*The procedure used to derive the five clusters is termed *factor analysis*. For a discussion of factor analysis, see Harman (1967).

Table 15.1 Measures of Adaptive Behavior

	Behavior assessed							Behavioral environment					Population type and size			Purpose			Examiner			Respondent			Reliability and validity data available	Scores		Administration time
Instrument	*Physical Development, Sensory Motor, and Locomotion*	*Self-Direction*	*Language and Communication*	*Vocational and Occupation*	*Economic*	*Social*	*Self-Help, Independent Functioning, and Self-Maintenance*	*With Peers*	*In School*	*In the Family*	*In the Community*	*Mixed*	*Age Range*	*Clinical*	*School*	*Screening*	*Placement*	*Programing*	*Teacher*	*Diagnostician*	*Paraprofessional*	*Teacher*	*Parent/Family*	*Child*		*Percentile*	*Scaled Score*	
AAMD Adaptive Behavior Scale-School Edition (Lambert & Windmiller, 1981)	×	×	×	×	×	×	×					×	3–17		×		×	×	×	×	×	×	×		Yes	×	×	45 minutes to 1 hour
Adaptive Behavior Inventory for Children (Mercer & Lewis, 1978)				×	×	×	×	×	×	×	×		5–11		×		×			×	×		×		Yes	×	×	1 hour
Camelot (Foster, 1974)	×	×	×	×	×	×	×						2–adult				×	×	×	×	×	×	×		Yes			1 hour
Children's Adaptive Behavior Scale (Richmond & Kicklighter, 1980)		×	×	×	×	×	×						5–10		×	×	×			×				×	Yes	×		30 minutes to 1 hour
Social and Prevocational Information Battery (Halpern et al., 1975)		×	×	×	×	×	×						junior–senior high school		×		×	×	×	×	×			×	Yes	×		1–2 hours
Vineland Adaptive Behavior Scale (Sparrow et al., 1984)		×	×	×	×	×	×						birth–18-11	×	×		×			×		×	×		Yes			20 minutes

From "Assessment and Interventions for Mildly Retarded and Learning Disabled Children" by T. Oakland and D. Goldwater, 1979, in G. Phye and D. Reschly (Eds.), *School Psychology: Perspectives and Issues* (p. 147), New York: Academic Press. Copyright 1979 by Academic Press. Adapted by permission.

Table 15.2 Domains and Subdomains from the ABS-SE

Part One Domains and Subdomains	Part Two Domains
Domain 1 Independent Functioning	*Domain 10* Aggressiveness
Eating Subdomain	*Domain 11* Antisocial vs. Social Behavior
Toilet Use Subdomain	*Domain 12* Rebelliousness
Cleanliness Subdomain	*Domain 13* Trustworthiness
Appearance Subdomain	*Domain 14* Withdrawal vs. Involvement
Care of Clothing Subdomain	*Domain 15* Mannerisms
Dressing & Undressing Subdomain	*Domain 16* Interpersonal Manners
Travel Subdomain	*Domain 17* Acceptability of Vocal Habits
Other Independent Functioning Subdomain	*Domain 18* Acceptability of Habits
Domain 2 Physical Development	*Domain 19* Activity Level
Sensory Development Subdomain	*Domain 20* Symptomatic Behavior
Motor Development Subdomain	*Domain 21* Use of Medications
Domain 3 Economic Activity	
Money Handling & Budgeting Subdomain	
Shopping Skills Subdomain	
Domain 4 Language Development	
Expression Subdomain	
Comprehension Subdomain	
Social Language Development Subdomain	
Domain 5 Numbers & Time	
Domain 6 Prevocational Activity	
Domain 7 Self-Direction	
Initiative Subdomain	
Perseverance Subdomain	
Leisure Time Subdomain	
Domain 8 Responsibility	
Domain 9 Socialization	

From *AAMD Adaptive Behavior Scale–School Edition* by N. Lambert and M. Windmiller, 1981, Monterey, CA: CTB/McGraw-Hill. Copyright 1981 by American Association on Mental Deficiency. Reprinted by permission.

Furthermore, since the factors are composed of several items and the domains are composed of only a few, the factors are much more stable and reliable indicators of a child's functioning and thus more appropriate for diagnostic and classification decisions. The domain sources, which are more behavioral, may be most useful for instructional planning.

The factors can be described briefly as follows:

1. *Personal Self-Sufficiency:* This cluster reflects the degree to which a child is able to handle personal needs such as eating, drinking, and toilet use.
2. *Community Self-Sufficiency:* This factor assesses the extent to which a child can function appropriately in situations such as traveling about the

Variable	Factor 1 Personal Self-Sufficiency	Factor 2 Community Self-Sufficiency	Factor 3 Personal-Social Responsibility	Factor 4 Social Adjustment	Factor 5 Personal Adjustment
ITEM 1 Use of Table Utensils	●				
ITEM 2 Eating in Public		●			
ITEM 3 Drinking	●				
ITEM 5 Toilet Training	●				
ITEM 6 Washing Hands & Face	●				
ITEM 7 Bathing	●				
ITEM 8 Personal Hygiene		●			
ITEM 10 Clothing		●			
ITEM 11 Care of Clothing		●			
ITEM 12 Dressing	●				
ITEM 13 Shoes	●				
ITEM 14 Sense of Direction		●			
ITEM 15 Public Transportation		●			
ITEM 16 Telephone		●			
ITEM 17 Miscellaneous Independent Functioning		●			
DOMAIN 2 Physical Develop	●				
DOMAIN 3 Econ Activity		●			
DOMAIN 4 Language Development		●			
DOMAIN 5 Numbers & Time		●			
ITEM 40 Job Complexity		●			
ITEM 41 School Job Performance			●		
ITEM 42 School or Work Habits			●		
DOMAIN 7 Self Direction			●		
DOMAIN 8 Responsibility			●		
ITEM 50 Cooperation			●		
ITEM 51 Consideration for Others			●		
ITEM 52 Awareness of Others			●		
ITEM 53 Interaction with Others			●		
ITEM 54 Participation in Group Activities			●		
DOMAIN 10 Aggressiveness				●	
DOMAIN 11 Antisoc vs Soc Beh				●	
DOMAIN 12 Rebelliousness				●	
DOMAIN 13 Trustworthiness				●	
DOMAIN 14 Withdrawal			●		
DOMAIN 15 Mannerisms					●
DOMAIN 16 Appropriateness of Interpersonal Manners					●
DOMAIN 17 Vocal Habits					●
DOMAIN 18 Habits				●	
DOMAIN 19 Activity Level				●	
DOMAIN 20 Symptomatic Beh				●	

Figure 15.1 The five ABS-SE factors. (From *AAMD Adaptive Behavior Scale–School Edition* by N. Lambert and M. Windmiller, 1981, Monterey, CA: CTB/McGraw-Hill. Copyright 1981 by American Association on Mental Deficiency. Reprinted by permission.)

neighborhood, communicating with others, and engaging in economic activity.

3. *Personal-Social Responsibility:* Items within this factor reflect relatively high-level social interaction skills, including getting to school or work on time, showing initiative in school or job settings, interacting cooperatively with others, and assuming responsibility for one's own actions.
4. *Social Adjustment:* This factor is composed of items exclusively from Part Two of the ABS-SE. The problem behaviors assessed include those in which a child is inappropriately interacting with others (for example, being aggressive, lying, or cheating). Such behaviors are characteristic of acting-out or behavior-disordered children.
5. *Personal Adjustment:* Items in this cluster reflect three areas of inappropriate contact with others, such as excessing hugging, touching, or kissing, and unacceptable vocal habits, such as echolalia or talking too loudly.

The first three factors are arranged in virtually a developmental progression from least complex to most complex. Skills assessed by Factor 1 are typically developed early in life and are responsive to training. By contrast, the skills assessed by Factors 2 and 3 represent more complex forms of learning that require children to generalize skills learned in one situation to new settings. Factors 4 and 5 are relatively independent of chronological age but instead represent inappropriate behaviors that can occur at almost any developmental stage.

The ABS-SE is designed for use with children aged three years, three months, to seventeen years, two months. It is administered either by reading the items to someone who knows the child well (such as a parent or classroom aide) or by someone who knows the child *and* who has been trained in use of the test. First-person assessments require fifteen to forty-five minutes, but third-party interviews can last over an hour. The test's authors encourage users to obtain ratings from both teachers and parents whenever possible.

Figure 15.2 illustrates two items from ABS-SE. Note that both are arranged in order of difficulty, as are most items in Part One; the rater is supposed to circle the statement that describes best the most difficult task the child can perform. Items on the ABS-SE can be criticized on two counts. First, some are vague and difficult to interpret. On Item 53 (see Figure 15.2), for example, what is the meaning of "a short period of time" in the second statement and "with little interaction" in the third statement? Second, an inadequate number of items assess the higher-order social interaction skills required of older children. There are numerous items that reflect self-care skills and self-sufficiency, but a relative lack of items to measure the skills expected of adolescents.

Standardization sample and norms. The ABS-SE was standardized over a period of seven years (1972–79) on 6,523 subjects from three to seventeen years of age. The sample contained children from two states (California and

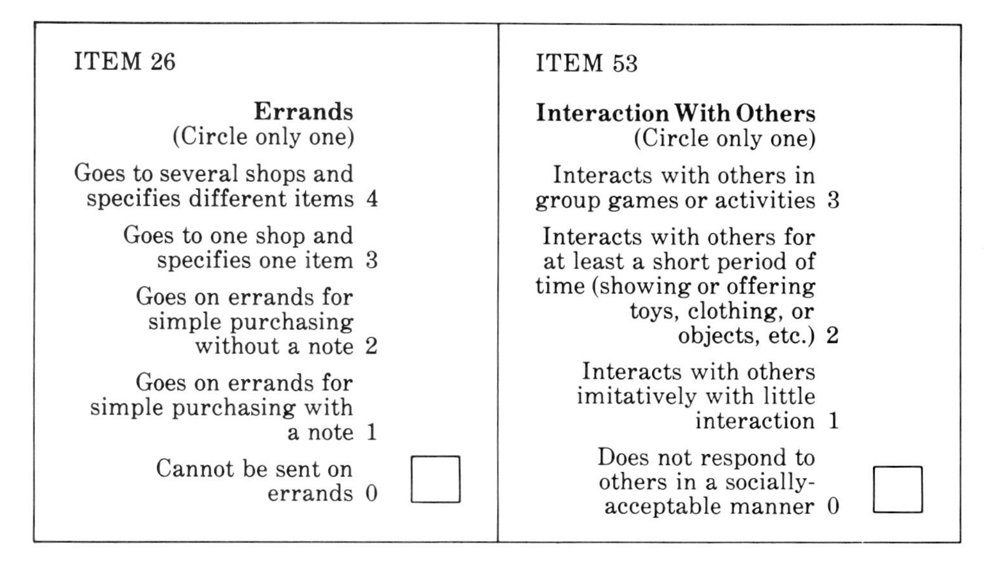

ITEM 26

Errands
(Circle only one)

Goes to several shops and specifies different items 4

Goes to one shop and specifies one item 3

Goes on errands for simple purchasing without a note 2

Goes on errands for simple purchasing with a note 1

Cannot be sent on errands 0 ☐

ITEM 53

Interaction With Others
(Circle only one)

Interacts with others in group games or activities 3

Interacts with others for at least a short period of time (showing or offering toys, clothing, or objects, etc.) 2

Interacts with others imitatively with little interaction 1

Does not respond to others in a socially-acceptable manner 0 ☐

Figure 15.2 Sample items from the ABS-SE. (From *AAMD Adaptive Behavior Scale–School Edition* by N. Lambert and M. Windmiller, 1981, Monterey, CA: CTB/McGraw-Hill. Copyright 1981 by American Association on Mental Deficiency. Reprinted by permission.)

Florida) who were either regular education, educable mentally retarded (EMR) or trainable mentally retarded (TMR) students. Representatives from various ethnic groups (black, Spanish-surnamed, white, and others) and from cities of various population densities (urban, suburban, and rural) were included. Although the sample did not represent all geographic areas of the country, its size and diversity were admirable relative to those of most other adaptive behavior scales.

Separate norms are provided for three reference groups (regular education, EMR, and TMR). Depending upon whether they are going to be used for classification or instructional planning, scores can be transformed into either percentiles or scaled scores.

Data obtained. Responses to individual items are recorded in an Assessment Booklet. Following completion of the scale, total scores for each domain are calculated by summing items within the domain. Depending upon the purpose for which the ABS-SE is being used, scores are transferred from the booklet to a Diagnostic Profile or an Instructional Planning Profile or both. Because these two profiles are in booklets separate from the Assessment Booklet, transferring scores is tedious.

If the ABS-SE is to be used to make a classification or diagnostic decision (for example, Is this child's adaptive behavior consistent with a diagnosis of mental retardation?), raw scores from the Assessment Booklet are converted

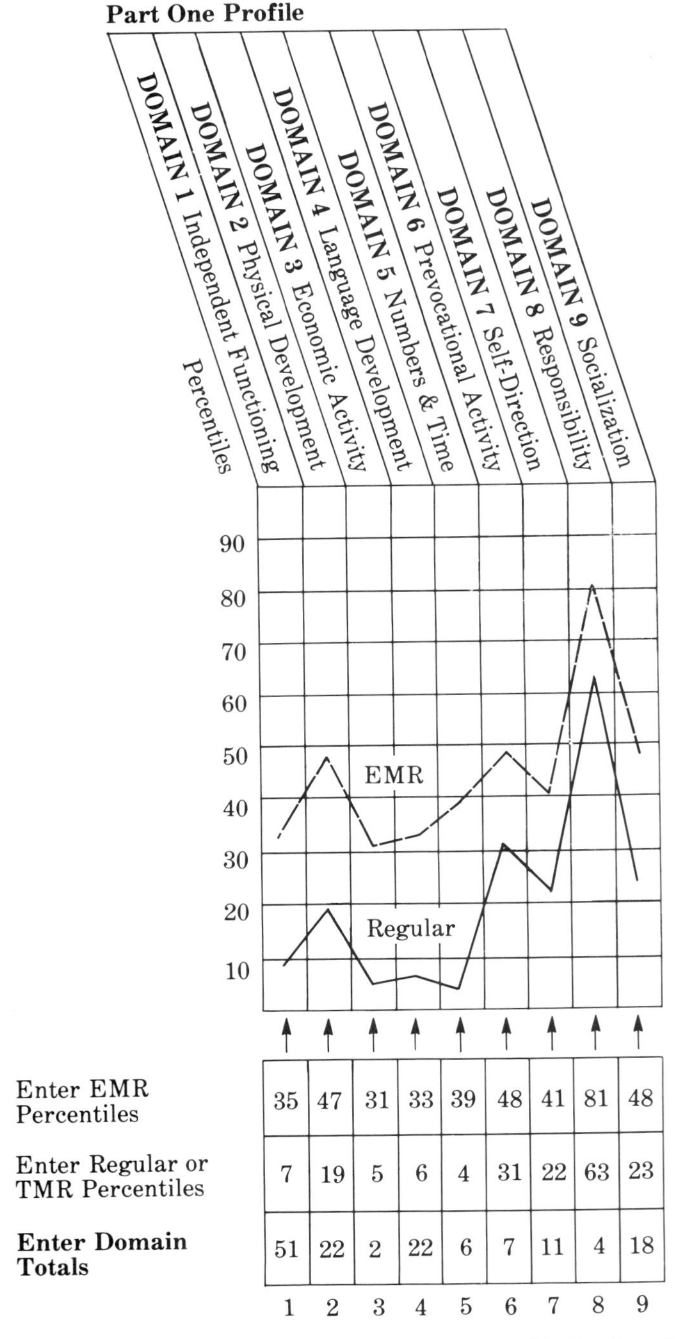

Figure 15.3 Sample instructional planning profile for Part One of the ABS-SE. (From *AAMD Adaptive Behavior Scale–School Edition* by N. Lambert and M. Windmiller, 1981, Monterey, CA: CTB/McGraw-Hill. Copyright 1981 by American Association on Mental Deficiency. Reprinted by permission.)

to scaled scores by referencing the normative tables provided. Two types of scores can be obtained. The first type is a factor score for each of the five factors. Obtaining factor scores is an eight-step process involving several score transformations and transferences from one booklet to another. The outcome is a profile of how the child compares to any one or all of the three normative groups (regular education, EMR, and TMR students).

Figure 15.3 illustrates the use of the ABS-SE factor scores. Note that factor scores have been plotted according to both regular education and EMR reference groups. The scores in the example appear more "average" when compared to the EMR group rather than to the regular education group. Thus, the child's adaptive behavior would be considered in the EMR range. In general, factor scores below 7 represent a significant deviation from the reference group.

The second type of score available for classification and diagnostic decisions is the Comparison Score, which is derived by combining the scores from the Personal Self-Sufficiency, Community Self-Sufficiency, and Personal-Social Responsibility factors. Recall that these three scales most closely represent what has traditionally been called adaptive behavior. The Comparison Score is useful if an overall or summary score is needed to describe a particular child's functioning. By consulting the norm tables, the Comparison Score can be converted into a percentile.

If results from the ABS-SE are going to be used for instructional planning, scores from the Assessment Booklet can be transferred to the Instructional Planning Profile. Unlike the Diagnostic Profile, which contained factor scores, the Instructional Planning Profile is used to plot percentiles for each of the twenty-one domains (see Table 15.2). The ABS-SE comes with a ninety-page guide that describes a large number of commercially available instructional materials that can be used to remediate deficits in areas targeted by the test.

In sum, the effective use of the ABS-SE is thus facilitated by its comprehensive array of accompanying materials, including a fifteen-page Assessment Booklet that contains the items, a ninety-page Administration and Planning Manual, an eighty-three page Diagnostic and Technical Manual, an Instructional Planning Profile, a Diagnostic Profile, and a *Parents Guide*, which not only discusses the measure but provides information about adaptive behavior in general.

Reliability and validity. Reliability data are extremely limited for an instrument that has had so much effort and expense put into other areas of its development. The only such information presented is for internal consistency. Although reliability is adequate with respect to this one type, it is surprising that test-retest and interrater reliabilities were not reported. Furthermore, information on reliability is available only for the factor scores and not the domain scores.

Two major types of validity data were presented by the authors: (a) data on the degree to which the scores on the ABS-SE are correlated with intelligence, and (b) data on the degree to which the ABS-SE can predict the appropriate classification for regular and mildly retarded children. Scores on most domains on the ABS-SE have low to moderate correlations with IQ scores, except from those domains that overlap with intelligence test content (for example, language development) and have a strong association with IQ scores and those domains from Part Two that have near-zero correlations with IQ scores, as would be expected.

The capacity of the ABS-SE to categorize children correctly has also been evaluated by assessing children who were already placed in classrooms for either regular education, EMR, or TMR students. The results of several such studies suggested that children assigned to such programs were significantly different with respect to adaptive behavior as measured by the ABS-SE.

Summary. Technically, the ABS-SE is an excellent instrument that is superior to most other measures of adaptive behavior. It is a well-organized test that is accompanied by a wide array of ancillary materials. Limitations of the ABS-SE include the use of items that can be easily misinterpreted and its inadequate assessment of EMR adolescents. Although administration and full interpretation of the ABS-SE can be time-consuming when done by hand, the scope and depth of the data yielded by this process are impressive.

Adaptive Behavior Inventory for Children

Overview and purpose. It is important to know that the Adaptive Behavior Inventory for Children (ABIC) was developed by a sociologist — Jane Mercer — and her colleagues (Mercer & Lewis, 1978). Her socioecological perspective is that a child's adaptive behavior can be evaluated only in relationship to the role expectations of the family, the community, the peer group, the school, and the economy and self-maintenance roles. The ABIC is an outgrowth of the research by Mercer and others into the processes used to diagnose individuals as mentally retarded (Mercer, 1970). Because she concluded from her data that available tests inadequately measured adaptive behavior, she developed a comprehensive assessment system — the System of Multicultural Pluralistic Assessment (SOMPA) — of which the ABIC is an integral part.

The ABIC can be best understood by reference to the unique rhetoric of Mercer (1979):

> Adaptive behavior is conceptualized as achieving an adaptive fit in social systems through the development of interpersonal ties and the acquisition of specific skills required to fulfill the task functions associated with particular roles. . . . The preschool child's experience is limited mainly to the family and neighborhood. Therefore, questions in the ABIC for young children are concerned mainly with roles in the family and in the immediate neighborhood and peer group. As the child moves into the social system of the school, there are questions concerning performance in nonacademic

> school roles and interaction with peers at school. . . . As the child grows older, the child assumes more community roles, ranges over a larger geographic territory, learns to function in earner and consumer roles, and assumes greater responsibility for protection of his or her own health and welfare. The developmental sequencing is reflected in the sequencing of ABIC items. (p. 93)

The ABIC consists of 242 questions that are administered in an interview to either a caretaker who knows the child well or, preferably, a parent. It yields scores for six scales: Family, Community, Peer Relations, Nonacademic School Roles, Earner/Consumer, and Self-Maintenance. Optimally, the interview takes place in the child's home and is conducted by someone with whom the parent or other caretaker is comfortable. Thus, interviewers are instructed to wear simple clothing that is similar to that worn by those in the same social class as the parent or caretaker. The interview should also be conducted in the primary language of the home. School districts that use the ABIC often find it useful to train paraprofessionals who already fit into a particular social system in the administration of the SOMPA.

Items are structured to assess the *frequency* with which a child performs certain activities. A typical item in terms of format and degree of vagueness of wording is: "Does [name of child] take telephone and other messages correctly and give them to the right person? 1. Sometimes; 2. Regularly; or 3. Never." Respondents are repeatedly asked to distinguish between words such as *sometimes*, *often*, *occasionally*, and *frequently*. Since these words may have different meanings to various respondents, the significance of the test results is also called into question. Another problem is that the interviewer must read *all* items appropriate for a child's age, even if the answer is known before the question is asked. Thus, an interviewer sitting in a house with a dirt floor, no electricity, and no running water may feel uncomfortable asking the parent about the child's television habits when obviously there is no television in the home.

Standardization sample and norms. The ABIC was standardized on a stratified random sample of 2,085 California school children. The sample was stratified according to age, gender, ethnic group (there were equal numbers of whites, blacks, and Hispanics), and community size. Sample selection appears to have been more carefully conducted than for the other measures of adaptive behavior.

Norms are provided for children aged five years, zero months to eleven years, eleven months. This age span was divided into three-month intervals, with separate norm tables provided for each. The norms are used to convert raw scores into scaled scores for each of the six areas assessed by the ABIC.

Data obtained. Scoring procedures for the ABIC contain some built-in safeguards to help insure its validity. The most prominent of these is a Veracity

Scale, which contains twenty-four items that involve activities performed only by older adolescents and would not be at all typical of the five- to eleven-year-old children for whom the ABIC is designed. The validity of a child's scores are questioned if high scores are obtained on too many of these high-level skills. The number of times the respondent answered "don't know" to questions represents another validity check. It is assumed that too many responses of this type suggest that the respondent doesn't know the child well enough to give reliable results.

Raw scores for each of the six scales of the ABIC are converted to scaled scores, which correspond closely to percentiles. A more global indicator of adaptive functioning can be obtained by simply averaging the six scaled scores. The primary use for data obtained from the ABIC is to assist in diagnosis and classification decisions. It is far less useful than other instruments for the design of educational programs.

Reliability and validity. Two types of reliability data are available for the ABIC. First, the split-half procedure was utilized to assess reliability using the entire standardization sample. This analysis indicated that reliability was generally above .75 for the six scales and above .95 for the Average Scaled Score across all age groups for which the instrument is appropriate.

Second, the interrater agreement between individuals who heard the same interview was measured at workshops designed to train people to use the ABIC. Near the end of the training, workshop participants listened to an interview conducted by the instructor. Each participant scored the interview independently, and the degree to which the scores differed was assessed. Across a series of ten such interviews, with different parents and in different communities, there was very high interobserver agreement.

The technical manual for the ABIC contains very little information relevant to its validity. In fact, Mercer (1979) states that traditional psychometric methods are inappropriate for the validation to the ABIC:

> For example, it would not be logical to validate the mother's report of the child's performance in the peer group with the teacher's report of peer group performance since neither the mother nor the teacher are members of the peer group. Likewise, it would be even less defensible to "validate" the mother's report of the child's family role performance against the teacher's responses to the questions in the Family Scale. The validity of the ABIC is judged by its ability to reflect accurately the extent to which the child is meeting the expectations of the members of the social systems covered in the scales, not by its correlation with teacher judgments, school performance, or performance on measures of achievement tests, aptitude tests, or "intelligence" tests. (p. 109)

Just how to assess whether the ABIC actually reflects the degree to which the child is meeting societal expectations is not known. Lacking such a methodology, other researchers have applied more traditional psychometric criteria to the test (Oakland, 1979). Their research suggests the correlation between scores on the ABIC and either intelligence tests or achievement tests is so low as to indicate that the ABIC is relatively independent of either intelligence or achievement. This suggests that the ABIC cannot be used in predicting progress in school. Mercer would probably not be surprised by this finding, given that the purpose of the ABIC is to predict acceptance by a social system rather than success in school. Currently, we know of no research indicating how the ABIC is related to other adaptive behavior instruments.

Because of the lack of research on the ABIC, it is impossible to determine exactly what the instrument is measuring. Studies do suggest what it is *not* measuring (intelligence and school achievement). Until it can be established whether it measures some aspect of adaptive behavior that would be useful in schools, its use for this purpose is highly suspect.

Summary. The ABIC was designed from a socioecological perspective to try to improve the process of diagnosing mild mental retardation in elementary school children. Because its primary purpose is as a diagnostic instrument, the ABIC is less useful for developing educational plans. However, given the lack of suitable validity data, its use even for diagnostic purposes is questionable. The ABIC has the potential to be a very useful addition to the list of measures for assessing adaptive behavior, but full potential of this instrument must await additional research.

Children's Adaptive Behavior Scale

Overview and purpose. Unlike most other measures of adaptive behavior, the Children's Adaptive Behavior Scale, or CABS (Richmond & Kicklighter, 1980) is designed to assess *directly* a child's ability to perform adaptively. Administration of the CABS is similar to the procedure used with the individually administered intelligence tests in that the "testing" is conducted by a qualified examiner in a one-to-one setting. During the process the child is asked to perform various tasks and to respond to questions in five major domains:

1. *Language Development:* This area assesses "socially essential, rather than desirable, levels of development" (Richmond & Kicklighter, 1980, p. 5). Although its primary focus is oral expressive language (for example, the child is asked to name something that can be eaten), some items require the child to read and write.
2. *Independent Functioning:* This domain measures the extent to which a child can assume responsibility for tasks encountered daily during normal living. Children are asked questions such as, "Why should you brush your teeth?"
3. *Family Role Performance:* This area assesses how well a child is capable of coping with the normal demands of a home environment. Items focus on the family ("How many people are in your family?") and duties usually performed at home (e.g., "Tell me two ways to cook an egg.")

4. *Economic-Vocational Activity:* This area assesses knowledge of working, earning, and spending. A majority of the items pertain to money concepts, money usage ("About how much does a small can of Coke cost?"), and vocational concepts ("Where does a nurse usually work?").
5. *Socialization:* This domain assesses the degree to which a child interacts appropriately with others.

The CABS is designed to be used with children from five to ten years of age. Since the instrument is directly administered, third-party interviews are not required. This may be an advantage, especially in the light of indications that the information elicited from a third party may be subject to bias (Coulter & Morrow, 1978). Administration requires approximately thirty minutes, which is considerably less than is needed for many other measures of adaptive behavior.

Standardization sample and norms. The standardization group for the CABS consisted of only 250 mildly retarded children in South Carolina and Georgia. Norms were included at each age level. Although the authors indicate that the test is appropriate for children five years of age, no five year olds were included in the sample.

Because the standardization inadequately represents the national population, the authors recommend that users construct local norms. A possible source of confusion in the use of the norms is that they are referenced to a group of mildly retarded children. The instrument is interpreted by comparing an individual's domain scores with the age norms for the reference group. If there is close correspondence between the child and the reference group, the subject is presumed to display adaptive behavior consistent with a diagnosis of mild mental retardation. Unfortunately, it is unclear just how close to the norms a child must be for this diagnosis. Likewise, it is not clear how far above the mean for mildly retarded children a child must be for his adaptive behavior to be considered inconsistent with such a diagnosis.

Data obtained. The data obtained from the CABS are in the form of age equivalent scores for each of the five major domains. The authors indicate that the domains are relatively independent and suggest using five domain scores diagnostically. Thus, a child who scores well in the Socialization domain but performs poorly on the Language domain may be a candidate for language programing.

Reliability and validity. Internal consistency reliability coefficients were reported for a sample of 250 mildly retarded children and ranged from a low of .63 for Language Development and Socialization to a high of .83 for Independent Functioning. Reliability coefficients in this range suggest that using the CABS for making important decisions is a questionable practice.

Although the CABS is designed to reflect adaptive behavior, there is some question of whether it may be more highly associated with intelligence than is desirable and to a greater degree than other measures of such behavior. Part of the problem is that because with the CABS a child is evaluated in a one-to-one setting, we must *infer* that behavior in that setting reflects how the child actually performs outside the testing situation. For example, many items on the CABS assess whether a child *knows* how to perform under given circumstances. It is thus assumed that there is a correspondence between knowing and *doing*. However, it is possible, and in fact probable, that such a relationship does not exist in many instances.

Correlations between the CABS total score and the Wechsler Intelligence Scale for Children-Revised (WISC-R; Wechsler, 1974) are .57 for Verbal IQ, .33 for Performance IQ, and .51 for Full-Scale IQ. This would suggest the CABS has a relatively strong relationship to intelligence, especially verbal intelligence. Such a relationship has disturbing implications. Recall that a primary reason for assessing adaptive behavior is to prevent children with language problems from being inappropriately labeled as mentally retarded. With the verbal format of the CABS, however, the true adaptive functioning of children with poor language skills may be markedly underestimated. Contrast this with the ABIC, which has near-zero correlations with IQ test scores (Mercer & Lewis, 1979).

Additional evidence that the CABS is measuring something different from other measures of adaptive behavior is that the correlations between CABS and other instruments are low to moderate; the test authors reported that such correlations were statistically significant in forty-two of sixty possible comparisons. However, most of these correlations were below .40, suggesting the two instruments are not highly related.

Summary. The CABS is unique in being a *direct* measure of adaptive functioning in children. However, because of sketchy reliability data and validity studies that suggest moderate correlations with verbal IQ test scores, the CABS should be used only in conjunction with measures of adaptive behavior that rely on third-party interviews. In such cases the CABS can broaden the range of skills examined in a comprehensive assessment of adaptive behavior.

Vineland Adaptive Behavior Scales

Overview and purpose. The purpose of the Vineland Adaptive Behavior Scales (Sparrow, Balla, & Cicchetti, 1984) (VABS) is to assess handicapped and nonhandicapped individuals from birth to adulthood in four behavior domains: Communication, Daily Living, Socialization, and Motor Skills. Three versions of the scales exist, including the Survey Form, which has 297 items; the Expanded Form, which has 577 items; and the classroom edition, which has 244 items. Administration requires that someone familiar with the child be interviewed. The technical information pertaining to the VABS pertains primarily to the Survey Form.

Standardization sample and norms. The VABS was standardized on 3,000 individuals ranging in age from birth to eighteen years, eleven months. The stratification of the sample is very good with respect to all major demographic variables, including age, geographic region, parental education, race or ethnic group, community size, and educational placement.

Norms are provided in a number of different forms for a wide variety of populations. A useful feature is that standard score equivalents are available for the raw scores for each behavior domain and for overall functioning. This latter score, the Adaptive Behavior Composite Standard, has a mean of 100 and a standard deviation of 15, thus facilitating comparisons with intelligence tests. Other available norms include percentile ranks and stanines, age equivalent scores, and maladaptive level scores for the optional Maladaptive Behavior domain. Supplemental norms are provided for comparison of older individuals up to age 40 as well as those who are emotionally disturbed, hearing impaired, and visually impaired.

Data obtained. The VABS yields scores for the Communication domain (including subdomain scores for Receptive, Expressive, and Written Language), the Daily Living domain (including subdomain scores for Personal, Domestic, and Community Living), the Socialization domain (including subdomain scores for Interpersonal Relationships, Play and Leisure Time, and Coping Skills), and the Motor Skills domain (including subdomain scores for Gross and Fine Motor Skills). The Adaptive Behavior Composite Standard is based upon functioning in each of the four behavior domains and reflects overall adaptive behavior. The Maladaptive Behavior domain indicates the extent to which the frequency of someone's inappropriate behavior is significantly different from that of the normative group.

Reliability and validity. Reliability of the VABS appears to be adequate for the four behavior domains and poor to adequate for the subdomains. Median split-half reliability coefficients across ages ranged from .83 for the Motor Skills domain to .90 for the Daily Living domain. Interrater reliability for the domains were lower and ranged from .62 to .78. The reliability of the subdomains is very questionable for some age groups, and diagnostic decisions should probably not be based on them.

Primarily because of the recent publication of the VABS, validity data are somewhat sparse. Existing data do suggest the instrument is moderately correlated with other adaptive behavior scales and predictably has relatively low correlations with intelligence tests. A large number of validation studies will no doubt appear over the next few years.

Summary. The VABS is one of the better adaptive behavior tests available. Its psychometric properties are as good or better than those of any other instrument. In addition, it is one of the more useful instruments for making intervention programing decisions.

Social and Prevocational Information Battery

Overview and purpose. A variety of tests assess the adaptive behavior of children who are twelve years old and younger. However, the range of instruments that assess someone who is in junior or senior high school is much more limited. The Social and Prevocational Information Battery, or SPIB (Halpern, Raffeld, Irvin, & Link, 1975), is one of the most comprehensive scales available for adolescents.

Although it is not billed as an adaptive behavior scale, the SPIB comprehensively assesses the skills needed to develop personal and social responsibility. More specifically, it is designed to assess five areas widely regarded as central to the community adjustment of educable mentally retarded students:

1. *Economic Self-Sufficiency:* Tests in this domain measure a student's ability in banking, budgeting, and purchasing. Individual items focus on understanding money, establishing a checking account, and paying bills.
2. *Employability:* This section contains items that assess job-related behaviors and job-search skills. The job-related behaviors include how to get along with a boss, how to ask for help, and how to interact with the public. Job-search skills such as completing employment applications and interviewing are also assessed.
3. *Family Living:* This area measures skills related to home management and physical health. A student is questioned about putting out accidental fires, washing clothing, and handling minor illnesses and injuries.
4. *Personal:* This domain assesses knowledge of personal hygiene and grooming, such as showering and changing clothing.
5. *Communications:* This domain exclusively tests the ability to read and interpret functional signs such as ENTER, EXIT, MEN, and POISON.

The SPIB contains a total of 277 items, which are orally administered to one or more students who mark their responses on answer sheets. Because the response format is true-false or picture selection, students are not penalized for reading difficulties. Testing requires three sessions (preferably on separate days) lasting approximately one hour each. The directions for administering the SPIB are highly structured and well organized.

Standardization sample and norms. The SPIB was standardized on a sample of 906 junior and senior high school students, stratified according to school size and geographic region. Unfortunately, the entire sample was taken from Oregon. The students were all diagnosed as educable mentally retarded (mean IQ = 68) and ranged in age from fourteen to twenty years. The test manual indicates the majority of the sample group was Caucasian but does not provide actual numbers of various ethnic groups. Separate norms are provided for students in junior high (grades seven to nine) and senior high (grades ten to twelve). Since the reference group was entirely composed of diagnosed educable mentally retarded students, a student who scores at the 50th percentile is average with respect to the norm group and *not* with respect to the general population.

Data obtained. By using the norms, raw scores can be converted into percentiles for each of the major areas measured by the SPIB. It is also possible to analyze the individual items to discover more specific areas of weakness. The results can then be translated into educational objectives.

Reliability and validity. Two forms of reliability data are reported for the SPIB: internal consistency and test-retest. For both types, reliability was in the mid-.80s for total test scores. Such figures are slightly lower than desirable for the subtest scores but excellent for the total test score.

Several types of validity data are discussed in the manual. Predictive validity was examined by comparing the scores of graduating seniors with counselor ratings of the students one year later. The results of this comparison suggested that the SPIB predicts community adjustment reasonably well.

Correlations between the SPIB and IQ scores from both the WISC-R indicated a moderate positive relationship. Correlations between individual subtests on the SPIB and Full-Scale IQ scores ranged from .37 to .51, with a median of .49. This suggests that whatever the SPIB is measuring is somewhat similar to what IQ tests measure; in part this is to be expected, for the positive adaptive behavior of mildly retarded adolescents does require some of the skills measured by intelligence tests.

Summary. The SPIB is designed to assess skills associated with the ultimate community adjustment of junior and senior high school students. It is one of the few useful measures of the adaptive behavior of adolescents, for predictive validity data suggest the instrument does adequately predict personal and social adjustment in a community setting.

Problems and Issues in the Assessment of Adaptive Behavior

The strong need to assess adaptive behavior that arose during the early 1970s resulted in the proliferation of well over 100 scales and check lists (Meyers, Nihira, & Zetlin, 1979), some of which have been reviewed here. With this new technology came the inevitable need to evaluate the effects of over a decade of research and practice. Thus, we conclude our discussion of adaptive behavior by reviewing two of the most important issues that have evolved in the assessment of adaptive behavior.

Declassification of Students

The most pressing practical problem that has resulted from the use of adaptive behavior instruments is that some children who once qualified for special education placement as mentally retarded are no longer eligible. Before we began assessing adaptive behavior, children needed markedly low scores on *only* intelligence tests to be placed in special programs. Now they need low scores on *both* intelligence tests and measures of adaptive behavior, which is less likely to occur. The declassification of students that may result can produce exceedingly difficult situations. For example, a multidisciplinary team may learn that a particular child has an IQ test score of 69, which is in the mildly retarded range, but has scored in the normal range on an adaptive behavior scale. If the IQ test score is at all predictive of functioning, the child will have difficulty succeeding in school. However, since the child has normal adaptive behavior, a diagnosis of mental retardation may be contrary to state laws and regulations governing handicapped children.

One possible outcome for a child who performs in the mildly retarded range on a measure of intelligence but who has average adaptive behavior is that no special education is provided at all. This is perhaps the most conservative legal option available. An alternative is to ignore the information concerning adaptive behavior and place the child in a program for mildly retarded children. Perhaps the most satisfying option is to develop and provide alternate programing for children who are comprehensively retarded rather than those who have difficulty only at school. Unfortunately, such alternatives are not widely available.

It is ironic that the declassification issue arose because of "do-gooders" on one side who wanted to provide special education services to mentally retarded children and "do-gooders" on the other side who wanted to prevent abuses such as "the six-hour retarded child" (that is, a child who is considered mentally retarded for the six hours spent at school but functions well outside of school in his or her home and community — see President's Committee on Mental Retardation, 1970). This issue exemplifies the type of legalistic game playing which is unfortunately all too common in current special education practice. This "hardening of the categories" often prevents the provision of services to children who really need them. The real culprit here is the education system — those administrators and school boards who believe that children must be diagnosed before receiving services. However, if children who function poorly in school can be offered a continuum of special services, there would be no need to debate the diagnosis of a particular child. Instead, the debate would center around what *type* of services to provide.

Relationship Between Adaptive Behavior and Intelligence

What is the optimal relationship between instruments that measure adaptive behavior and those that assess intelligence? Should there be a strong relation-

FOCUS ON PRACTICE
Declassification — A Suggestion from Dan Reschley

How adaptive behavior is conceptualized and measured along with the available special education service options will have a significant influence on the classification/placement decisions that are made. I suggest that the adaptive behavior dimension for school-age children be conceptualized as two separate components. One component should involve performance in the public school setting with primary emphasis on academic achievement in the classroom. The other component should be role performance in social systems outside of the public school such as the home, neighborhood, and community. Separating the adaptive behavior dimension into two components is advisable because recently published data suggest that adaptive behavior in academic settings and social role performance outside of school are largely unrelated for many students. . . .

The different combinations of adaptive behavior and intelligence have implications for classification and placement decisions. Adaptive Behavior-School (AB-S) should be based on a complete educational evaluation including observation in the classroom, examination of samples of daily work, teacher interview, and the results of individually administered standardized achievement tests. Adaptive Behavior-Outside School (AB-OS) should be based on information from formal inventories . . . or informal data collection procedures.

Of particular interest are the children who exhibit the pattern of very low intelligence, very low AB-S, and normal AB-OS. A major current dilemma is whether these children should be classified and placed in special education programs. Such children are "six-hour retarded children" almost by definition. If they are classified and placed in special education programs we will almost inevitably overrepresent minority children. In my view these children should be served in special education programs in most instances because they do, in fact, have extreme educational needs that are typically beyond the scope of regular classroom instruction. The solution of "delabeling" these children does not address these needs. However, the segregated special class for the mildly retarded, which has often been the placement used because in many cases it was the only alternative, is an equally inappropriate solution.

Refining the classification system would be beneficial in resolving this dilemma. The terms "comprehensive" and "quasi" are probably as objectionable as the term "mental retardation." Using terms like "educational retardation," "educationally handicapped," or some other term that is as behaviorally descriptive as possible of the quasi-retarded pattern would be preferable. Greater refinement in the classification system is useful only if there are implications for placement decisions and educational programming. The change suggested may have such implications.

The "quasi-retarded" do need special services. However, if special education services are to be provided, the objectives should be oriented toward specific academic needs rather than broad social competencies. In most instances the resource program involving remedial and compensatory tutorial services is a more appropriate option than the special class. Special class programs for the mildly retarded have traditionally placed considerable emphasis on broadly defined social competencies and "functional" academic skills [O. Kolstoe, 1976, *Teaching Educable Mentally Retarded Children*, 2nd ed., New York: Holt, Rinehart and Winston]. This emphasis

continued

FOCUS ON PRACTICE *continued*

is clearly appropriate for the comprehensively retarded, but is probably misdirected for most of the quasi-retarded. With few exceptions the quasi-retarded, if placed in special education, should be placed in resource programs.

Using the resource option for the quasi-retarded would alleviate many of the concerns expressed by federal district courts in the placement litigation. The amount of time spent outside of the educational mainstream is minimized by the resource option thus reducing the very proper concern about racial segregation. Placement in the resource option regardless of classification used may have the additional advantage of being less stigmatizing. Analysis of outcome data must, of course, be the ultimate criteria against which this or any other classification/placement system must be validated.

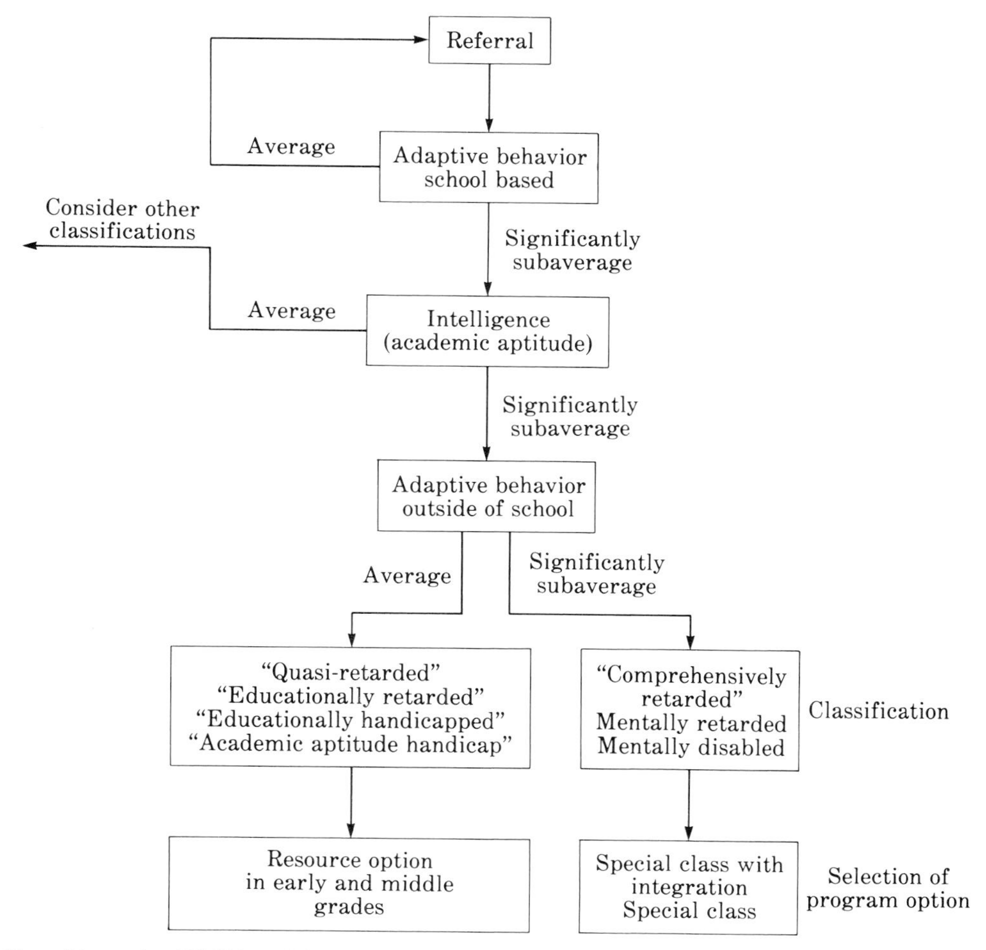

From "Assessing Mild Mental Retardation: The Influence of Adaptive Behavior, Sociocultural Status, and Prospects for Nonbiased Assessment" by D. J. Reschley in *The Handbook of School Psychology* (pp. 209–242), by C. R. Reynolds and T. B. Gutkin (Eds.), 1982, New York: John Wiley and Sons.

ship or no relationship at all? Do adaptive behavior instruments actually measure some construct that everyone agrees is adaptive behavior? The answers to these questions are anything but straightforward. The problem is compounded because both intelligence and adaptive behavior are hypothetical constructs that are difficult to measure. We will approach this issue of how the two constructs are related by examining first how they are different and then how they are alike.

There are several differences between instruments that assess adaptive behavior and those that assess intelligence. First, adaptive behavior scales are most concerned with everyday behaviors, whereas intelligence tests tend to reflect thinking processes. Because of this, adaptive behavior instruments tend to focus on common or typical behaviors and intelligence tests are concerned primarily with a child's potential. Thus intelligence tests assess verbal and quantitative learning and higher-order thinking skills, whereas adaptive behavior instruments reflect the degree to which a child can adapt to environmental demands. In sum, IQ scores are secured by a process that samples the subject's best possible performance and that interprets the results in terms of a trait system, with a presumption of stability in the obtained scores. In contrast, adaptive behavior scales secure descriptions of everyday adaptations without necessarily determining best possible performances; in some scales, little or no regard for trait inference is intended. Further, the data on adaptive behavior measurement deny any unitary or general factor (Meyers, Nihira, & Zetlin, 1979, p. 434).

Despite the difference between instruments that assess adaptive behavior and intelligence, some adaptive behavior scales have very high correlations (up to .83) with intelligence tests. Thus, one would expect the constructs to be somewhat similar. In one review, adaptive behavior/IQ correlations ranged from a low of .09 for the ABIC to a high of .83 for the old Vineland Social Maturity Scale (Doll, 1965). Such a wide range of correlations results from the types of skills measured by various adaptive behavior instruments and the manner in which they are measured. Scales with a preponderance of items that assess communication skills and cognitive development generally have higher correlations with IQ tests than those that focus on self-help skills and independent functioning. Likewise, adaptive behavior instruments that are directly administered to the child rather than to a third-party informant have higher correlations with IQ tests because the format of the items, the skills assessed, and the method of administration more closely approximate those on IQ measurements.

What should be the relationship between IQ and adaptive behavior? This answer has been summarized by Lambert (1981):

> There is an obvious relationship between adaptive behavior and intelligence. Children with higher levels of intelligence generally learn to perform independent skills sooner, are able to assume greater responsibility, and have a greater capacity for social adjustment than children with lower levels. Yet, it is also true that there are mentally retarded and develop-

> mentally delayed children who do not have high levels of intelligence but who show potential for high levels of adaptive behavior. Such a discrepancy indicates that low to moderate correlations between adaptive behavior and intellectual functioning would be expected. An instrument designed to measure adaptive behavior should yield scores that indicate it assesses a dimension or construct that is separate from but related to intelligence since both measures provide evidence of psychological development. (p. 75)

Summary

Our review of adaptive behavior has summarized the major factors influencing assessment theory and practice in this area. However, several major issues were not resolved. For example, what is adaptive behavior? What is the *best* way to assess it? Are there reliable instruments for measuring adaptive behavior? What do we do with the declassified child? We will be better able to address these questions as research continues to accumulate. At the present, however, measurement of adaptive behavior is difficult at best. Because of the fluctuations in their everyday adaptations, it may not be possible to develop a measure that will predict adaptive behaviors across situations and time; however, it is possible to insure that those measures that are constructed have a truly representative norm sample and high internal consistency. Furthermore, those who use measures of adaptive behavior can be sure that they select those instruments that are in the best interest of children.

Chapter 16

Low-Incidence Handicapping Conditions

Learning Objectives

1. List three general considerations in the assessment of children with low-incidence handicaps.
2. Describe special preparations that can increase the validity of assessments of severely and profoundly handicapped children.
3. List and describe major issues in the assessment of severely and profoundly handicapped children.
4. List and describe major issues in the assessment of hearing impaired children.
5. List and describe major issues in the assessment of visually impaired children.

All of Colleen's undergraduate and graduate training had barely prepared her for what she was facing on the first day of her internship at a school for multiply handicapped and severely retarded children. Colleen was in the process of assisting her supervisor in the evaluation of Louise. The staff had requested this evaluation because even though Louise had been diagnosed as severely retarded, they saw some "spark" in her eyes that suggested higher potential.

It was immediately obvious to Colleen that most forms of standard testing would be impossible to complete. Louise, who was eight years old, had to be strapped in a special adaptive wheelchair to sit upright. Records indicated she had spastic cerebral palsy; this meant Louise had virtually no voluntary control of her limbs, which moved in erratic, jerking movements, but she did have some head control. For many years children such as Louise were described in many psychologists' reports as "untestable." Now these children attend school, where assessments are done.

Colleen's supervisor was a good one. He asked Colleen to assume that Louise's thinking, ability to reason, and language were all normal. But how could this assumption be tested if Louise could not talk or point or communicate a correct answer in any of the usual ways? Colleen was dumbfounded. Every test she proposed to administer would be inappropriate, as her supervisor quickly pointed out. Finally, she hit upon the Columbia Mental Maturity Test (Burgemeister, Blum & Lorge, 1972). The response format for this test requires only that the child point to the correct answer. However, since even pointing was a problem for Louise, Colleen placed a hatlike pointer with an extended stick on Louise's head so she could indicate her responses. Louise scored in the mildly retarded range, which was significantly above previous clinical estimates of her ability.

Colleen's story is typical in that modifications and adaptations may be needed before testing children with severe mental, physical, or sensory handicaps. The evaluation she conducted was not typical because teachers are most often not looking for an indication of cognitive functioning (such as IQ) but rather for what the child can and cannot do so that educational programs can be instituted.

General Considerations in the Assessment of Low-Incidence Handicaps

Children with low-incidence handicaps have been diagnosed as belonging in one of five categories: (a) severely or profoundly handicapped, (b) multiply handicapped, (c) visually impaired, (d) hearing impaired, and (e) severely behavior disordered. Such handicaps occur relatively infrequently in the general population. In this chapter we discuss each of the low-incidence handicaps separately. We have, however, combined the severely or profoundly retarded category and the multiply handicapped category because assessment procedures utilized with these two groups are quite similar. We are well aware that severely and profoundly retarded children differ from multihandicapped and from each other, but part of assessment is to reveal such differences. The assessment of behavior disorders was discussed in Chapter 14.

Before we begin our discussion of the assessment procedures appropriate for each of the subgroups, we will specify some general considerations for assessing children with low-incidence handicaps. These guidelines are offered primarily to facilitate and encourage an approach to the assessment of severely handicapped children that *qualitatively* differs from that typically used with mildly handicapped children.

FOCUS ON PRACTICE
The Case of Leslie Lemke

Leslie Lemke was about to play the piano before a full house at Milwaukee's Mount Carmel Lutheran Church, and he had a case of preconcert jitters. His 84-year-old foster mom, May, exuberantly steered guests over to meet her "little miracle boy," pointing to the six-footer sitting stoically in a beige wood pew. Suddenly he reached out in a frantic search to locate his foster father. "Daddy's right here," said Joe Lemke, 80, taking his son's hand. "I know Daddy's right here," repeated Leslie, who is blind, severely retarded and crippled by cerebral palsy. He is 32 years old.

As the audience soon learned, Leslie is also astonishingly gifted. Though his mind functions at about the level of a 3-year-old and though he has never seen a sheet of music, his foster mother long ago suspected that Leslie might be a musical prodigy. Hadn't she discovered him one day strumming rhythmically on the steel springs of his bed?

Joe and May scraped together $250 for a used piano, and to their amazement late one night, when Leslie was 16, he crawled over to the piano and started playing a Tchaikovsky concerto. He had heard Liberace play the music on television. Leslie had never played anything before, but it soon became evident that, after hearing any piece of music just once, he could unerringly reproduce it on the keyboard. Later he learned to sing as he played.

If there were skeptics in that Milwaukee audience two weeks ago, their doubts were dispelled when Leslie launched into a remarkably polished version of *Rhapsody in Blue* and a Louis Armstrong-like vocal rendition of *Hello, Dolly!* In a clear, resonant baritone, he belted out *I Believe*, his favorite song, and when he played *Somewhere My Love*, his foster parents danced together at the front of the church. Then, while many of his listeners fought back tears, Leslie tilted his head back and,

continued

Use a Variety of Techniques, Strategies, and Instruments

Obtaining valid and comprehensive assessments of children with severe or multiple handicaps is extremely difficult and makes it imperative to utilize an array of assessment strategies. Three factors that contribute to assessment difficulty are: (a) the possible presence of splinter skills, (b) problems in test stimuli presentation, and (c) problems in responding.

The concept of splinter skills refers to an unevenness in development that is sometimes seen in children with severe handicaps. Perhaps the most extreme (and rare) form of splinter skills are those present in the Idiot Savant (see Focus on Practice). Other severely handicapped persons may have less spectacular splinter skills, so the use of a variety of measures decreases the likelihood that splinter skills will go undetected. For three major categories of assessment strategies (standardized tests, developmental scales, and system-

FOCUS ON PRACTICE *continued*

with emotion, sang *Amazing Grace* and *He Touched Me*. In medical terms Leslie exemplifies the phenomenon known as the savant syndrome, an exceedingly rare condition in which a person with severe mental handicaps demonstrates a singular, spectacular talent. Scientists can only speculate on how the Leslie Lemkes do what they do.

In medical literature only about 100 such cases of spectacular abilities have been reported since 1865, according to Dr. Darold Treffert, 51, who headed the Winnebago Mental Health Institute in Wisconsin for 15 years and is now in private psychiatric practice in Fond du Lac. Treffert is nationally recognized as an expert on the savant syndrome (the older, cruel description, "idiot savant," is now discarded). In all, Treffert has seen about a dozen people with savant characteristics, including one who could pop basketball free throws one after the other without missing and another who memorized the Milwaukee bus system. "If you told him the number of the bus that was passing and the time of day," says Treffert, "he could tell you what corner in the city you were standing on."

About one of every 2,000 severely retarded people demonstrates some savant characteristics, Treffert declares, and unaccountably, male savants outnumber their female counterparts about six to one. "There is a gradation of savant abilities, ranging from someone who may have good recall of history to one with the extraordinary talent that Leslie Lemke has."

Treffert believes that a savant possesses an idiosyncratic brain circuitry giving him "access to portions of the brain, particularly memory, that the rest of us don't have." But, Treffert admits, "we have not had the technology to find out why these people have this memory access."

Excerpted from the July 2, 1984 issue of *People Weekly* Magazine, written by Giovanna Brev/Time Inc.

atic observation), there are significant correlations between the measures, but the data derived from each source do make unique and nonoverlapping contributions (Diebold, Curtis, & DuBose, 1978; Simeonsson, Huntington, & Parse, 1980).

A second reason for multiple assessment stems from problems in the presentation of test stimuli to some children. This point is so obvious that it hardly merits stating; nevertheless, a child must understand what is expected on a particular task while the chance of inadvertent cueing is reduced as much as possible:

> This does not pose a serious problem when assessing nonphysically handicapped children, because many language concepts found in normative-based tests are utilized frequently in their natural environment. It is also not difficult to determine if they understand the examiner's language, be-

> cause nonhandicapped learners will usually tell the examiner that they do not understand or have puzzled looks on their faces. Physically handicapped children may be unable to exhibit either response. The child should then be required to perform several sample tests prior to beginning the formal evaluation. (Duncan, Sbardellati, Maheady, & Sainato, 1980, p. 21)

A common problem is that test stimuli that are designed for a child's age may not be suitable for the child's developmental level (for example, it is inappropriate to administer the Wechsler Intelligence Scale for Children-Revised, to a profoundly retarded seven-year-old because there is a very low probability of eliciting even one correct answer). One solution is to administer tests designed for infants. However, this may provide results that are not valid if handicapped children were not included in the standardization sample and if the norm tables do not accommodate the extreme ages and scores obtained by older handicapped children (Simeonsson, 1977). One may use infant scales, however, if they have been validated for severely retarded adolescents and adults and if the literature, such as the *American Journal of Mental Deficiency*, offers reports of numerous validation studies. For assessing some skills, an examiner may be left with the options of using a checklist, creating instruments, using an inappropriate test, or making unvalidated modifications in existing instruments. Because none of these options alone is sufficient, the use of a variety of assessment methodologies helps one gain an understanding of a student.

Many children may have problems in responding. Blind children will have difficulty responding to visual stimuli, hearing impaired children may have difficulty responding to auditory stimuli, and some physically handicapped children may be unable to answer questions that require motor responses. Children who are without these deficits can be tested through a variety of modalities, and if there is a convergence of information across modalities, even if it is within the same test, one can be reasonably confident of the results. Because some children can be assessed through only one modality, an examiner cannot be as confident that the results are valid unless results from one type of assessment are supported by results of other assessment strategies.

Use a Developmental Perspective

A thorough knowledge of child development is valuable in assessing handicapped children for two reasons. First, the evaluation specialist should continually ask, "What could normal children reasonably be expected to do in this situation or on this task?" For example, a parent may be concerned that a five-year-old child diagnosed as brain injured is hyperactive and wants advice on how to deal with the hyperactivity. An initial observation suggests to the examiner that the child's "hyperactivity" is well within normal limits for the child's age. Thus, it was the parent's *perception* that was the problem, not the child's *behavior*. Such perceptions among family members and other care givers may be more common for children diagnosed as handicapped than for normal children. There is a tacit assumption among many that *any* behavior that the care giver does not like, that represents a change from the child's usual actions, or that *appears* to be deviant from the normal population is attributable to the handicapping conditioning. Thus, a blind child who seems unusually frustrated over a period of a month may be referred for evaluation with the assumption that the frustration is caused by the blindness. Individuals who attribute this sort of blame to the handicap fail to recognize that normal children are hyperactive, become frustrated, and have many other problems that usually disappear without any treatment at all. A knowledge of normal development allows the specialist to determine when a "problem" really is a problem.

Second, a knowledge of child development can serve to guide assessment activities. Using developmental norms as a basis, the skills a child must acquire can be viewed as resting along a continuum from incompetent infant to competent adult. For the most part, skills along this continuum are learned in sequential order. If we can determine where a particular child falls with respect to this sequence of skills, we can provide quite relevant information to instructional specialists. For example, direct-care staff may have initiated an evaluation because an older child was not responding to toilet training. The evaluation may suggest that instruction in toilet training is likely to continue to be unsuccessful until specific skills in the sequence are learned first. In other words, there are several skills prerequisite to toilet training which still remain to be learned. The obvious recommendation would be to initiate instruction focusing on those prerequisite skills. The exact nature of the skills would be determined by referring to a good developmental skill sequence.

Use a Process Orientation to Evaluation

A major theme of this text has been that test scores are not likely to reveal a complete picture of a particular child. We have repeatedly emphasized that specific behavioral characteristics of learners can be identified by the careful observation of behavior and informal assessment. Nowhere is such a process orientation more appropriate than with children who exhibit sensory deficits or who are severely handicapped in cognition. A process orientation to the assessment of a severely or profoundly retarded child would require answers to at least the following questions:

- Does the child appear to favor certain toys, objects, or activities?
- How does the child interact with others? Does the child play? Fight? Withdraw?
- Does the child seek interaction or wait for others to initiate contact?
- Is there a difference between how the child interacts with children versus adults? Does the child, for example, play with adults but withdraw from children?
- Does the child appear to favor males over females, in adults or children?

- How does the child respond to different auditory, visual, and tactile stimuli?
- Are there certain activities the child seems particularly to enjoy? Are these directed toward the self (e.g., self-stimulatory repetitive behavior such as rocking) or outer-directed (e.g., playing with trains or coloring)?
- How long does the child generally remain with one activity or one object?
- Is the child easily distracted by various events in the room, such as voices, people passing by, school bells, or other students?
- Does the child perform certain behaviors independently, but not under adult cues? Or vice versa.
- Are there certain obvious educational programing priorities that can be identified immediately?
- Does the child demonstrate an understanding and awareness of the surroundings?
- How does the child explore the environment? Does the child primarily rely on visual, auditory, or tactile means to investigate the environment?
- How does the child respond to different reinforcers? What consequences seem to work best for inappropriate behavior? (Van Etten, Arkell, & Van Etten, 1980)

The primary advantage to a process orientation is that it broadens the scope of assessment activities and helps to insure the evaluation will be instructionally relevant.

Evaluations Must Have Treatment Validity

Evaluations of children with low-incidence handicaps are relatively straightforward with respect to classification because it is usually very easy to determine that the child has a problem (for example, is blind or severely mentally retarded) and qualifies for some type of special education program. In fact, many children will already have a medical diagnosis before they enter school. Thus, when a child is referred for evaluation because of a specific problem or for a periodic reevaluation, it is not very useful to respond with only a diagnosis. The teachers who work daily in small groups with severely handicapped children already have a very good idea of the level at which the child is functioning. What they may not know, however, is which skills to teach next and which strategies to use in teaching the skills. Evaluations that can provide such information are invaluable.

Specialists who conduct educational evaluations can often "get by" with evaluations that only categorize a child if a primary purpose of the evaluation is to determine eligibility for special education. However, children with severe handicaps do not need relabeling. What they need are specific recommendations for treatment. Evaluations that fail to provide such recommendations are virtually worthless.

Evaluating Severely and Profoundly Handicapped Children

Definitional Issues

Most but not all severely handicapped children function cognitively at moderate to profound retardation levels. Until recently the severely and profoundly handicapped were so classified according to definitions that utilized scores on intelligence tests as a major determining factor. The most common system of classification is that utilized by the American Association on Mental Deficiency (AAMD) whereby children are classified as mildly, moderately, severely, or profoundly retarded (Grossman, 1977). In the past American educators used a system in which children with IQs between 50 and 75 were diagnosed as educable mentally retarded (EMR) and those with IQs between 35 and 50 were referred to as trainable mentally retarded (TMR). Although IQ can no longer be used as the sole criterion for classification and adaptive behavior must be considered as well, it still carries a significant weight in decision making, in part because measures of intelligence are far more reliable than measures of adaptive behavior and in part because children are rarely referred for measurement of intellectual functioning unless they have already displayed adaptive behavior deficits.

Issues in the Assessment of Severely and Profoundly Handicapped Children

In addition to the general considerations for assessing all children with low-incidence handicaps presented earlier, there are several issues that are most important when evaluating the severely and profoundly handicapped. These include special preparations for assessment and finding a reliable response mode.

Special preparations for assessment. It is apparent to anyone who has ever worked with severely and profoundly handicapped children that one cannot typically just walk in with a test kit and launch into an assessment. Instead, it is usually necessary to obtain a considerable amount of information about the child prior to face-to-face assessment. Many children will be physically handicapped and unable to respond in the usual manner. These children may require a special chair or other device to support the body. Some will not perform for strangers, and the enlistment of a familiar adult may be necessary. Other children may require primary reinforcers (such as small bits of fruit) to maintain optimal performance. However, there is sometimes no quicker way

Table 16.1 Considerations Prior to Testing Severely and Profoundly Handicapped Children

1. Sensory and motor skills
   a. What sensory impairment does the student *obviously* display that may interfere with ability to execute test demands?
   b. Are gross and fine motor movements intact?
   c. Can the student execute bilateral movements? If not, can the student compensate adequately for testing purposes with unilateral movements?
   d. Does respiration appear adequate, or is there difficult breathing, congestion, or wheezing?
   e. What body parts can the student use most effectively to execute test demands?
2. Attentiveness
   a. Can the student make eye contact on a basis sufficient for testing?
   b. If eye contact is not in the student's repertoire, can he or she attend auditorally?
   c. Can tactile prompts be used with the student effectively for testing purposes?
   d. What is the approximate duration of attention span?
   e. Can physical or social reinforcers be effectively used for testing purposes? If so, how do reinforcers differentially affect the student's responses?
3. Communication skills
   a. Is the student verbal? To what degree are expressive and receptive language adequate?
   b. If the student is nonverbal, what is the mode of communication?
   c. Does the student respond (verbally or nonverbally) spontaneously?
   d. What prompts appear to be most effective in eliciting communication responses?

From *The Severely and Profoundly Handicapped: Programs, Methods, and Materials* (p. 45) by G. Van Etten, C. Arkell, and C. Van Etten. Copyright © 1980 by Dr. Glen Van Etten. Published by C. V. Mosby. Reprinted by permission of Dr. Glen Van Etten.

to lose rapport with a school or institutional staff than by giving food rewards to children whose diet is restricted. A list of other variables to consider prior to testing, as developed by Van Etten et al. (1980), is presented in Table 16.1.

Hart (1977) has proposed that children be assessed in five settings that range from the informal to formal:

1. *Unstructured Setting:* Child is placed in a room with a variety of toys and/or other age-appropriate stimuli. Through a one-way mirror or from a corner of the room, the examiner observes to see with which stimuli and in what manner the child interacts.
2. *Stimulus-Oriented Setting:* Using the same room as for the unstructured setting, the examiner presents stimuli to the child to determine the child's reaction when forced to interact with various materials.
3. *Interpersonal Setting:* A familiar adult is provided with instructions for eliciting verbal interactions with the child.
4. *Task-Oriented Setting:* A familiar adult is asked to facilitate the child's display of special talents or abilities. In addition to seeing the child perform

under optimal conditions, the examiner has the opportunity to determine how well the child responds to instructions and attends to the tasks.

5. *Formal Learning Setting:* With the familiar adult present, the examiner requests the child to perform specific tasks based upon strengths and weaknesses noted from observations in previous settings.

Determining and using a reliable response mode. An important prerequisite in the assessment of severely and profoundly handicapped children is to determine a reliable response mode. According to Duncan, Sbardellati, Maheady, and Sainato (1980), it is essential that a child have some way "to vocalize or move as a reliable response to stimuli without *any* subjective interpretation on the part of the examiner" (p. 18). Children differ in their capability to respond to a question or some other stimulus. Duncan et al. (1980) presented the following hierarchy of possible responses:

1. *Expressive Language Response:* Displayed by children who possess easily understood, expressive language. They can be assessed at the recall ("From what animal do we get milk?") versus a recognition level ("Point to the picture of the animal that gives milk.").
2. *Pointing Response:* Shown by children who can reliably point to the correct answer, usually from a small array of stimuli. All too frequently, however, physically handicapped children have a pointing response that is unreliable and difficult to score. For example, if two stimuli are close together, a child who has jerking hand movements may not be able to indicate reliably to which of two stimuli he is pointing. Also, children become extremely adept at perceiving small cues from an examiner concerning the correctness of a particular response and may switch quickly back-and-forth between alternatives.
3. *Using an Existing Motor Response:* Used by some children who have neither expressive language nor a pointing response yet are nevertheless capable of answering "yes" or "no" using responses that are idiosyncratic to their own physical mobility. Usually adults familiar with the child can describe these responses, which may include small movements of some body part or noises. Such responses are usually designed to signal *either* "yes" or "no." Occasionally a child may have separate responses for "yes" and "no" but more often can communicate only one or the other.
4. *Training an Existing Inconsistent Response:* Occasionally it is necessary to institute a training program to increase the reliability of an inconsistent response. For example, a child may use a head movement to indicate "yes." However, the same head movement may occur when the child is angry or under stress. Thus, it becomes impossible for an examiner to interpret a child's intent. The process of teaching a consistent response usually involves placing the child on a shaping program. For example, a child who raises a finger to indicate "yes" could be taught to raise the entire arm.
5. *Teaching a Nonexistent Response:* Some children have no method of communicating or interacting with the environment. According to Duncan et al.

(1980), this may result in "learned helplessness" because "their environment has been structured in such a way that they perceive no connection between their actions and the consequences they receive" (p. 20). Training a child to respond to stimuli after that child has been without such skills for *years* is exceedingly difficult. Because of the long-term nature of such training, it is best accomplished through the child's educational program.

6. *Using a Nonvoluntary Response:* At some point it may become obvious to the multidisciplinary evaluation team that a child is unlikely to develop voluntary control of responding (that is, given a stimulus, the child does not respond in any meaningful way). An evaluation of the children may encompass the assessment of *elicited* rather than *emitted* responses. In one sense, a child has voluntary control over emitted responses (for example, the child points to a picture of a fork when given the appropriate verbal cue), but elicited response occurs in reaction to stimuli (for example, smelling salts placed under the nose will usually result in an involuntary turning away from the stimulus). Thus, evaluation may include noting the types of stimuli to which the child responds, including light, vibration, heat, cold, loud noises, pinpricks, salt, and sugar. However, in certain situations it may be unethical, against institutional rules, or even illegal to utilize some of these stimuli.

Individuals who have not interacted with severely and profoundly handicapped children may not anticipate the complexities of such an evaluation. Dubose (1976) has referred to such an evaluation as "the diagnostician's challenge" and suggests that as the number and severity of impairments increase, the resulting increases in the complexity of the evaluation are multiplicative.

Evaluation Methodologies for Severely and Profoundly Handicapped Children

The comprehensive evaluation of severely and profoundly handicapped children involves the assessment of cognitive development, adaptive behavior, communication skills, motor development, social-emotional functioning, and vocational skills. The primary assessment strategies used to yield information about these areas of functioning include: (a) interviews, (b) checklists and rating scales, (c) formal tests, (d) observation, (e) behavioral assessment. Since the latter two have been discussed earlier in the text, we will describe only interviews, rating scales, and formal tests in the section that follows.

Interviews. An excellent starting point for assessment is to interview individuals with whom the child has frequent interaction, such as parents and teachers. Interviews can accomplish five primary goals. First, they can yield information that clearly defines the purposes and goals of assessment. What problems prompted the assessment? How will the assessment information be used? Second, interviews can provide information about *how* to assess a child. Many severely and profoundly handicapped children have idiosyncratic response modes or styles of interaction. Interviews with those knowledgeable of these styles can prove invaluable in conducting a comprehensive evaluation. Third, interviews not only guide other types of assessment but they are also an important form of evaluation in and of themselves. For example, many adaptive behavior scales utilize third-party interviews to obtain information about what a child can and cannot do. Fourth, interviews have been used traditionally to elicit information about a child's developmental history, family resources, siblings, and medical status. Finally, many specialists utilize interviews to conduct a functional analysis of the child's behavior, that is, an examination of the child's behavioral excesses and deficits and the environmental stimuli that control these behaviors. For example, with a child who engages in self-abusive behavior such as head banging, it is important to determine the factors that maintain this behavior (although the more remote "cause" will probably be elusive).

Checklists and rating scales. Because many severely and profoundly handicapped children are difficult to evaluate through a direct question-and-answer format, a number of checklists and rating scales have emerged that minimize the amount of direct interaction with the child. These are typically completed by someone who knows the child well or through an interview with such a person. The respondent is asked to indicate either the presence or absence of a particular behavior or the degree to which the behavior is present.

Checklists and rating scales offer several advantages (Wells, 1981). They are quick, economical and efficient, and most examine a wide range of behaviors. A primary disadvantage is that perceptions of behavior often differ markedly from actual observations (Whalen & Henkler, 1976).

The existing checklists and rating scales vary along three important dimensions: informant, scope, and structure (McMahon, 1984). The *informant* dimension pertains to who completes the instrument. The type of information desired helps to dictate the informant used. The most typical informants are teachers and parents. The *scope* of an instrument refers to the extent to which it reflects a narrow versus a wide range of behaviors. Some instruments may be useful only for self-help skills, while others may also evaluate vocational skills, language development, maladaptive behaviors and a number of other domains. Finally, the *structure* dimension refers to length, format, and specificity of the scale or checklist. Some are quite global in their descriptions (for example, the child is capable of taking care of herself), whereas others are more specific ("the child can put on a shirt without assistance"). The length can range from five to several hundred items. Formats can vary from requiring only a "yes" or "no" response for indicating the presence or absence of a skill to asking the rater to indicate on a 1 to 5 scale the degree to which a particular skill is present. A sample behavioral checklist is presented in Table 16.2.

Table 16.2 Sample Behavioral CheckList for Drinking

1. Opens mouth when physically stimulated
2. Closes mouth when physically stimulated
3. Sucks liquid from straw
4. Takes liquids from cup/glass held by another
5. Swallows liquids when physically stimulated
6. Swallows liquids independently
7. Retains liquids in mouth without drooling
8. Touches with hands cup/glass held by adult while drinking
9. Tips cup/glass to drink held by adult
10. Holds cup/glass to drink when placed in both hands
11. Reaches for cup/glass independently
12. Grasps cup/glass independently
13. Picks up cup/glass independently with some spilling
14. Picks up cup/glass independently without spilling
15. Drinks from cup/glass held to mouth by adult, using both hands, with some spilling
16. Drinks from cup/glass held to mouth by adult, using both hands, without spilling
17. Reaches for cup/glass, grasps, brings to mouth to drink, independently
18. Reaches for cup/glass, grasps, brings to mouth, tips to drink, independently with some spilling
19. Reaches for cup/glass, grasps, brings to mouth, tips to drink, independently without spilling
20. Reaches for cup/glass, grasps, brings to mouth, tips to drink, drinks, independently with some spilling
21. Reaches for cup/glass, grasps, brings to mouth, tips to drink, drinks, independently without spilling

From *The Severely and Profoundly Handicapped: Programs, Methods, and Materials* (p. 54) by G. Van Etten, C. Arkell, and C. Van Etten.

Formal tests. Formal tests designed specifically for use with severely and profoundly handicapped children are relatively rare. Tests designed for other purposes are more commonly utilized. For example, it is not uncommon to use infant intelligence tests such as the Bayley Scales of Infant Development (Bayley, 1969) with severely and profoundly retarded children. The problems of using such tests with children for whom they were not specifically standardized have been discussed earlier in this chapter. Bayley specifically cautions in her manual against such misuse; however, validation studies of this test have been conducted with retarded adults.

Among the formal tests that have response formats that are useful when assessing severely and profoundly handicapped children is the Columbia Mental Maturity Scale (Burgemeister et al., 1972), which requires a child to select from an array of objects on a printed card the one that is different from the others. The test is intended to assess nonverbal reasoning, and all the child need do is *point* to the correct answer. Verbal responses are not required. The stimulus cards are large enough so that many physically handicapped children with minimal muscle control can respond.

Evaluating Hearing Impaired Children

Definitional Issues

To understand hearing loss one must first understand the nature of sound. Essentially, sound is measured by two primary components: intensity and frequency. In everyday language the intensity of sound refers to how loud it is. Assessment of intensity is generally in terms of decibels (dB), with 0 dB being the softest sound that a normal person can perceive and sounds greater than about 125 dB causing pain. Table 16.3 illustrates the dB levels corresponding to various levels of hearing loss. Sound frequency refers to the degree a sound is low or high pitched. Frequency was formerly assessed in terms of cycles per second but has more recently been measured in hertz units. To understand speech sounds, we must be able to hear sounds in the 300 to 4,000 hertz range. On a piano this would correspond to approximately middle C on the low end to the highest piano note at the high end.

Degree of hearing loss (see Table 16.3) is important because it is highly correlated with the acquisition of speech and is a major factor in educational placements (Spragins, 1980). Obviously the degree of loss is also important in planning and interpreting an evaluation. Children with mild to moderate hearing loss would probably be evaluated differently than children with a severe or profound loss. In addition, the interpretation of the results must be evaluated in view of the "normal" expectations within a certain degree of hearing loss. For example, expectations for the extent of language development change drastically as the extent of hearing loss increases.

Issues in the Assessment of Hearing Impaired Children

Screening for hearing defects is done with an audiometer, usually by a school nurse; full examination is done by audiologists or medical specialists. The major problems in the educational assessment of hearing impaired children involve language competence and communications abilities that can present difficulties in obtaining a valid evaluation. If hearing impaired children are not properly evaluated and classified, they will be unlikely to receive appropriate education. Careful consideration must be given to two basic issues: (a) evaluating the impact of the impairment on other (especially cognitive) areas of functioning, and (b) determining an appropriate communication mode.

Evaluating the impact of hearing impairment on other abilities. If a child with severe hearing loss earns a score of 88 on a verbally administered intelligence test, the prudent examiner must consider a number of alternative ex-

Table 16.3 Effects of Hearing Impairments

Faintest sound heard	Effect on the understanding of language and speech	Educational needs and programs
Slight		
27 to 40 dB	May have difficulty hearing faint or distant speech. Will not usually have difficulty in school situations.	May benefit from a hearing aid as loss approaches 40 dB. Attention to vocabulary development. Needs favorable seating and lighting. May need speechreading instruction. May need speech correction.
Mild		
41 to 55 dB	Understands conversational speech at a distance of 3 to 5 feet (face to face). May miss as much as 50% of class discussions if voices are faint or not in line of vision. May have limited vocabulary and speech anomalies.	Should be referred to special education for educational follow-up. May benefit from individual hearing aid by evaluation and training in its use. Favorable seating and possible special class placement, especially for primary age children. Attention to vocabulary and reading. May need speechreading instruction. Speech conservation and correction, if indicated.
Marked		
56 to 70 dB	Conversation must be loud to be understood. Will have increasing difficulty with school group discussions. Is likely to have defective speech. Is likely to be deficient in language use and comprehension. Will have limited vocabulary.	Will need resource teacher or special class. Should have special help in language skills, vocabulary development, usage, reading, writing, grammar, etc. Can benefit from individual hearing aid by evaluation and auditory training. Speechreading instruction. Speech conversation and speech correction.

Table 16.3, *continued*

Faintest sound heard	Effect on the understanding of language and speech	Educational needs and programs
Severe		
71 to 90 dB	May hear loud voices about 1 foot from the ear. May be able to identify environmental sounds. May be able to discriminate vowels but not all consonants. Speech and language defective and likely to deteriorate. Speech and language will not develop spontaneously if loss is present before 1 year of age.	Will need full-time special program for deaf children, with emphasis on all language skills, concept development, speechreading, and speech. Program needs specialized supervision and comprehensive supporting services. Can benefit from individual hearing aid by evaluation. Auditory training on individual and group aids. Part-time in regular classes only as profitable.
Extreme or profound		
91 dB or more	May hear some loud sounds but is aware of vibrations more than tonal pattern. Relies on vision rather than hearing as primary avenue for communication. Speech and language defective and likely to deteriorate. Speech and language will not develop spontaneously if loss is present before one year of age.	Will need full-time special program for deaf children, with emphasis on all language skills, concept development, speechreading, and speech. Program needs specialized supervision and comprehensive supporting services. Continuous appraisal of needs in regard to oral or manual communication. Auditory training on individual and group aids. Part-time in regular classes only for carefully selected children.

From *Exceptional Children*, 2nd ed., by William L. Heward and Michael D. Orlansky, 1984, Columbus, OH: Charles E. Merrill. Copyright 1984, Charles E. Merrill Publisher. Reprinted by permission of the publisher.

planations for this below-average score. For example, how much of the low score is due to the child being penalized for having a hearing impairment? Perhaps the child missed key words in some of the questions because of poor hearing. At a more general level, the child has probably missed a considerable amount of environmental stimulation, especially in the area of language, because of the impairment and therefore may not have acquired skills that otherwise could have been learned. Spragins (1980) has listed a series of related issues:

1. What is the impact of auditory deprivation on intellectual development and functioning?
2. Is language a primary vehicle of intellectual development or is there independence of linguistic and intellectual development?
3. Is the developmental lag that hearing impaired children manifest on cognitive tasks, in actuality, a general experiential deficit?
4. Granted the fact that thinking is clearly possible without verbal language, is enculturation possible without language? (p. 58)

None of these issues is easily resolved. However, each must be raised whenever evaluating hearing impaired children. It is inappropriate to assume that hearing impaired children are otherwise normal children who are difficult to evaluate simply because of sensory deficits. This assumption would lead us to believe that if we could just find a way to communicate properly during the evaluation, we could somehow tap the child's "true" potential. Unfortunately, hearing impairment is not just a sensory deficit, for it brings with it serious linguistic limitations (Sullivan & Vernon, 1979).

Determining an appropriate communication mode. Depending on the degree of hearing impairment, communication with hearing impaired children can be attempted through a variety of modalities: gesture, sign language, pantomime, vocalization, and expressive speech. Usually, the most acceptable form of communication can be determined prior to the evaluation. In the past it seems that children were evaluated in the mode that was most convenient and comfortable to the examiner. There is a growing realization, however, that the hearing impaired should be evaluated in the mode that is most useful for communication.

The most frequent problem occurs when the child is fluent in sign language but the examiner is not (Levine, 1974). Because this can lead to invalid results, it is negligent for the examiner to use the results to make important decisions about the child. As Sullivan and Vernon (1979) point out, "deaf children are linguistically proficient in the syntax, morphology, and semantics of sign language. This is their 'native' tongue which they naturally acquire. . . . English is learned as a second language by most hearing impaired children" (p. 271).

Evaluation Methodologies for Hearing Impaired Children

Cognitive and intellectual assessment of processes. So few tests have been specifically designed for hearing impaired children that common practice has been to select instruments that require a performance rather than a verbal response format (Spragins, 1980). Accordingly, the performance sections of the

WISC-R (Wechsler, 1974) have been routinely administered to hearing impaired children. According to Levine (1974), a variety of other instruments are also commonly utilized, including the Columbia Mental Maturity Scale (Burgemeister et al., 1972), Hiskey-Nebraska Test of Learning Aptitude (Hiskey, 1966), and the Leiter International Performance Scale (Leiter & Arthur, 1955) although several have problems in terms of predictive validity, norm samples, or reliability. Since hearing impaired children were not included in the standardization of many of these instruments, results must be cautiously interpreted because hearing impaired children may be disadvantaged even on performance tasks. For example, the average score for hearing impaired children on the Picture Arrangement subtest of the WISC-R is over 2 points lower than for the normal population (Anderson & Sisco, 1977). Some tests, designed for hearing children can be adapted to the needs of hearing impaired children. For example, during test administration children can easily learn what is expected of them through modeling and pantomine instructions, if this change in instructions has been validated.

Given that so few tests exist specifically for hearing impaired children and that the use of tests designed for other purposes is questionable, the best approach for evaluating such children would appear to be a cautious use of several formal tests. A growing research literature has assessed the effects of such an approach (cf. Sullivan & Vernon, 1979), which may make it possible to ascertain the deleterious impacts, if any, of administering various instruments to hearing impaired children. Among the cognitive measures used with these children, it appears that only the WISC-R, which was restandardized on hearing impaired children (Anderson & Sisco, 1977), and the Hiskey-Nebraska, which is now becoming somewhat dated, have norms based on a hearing impaired population.

Assessment of Academic Achievement

The problems associated with cognitive and intellectual assessment are also applicable to the testing of academic achievement. Since reading is a language-based skill, it is not surprising that hearing impaired children perform significantly lower in this and related areas (such as language arts and social studies) than do their nonhandicapped counterparts (Trybos & Karchmer, 1977). Informal assessment, task analysis, and test-teach-test strategies are preferred with hearing impaired children.

Assessment of Language and Communication Skills

Most children who cannot hear speech well have difficulty developing language. This area is routinely assessed in the evaluation of hearing impaired children. The two most important factors to evaluate are: (a) speech intelligibility and (b) receptive and expressive manual and oral communication skills

(Spragins, 1980). Speech intelligibility can be assessed in terms of how understandable the speech is or the percent of time it is understandable. Primarily a function of degree of hearing loss, it does not improve markedly with increased age or training (Karchmer & Trybus, 1978). Communication skills can be assessed through formal tests, informal evaluation, or ongoing language curriculum.

Evaluating Visually Impaired Children

Definitional Issues

The three components that must be assessed to determine visual impairment in students are visual acuity, field of vision, and functional vision. Screening for visual acuity is conducted in schools by a school nurse who uses Snellen charts at a distance of twenty feet and at reading distance. Full examinations are given by ophthalmologists, optometrists, or opticians. *Visual acuity* reflects the degree to which individuals can differentiate objects and discriminate details. In screening tests (for example, Snellen charts), a child is typically presented with an eye chart placed 20 feet away and asked to identify letters printed on the chart in varied sizes. The standard criterion for ruling out visual acuity problems is 20/20 vision, meaning that one reads the line of the type size labeled 20 while standing twenty feet away. Those with visual acuity of less than 20/200 in their best eye after correction are classified as legally blind.

The second type of definition focuses upon *field of vision*, or the extent to which a child can see a full range of stimuli (that is, has peripheral vision). Some children, for example, have excellent visual acuity but their field of vision may be so restricted that they can see only one or two letters simultaneously on a printed page.

The third type of assessment for visual impairment is based upon the degree to which a person has *functional vision*. Most individuals with some vision, even some classified as legally blind, can be trained to use large print and other visual materials. Using this criterion, children are classified as blind when they cannot make use of partial sight and must be educated using braille or auditory materials; those who can be educated through the visual modality are termed partially sighted. Assessment for functional vision is clinical, requiring direct observations of the child's behavior.

Issues in the Assessment of Visually Impaired Children

Just as the educational assessment of hearing impaired children is not a matter of simply making auditory instructions and stimuli understandable, so the assessment of visually impaired children is more than avoiding the use of visual test stimuli. Visual impairments represent a handicap that markedly decreases the amount and type of information available to a child during development.

Thus, in some areas a normally functioning child with serious, uncorrected visual impairments may perform at levels below those of children with normal vision. Several problems exist with the use of psychoeducational assessment instruments designed for sighted populations. Some assessors have used verbal tests (for example, the WISC-R Verbal section) or written tests translated into braille to evaluate visually handicapped children. However, Baker (n.d.) has identified a number of problems with this approach:

1. Visually handicapped children may be at a disadvantage when required to remember lengthy instructions or numerous multiple-choice responses.
2. Translations of tests designed for sighted individuals for use with the visually handicapped must necessarily omit certain components such as maps and diagrams.
3. Visualization is the key component of some tests.
4. Tests may require knowledge that is only available visually and is not a part of any curriculum that would be specifically taught to a visually handicapped child.

Another problem is that norms developed from a sighted population do not apply when standardized administration procedures are altered. However, many visually impaired children retain some residual sight that can be utilized through large-print materials or electronic magnification devices. It may be possible, with only very slight modification, to adapt some visual materials for use during assessment. The Focus on Practice provides some practical suggestions for establishing rapport with and evaluating visually handicapped children. However, the statement that you should "expect language and motor delays" is not substantiated by research evidence.

Evaluation Methodologies for Visually Impaired Children

A wide variety of tests have been designed or can be adapted for use with visually impaired children. It is also possible to utilize interviews, and informal and behavioral assessment techniques that have been discussed elsewhere in this chapter and throughout the text.

It is the exception rather than the rule to find well-standardized and -validated tests that have been normed on visually handicapped populations. Because of this, Baker (n.d.) has suggested that the principle that should guide users of such tests is *caveat emptor*. The following list of potential problems (adapted from Baker) should be considered in evaluating assessment instruments for visually impaired children:

1. Overall test quality is sometimes poor because many tests were developed as part of master's theses or doctoral dissertations and may not have received the careful research and revision characteristically given to the instruments developed by major test publishing companies.

FOCUS ON PRACTICE
Establishing Rapport with and Evaluating a Visually Impaired Child

When establishing rapport with a child who cannot see well, the psychologist's friendly smile will be in vain. Other techniques must be developed. A handshake, hand on shoulders or other "hands on" approach is a quick way to connect with that person. He may wish to be guided by holding on to your elbow. We take in a new room by looking around; allow the child to explore by touching or describing the setting, including the test equipment.

As you settle in, take a moment to discuss his vision problem. For some children, bright contrast is preferred. Others work best in diffuse, natural light and some children need dimness. Small print may be better than large print. For most blind people, minimal distraction by sounds or smell is preferred. Sounds we may ignore, such as a ticking stopwatch, a motor or sniffling will pose a direct distraction to those who do not see. Offer to adjust the lighting, explain sounds and ask him to let you know when he needs help. It's easiest to be frank because it allows him that privilege as well. A few people feel they need to shout or speak slowly to blind people, but obviously this doesn't help much. Use your regular vocabulary, including references to "seeing." Blind persons use these words too.

In addition, be sure your paper is off white or yellow to reduce glare. Provide a choice of pens and pencils for him to choose. A soft #2 pencil or felt tip is often desired. Then after you are both comfortable, begin to test.

Evaluating a visually impaired preschooler requires common sense and clinical skills. Remember to expect language and motor delays as well as possibly some autistic-like symptoms. One may be left wondering how to get an accurate feel for this child's potential. Unfortunately there is no magic way to find out. We have little else but several standard tests, behavioral observation and our clinical judgment to use.

2. Norms may be based upon small numbers.
3. Because institutionalized populations are readily available during standardization, these groups may be overrepresented in the normative sample.
4. Norms are typically not provided for various degrees of visual impairment (for example, partially sighted versus blind), even though performance expectations across the range of impairments differ markedly.
5. Test instructions may be poorly standardized or difficult to interpret and introduce an unwanted source of variation in scores due to examiner interpretation (or misinterpretation!) of instructions.

6. Often there is very little supporting documentation and research to establish the reliability or validity of the instrument.

The prudent test user will consider each of these factors in light of the particular information desired and the specific characteristics of an individual client. Readers wanting more information on the assessment of the visually impaired are referred to other sources (Bauman & Kropf, 1979; Goldman & Duda, 1980).

Summary

This chapter has summarized a variety of approaches for assessing children with low-incidence handicaps, including severely and profoundly handicapped children (most of them functioning at seriously retarded levels), hearing impaired children, and visually impaired children. For the astute reader, it will be apparent that the *processes* of assessing these diverse groups are more similar than different. What are the commonalities of the processes? Are the processes really that much different from those used in the assessment of children with less severe or disabling handicaps? The answers to these questions should help to put the assessment of low-incidence children in perspective with assessment in general. Our view is that *all* children range along a normal-abnormal continuum and that one does not necessarily adopt a completely different approach when moving from one type of assessment to another. We may use different *methods* but the process and the guiding philosophy remain remarkably consistent.

References

Achenbach, T. M. (1982). *Developmental psychopathology.* New York: Wiley.

Achenbach, T. M., & Edelbrock, C. (1981). Behavioral problems and competencies reported by parents of normal and disturbed children 4 through 16. *Monographs of the Society for Research in Child Development, 46* (Serial No. 188).

Achenbach, T. M., & Edelbrock, C. (1983). *Manual for the Child Behavior Checklist and Revised Child Behavior Profile.* Burlington, VT: University of Vermont.

Ackerman, P. R., & Moore, M. G. (1976). Delivery of educational services for preschool handicapped children. In T. D. Tjossem (Ed.), *Intervention strategies for high risk infants and young children* (pp. 268–311). Baltimore: University Park Press.

Adams, R. S., & Biddle, B. J. (1970). *Realities of teaching.* New York: Holt, Rinehart & Winston.

Affleck, J. O., Lowenbraum, S., & Archer, A. (1980). *Teaching mildly handicapped in the regular classroom* (2nd ed.). Columbus, OH: Charles Merrill.

Alessi, G. (1980). Behavioral observation for the school psychologist: Response discrepancy model. *School Psychology Review, 9,* 31–45.

Alessi, G., & Kaye, J. (1983). *Behavioral assessment for school psychologists.* Kent, OH: National Association of School Psychologists.

Algozzine, B. (1977). The emotionally disturbed child: Disturbed or disturbing. *Journal of Abnormal Child Psychology, 5,* 205–211.

American Guidance Service. (1985). *K-ABC ASSIST* (computer program). Circle Pines, MN: Author.

American Guidance Service. (1985). *Woodcock ASSIST* (computer program). Circle Pines, MN: Author.

American Psychological Association. (1985). *Joint standards for educational and psychological testing* (3rd ed.). Washington, DC: Author.

American Psychological Association. (1986). *Guidelines for computer based tests and interpretation.* (Available from the American Psychological Association, 1200 Seventeenth Street, NW, Washington, DC 20036.)

Ames, L. B., Metraux, R., Rodell, J., & Walker, R. (1974). *Child Rorschach responses.* New York: Brunner/Mazel.

Anastasi, A. (1981). Coaching, test sophistication, and developed abilities. *American Psychologist, 36*, 1086–1093.

Anastasi, A. (1982). *Psychological testing* (5th ed.). New York: Macmillan.

Anderson, L. M., Evertson, C. M., & Brophy, J. E. (1979). An experimental study of effective teaching in first grade reading groups. *Elementary School Journal, 79*, 193–222.

Anderson, R. C. (1972). How to construct achievement tests to assess comprehension. *Review of Educational Research, 42*, 145–170.

Anderson, R. C., Reynolds, R. E., Schallert, D. L., & Goetz, E. T. (1977). Frameworks for comprehending discourse. *American Educational Research Journal, 14*, 367–381.

Anderson, R. J., & Sisco, F. H. (1977). *Standardization of the WISC-R performance scale for deaf children* (Series T, Number 1). Washington, DC: Gallaudet College Office of Demographic Studies.

Asher, S. R., & Hymel, S. (1981). Children's social competence in peer relations: Sociometic and behavioral assessment. In J. D. Wine & M. D. Smyt (Eds.), *Social competence* (pp. 125–167). New York: Guilford Press.

Asher, S. R., & Taylor, A. (1981). The social outcomes of mainstreaming: Sociometric assessment and beyond. *Exceptional Education Quarterly, 1*, 13–30.

Axelrod, S., Hall, R. V., & Tams, A. (1972, May). *A comparison of common seating arrangements in the classroom.* Paper presented at the Kansas Symposium of Behavior Analysis in Education, Lawrence, KS.

Baer, D. M. (1974). A note on the absence of Santa Claus in any known ecosystem: A rejoiner to Willems. *Journal of Applied Behavior Analysis, 7*, 167–170.

Baker, R. M. (no date). *The psychological assessment of the visually handicapped.* Colorado Springs: Colorado School for the Deaf and Blind.

Balow, I. H., Farr, R., Hogan, T. D., & Prescott, G. A. (1978). *Metropolitan Achievement Test.* San Antonio, TX: The Psychological Corporation.

Bandura, A. (1974). Behavior theory and the models of man. *American Psychologist, 29*, 859–869.

Bandura, A. (1977). Self-efficacy: Toward a unifying theory of behavioral change. *Psychological Review, 84*, 191–215.

Bandura, A. (1978). The self-system in reciprocal determinism. *American Psychologist, 33*, 344–358.

Barker, R. G. (1968). *Ecological psychology.* Palo Alto, CA: Stanford University Press.

Barlow, B. (1979). Definitional and prevalence problems in behavior disorders of children. *School Psychology Digest, 8*, 348–354.

Barrie-Blackey, S. (1973). Six-year-old children's understanding of sentences adjoined with time adverbs. *Journal of Psycholinguistic Research, 2*, 153–156.

Barton, E. J., & Ascione, F. R. (1984). Direct observation. In T. Ollendick & M. Hersen (Eds.), *Child behavioral assessment* (pp. 166–194). New York: Pergamon Press.

Bauman, M. K., & Kropf, C. A. (1979). Psychological tests used with blind and visually handicapped persons. *School Psychology Review, 8*, 257–270.

Bayley, N. (1969). *Bayley Scales of Infant Development.* New York: Psychological Corporation.

Beatty, L. L., Madden, R., Gardner, E. F., & Karlsen, B. (1976). *Stanford Diagnostic Mathematics Test.* New York: Harcourt Brace Jovanovich.

Becker, W. C. (1977). Teaching reading and language to the disadvantaged — What have we learned from field research. *Harvard Educational Review, 47*, 518–543.

Becker, W. C., & Carnine, D. (1980). Direct instruction: An effective approach to educational intervention with disadvantaged and low performers. In B. B. Lahey & A. E. Kazdin, *Advances in clinical child psychology* (Vol. 3, pp. 429–463). New York: Plenum Press.

Beery, K., & Buktenica, N. (1982). *Developmental Test of Visual-Motor Integration.* Chicago: Follett Educational Corporation.

Bender, L. (1938). *The Bender Visual Motor Gestalt Test for Children.* New York: American Orthopsychiatric Association.

Bennett, R. E., & Shepard, M. J. (1982). Basic measurement proficiency of learning disability specialists. *Learning Disability Quarterly, 5*, 177–184.

Benton, A. (1963). *Benton Visual Retention Test* (rev. ed.). New York: Psychological Corporation.

Bergan, J. (1977). *Behavioral consultation.* Columbus, OH: Charles Merrill.

Bergan, J., Byrnes, T., & Kratochwill, T. (1979). Effects of behavioral and medical models of consultation on teacher expectancies and instruction of a hypothetical child. *Journal of School Psychology, 17*, 307–316.

Bergan, J., & Tombari, M. (1975). The analysis of verbal interactions occurring during consultation. *Journal of School Psychology, 13*, 209–266.

Bersoff, D. N. (1983). Social and legal influences on test development and usage. In B. Plake, *Buros/Nebraska symposium on measurement and testing* (Vol. 1, pp. 126–161). Hillsdale, NJ: Lawrence Erlbaum Associates.

Betts, E. A. (1946). *Foundations of reading instruction.* New York: American Book.

Biber, B. (1984). *Early education and psychological development.* New Haven: Yale University Press.

Biehler, R. (1954). Companion choice behavior in the kindergarten. *Child Development, 25*, 45–50.

Bijou, S., & Baer, D. (1961). *Child development I: A systematic and empirical theory.* Englewood Cliffs, NJ: Prentice-Hall.

Bliss, L. S., Allen, D. V., & Wrasse, K. W. (1978). A story completion approach as a measure of language development in children. *Journal of Speech and Hearing Research, 20,* 358–372.

Blood, D. F., & Budd, W. C. (1972). *Educational measurement and evaluation.* New York: Harper & Row.

Bloom, L. (1973). *One word at a time.* The Hague: Mouton.

Bloom, L. (1975). Language development. In F. D. Horowitz (Ed.), *Review of child development research* (Vol. 4). Chicago: University of Chicago Press.

Boring, E. G. (1950). *A history of experimental psychology* (2nd ed.). New York: Appleton-Century-Crofts.

Bormuth, J. R. (1969). Factor validity of cloze tests as measures of reading comprehension ability. *Reading Research Quarterly, 4,* 358–365.

Bracken, B. A. (1985). A critical review of the Kaufman Assessment Battery for Children (K-ABC). *School Psychology Reviews, 14,* 21–36.

Bracken, B. A., Prasse, D. P., & McCallum, R. S. (1984). Peabody Picture Vocabulary Test-Revised: An appraisal and review. *School Psychology Review, 13,* 49–60.

Brewer, M., & Collins, B. E. (1981). Perspectives on knowing: Six themes from Donald T. Campbell. In M. Brewer & B. E. Collins (Eds.), *Scientific inquiry and the social sciences* (pp. 1–9). San Francisco: Jossey-Bass.

Brigance, A. (1977). *Diagnostic Inventory of Basic Skills.* North Billerica, MA: Curriculum Associates.

Brophy, J. E. (1981). Teacher praise: A functional analysis. *Review of Educational Research, 51,* 5–32.

Brophy, J. E., & Evertson, C. M. (1976). *Learning from teaching: A developmental perspective.* Boston: Allyn & Bacon.

Brophy, J. E., & Good, T. (1974). *Teacher-student relationships: Causes and consequences.* New York: Holt, Rinehart & Winston.

Brown v. *Board of Education,* 347 U.S. 483 (1954).

Brown, F. G. (1983). *Principles of educational and psychological testing* (3rd ed.). New York: Holt, Rinehart & Winston.

Brown, J. I., Bennett, J. M., & Hanna, G. S. (1981). *The Nelson-Denny Reading Test.* Chicago: Riverside.

Brown, J. S., & Burton, R. R. (1978). Diagnostic models for procedural bugs in basic mathematical skills. *Cognitive science, 2,* 155–192.

Brown, L., & Hammill, D. D. (1978). *Manual for the Behavior Rating Profile.* Austin, TX: PRO-ED.

Brown, R. (1973). *A first language: The early stages.* Cambridge, MA: Harvard University Press.

Brown, V. L., & McEntire, E. (1984). *Test of Mathematical Abilities.* Austin, TX: PRO-ED.

Brueckner, L. J., & Bond, G. L. (1955). *The diagnosis and treatment of learning difficulties*. Englewood Cliffs, NJ: Prentice-Hall.

Bruner, J. S. (1960). *The process of education*. New York: Vintage.

Bryen, D. N., & Gallagher, D. (1983). Assessment of language and communication. In K. D. Paget & B. A. Bracken (Eds.), *The psychoeducational assessment of preschool children*. New York: Grune & Stratton.

Buck, J. T. (1948). The H-T-P technique: A qualitative and quantitative scoring manual. *Journal of Clinical Psychology, 4*, 317–396.

Burgemeister, B. B., Blum, L. H., & Lorge, I. (1972). *Columbia Mental Maturity Scale* (3rd ed.). New York: Harcourt Brace Jovanovich.

Burns, G. (1980). Indirect measurement and behavioral assessment: A case of social behavioral psychometrics. *Behavioral Assessment, 2*, 197–206.

Buros, O. K. (Ed.). (1961). *Tests in print*. Highland Park, NJ: Gryphon Press.

Buros, O. K. (Ed.). (1974). *Tests in print II*. Highland Park, NJ: Gryphon Press.

Buros, O. K. (Ed.). (1978). *Eighth mental measurements yearbook*. Highland Park, NJ: Gryphon Press.

Buswell, G. T., & John, L. (no date). *Buswell-John Diagnostic Chart for Individual Difficulties in Fundamental Processes Arithmetic*. Indianapolis: Bobbs-Merrill.

Cain, L. F., Levine, S., & Elzey, F. F. (1963). *Cain-Levine Social Competency Scale*. Palo Alto, CA: Consulting Psychologists Press.

Cairns, H. S., & Hsu, J. R. (1978). Who, why, when and how: A developmental study. *Journal of Child Language, 5*, 477–488.

Campbell, D., & Fiske, D. (1959). Convergent and discriminant validation by the multitrait-multimethod matrix. *Psychological Bulletin, 56*, 81–105.

Carlberg, C., & Kavale, K. (1980). The efficacy of special versus regular class placement for exceptional children: A meta-analysis. *The Journal of Special Education, 14*, 295–309.

Carnine, D., & Silbert, J. (1979). *Direct instruction reading*. Columbus, OH: Charles Merrill.

Carroll, A. W. (1974). The classroom as an ecosystem. *Focus on Exceptional Children, 6*, 4.

Carroll, J. B. (1971). Defining language comprehension: Some speculations. In R. O. Freddle & J. B. Carroll (Eds.), *Language comprehension and the acquisition of knowledge*. Washington, DC: V. H. Winston and Sons.

Carroll, J. B. (1972). A review of the Illinois Test of Psycholinguistic Abilities. In O. K. Buros (Ed.), *Seventh mental measurement yearbook*. Highland Park, NJ: Gryphon Press.

Carrow, E. (1973). *Carrow Elicited Language Inventory*. Austin, TX: Learning Concepts.

Carrow-Woolfolk, E. (1973). *Test for Auditory Comprehension of Language*. Hingham, MA: Teaching Resources.

Case, R. (1974). Structures and strictures: Some functional limitations on the course of cognitive growth. *Cognitive Psychology, 6*, 544–574.

Cawley, J. F. (1978). An instructional design in mathematics. In L. Mann, L. Goodman, & J. L. Wiederholt (Eds.), *Teaching the learning disabled adolescent*. Boston: Houghton Mifflin.

Centra, J. A., & Potter, D. A. (1980). School and teacher effects: An instructional model. *Review of Educational Research, 50*, 273–292.

Chall, J. S. (1967). *Learning to read: The great debate*. New York: McGraw-Hill.

Chapman, R. N., Larsen, S. L., & Parker, R. M. (1979). Interactions of first-grade teachers with learning disordered children. *Journal of Learning Disabilities, 12*, 225–230.

Chappell, G. E., & Johnson, G. A. (1976). Evaluation of cognitive behavior in the young nonverbal child. *Language, Speech and Hearing Services in Schools, 1*, 17–24.

Chipman, H., & deDardel, C. (1974). Developmental study of comprehension and production of the pronoun it. *Journal of Psycholinguistic Research, 3*, 91–99.

Clark, E. (1973). What's in a word? In T. E. Moore (Ed.), *Cognitive development and the acquisition of language*. New York: Academic Press.

Clark, L. C., Gresham, F. M., & Elliott, S. N. (1985). Development of a social skills assessment measure: The TROSS-C. *Journal of Psychoeducational Assessment, 3*, 347–356.

Colarusso, R. P., & Hammill, D. D. (1972). *Motor-Free Visual Perception Test*. Novato, CA: Academic Therapy Publications.

Colbourne, M. J., & McLeod, J. (1983). Computer-guided educational diagnosis: A prototype expert system. *Journal of Special Education Technology, 6*, 30–39.

College Board. (1981). *Degrees of reading power*. New York: Author.

Cone, J. (1977). The relevance of reliability and validity for behavioral assessment. *Behavior Therapy, 8*, 411–426.

Cone, J. (1978). The Behavioral Assessment Grid (BAG): A conceptual framework and taxonomy. *Behavior Therapy, 9*, 882–888.

Cone, J. (1979). Confounded comparisons in triple response mode assessment. *Behavioral Assessment, 1*, 85–96.

Cone, J. (1981). Psychometric considerations. In M. Hersen & A. Bellack (Eds.), *Behavioral assessment: A practical handbook* (2nd ed.) (pp. 38–70). New York: Pergamon Press.

Cone, J., & Hawkins, R. (Eds.). (1977). *Behavioral assessment: New directions in clinical psychology*. New York: Brunner/Mazel.

Conners, K. (1973). Rating scales for use in drug studies with children. *Psychopharmacology Bulletin, 24*, 24–84.

Connolly, A. J., Nachtman, W., & Pritchett, E. M. (1976). *KeyMath Diagnostic Arithmetic Test*. Circle Pines, MN: American Guidance Service.

Coulter, A., & Morrow, H. (1978). *The concept and measurement of adaptive behavior.* New York: Grune & Stratton.

Cratty, B. J. (1970). *Perceptual and motor development in infants and young children.* New York: Macmillan.

Cronbach, L. J. (1970). *Essentials of psychological testing.* New York: Harper & Row.

Cronbach, L. J., Glaser, G., Nanda, H., & Rajaratman, N. (1972). *The dependability of behavioral measures.* New York: Wiley.

Cronbach, L. J., & Snow, R. E. (1969). *Final report: Individual differences in learning ability as a function of instructional variables.* Stanford, CA: Stanford University.

Cronbach, L. J., & Snow, R. E. (1977). *Aptitudes and instructional methods.* New York: Irvington.

CTB/McGraw-Hill. (1977). *The California Achievement Tests.* Monterey, CA: Author.

CTB/McGraw-Hill. (1979). *The California Achievement Tests.* Monterey, CA: Author.

Cullinan, D., Epstein, M., & McLinden, D. (1986). Status and change in state administrative definitions of behavior disorders. *School Psychology Review, 15,* 383–392.

Cummings, J. A. (1979). Linguistic interdependence and the educational development of bilingual children. *Review of Educational Research, 49,* 222–251.

Cummings, J. A. (1985). [Review of *Woodcock-Johnson Psychoeducational Battery*]. In J. V. Mitchell, Jr., *Ninth mental measurements yearbook.* Lincoln, NE: Buros Institute of Mental Measurements.

Cummings, J. A., & Moscato, E. M. (1984). Research on the Woodcock-Johnson Psycho-Educational Battery: Implications for practice and future investigations. *School Psychology Review, 13,* 33–40.

Dale, E., & Chall, J. S. (1948). A formula for predicting readability. *Educational Research Bulletin, 27,* 11–20, 37–54.

Dale, P. (1976). *Language development: Structure and function.* New York: Prentice-Hall.

Das, J. P., Kirby, J. R., & Jarman, R. F. (1979). *Simultaneous and successive cognitive processes.* New York: Academic Press.

Davis, S. E., & Kramer, J. J. (1985). Comparison of the PPVT-T and WISC-R: A validations study with second-grade students. *Psychology in the Schools, 22,* 29–32.

deHirsch, D., Jansky, J. J., & Langford, W. S. (1966). *Predicting reading failure.* New York: Harper & Row.

De Oreo, K. (1980). Refining locomotor skills. In C. Corbin (Ed.), *A textbook of motor development* (pp. 59–67). Dubuque, IA: Wm. C. Brown.

Diebold, M. H., Curtis, W. S., & Dubose, R. F. (1978). Relationships between psychometric and observational measures of performance in low-functioning children. *AAESPH Review, 3,* 123–128.

Doll, E. A. (1965). *Vineland Social Maturity Scale.* Circle Pines, MN: American Guidance Services.

Doll, E. A. (1966). *Preschool Attainment Record.* Circle Pines, MN: American Guidance Services.

Drabman, R., Hammer, D., & Rosenbaum, M. (1979). Assessing generalization in behavior modification with children: The generalization map. *Behavioral Assessment, 1,* 103–220.

Dubose, R. F. (1976). Predictive value of infant intelligence scales with multiply handicapped children. *American Journal of Mental Deficiency, 81,* 388–390.

Duncan, D., Sbardellati, E., Maheady, F., & Sainato, D. (1980). Nondiscriminatory assessment of severely physically handicapped individuals. *The Journal of the Association of the Physically Handicapped, 6,* 17–22.

Dunn, L. M. (1965). *Peabody Picture Vocabulary Test.* Circle Pines, MN: American Guidance Service.

Dunn, L. M., & Dunn, L. M. (1981). *Peabody Picture Vocabulary Test-Revised.* Circle Pines, MN: American Guidance Service.

Dunn, L. M., & Markwardt, F. C. (1970). *Peabody Individual Achievement Test.* Circle Pines, MN: American Guidance Service.

Durrell, D. D. (1955). *Durrell Analysis of Reading Difficulty.* New York: Harcourt Brace Jovanovich.

Dwyer, C. A. (1973). Sex differences in reading: An evaluation and a critique of current theories. *Review of Educational Research, 43,* 455–468.

Eaves, R. C., & McLaughlin, P. A. (1977). A systems approach for the assessment of the child and his environment: Getting back to basics. *Journal of Special Education, 2,* 99–111.

Ebel, R. L. (1966). Some measurement problems in a national assessment of educational progress. *Journal of Educational Measurement, 3,* 11–17.

Ebel, R. L. (1975). Educational tests: Valid? Biased? Useful? *Phi Delta Kappan, 57,* 83–89.

Edelbrock, C. (1983). Problems and issues in using rating scales to assess child personality and psychopathology. *School Psychology Review, 12,* 253–299.

Education for All Handicapped Children Act of 1975. (1977). *Federal Register, 197,* 42474–42518.

Elliott, S. N., & Bretzing, B. H. (1980). Using and updating local norms. *Psychology in the Schools, 17,* 196–201.

Elliott, S. N., & Piersel, W. C. (1982). Direct assessment of reading skills: An approach which links assessment to intervention. *School Psychology Review, 11,* 257–280.

Engler, L., Hannah, E., & Longhurst, T. (1973). Linguistic analysis of speech samples: A practical guide for clinicians. *Journal of Speech and Hearing Disorders, 38,* 192–204.

Enright, B. E. (1983). *ENRIGHT Diagnostic Inventory of Basic Arithmetic Skills.* North Billerica, MA: Curriculum Associates.

Epstein, M., Cullinan, D., & Sabatino, D. (1977). State definitions of behavior disorders. *Journal of Special Education, 11,* 417–425.

Erikson, E. (1963). *Childhood and society* (2nd ed.). New York: Norton.

Exner, J. E. (1974). *The Rorschach: A comprehensive system* (Vol. 1). New York: Wiley.

Eysenck, H. J., & Kamin, L. (1981). *The intelligence controversy.* New York: Wiley.

Family Educational Rights and Privacy Act, P. L. 93–380, 20 U.S.C.A., 45 C.F.R.

Farr, R. C. (1970). *Reading: What can be measured?* Newark, DE: International Reading Association.

Farr, R. C., Prescott, G. A., Balow, I. H., & Hogan, T. P. (1978). *Metropolitan Achievement Tests: Reading Instructional Battery.* New York: Psychological Corporation.

Feldt, S. L., Forsyth, R. A., Lindquist, E. F., with the assistance of Alnot, S. D., & Belgrade, P. S. (1982). *Iowa Test of Basic Skills.* Chicago: Science Research Associates.

Fenton, K. S., Yoshida, R. K., Maxwell, J. P., & Kaufman, M. T. (1979). Recognition of team goals: An essential step toward rational decision-making. *Exceptional Children, 45*, 638–644.

Flanders, N. A. (1970). Interaction analysis: A technique for quantifying teacher influences. In H. G. Clarizio, R. C. Craig, & W. A. Mehrens (Eds.), *Contemporary issues in educational psychology* (2nd ed.). Boston: Allyn & Bacon.

Fluharty, N. B. (1978). *Fluharty Preschool Speech and Language Screening Test.* Hingham, MA: Teaching Resources.

Forehand, R., Breiner, J., McMahon, R. J., & Davies, G. (in press). Predictors of cross-setting behavior change in the treatment of child problems. *Journal of Child Clinical Psychology.*

Foster, R. (1974). *Camelot Behavioral Checklist.* Parsons, KS: Camelot Behavioral Systems.

Foster, S., & Cone, J. (1980). Current issues in direct observation. *Behavioral Assessment, 2*, 313–338.

Fox, R., Luszhi, M. B., & Schumch, R. (1966). *Diagnosing classroom learning environments.* Chicago: Science Research Associates.

Frankenburg, W. K., & Dodds, J. B. (1967). *The Denver Developmental Screening Test.* Denver: University of Colorado Medical Center.

Frankenburg, W. K., Van Doorninck, W. J., Liddell, T. N., & Dick, N. P. (1976). The Denver Prescreening Developmental Questionnaire. *Journal of Pediatrics, 57*, 744–753.

Freund, J. H., Bradley, R. H., & Caldwell, B. M. (1979). The home environment in the assessment of learning disabilities. *Learning Disabilities Quarterly, 2*, 39–51.

Freud, S. (1933). *New introductory lectures on psychoanalysis.* New York: Norton.

Fry, M., & Lagomarsino, L. (1982). Factors that influence reading: A developmental perspective. *School Psychology Review, 11*, 239–250.

Gardner, E. F., Callis, R., Merwin, J. C., & Rudman, H. C. (1982). *Stanford Test of Academic Skills.* San Antonio, TX: Psychological Corporation.

Gardner, E. F., Rudman, H. C., Karlen, B., & Merwin, J. C. (1982). *Stanford Achievement Test*. San Antonio, TX: Psychological Corporation.

Gardner, M. F. (1983). *Upper-Extension Expressive One-Word Picture Vocabulary Test*. Novato, CA: Academic Therapy Publications.

Gates, A. I., & McKillop, A. S. (1962). *Gates-McKillop Reading Diagnostic Tests*. New York: Teacher's College Press.

Gates, A. I., McKillop, A. S., & Horowitz, E. C. (Eds.). (1981). *Reading Diagnostic Tests*. New York: Teacher's College Press.

Gessell, J. K. (1977). *Diagnostic Mathematics Inventory*. Monterey, CA: CTB/McGraw-Hill.

Gesten, E. L., Cowen, E. L., DeStefano, M. A., & Gallaghen, R. (1978). Teachers' judgements of class-related and teaching-related problem situations. *Journal of Special Education, 12*, 15–20.

Gibson, E. J. (1969). *Principles of perceptual learning and development*. New York: Appleton-Century-Crofts.

Gibson, E. J., & Levin, H. (1975). *The psychology of reading*. Cambridge, MA: The MIT Press.

Ginsburg, H. P., & Baroody, A. J. (1983). *The Test of Early Mathematics Ability*. Austin, TX: PRO-ED.

Ginsburg, H. P., & Mathews, S. C. (1984). *Diagnostic Test of Arithmetic Strategies*. Austin, TX: PRO-ED.

Gittelman, R. (1980). The role of psychological tests for differential diagnosis in child psychiatry. *Journal of the American Academy of Child Psychiatry, 19*, 413–438.

Gleitman, H. (1981). *Psychology*. New York: Norton.

Glover, R., Bruning, R., & Filbeck, R. (1983). *Educational psychology*. Boston: Little, Brown.

Glucksberg, S., & Krauss, R. M. (1967). What do people say after they have learned how to talk? Studies of the development of referential communication. *Merrill-Palmer Quarterly, 13*, 309–316.

Goh, D. S., Telzrow, C. J., & Fuller, G. B. (1981). The practice of psychoeducational assessment among school psychologists. *Professional Psychology, 12*, 696–706.

Goldberg, L. R. (1970). Man vs. model of man: A rationale, plus some evidence for a method of improving clinical inference. *Psychological Bulletin, 73*, 422–432.

Goldfried, M., & Kent, R. (1972). Traditional versus behavioral personality assessment: A comparison of methodological and theoretical assumptions. *Psychological Bulletin, 77*, 409–420.

Goldman, F. H., & Duda, D. (1980). Psychological assessment of the visually impaired child. In R. K. Mulliken & M. Evans (Eds.), *Assessment of children with low-incidence handicaps*. Kent, OH: National Association of School Psychologists.

Goldman, R., & Fristoe, M. (1972). *Goldman-Fristoe Test of Articulation*. Circle Pines, MN: American Guidance Service.

Goldman, R., Fristoe, M., & Woodcock, R. (1980). *The Goldman-Fristoe-Woodcock Test of Auditory Discrimination.* Circle Pines, MN: American Guidance Service.

Goldstein, K. (1939). *The organism.* New York: American Book Company.

Goldstein, K. (1948). *After-effects of brain injuries in war.* New York: Grune & Stratton.

Good, T. L. (1979). Teacher effectiveness in the elementary school. *Journal of Teacher Education, 30,* 52–64.

Good, T.L., & Brophy, J. (1978). *Looking into classrooms.* New York: Harper & Row.

Gordon, I. (1976). *What are effective learning environments for school age children?* Gainesville, FL: Institute for Development of Human Resources Conference, University of Florida.

Goslin, D. A. (1963). *The search for ability: Standardized testing in social perspective.* New York: Russell Sage Foundation.

Graham, F., & Kendall, B. (1960). Memory for Designs Test: Revised general manual. *Perceptual and Motor Skills, 11,* 147–188.

Gresham, F. M. (1981a). Assessment of children's social skills. *Journal of Child Psychology, 19,* 120–133.

Gresham, F. M. (1981b). Social skills training with handicapped children: A review. *Review of Educational Research, 52,* 139–176.

Gresham, F. M. (1981c). Validity of social skills measures for assessing social competence in low-status children: A multivariate investigation. *Developmental Psychology, 17,* 390–398.

Gresham, F. M. (1982a). A model for the behavioral assessment of behavior disorders in children: Measurement considerations and practical application. *Journal of School Psychology, 20,* 131–144.

Gresham, F. M. (1982b). Social interactions as predictors of children's likeability and friendship patterns: A multiple regression analysis. *Journal of Behavioral Assessment, 4,* 39–54.

Gresham, F. M. (1983). Social validity in the assessment of children's social skills: Establishing standards for social competency. *Journal of Psychoeducational Assessment, 1,* 297–307.

Gresham, F. M. (1984). Behavioral interviews in school psychology: Issues in psychometric adequacy and research. *School Psychology Review, 13,* 17–25.

Gresham, F. M. (1985a). Behavior disorder assessment: Conceptual, definitional, and practical considerations. *School Psychology Review, 14,* 495–509.

Gresham, F. M. (1985b). Social skills assessment and training. In J. Ysseldyke (Ed.), *School psychology: The state of the art.* Minneapolis: National School Psychology Inservice Training Network.

Gresham, F. M., & Elliott, S. N. (1984). Assessment and classification of children's social skills: A review of methods and issues. *School Psychology Review, 13,* 292–301.

Gresham, F. M., & Elliott, S. N. (1987). The relationship between adaptive behavior and social skills: Issues in definition and assessment. *Journal of Special Education, 21*, 167–181.

Gresham, F. M., & Nagle, R. J. (1980). Social skills training with children: Responsiveness to modeling and coaching as a function of peer orientation. *Journal of Consulting and Clinical Psychology, 48*, 718–729.

Grossman, H. (Ed.). (1973). *Manual on terminology and classification in mental retardation* (Special Publication No. 2). Washington, DC: American Association on Mental Deficiency.

Grossman, H. (1977). *Manual on terminology and classification in mental retardation* (rev. ed.). Washington, DC: American Association on Mental Deficiency.

Grossman, H. (1981). *Manual on terminology and classification in mental retardation.* Washington, DC: American Association on Mental Deficiency.

Grossman, H. (1983). *Manual on terminology and classification in mental retardation.* Washington, DC: American Association on Mental Deficiency.

Guadalupe Organization v. *Tempe Elementary School District*, 71-435, District Court for Arizona, January 1972.

Guerin, G. R., & Maier, A. S. (1983). *Informal assessment in education.* Palo Alto, CA: Mayfield.

Guilford, J. P. (1967). *The nature of human intelligence.* New York: McGraw-Hill.

Gutkin, T. B., & Curtis, M. J. (1982). School-based consultation: Theory and techniques. In C. R. Reynolds & T. B. Gutkin (Eds.), *The handbook of school psychology* (pp. 796–828). New York: Wiley.

Hallahan, D. P., & Cruickshank, W. M. (1973). *Psychoeducational foundations of learning disabilities.* Englewood Cliffs, NJ: Prentice-Hall.

Hallahan, D. P., & Kauffman, J. M. (1982). *Exceptional children.* Englewood Cliffs, NJ: Prentice-Hall.

Halpern, A., Raffeld, P., Irvin, L. K., & Link, R. (1975). *Social and Prevocational Information Battery.* Monterey, CA: CTB/McGraw-Hill.

Hammill, D. D., & Bartel, N. R. (1975). *Teaching children with learning and behavior problems.* Boston: Allyn & Bacon.

Hammill, D. D., & Larsen, S. C. (1974a). The effectiveness of psycholinguistic training. *Exceptional Children, 7*, 429–436.

Hammill, D. D., & Larsen, S. C. (1974b). The relationship of selected auditory perceptual skills and reading ability. *Journal of Learning Disabilities, 7*, 429–436.

Hammill, D. D., & Larsen, S. C. (1983). *Tests of Written Language.* Austin, TX: PRO-ED.

Handin, V. (1978). Ecological assessment and intervention for learning disabled students. *Learning Disabilities Quarterly, 1*, 15–20.

Hargrove, L. J., & Poteet, J. A. (1984). *Assessment in special education: The education evaluation.* Englewood Cliffs, NJ: Prentice-Hall.

Harman, H. H. (1967). *Modern factor analysis.* Chicago: University of Chicago Press.

Harris, A. J. (1970). *How to increase reading ability.* New York: David McKay.

Harris, J., & Harris, L. (1982). Basal reading programs and the school psychologist. *School Psychology Review, 11*, 290–298.

Hart, V. (1977). Perceptual skills. In N. G. Hairing (Ed.), *Developing effective individualized education programs for severely handicapped children and youth.* Washington, DC: Bureau of Education for the Handicapped.

Hasselbring, T. S. (1984). Computer-based assessment of special needs students. In R. E. Bennett & C. A. Maher (Eds.), *Microcomputers and exceptional children* (pp. 7–19). New York: Haworth.

Hasselbring, T. S. (1985, August). *Computer-based assessment in the schools: Expert systems applications.* Paper presented at the American Psychological Association annual meeting. Los Angeles, CA.

Hauger, J. (1985). *Compuscore for the Woodcock-Johnson Psychoeducational Battery* (computer program). Allen, TX: DLM Teaching Resources.

Hawkins, R. P. (1979). The functions of assessment: Implications for selection and development of devices for assessing repertoires in clinical, educational, and other settings. *Journal of Applied Behavior Analysis, 1*, 97–106.

Haynes, S., & Jensen, B. (1979). The interview as a behavioral assessment instrument. *Behavioral Assessment, 1*, 97–106.

Heber, R. (1961). *A manual on terminology and classification in mental retardation.* Washington, DC: American Association on Mental Deficiency.

Hendrick Hudson District Board of Education v. *Rowley.* 347 U.S. 483 (1982).

Heron, T. E., & Heward, W. L. (1982). Ecological assessments: Implications for teachers of learning disabled students. *Learning Disabilities Quarterly, 5*, 117–125.

Herrnstein, R. J. (1982). IQ testing and the media. *The Atlantic Monthly, 6*, 68–74.

Hersen, M., & Bellack, A. (Eds.). (1981). *Behavioral assessment: A practical handbook* (2nd ed.). New York: Pergamon Press.

Hersh, R. H., & Walker, H. M. (1983). Great expectations: Making schools effective for all students. *Policy Studies Review, 2*, 147–188.

Hieronymous, A. N., Linquist, E. F., Hoover, H. D., et al. (1983). *Iowa Test of Basic Skills.* Chicago: Riverside.

Hills, J. R. (1976). *Measurement and evaluation in the classroom.* Columbus, OH: Charles Merrill.

Hiskey, M. S. (1966). *Hiskey-Nebraska Test of Learning Aptitude.* Lincoln, NE: Marshall Hiskey.

Hobbs, N. (Ed.). (1975). *Issues in the classification of children.* San Francisco: Jossey-Bass.

Hofer, P. J., & Green, B. F. (1985). The challenge of competence and creativity in computerized psychological testing. *Journal of Consulting and Clinical Psychology, 53*, 826–838.

Hoge, R. D. (1983). Psychometric properties of teacher-judgement measures of pupil aptitudes, classroom behaviors, and achievement levels. *Journal of Special Education, 17*, 401–429.

Holland, J. G., Solomon, C., Doran, J., & Frezza, D. A. (1976). *The analysis of behavior in planning instruction.* Reading, MA: Addison-Wesley.

Hopkins, K. D., & Glass, G. V. (1981). *Educational and psychological measurement and evaluation.* Englewood Cliffs, NJ: Prentice-Hall.

Howell, K. W., Kaplan, J. S., & O'Connell, C. Y. (1979). *Evaluating exceptional children: A task analysis approach.* Columbus, OH: Charles Merrill.

Hresko, W. P., Reid, D. K., & Hammill, D. D. (1981a). *Test of Early Language Development.* Austin, TX: PRO-ED.

Hresko, W. P., Reid, D. K., & Hammill, D. D. (1981b). *Test of Early Reading (TERA).* Austin, TX: PRO-ED.

Hull, F. M., et al. (1971). The National Speech and Hearing Survey: Preliminary results. *Journal of the American Speech and Hearing Association, 13*, 501–509.

Hunt, J. (1975). Reactions on a decade of early education. *Journal of Abnormal Child Psychology, 3*, 275–330.

Ingram, C. R. (1980). *Fundamentals of educational assessment.* New York: D. Van Nostrand.

Ingram, D. (1974). The relationship between comprehension and production. In R. L. Schieffelbusch & L. L. Lloyd (Eds.), *Language perspective — Acquisition, retardation, and intervention.* Baltimore: University Park Press.

Ireton, H., Lun, K. S., & Kampen, M. (1981). Minnesota Preschool Inventory: Identification of children at risk for kindergarten failure. *Psychology in the Schools, 18*, 193–501.

Ireton, H., & Thwing, E. (1974). *Minnesota Preschool Inventory.* Minneapolis: Behavior Science Systems.

Ireton, H., & Thwing, E. (1979). *Minnesota Preschool Inventory.* Minneapolis: Behavior Science Systems.

Jarman, R. F., & Das, J. P. (1977). Simultaneous and successive synthesis and intelligence. *Intelligence, 1*, 151–169.

Jastak, S., & Wilkinson, G. S. (1984). *Wide Range Achievement Test-Revised.* Wilmington, DE: Jastak Associates.

Jensen, A. R. (1980). *Bias in mental testing.* New York: The Free Press.

Jordon, B. T. (1974). *Jordon Left-Right Reversal Test.* San Rafael, CA: Academic Therapy Publications.

Just, M., & Carpenter, P. (1980). A theory of reading: From eye fixations to comprehension. *Psychological Review, 87*, 329–354.

Kamin, L. (1981). Some historical facts about IQ testing. In H. J. Eysenck & L. Kamin (Eds.), *The intelligence controversy* (pp. 90–97). New York: Wiley.

Katz, J. J., & Fodor, J. A. (1963). The structure of a semantic theory. *Language, 39*, 170–210.

Kaufman, A. S. (1975). Factor analysis of the WISC-R at 11 age levels between 6½ and 16½ years. *Journal of Consulting and Clinical Psychology, 43*, 135–147.

Kaufman, A. S. (1976a). A new approach to the interpretation of test scatter of the WISC-R. *Journal of Learning Disabilities, 9*, 160–168.

Kaufman, A. S. (1976b). Verbal-Performance IQ discrepancies of the WISC-R. *Journal of Consulting and Clinical Psychology, 44*, 739–744.

Kaufman, A. S. (1979). *Intelligent testing with the WISC-R*. New York: Wiley.

Kaufman, A. S., & Kaufman, N. L. (1983). *Kaufman Assessment Battery for Children*. Circle Pines, MN: American Guidance Service.

Kaufman, A. S., & Kaufman, N. L. (1985). *Kaufman Test of Educational Achievement*. Circle Pines, MN: American Guidance Service.

Kaufman, R. A. (1971). A possible integrative model for the systematic and measurable improvement of education. *American Psychologist, 26*, 250–256.

Kavale, K., & Mattison, P. D. (1982). "One jumped off the balance beam": Meta-analysis of perceptual-motor training. *Journal of Learning Disabilities, 26*, 121–134.

Kazdin, A. E. (1977). Assessing the clinical or applied importance of behavior change through social validation. *Behavior Modification, 1*, 427–451.

Kazdin, A. E. (1979). Situational specificity: The two-edged sword of behavioral assessment. *Behavioral Assessment, 6*, 57–76.

Kazdin, A. E. (1982). Applying behavioral principles in the schools. In C. R. Reynolds & T. B. Gutkin (Eds.), *The handbook of school psychology* (pp. 501–529). New York: Wiley.

Kazdin, A. E., & Matson, J. (1981). Social validation in mental retardation. *Applied Research in Mental Retardation, 2*, 39–53.

Kelley, M. F., & Surbeck, E. (1983). History of preschool assessment. In K. D. Paget & B. A. Bracken (Eds.), *The psychoeducational assessment of preschool children* (pp. 1–16). New York: Grune & Stratton.

Kelly, T. L. (1927). *Interpretation of educational measurements*. Yonkers-on-Hudson, NY: World Book.

Kent, R., & Foster, S. (1977). Direct observational procedures. In A. Ciminero, K. Colhoun, & H. Adams (Eds.), *Handbook of behavioral assessment* (pp. 279–328). New York: Wiley Interscience.

Kirk, S. A. (1963). Behavioral diagnosis and remediation of learning disabilities. *Proceedings of the annual meeting of the conference into the problems of the perceptually handicapped child* (Vol. 1). Urbana: University of Illinois Press.

Kirk, S., McCarthy, J., & Kirk, W. (1968). *Illinois Test of Psycholinguistic Abilities*. Urbana: University of Illinois Press.

Kleinmuntz, B. (1963). MMPI decision rules for the identification of college maladjustment: A digital computer approach [Special issue]. *Psychological Monographs, 77*.

Klopfer, W. G., & Taulbee, E. S. (1976). Projective tests. *Annual review of psychology*. Palo Alto, CA: Annual Reviews.

Kohlberg, L. (1976). Moral stages and moralization. The cognitive development approach. In T. Lickona (Ed.), *Moral development and moral behavior*. New York: Holt, Rinehart & Winston.

Koppitz, E. M. (1964). *The Bender-Gestalt Test for Young Children*. New York: Grune & Stratton.

Koppitz, E. M. (1968). *Psychological evaluation of children's human figure drawings*. New York: Grune & Stratton.

Koppitz, E. M. (1975). *The Bender-Gestalt Test for Young Children* (Vol. 2). New York: Grune & Stratton.

Kramer, J. J. (1985). *Computer-based test interpretation in psychoeducational assessment*. Trainers of School Psychologists meeting. Los Angeles, CA.

Kramer, J. J., Henning-Stout, M., Ullman, D. L., & Schellenberg, R. L. (1987). The viability of scatter analysis on the WISC-R and SBIS: Examining a vestige. *Journal of Psychoeducational Assessment*, *5*, 37–47.

Kramer, J. J., & Mitchell, J. V., Jr. (Eds.). (1985). Computer-based assessment and test interpretation: Promise, prospects, and pitfalls [Special issue]. *Computers in Human Behavior*, *1* (3 & 4).

Kratochwill, T. R. (1982). Advances in behavioral assessment. In C. Reynolds & T. Gutkin (Eds.), *Handbook of school psychology* (pp. 314–350). New York: Wiley Interscience.

Kratochwill, T. R., Doll, E. J., & Dickson, P. (1985). Microcomputers in behavioral assessment: Recent advances and remaining issues. *Computers in Human Behavior*, *1*, 277–291.

Kretschmer, R. R., & Kretschmer, L. W. (1978). *Language development and intervention with the hearing impaired*. Baltimore: University Park Press.

LaBerge, D., & Samuels, S. J. (1974). Toward a theory of automatic information processing in reading. *Cognitive Psychology*, *9*, 111–151.

Lambert, N., & Windmiller, M. (1981). *AAMD Adaptive Behavior: School edition*. Monterey, CA: McGraw-Hill.

Lamberts, F. (1979). Describing children's language behavior. In D. A. Sabatino & T. L. Miller (Eds.), *Describing learner characteristics of handicapped children and youth* (pp. 253–291). New York: Grune & Stratton.

Laosa, L. M. (1977). Nonbiased assessment of children's abilities: Historical antecedents and current issues. In T. Oakland (Ed.), *Psychological and educational assessment of minority children*. New York: Brunner/Mazel.

Larry P. v. *Wilson Riles et al.* (1974). United States District Court, Northern District of California, Case No. C-71-2270 RFP.

Larry P. et al. v. *Wilson Riles et al.* (1979). United States District Court, Northern District of California, Case No. C-71-2270 RFP. Injunction in 1972 & 1974. Opinion in October 1979.

Larsen, S. C., & Hammill, D. D. (1975). The relationship between selected visual skills and school learning. *Journal of Special Education, 9*, 281–291.

Laten, S., & Katz, G. (1975). *A theoretical model for assessment of adolescents: The ecological/behavioral approach*. Madison, WI: Madison Public Schools.

Learner, J. W. (1976). *Children with learning disabilities* (rev. ed.). Boston: Houghton Mifflin.

Lee, L. (1971). *Northwestern Syntax Screening Test*. Evanston, IL: Northwestern University Press.

Leinhardt, G., & Sewald, A. M. (1981). Student-level observation of beginning reading. *Journal of Educational Measurement, 18*, 171–177.

Leinhardt, G., Zigmond, N., & Cooley, W. W. (1981). Reading instruction and its effects. *American Educational Research Journal, 18*, 343–362.

Leiter, R. G., & Arthur, G. (1955). *Leiter International Performance Scale*. Chicago: Stoelting Company.

Leonard, L. B., Perozzi, J. A., Prutting, C. A., & Berkley, R. K. (1978). Nonstandardized approaches to the assessment of language behaviors. *American Speech and Hearing Association*, 371–379.

Levine, E. (1974). Psychological tests and practices with the deaf: A survey of the state of the art. *Volta Review, 76*, 298–319.

Levine, S., Elzey, F. F., & Lewis, M. (1969). *California Preschool Social Competency Scale*. Palo Alto, CA: Consulting Psychologists Press.

Lewin, K. (1951). *Field theory in the social sciences*. New York: Harper & Row.

Lichtenstein, R. (1982). New instrument, old problem for early identification. *Exceptional Children, 49*, 70–72.

Lichtenstein, R. (1984). Predicting school performance of preschool children from parent reports. *Journal of Abnormal Child Psychology, 12*, 79–94.

Lichtenstein, R., & Ireton, H. (1984). *Preschool screening: Identifying young children with developmental and educational problems*. Orlando, FL: Grune & Stratton.

Lillywhite, H. S. (1958). Doctor's manual of speech disorders. *Journal of American Medical Association, 167*, 850–858.

Lindeman, R. H., & Merenda, P. F. (1979). *Educational measurement*. Glenview, IL: Scott, Foresman.

Lindquist, G. T. (1982). Preschool screening as a means of predicting later reading achievement. *Journal of Learning Disabilities, 15*, 331–332.

Lippmann, W. (1976). The abuse of the tests. In N. Block & G. Dwokin (Eds.), *The IQ controversy*. New York: Pantheon. (Originally published in 1922).

Livingston, S. A., & Zieky, M. J. (1982). *Passing scores: A manual for setting standards of performance on educational and occupational tests*. Princeton, NJ: Educational Testing Service.

Lloyd, J. (1979). Ascertaining the reading skills of atypical learners. In D. A. Sabatino & T. L. Miller (Eds.), *Describing learner characteristics of handicapped children and youth*. New York: Grune & Stratton.

Lomax, R. (1980, April). *A generalizability study of the classroom observations of learning disabled students.* Paper presented at the annual meeting of the American Educational Research Association, Boston.

Lovitt, T. C., & Fantasia, K. (1980). Two approaches to reading program evaluation: A standardized test and direct assessment. *Learning Disability Quarterly, 3*, 77–87.

MacGinitie, W. (1978). *Gates-MacGinitie Reading Diagnostic Tests.* Boston: Houghton Mifflin.

Machover, K. (1949). *Personality projection in drawings of a human figure.* Springfield, IL: Charles C. Thomas.

MacMillan, D. (1982). *Mental retardation in school and society* (2nd ed.). Boston: Little, Brown.

MacMillan, D. L., & Meyers, C. E. (1980). Larry P.: An educational interpretation. *School Psychology Review, 9*, 136–148.

Mager, R. R. (1962). *Preparing instructional objectives.* Palo Alto, CA: Fearon.

Mardell, C., & Goldenberg, D. (1975). *Developmental Indicators for the Assessment of Learning (DIAL).* Edison, NJ: Childcraft Education Corporation.

Mardell-Czudnowski, C., & Goldenberg, D. (1984). Revision and restandardization of a preschool screening test: DIAL becomes DIAL-R. *Journal of the Division of Early Childhood*, Summer, 16–23.

Marshall, N. J. (1971). Environmental components of orientation toward privacy. In J. Archea & C. Eastman (Eds.), *ADRA Two.* Pittsburgh, PA: Carnegie Mellon University.

Mash, E., & Terdal, L. (Eds.). (1981). *Behavioral assessment of childhood disorders.* New York: Guilford Press.

Matarazzo, J. M. (1983, July). Computerized psychological testing. *Science, 221*, 323.

Matusiak, I. (1976). *Preschool screening for exceptional children's education needs in a large urban setting.* Milwaukee: Milwaukee Public Schools.

McCallum, R. S. (1985). [Review of *Peabody Picture Vocabulary Test-Revised*]. In J. V. Mitchell, Jr. (Ed.), *Ninth mental measurements yearbook.* Lincoln, NE: Buros Institute of Mental Measurements.

McCarthy, D. (1972). *Manual for the McCarthy Scales of Children's Abilities.* New York: Psychological Corporation.

McCracken, R. (1966). *Standard Reading Inventory.* Klamath Falls, OR: Klamath Printing.

McCullough, C. S., & Wenck, L. S. (Eds.). (1984). Computers in school psychology [Special issue]. *School Psychology Review, 13*, 421.

McDaniel, E. L. (1973). *Inferred Self-Concept Scale.* Los Angeles: Western Psychological.

McDermott, P. A. (1980). Congruence and typology of diagnoses in school psychology: An empirical study. *Psychology in the Schools, 17*, 12–24.

McDermott, P. A. (1981). Sources of error in the psychoeducational diagnosis of children. *Journal of School Psychology, 19*, 31–34.

McDermott, P. A. (1982). Actuarial assessment systems for the grouping and classification of school children. In C. R. Reynolds & T. B. Gutkin (Eds.), *The handbook of school psychology* (pp. 243–272). New York: Wiley.

McDermott, P. A., & Hale, R. L. (1982). Validation of a systems-actuarial computer process for multidimensional classification of child psychopathology. *Journal of Clinical Psychology, 38*, 477–486.

McDermott, P. A., & Watkins, M. W. (1979). A program to evaluate general and conditional agreement among categorical assignments of many raters. *Behavioral Research Methods and Instrumentation, 11*, 399–400.

McDermott, P. A., & Watkins, M. W. (1985). *McDermott-Multidimensional Assessment of Children* [Computer program]. Cleveland, OH: Psychological Corporation.

McMahon, R. J. (1984). Behavioral checklists and rating scales. In T. H. Ollendick & M. Hersen (Eds.), *Child behavioral assessment*. New York: Pergamon Press.

McPherson, K. S. (1985). On intelligence testing and immigration legislation. *American Psychologist, 40*, 242–243.

Meehl, P. E. (1954). *Clinical versus statistical predictions: A theoretical analysis and a review of the evidence*. Minneapolis: University of Minnesota Press.

Mehrens, W. A., & Lehmann, E. J. (1978). *Standardized tests in education*. New York: Holt, Rinehart & Winston.

Menyuk, P. (1969). *Sentences children use*. Cambridge, MA: MIT Press.

Menyuk, P. (1971). *The acquisition and development of language*. Englewood Cliffs, NJ: Prentice-Hall.

Menyuk, P. (1972). *The development of speech*. Indianapolis: Bobbs-Merrill.

Mercer, J. R. (1970). Sociological perspectives on mild mental retardation. In H. Haywood (Ed.), *Social-cultural aspects of mental retardation*. New York: Appleton-Century-Crofts.

Mercer, J. R. (1979). *SOMPA technical manual*. New York: Psychological Corporation.

Mercer, J. R., & Lewis, J. (1978). *The System of Multicultural Pluralistic Assessment*. New York: Psychological Corporation.

Merwin, J. C. (1966). The progress of exploration toward a national assessment of educational progress. *Journal of Educational Measurement, 3*, 5–10.

Messick, S. (1984). Abilities and knowledge in educational achievement testing. In B. S. Plake (Ed.), *Social and technical issues in testing*. Hillsdale, NJ: Lawrence Erlbaum Associates.

Meyers, C. E., Nihira, K., & Zetlin, A. (1979). The measurement of adaptive behavior. In N. R. Willis (Ed.), *Handbook of mental deficiency: Psychological theory and research*. Hillsdale, NJ: Lawrence Erlbaum Associates.

Miller, W. H. (1974). *Reading Diagnosis Kit*. New York: The Center for Applied Research in Education.

Mills v. *Board of Education of District of Columbia*, 348 F. Supp. 866 (D.D.C. 1972).

Mischel, W. (1968). *Personality and assessment.* New York: Wiley.

Mitchell, J. V., Jr. (1984). *Computer-based test interpretation and the public interest.* Paper presented at the annual meeting of the American Psychological Association. Toronto, Canada.

Moran, M. R. (1978). *Assessment of the exceptional learner in the regular classroom.* Denver: Love Publishing Company.

Moreland, K. L. (1985). Computer-based psychological assessment in 1985: A practical guide. *Computers in Human Behavior, 1*, 199–206.

Moreno, J. (1934). Who shall survive? *Nervous and Mental Disease Monograph* (Whole No. 58). Washington, DC: Society of Nervous and Mental Diseases.

Morgan, C. D., & Murray, H. A. (1935). A method of investigating fantasies: The Thematic Apperception Test. *Archive of Neurology and Psychiatry, 34*, 289–306.

Murray, H. A. (1971). *Thematic Apperception Test: Manual.* Cambridge, MA: Harvard University Press.

Myers, P. I., & Hammill, D. D. (1976). *Methods for learning disorders.* New York: Wiley.

Myers, P. I., & Hammill, D. D. (1982). *Learning disabilities: Basic concepts, assessment practices, and instructional strategies.* Austin, TX: PRO-ED.

Nagle, R. J. (1979). The McCarthy Scales of Children's Abilities: Research implications for the assessment of young children. *School Psychology Digest, 8*, 319–326.

Naslund, R. A., Thorpe, L. P., & Lefever, D. W. (1978). *SRA Achievement Series.* Chicago: Science Research Associates.

Nedler, S. E., & McAfee, O. D. (1979). *Working with parents: Guidelines for early childhood and elementary teachers.* Belmont, CA: Wadsworth.

Nelson, R. (1983). Behavioral assessment: Past, present, and future. *Behavioral Assessment, 5*, 195–206.

Nelson, R., & Bowles, P. C. (1975). The best of two worlds: Observation with norms. *Journal of School Psychology, 13*, 3–9.

Nelson, R., & Evans, I. (1977). Assessment of child behavior problems. In A. Ciminero, K. Calhoun, & M. Adams (Eds.), *Handbook of behavioral assessment* (pp. 603–682). New York: Wiley Interscience.

Nelson, R., & Hayes, S. (1979). Some current dimensions of behavior assessment. *Behavioral Assessment, 1*, 1–16.

Nelson, R., & Hayes, S. (1981). Nature of behavioral assessment. In M. Hersen & A. Bellack (Eds.), *Behavioral assessment: A practical handbook* (pp. 3–37). New York: Pergamon Press.

Newcomer, P., & Hammill, D. (1981). *The Test of Language Development.* Austin, TX: PRO-ED.

Nihira, D., Foster, R., Shellhaas, M., & Leland, H. (1974). *AAMD adaptive behavior.* Washington, DC: American Association on Mental Deficiency.

Oakland, T. (1979). Research on the Adaptive Behavior Inventory for Children and the estimated learning potential. *School Psychology Digest, 8*, 73–70.

Oakland, T. (1980). Nonbiased assessment of minority group children. *Exceptional Education Quarterly, 3*, 116–127.

O'Leary, K. D., & O'Leary, S. G. (1977). *Classroom management: The successful use of behavior modification* (2nd ed.). New York: Pergamon Press.

Ollendick, T., & Hersen, M. (Eds.). (1984). *Child behavioral assessment*. New York: Pergamon Press.

Page, E. B. (1985). Review of the Kaufman-Assessment Battery for Children. In J. V. Mitchell, Jr. (Ed.), *The ninth mental measurements yearbook*. Lincoln, NE: Buros Institute of Mental Measurements.

Paget, K. D., & Bracken, B. A. (1983). *The psychoeducational assessment of preschool children*. New York: Grune & Stratton.

Paraskevopoulos, J., & Kirk, S. A. (1969). *Development and psychometric characteristics of the Revised Illinois Test of Psycholinguistic Abilities*. Urbana, IL: University of Illinois Press.

Parents in Action on Special Education (PASE) v. *Joseph P. Hannon*. (1980, July). U.S. District Court, Northern District of Illinois, Eastern Division, no. 74 (3586).

Paris, S. (1973). Comprehension of language connectives and propositional logical relationships. *Journal of Experimental Child Psychology, 16*, 278–291.

Patterson, G. R. (1982). *Toddlers and delinquents: Variations on a theme of anti-social behavior*. Paper presented at the annual meeting of the American Psychological Association, Washington, DC.

Pennsylvania Association of Retarded Citizens v. *Commonwealth of Pennsylvania*. 343 F. Supp. 279 (E.D. Pa. 1972).

Peterson, D. W., & Batsche, G. M. (1983). School psychology and projective assessment: A growing incompatability. *School Psychology Review, 12*, 440–445.

Peterson, L., Homer, A., & Wonderlich, S. (1982). The integrity of independent variables in behavior analysis. *Journal of Applied Behavior Analysis, 15*, 477–492.

Pfeiffer, S. I. (1980). The school-based interprofessional team: Recurring problems and some possible solutions. *Journal of School Psychology, 18*, 388–394.

Pfeiffer, S. I. (1981). The problems facing multidisciplinary teams: As perceived by team members. *Psychology in the Schools, 18*, 330–333.

Piaget, J. (1954). *The construction of reality in the child* (M. Cook, Trans.). New York: Basic Books.

Piaget, J. (1963). *Origins of intelligence in children*. New York: Norton.

Piaget, J. (1970). *The science of education and the psychology of the child*. New York: Orion Press.

Piers, E., & Harris, D. (1969). *The Piers-Harris Children's Self Concept Scale*. Nashville: Counselor Recordings and Tests.

Pikulski, J. (1974, November). A critical review: Informal reading inventories. *The Reading Teacher*, 141–153.

Pollaway, E. A. (1985). [Review of *Test of Written Language*]. In J. V. Mitchell, Jr. (Ed.), *Ninth mental measurements yearbook*. Lincoln, NE: Buros Institute of Mental Measurements.

Potter, T. C., & Rae, G. (1981). *Informal reading diagnosis: A practical guide for the classroom teacher* (2nd ed.). Englewood Cliffs, NJ: Prentice-Hall.

Potts, M., Carlson, P., Cocking, R., & Copple, C. (1979). *Structure and development in child language*. Ithaca, NY: Cornell University Press.

Powell, W. (1971). Validity of the I.R.I. reading levels. *Elementary English*, *48*, 637–642.

Prasse, D. P. (1983). Legal issues underlying preschool assessment. In K. D. Paget & B. A. Bracken (Eds.), *The psychoeducational assessment of preschool children* (pp. 29–50). New York: Grune & Stratton.

Prasse, D. P., & Bracken, B. A. (1981). Comparison of the PPVT-R and WISC-R with urban educable mentally retarded students. *Psychology in the Schools*, *18*, 174–177.

President's Committee on Mental Retardation. (1970). *The six-hour retarded child*. Washington, DC: U.S. Government Printing Office.

Psychological Corporation. (1985). *WISC-R microcomputer-assisted interpretive report* (computer program). San Antonio, TX: Author.

Public Law 94-142. Education for All Handicapped Children Act of 1975 (1975, November 29).

Quay, H. C. (1983). A dimensional approach to behavior disorders: The Revised Behavior Problem Checklist. *School Psychology Review*, *12*, 244–249.

Quay, H. C., & Peterson, D. (1983). *Manual for the Revised Behavior Problem Checklist*. Coral Gables, FL: University of Miami.

Quay, H. C., & Werry, J. (1972). *Psychopathological disorders of childhood*. New York: Wiley.

Reger, R. (1972). The medical model in special education. *Psychology in the Schools*, *9*, 8–12.

Reid, D. K., Hresko, W. P., & Hammill, D. D. (1981). *The Test of Early Reading Ability*. Austin, TX: PRO-ED.

Reisman, F. K. (1978). *A guide to the diagnostic teaching of arithmetic*. Columbus, OH: Charles Merrill.

Reschly, D. J. (1979). Nonbiased assessment. In G. Phye & D. J. Reschly (Eds.), *School psychology: Perspectives and issues* (pp. 215–253). New York: Academic Press.

Reschly, D. J. (1980). Concepts of bias in assessment and WISC-R research with minorities. In H. Vance & F. Wallbrown (Eds.), *WISC-R: Research and interpretation*. Washington, DC: National Association of School Psychologists.

Reschly, D. J. (1980). School psychologists and assessment on the future. *Professional Psychology*, *11*, 841–848.

Reschly, D. J. (1982). Assessing mild mental retardation: The influence of adaptive behavior, sociocultural status, and prospects for nonbiased assessment. In C. R. Reynolds & T. B. Gutkin (Eds.), *The handbook of school psychology*. New York: Wiley.

Reschly, D. J., & Sabers, D. (1979). Analysis of test bias in four groups with the regression definition. *Journal of Educational Measurement, 16*, 1–6.

Resnick, L. B., Wang, M. C., & Kaplan, J. (1973). Task analysis in curriculum design: A hierarchically sequenced introductory mathematics curriculum. *Journal of Applied Behavior Analysis, 6*, 679–710.

Reynolds, C. R. (1982). The problem of bias in psychological assessment. In C. R. Reynolds & T. B. Gutkin (Eds.), *The handbook of school psychology* (pp. 178–208). New York: Wiley

Reynolds, C. R., & Elliott, S. N. (1983). Trends in commercial development and publication of educational and psychological tests. *Professional Psychology: Research and Practice, 14*, 554–558.

Reynolds, C. R., Gutkin, T. B., Elliott, S. N., & Witt, J. C. (1984). *School psychology: Essentials of theory and practice*. New York: Wiley.

Reynolds, C. R., & Paget, K. D. (1983). National normative and reliability data for the Revised Children's Manifest Anxiety Scale. *School Psychology Review, 12*, 324–336.

Reynolds, C. R., & Richmond, B. (1978). What I think and feel: A revised measure of children's manifest anxiety. *Journal of Abnormal Child Psychology, 6*, 271–280.

Richmond, B. O., & Kicklighter, R. H. (1980). *Children's Adaptive Behavior Scale*. Atlanta: Humanics.

Robeck, M. C., & Wilson, J. A. (1974). *Psychology of reading: Foundations of instruction*. New York: Wiley.

Robins, L. (1963). The accuracy of parental recall of aspects of child development and of child rearing practices. *Journal of Abnormal and Social Psychology, 66*, 261–270.

Robinson, D. Z. (1973). If you're so rich you must be smart. In C. Senna (Ed.), *The fallacy of IQ* (pp. 18–30). New York: The Third Press.

Rogers-Warren, A., & Warren, S. F. (1977). *Ecological perspective in behavioral analysis*. Baltimore: University Park Press.

Rogow, S. M. (1978). Considerations in assessment of blind children who function as severely or profoundly retarded. *Child: Care, Health, & Development, 4*, 327–335.

Roid, G. H. (1985). Computer-based test interpretation: The potential of quantitative aids to test interpretation. *Computers in Human Behavior, 1*, 207–219.

Roid, G. H. (1986). Computer technology in testing. In B. Plake & J. C. Witt (Eds.), *The future of testing*. Hillsdale, NJ: Lawrence Erlbaum Associates.

Rorschach, H. (1921). *Psychodiagnostic*. Bern: Bercher.

Rosenshine, B. (1976). Classroom instruction. In N. L. Gage (Ed.), *Psychology of teaching: The 77th yearbook of the National Society for the Study of Education*. Chicago: National Society for the Study of Education.

Ross, A. (1980). *Psychological disorders of children: A behavioral approach to theory, research, and therapy* (2nd ed.). New York: McGraw-Hill.

Ross, A., Lacey, H., & Partin, C. (1965). The development of a behavior checklist for boys. *Child Development, 36*, 1013–1027.

Ross, M., & Salvia, J. (1975). Attractiveness as a biasing factor in teaching judgements. *American Journal of Mental Deficiency, 80*, 96–98.

Salvia, J., & Ysseldyke, J. (1978). *Assessment in special and remedial education.* Boston: Houghton Mifflin.

Salvia, J., & Ysseldyke, J. (1981). *Assessment in special and remedial education* (2nd ed.). Boston: Houghton Mifflin.

Sampson, J. P. (Ed.). (1986). Computer applications in testing and measurement [Special issue]. *Measurement and Evaluation in Counseling and Development, 19* (1).

Sarason, S. B. (1982). *The culture of the school and the problem of change* (2nd ed.). Boston: Allyn & Bacon.

Sattler, J. (1982). *Assessment of children's intelligence and special abilities* (2nd ed.). Boston: Allyn & Bacon.

Saudargas, R., & Lentz, F. (1986). Estimating percent of time and rate via direct observation procedure and format. *School Psychology Review, 15*, 36–48.

Schwebel, A. I., & Cherlin, D. L. (1972). Physical and social distancing in teacher-pupil relationships. *Journal of Educational Psychology, 63*, 543–550.

Scott, M. (1980). Ecological theory and methods for research in special education. *Journal of Special Education, 14*, 279–294.

Shapiro, E. (1984). Self-monitoring procedures. In T. Ollendick & M. Hersen (Eds.), *Child behavioral assessment* (pp. 148–165). New York: Pergamon Press.

Shapiro, E. S., & Lentz, F. E. (1985). Assessing academic behavior: A behavioral approach. *School Psychology Review, 14*, 325–338.

Shepard, P., & McKinley, A. (1969). *The subversive science.* Boston: Houghton Mifflin.

Shouksmith, G. (1970). *Intelligence, creativity and cognitive style.* New York: Wiley.

Siegel, G. M., & Broen, P. A. (1976). Language assessment. In L. L. Lloyd (Ed.), *Communication assessment and intervention strategies* (pp. 73–122). Baltimore: University Park Press.

Silvaroli, N. J. (1965). *Classroom Reading Inventory.* Dubuque, IA: Wm. C. Brown.

Simeonsson, R. J. (1977). Infant assessment and developmental handicap. In B. M. Caldwell & D. J. Stedman (Eds.), *Infant education: A guide to helping handicapped children in first years of life.* New York: Walker & Company.

Simeonsson, R. J., Huntington, G. S., & Parse, S. A. (1980). Assessment of children with severe handicaps: Multiple problems — multivariate goals. *Journal of the Association of the Severely Handicapped, 5*, 55–72.

Sinclair, H. (1970). The transition from sensorimotor behavior to symbolic activity. *Interchange, 1*, 119–126.

Sindelar, P. T., & Deno, S. L. (1978). The effectiveness of special versus regular class placement for exceptional children: A meta-analysis. *The Journal of Special Education, 14*, 295–309.

Sitlington, P. L. (1970). *Validity of the Peabody Individual Achievement Test with educable mentally retarded adolescents.* Unpublished master's thesis. University of Hawaii, Honolulu, HI.

Skinner, B. F. (1953). *Science and human behavior.* New York: The Free Press.

Slate, J. R., & Saudargas, R. (1986). Differences in learning disabled and average student classroom behavior. *Learning Disability Quarterly, 9*, 61–67.

Smith, R. M., & Neisworth, J. T. (1975). *The exceptional child: A functional approach.* New York: McGraw-Hill.

Smith, R. M., Neisworth, J. T., & Greer, J. G. (1978). *Evaluating educational environments.* Columbus, OH: Charles Merrill.

Soli, S. D., & Devine, V. T. (1976). Behavioral correlates of achievement: A look at high and low achievers. *Journal of Educational Psychology, 68*, 335–341.

Solomon, D., & Kendall, A. J. (1979). *Children in the classroom.* New York: Praeger.

Sommer, R., & Sommer, B. A. (1983). Mystery in Milwaukee: Early intervention, IQ, and psychology. *American Psychologist, 38*, 982–985.

Spache, G. D. (1972). *Diagnostic Reading Scales.* Circle Pines, MN: American Guidance Service.

Sparrow, S. S., Balla, D. A., & Cicchetti, D. V. (1984). *Vineland Adaptive Behavior Scales.* Circle Pines, MN: American Guidance Service.

Spearman, C. E. (1927). *The abilities of man.* New York: Macmillan.

Spivack, G., & Seift, M. (1967). *Devereux Elementary School Behavioral Rating Scale.* Devon, PA: The Devereux Foundation.

Spragins, A. B. (1980). Psychological assessment of the school age hearing impaired child. In R. K. Mulliken and Maryrose Evans (Eds.), *Assessment of children with low-incidence handicaps.* Kent, OH: National Association of School Psychologists.

Staats, A. (1981). Paradigmatic behaviorism, unified theory construction methods, and the zeitgeist of separatism. *American Psychologist, 36*, 239–256.

Stallings, J., Needles, M., & Stayrook, W. (1979). *How to change the process of teaching basic reading skills in secondary schools.* Menlo Park, CA: SRI International.

Stanley, J. C. (1976). Test better finder of great math talent than teachers are. *American Psychologist, 31*, 313–314.

Steenburgen, F. (1978). *The Steenburgen Diagnostic-Prescriptive Math Program.* Novato, CA: Academic Therapy Publications.

Stephens, T. M. (1978). *Social skills in the classroom.* Columbus, OH: Cedars Press.

Sternberg, R. J. (1979). [Review of "Six authors in search of a character: A play about intelligence tests in the year 2000"]. In R. J. Sternberg & D. K. Detterman (Eds.), *Human intelligence: Perspectives on its theory and measurement* (pp. 257–268). Norwood, NJ: Ablex Publishing.

Sternberg, R. J. (1982). Who's intelligent? *Psychology Today, 16*, 30–36.

Sternberg, R. J. (1984a). *Beyond IQ: A triarchic theory of human intelligence.* New York: Cambridge University Press.

Sternberg, R. J. (1984b). What should intelligence tests test? Implications of a triarchic theory of intelligence for intelligence testing. *Educational Researcher, 13*, 5–15.

Sternberg, R. J., & Davidson, J. E. (1982). The mind of the puzzler. *Psychology Today, 16*, 37–44.

Stevens, R., & Rosenshine, B. (1981). Advances in research on teaching. *Exceptional Education Quarterly, 3*, 1–9.

Strain, R. S., Shores, R., & Kerr, M. M. (1976). An experimental analysis of "spillover" effects on the social interaction of behaviorally handicapped preschool children. *Journal of Applied Behavior Analysis, 9*, 31–40.

Strauss, A. A., & Lehtinen, L. (1947). *Psychopathology and education of the brain-injured child.* New York: Grune & Stratton.

Sullivan, P. M., & Vernon, M. (1979). Psychological assessment of hearing impaired children. *School Psychology Review, 8*, 271–290.

Szasz, T. S. (1960). The myth of mental illness. *American Psychologist, 15*, 113–118.

Taylor, G. R. (1970). *The doomsday book.* New York: World Publishing Company.

Terman, L. M., & Merrill, M. (1973). *Stanford-Binet Intelligence Scale: 1973 norms edition.* Boston: Houghton Mifflin.

Tharinger, D. J., Laurent, J., & Best, L. R. (1986). Classification of children referred for emotional and behavioral problems: A comparison of P.L. 94-142 SED criteria, DSMIII and the CBCL system. *Journal of School Psychology, 24*, 111–121.

Thorndike, R. L. (1972). Wide Range Achievement Test. In O. K. Buros (Ed.), *Seventh mental measurements yearbook* (Vol. 1, pp. 67–68). Highland Park, NJ: Gryphon Press.

Thorndike, R. L., & Hagen, E. P. (1982). *Cognitive Abilities Test.* Chicago: Riverside.

Thorndike, R. L., Hagen, E. P., & Sattler, J. M. (1986). *Stanford-Binet Intelligence Scale* (4th ed.). Chicago: Riverside.

Thurman, S. K. (1977). Congruence of behavioral ecologies: A model for special education programming. *Journal of Special Education, 11*, 329–333.

Thurstone, L. L. (1938). Primary mental abilities. *Psychometric Monographs* (Whole No. 1).

Tomlinson, J. R., Acker, N. E., & Mathieu, P. J. (1984). *The behavior manager* [computer program]. Minneapolis, MN: ATM.

Trachtman, G. M. (1972). Pupils, parents, privacy, and the school psychologist. *American Psychologist, 17*, 32–45.

Trybos, R. J., & Karchmer, M. A. (1977). School achievement scores of hearing impaired children: National data on achievement status and growth patterns. *American Annals of the Deaf, 122*, 62–69.

Tucker, J. (1977). Operationalizing the diagnostic-intervention process. In T. Oakland (Ed.), *Psychological and educational assessment of minority children* (pp. 91–111). New York: Brunner/Mazel.

Tyack, D., & Gottsleben, R. (1974). *Language sampling, analysis, and training: A handbook for teachers and clinicians.* Palo Alto, CA: Consulting Psychological Press.

Tyler, R. W. (1966). The objectives and plans for a national assessment of educational progress. *Journal of Educational Measurement, 3,* 1–4.

Ullman, L., & Krasner, L. (1969). *A psychological approach to abnormal behavior.* Englewood Cliffs, NJ: Prentice-Hall.

Van Etten, G., Arkell, C., & Van Etten, C. (1980). *The severely and profoundly handicapped: Programs, methods, and materials.* St. Louis: Mosby.

Van Hattum, R. J. (Ed.). (1980). *Communication disorders: An introduction.* New York: Macmillan.

Van Houten, R. (1979). Social validation: The evolution of standards of competency for target behaviors. *Journal of Applied Behavior Analysis, 12,* 581–591.

Van Melle, W. (1977). MYCIN: A knowledge-based consultation program for infectious disease diagnosis. *International Journal of Man-Machine Studies, 10,* 313–322.

Venesky, R. L. (1976). Prerequisites for learning to read. In J. R. Levin & V. L. Allen (Eds.), *Cognitive learning in children.* New York: Academic Press.

Wahler, R., House, A., & Stambaugh, E. (1976). *Ecological assessment of child problem behavior: A clinical package for home, school, and motivational settings.* New York: Pergamon Press.

Walker, H. M. (1976). *Walker Problem Behavior Identification Checklist* (Rev. 1976). Los Angeles, CA: Western Psychological Services.

Walker, H. M., & Hops, H. (1976). Use of normative peer data as a standard for evaluating classroom treatment effects. *Journal of Applied Behavior Analysis, 9,* 159–168.

Walker, H. M., & Rankin, R. (1983). Assessing the behavioral expectations of least restrictive settings. *School Psychology Review, 12,* 274–284.

Walker, R., & Fox, J. (1981). Setting events in applied behavior analysis: Conceptual and methodological expansion. *Journal of Applied Behavior Analysis, 14,* 327–338.

Wallace, C., & Kauffman, J. (1978). *Teaching children with learning problems* (2nd ed.). Columbus, OH: Charles Merrill.

Wallace, G., & Larsen, S. C. (1978). *Educational assessment of learning problems: Testing for teaching.* Boston: Allyn & Bacon.

Wechsler, E. (1974). *Manual for the Wechsler Intelligence Scale for Children-Revised.* New York: Psychological Corporation.

Weinstein, C. S. (1979). The physical environment of the schools: A review of research. *Review of Educational Research, 49,* 577–610.

Weiss, C. E., & Lillywhite, H. S. (1976). *Communication disorders: A handbook for prevention and early intervention.* St. Louis: Mosby.

Wells, K. C. (1981). Assessment of children in outpatient settings. In M. Hersen & A. S. Bellack (Eds.), *Behavioral assessment.* New York: Pergamon Press.

Wepman, J. (1973). *The Auditory Discrimination Test.* Chicago: Language Research.

Western Psychological Corporation. (1985). *WPS test report: Luria-Nebraska Neuropsychological Battery microcomputer diskette* (computer program). Los Angeles, CA: Author.

Whalen, C. K., & Henkler, B. (1976). Psychostimulants and children: A review and analysis. *Psychological Bulletin, 83*, 1113–1130.

White, M., & Miller, S. R. (1983). Dyslexia: A term in search of a definition. *Journal of Special Education, 17*, 5–10.

Wicker, A. C. (1979). Ecological psychology: Some recent and prospective developments. *American Psychologist, 34*, 755–765.

Wilen, D. K., & Sweeting, C.V.M. (1986). Assessment of limited English proficient Hispanic students: Recommendations for school psychology practice. *School Psychology Review, 15*, 59–75.

Wilkens, G., & Sasko, G. (1984). *The DESB II computer program* (computer program). Devon, PA: The Devereux Foundation.

Williams, H. G. (1983). Assessment of gross motor functioning. In K. D. Paget & B. A. Bracken (Eds.), *The psychoeducational assessment of preschool children* (pp. 225–260). New York: Grune & Stratton.

Williams, R. T. (1985). [Review of *Test of Written Language*]. In J. V. Mitchell, Jr. (Ed.), *Ninth mental measurements yearbook*. Lincoln, NE: Buros Institute of Mental Measurements.

Winne, P. H. (1979). Experiments relating teachers' use of higher cognitive questions to student achievement. *Review of Educational Research, 49*, 13–50.

Wise, S. L. (1985). *Determining cutoff scores for the PPST*. Unpublished manuscript. University of Nebraska-Lincoln, Lincoln, NE.

Witt, J. C., & Elliott, S. N. (1983). Assessment in behavioral consultation: The initial interview. *School Psychology Review, 12*, 42–49.

Witt, J. C., & Elliott, S. N. (1985). Acceptability of classroom management strategies. In T. R. Kratochwill (Ed.), *Advances in school psychology* (Vol. 4, pp. 251–288). Hillsdale, NJ: Lawrence Erlbaum Associates.

Witt, J. C., & Gresham, F. M. (1985). [Review of the *Wechsler Intelligence Scale for Children-Revised*.] In J. V. Mitchell, Jr. (Ed.), *Ninth mental measurements yearbook* (pp. 1716–1719). Lincoln, NE: Buros Institute of Mental Measurements.

Wolf, M. M. (1978). Social validity: The case for subjective measurement or how applied behavior analysis is finding its heart. *Journal of Applied Behavior Analysis, 11*, 203–214.

Woodcock, R. W. (1973). *Woodcock Reading Mastery Tests*. Circle Pines, MN: American Guidance Service.

Woodcock, R. W. (1978). *Woodcock-Johnson Psychoeducational Battery*. Allen, TX: DLM Teaching Resources.

Woodcock, R. W. (1980). *Woodcock Language Proficiency Battery*. Hingham, MA: Teaching Resources.

Woodcock, R. W. (1984). A response to some questions about the Woodcock-Johnson I: The mean score discrepancy issue. *School Psychology Review, 13*, 342–354.

Wright, D., & Piersel, W. C. (1987). Group administered tests for decision making: How useful? Depends on the question. *Journal of School Psychology, 25*, 63–71.

Wyne, M. D., & O'Connor, P. D. (1979). *Exceptional children: A developmental view.* Lexington, MA: D. C. Heath.

Wyne, M. D., & Stuck, G. B. (1979). Time-on-task and reading performance in under-achieving children. *Journal of Reading Behavior, 11*, 119–128.

Yarrow, M. R., Campbell, J., & Burton, R. (1963). Reliability of maternal retrospection: A preliminary report. *Family Process, 3*, 207–218.

Ysseldyke, J. E. (1973). Diagnostic-prescriptive teaching: The search for aptitude-treatment interactions. In L. Mann & D. Sabatino (Eds.), *The first review of special education* (Vol. 1). Philadelphia: Journal of Special Education Press.

Ysseldyke, J. E. (1977). Aptitude-treatment interaction research with first grade children. *Contemporary Educational Psychology, 2*, 1–9.

Ysseldyke, J. E. (1979). Issues in psychoeducational assessment. In G. Phye & D. J. Reschly (Eds.), *School psychology: Perspectives and issues.* New York: Academic Press.

Ysseldyke, J. E., & Algozzine, B. (1982). *Critical issues in special and remedial education.* Boston: Houghton Mifflin.

Ysseldyke, J. E., & Mirkin, P. (1982). The use of assessment information to plan instructional interventions. A review of the research. In C. Reynolds & T. Gutkin (Eds.), *Handbook of school psychology* (pp. 395–409). New York: Wiley.

Ysseldyke, J. E., & Thurlow, M. L. (1984). Assessment practices in special education: Adequacy and appropriateness. *Educational Psychologist, 9*, 123–136.

Zimmerman, I., Steiner, V., & Evatt, R. (1970). *Preschool Language Scale.* Columbus, OH: Charles Merrill.

Zintz, M. W. (1975). *The reading process, the teacher and the learner* (2nd ed.). Dubuque, IA: Wm. C. Brown.

Zubin, J. (1967). Classification of behavior disorders. *Annual Review of Psychology, 18*, 373–406.

Index